BASS GUITAR SCALES 365
BY KIRK TATNALL

HOW TO GET THE AUDIO	
INTRODUCTION	4
HOW TO USE THIS BOOK	5
WEEK 1: A MAJOR	6
WEEK 2: A MINOR	9
WEEK 3: A MAJOR PENTATONIC	12
WEEK 4: A MINOR PENTATONIC	15
WEEK 5: B♭ MAJOR	18
WEEK 6: B♭ MINOR	21
WEEK 7: B♭ MAJOR PENTATONIC	24
WEEK 8: B♭ MINOR PENTATONIC	27
WEEK 9: B MAJOR	30
WEEK 10: B MINOR	33
WEEK 11: B MAJOR PENTATONIC	36
WEEK 12: B MINOR PENTATONIC	39
WEEK 13: C MAJOR	42
WEEK 14: C MINOR	45
WEEK 15: C MAJOR PENTATONIC	48
WEEK 16: C MINOR PENTATONIC	51
WEEK 17: C♯ MAJOR	54
WEEK 18: C♯ MINOR	57
WEEK 19: C♯ MAJOR PENTATONIC	60
WEEK 20: C♯ MINOR PENTATONIC	63
WEEK 21: D MAJOR	66
WEEK 22: D MINOR	69

ISBN: 978-1-969094-00-2
COPYRIGHT © 2025 KIRK TATNALL & TROY NELSON MUSIC LLC
International Copyright Secured. All Rights Reserved.

No part of this publication may be reproduced without the written consent of the author, Kirk Tatnall, and the publisher, Troy Nelson Music LLC. Unauthorized copying, arranging, adapting, recording, Internet posting, public performance, or other distribution of the printed or recorded music in this publication is an infringement of copyright. Infringers are liable under the law.

WEEK 23: D MAJOR PENTATONIC	**72**
WEEK 24: D MINOR PENTATONIC	**75**
WEEK 25: E♭ MAJOR	**78**
WEEK 26: E♭ MINOR	**81**
WEEK 27: E♭ MAJOR PENTATONIC	**84**
WEEK 28: E♭ MINOR PENTATONIC	**87**
WEEK 29: E MAJOR	**90**
WEEK 30: E MINOR	**93**
WEEK 31: E MAJOR PENTATONIC	**96**
WEEK 32: E MINOR PENTATONIC	**99**
WEEK 33: F MAJOR	**102**
WEEK 34: F MINOR	**105**
WEEK 35: F MAJOR PENTATONIC	**108**
WEEK 36: F MINOR PENTATONIC	**111**
WEEK 37: F♯ MAJOR	**114**
WEEK 38: F♯ MINOR	**117**
WEEK 39: F♯ MAJOR PENTATONIC	**120**
WEEK 40: F♯ MINOR PENTATONIC	**123**
WEEK 41: G MAJOR	**126**
WEEK 42: G MINOR	**129**
WEEK 43: G MAJOR PENTATONIC	**132**
WEEK 44: G MINOR PENTATONIC	**135**
WEEK 45: A♭ MAJOR	**138**
WEEK 46: A♭ MINOR	**141**
WEEK 47: A♭ MAJOR PENTATONIC	**144**
WEEK 48: A♭ MINOR PENTATONIC	**147**
WEEK 49: THE BLUES SCALE	**150**
WEEK 50: HARMONIC MINOR	**153**
WEEK 51: MELODIC MINOR	**156**
WEEK 52: THE MODES	**159**
WEEK 53: DAY 365	**164**
ABOUT THE AUTHOR	165

HOW TO GET THE AUDIO

The audio files for this book are available for free as downloads or streaming on *troynelsonmusic.com*.

We are available to help you with your audio downloads and any other questions you may have. Simply email *help@troynelsonmusic.com*.

See below for the recommended ways to listen to the audio:

Download Audio Files	Stream Audio Files
• Download Audio Files (Zipped)	• Recommended for CELL PHONES & TABLETS
• Recommended for COMPUTERS on WiFi	• Bookmark this page
• A ZIP file will automatically download to the default "downloads" folder on your computer	• Simply tap the PLAY button on the track you want to listen to
• Recommended: download to a desktop/laptop computer *first*, then transfer to a tablet or cell phone	• Files also available for streaming or download at *soundcloud.com/troynelsonbooks*
• Phones & tablets may need an "unzipping" app such as iZip, Unrar or Winzip	
• Download on WiFi for faster download speeds	

**To download the companion audio files for this book,
visit:** troynelsonmusic.com/audio-downloads/

INTRODUCTION

Welcome to *Bass Guitar Scales 365*. The goal of this book is to provide a clear path to learning the essential scale patterns needed to make music, one day at a time. With just a few minutes of daily practice, you will unlock the fretboard and be able to use these scales in all 12 keys.

WHAT IS A SCALE?

As defined by *Merriam-Webster,* a scale is "a graduated series of musical tones ascending or descending in order of pitch according to a specified scheme of their intervals." More simply, you might think of a scale as being a musical alphabet of notes that songs are composed from, or a group of notes that will fit a song or chord progression for creating a bass line. The sound of a scale is defined by how far apart each note is from the next.

WHOLE AND HALF STEPS

Half steps and *whole steps* are used to measure the distance between notes. A *half step* (H) is the smallest distance you can move; it's equivalent to moving up or down one key at a time on the piano, or one fret at a time on the bass. A *whole step* (W) is equal to two half steps and is equivalent to moving two keys on the piano or two frets on the bass. Since the distance between notes defines a scale, they are often represented this way: W W H W W W H. When the need for three half steps occurs, we will use W+H throughout the book.

READING SCALE DIAGRAMS

Scale diagrams are used to visually represent the bass fretboard and show how scale patterns fit on it. The strings run horizontally, with the 4th string on the bottom of the diagram, and the 1st string at the top. You'll notice that string 4 is thicker than string 1 in the diagram, just like your bass. The vertical lines represent frets. Use the fret numbers below the diagram and the grey fretboard dots to move the diagram to the correct location along the fretboard. The white dots represent the root note (1st note and name of the scale), and black dots represent all others. Inside each dot will be either a finger number or a note name.

A MAJOR PENTATONIC – FINGERINGS

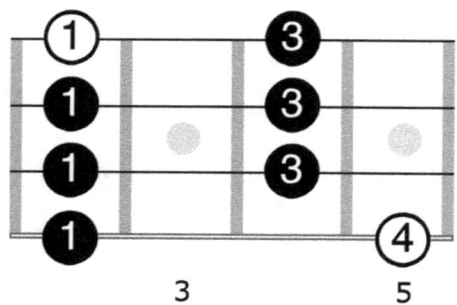

C MAJOR PENTATONIC – NOTE NAMES

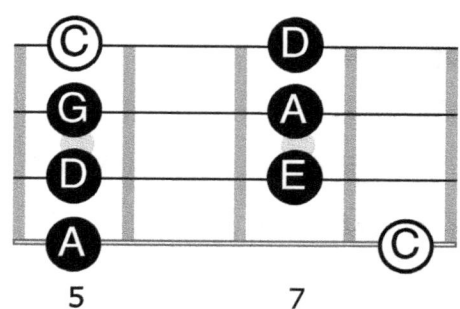

READING BASS TABLATURE

In addition to standard notation, this book uses a numeric notation system called *tablature*, or *tab*. In tab, the four horizontal lines represent the four strings of the bass. The top line is your 1st string, and the bottom line is your 4th string. The numbers placed on the lines indicate the fret on which the note should be played. For example, a "5" placed on the top line indicates that you play string 1, fret 5. An "8" on the bottom line indicates that you play string 4, fret 8. Open strings are indicated with a "0." For example, when placed on the 3rd line from the top, a "0" would mean that you play your 3rd (A) string open (i.e., with no fingers).

HOW TO USE THIS BOOK

The concept of this book is to have one small task to do every day. Doing so will cement the scale patterns into memory and enable you to recall and use them while making music. Simply follow these 3 steps:

1. **Play the scale example as written.** Each scale pattern example begins from its root note and is designed to repeat in a way that helps you hear the sound of the scale.

2. **Use the entire scale pattern.** While the daily examples focus on the main octave of each pattern, it's important to explore the entire fingering, as bass lines and melodies will go up and down beyond the root. Locate the root of a scale (white dots) and ascend within the pattern to its highest note. Next, descend to the lowest note within the pattern, then turn around and ascend to the root note from which you began. Beginning and ending on the root will ensure that you are hearing the scale correctly.

3. **Have fun with the scale pattern!** While ascending and descending scales for memorization is absolutely necessary, bass lines involve much more variety, such as skipping notes, changing direction, and varying rhythms. Throughout this book, Sundays will offer different ways to be musical with scales—and you can create your own, as well! A simple YouTube search for something like "G major backing track" or "C minor backing track" will yield many opportunities to use the scale pattern you're learning in a musical environment. Even going up and down a pattern while playing with a backing track is fun and will help you absorb the scales sound.

PRACTICE TIPS

The most important aspect of this book is to play the scales daily. A small amount of daily practice is much better than two hours one day and nothing the rest of the week! In fact, you can accomplish all three steps in 5–10 minutes of practice. As you're first learning the patterns, they will naturally be more difficult, but by the time you've made it through a couple of keys, the fingerings will become familiar. Don't fret over memorizing the patterns—this will happen naturally as you continue to cycle through new keys. Lastly, feel free to experiment with scale fingerings. Although you'll want to adhere to most of the indicated fingerings, as they are the most efficient and logical, some may be too difficult or uncomfortable due to smaller hands, so audition fingerings until you find the one that is right for you.

WEEK 1: A MAJOR

The *major scale* is the most important scale to learn, as many other scales originate from it. Let's examine how it is constructed and how it is laid out across the fretboard.

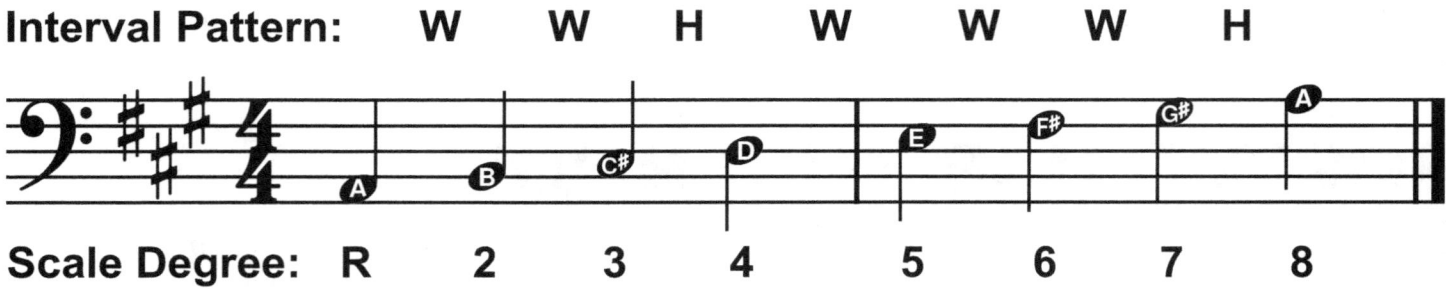

MONDAY: OPEN-STRING PATTERN   1

Remember to use the 3-step method from "How to Use This Book." Sometimes the best pattern for a bass line utilizes open strings. Throughout this book, we'll begin by exploring the most practical scale pattern that uses open strings or is closest to the nut. Our first pattern is an amalgam of Pattern 1 and Pattern 5. Notice how the notes on frets 2 and 4 are shared with Pattern 1, and the open strings are the same as Pattern 5.

TUESDAY: PATTERN 1   2

WEDNESDAY: PATTERN 2

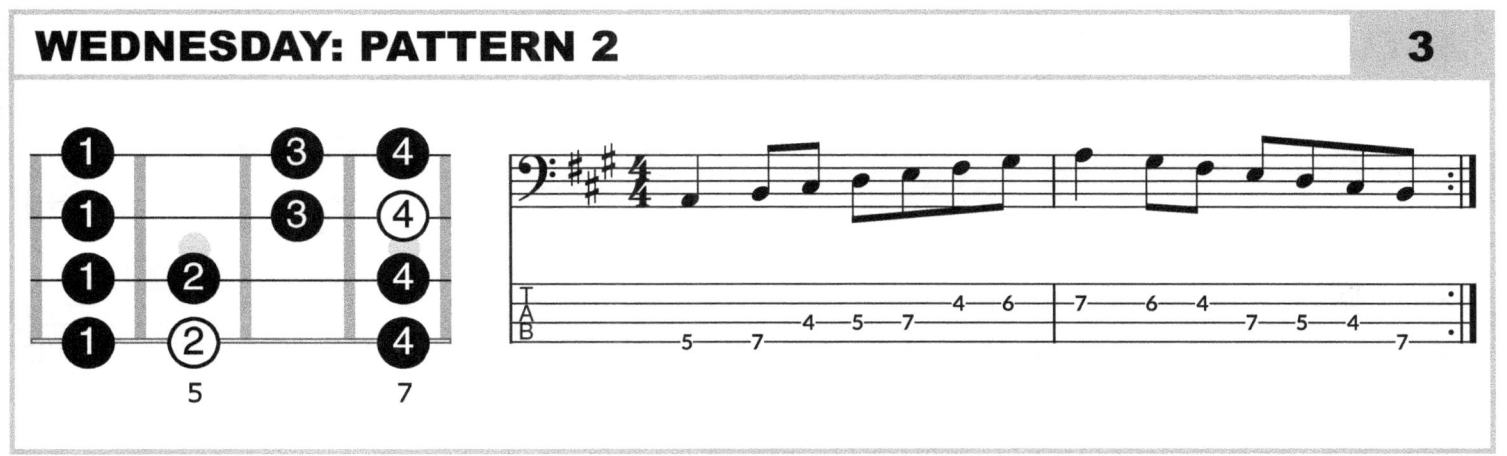

THURSDAY: PATTERN 3

FRIDAY: PATTERN 4

SATURDAY: PATTERN 5

SUNDAY: SCALE APPLICATION

In many musical situations, bass players play the root note of a chord first to establish a foundation for the music. Among the most commonly used chords throughout history are the 1, 4, 5, and 6-minor chords. Today, we'll focus on identifying these notes within the open-string pattern. The term "chord progression" simply means the order that chords appear in a song or song section. Our progression below would be labeled as 1, 5, 6- (minor), 4—or A, E, F#m, D when written as chord symbols.

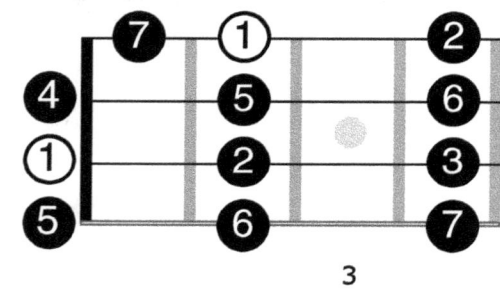

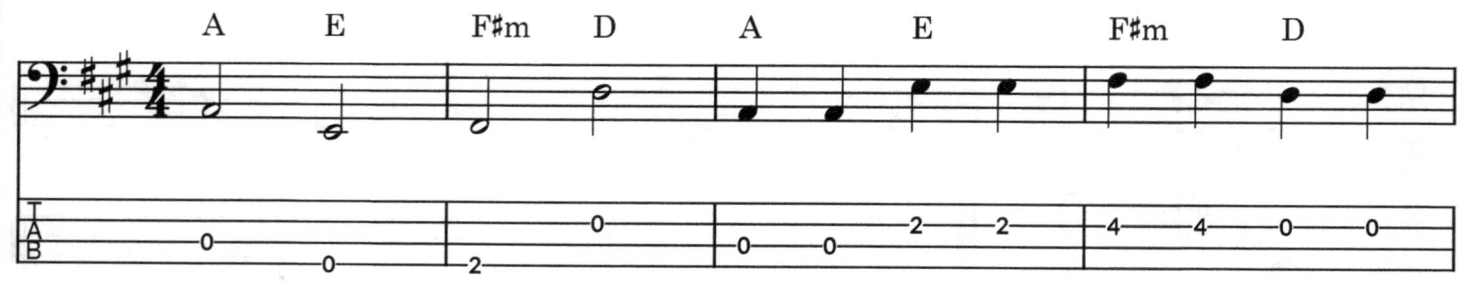

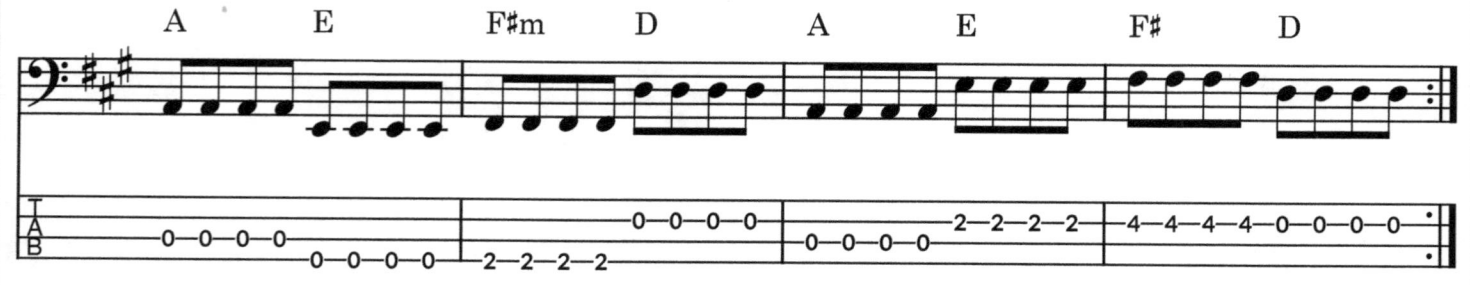

WEEK 2: A MINOR

The *natural minor scale* is created by shifting the starting (root) note of its relative major scale to the 6th degree (C to A in the case of C major/A minor). Let's examine its interval pattern (the flatted 3rd, 6th, and 7th are the alterations required to turn A major into A minor) and how it lays across the fretboard.

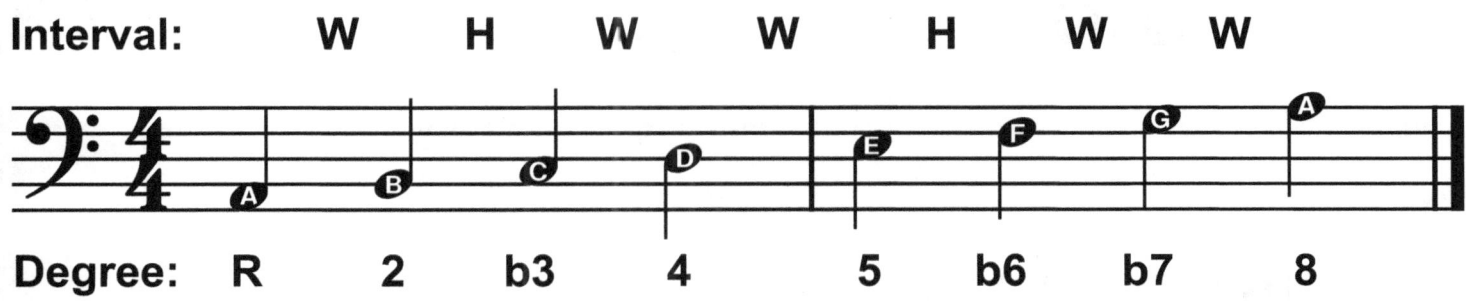

MONDAY: OPEN-STRING PATTERN 4   8

As mentioned in the previous week, we'll always begin with the pattern that is closest to the nut and headstock of the bass. In A minor, this is accomplished by using Pattern 4, with open strings replacing the 1st-finger notes.

TUESDAY: PATTERN 5   9

WEDNESDAY: PATTERN 1

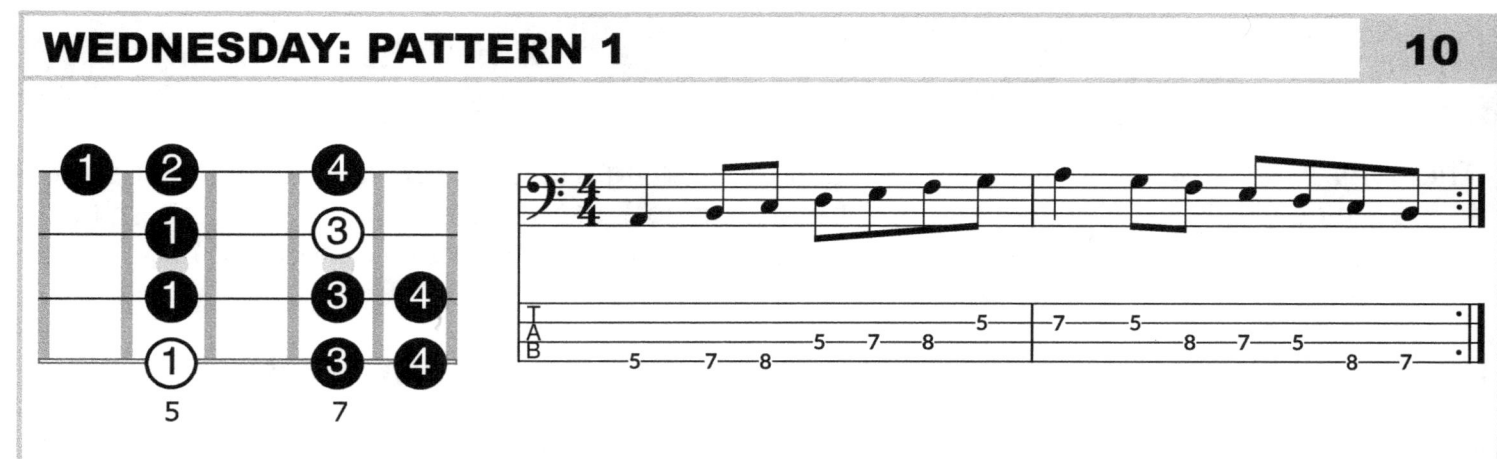

THURSDAY: PATTERN 2

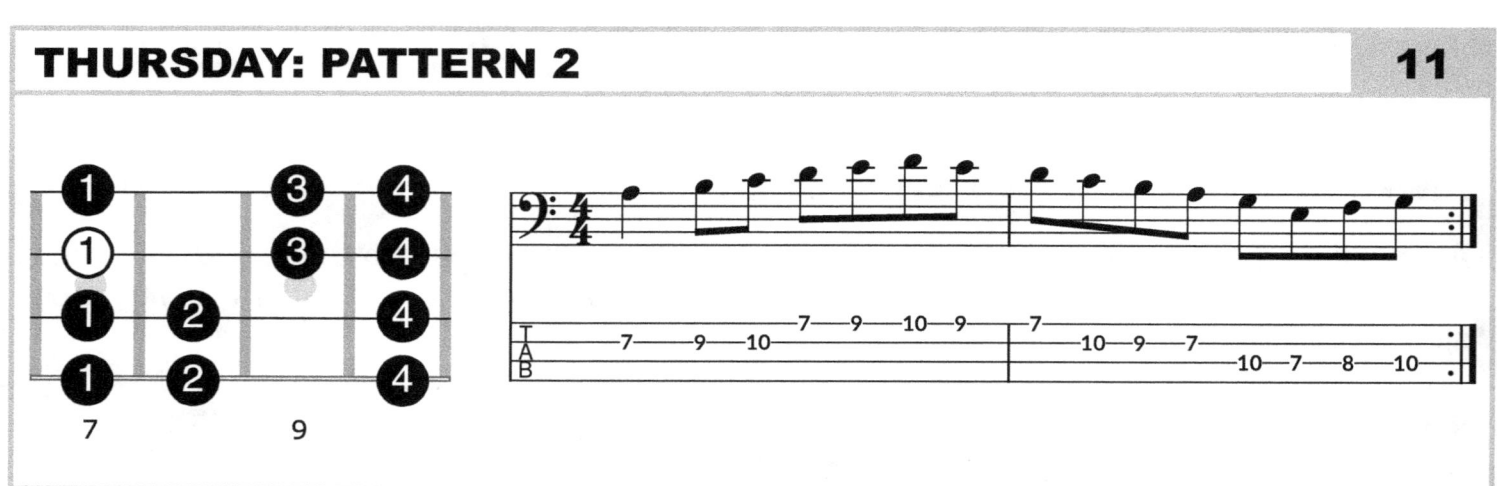

FRIDAY: PATTERN 3

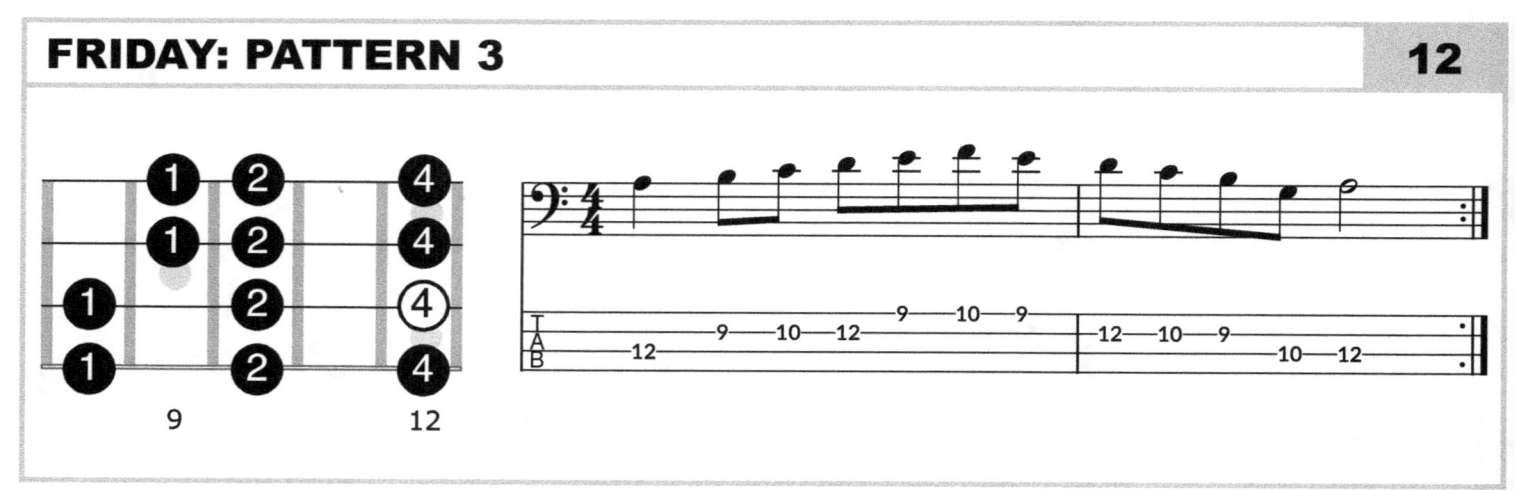

SATURDAY: PATTERN 4

Observe how the first finger replaces notes that were open strings on Monday.

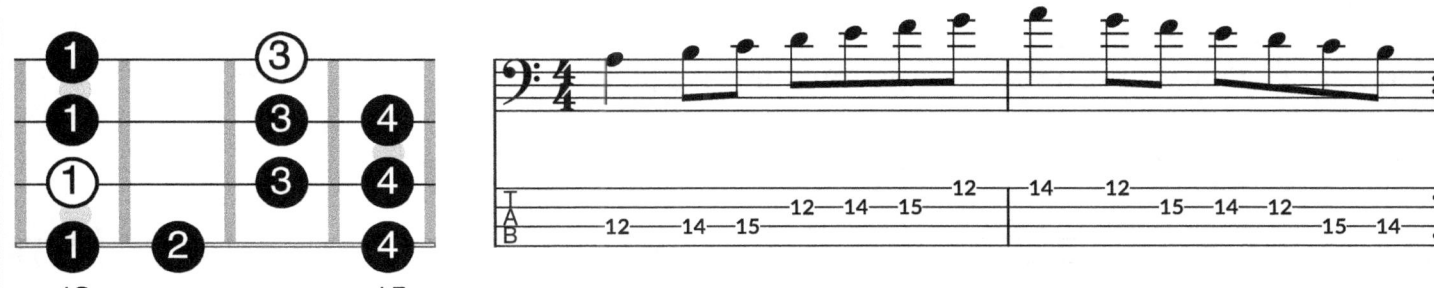

SUNDAY: SCALE APPLICATION

Chord progressions can also originate from the minor scale. Although the scale is created by shifting the starting note of its relative major scale to the 6th degree, the chords in the progression are still labeled according to the relative major scale—in our case, C major. So, today's progression, Am F C G, would be labeled 6- 4 1 5.

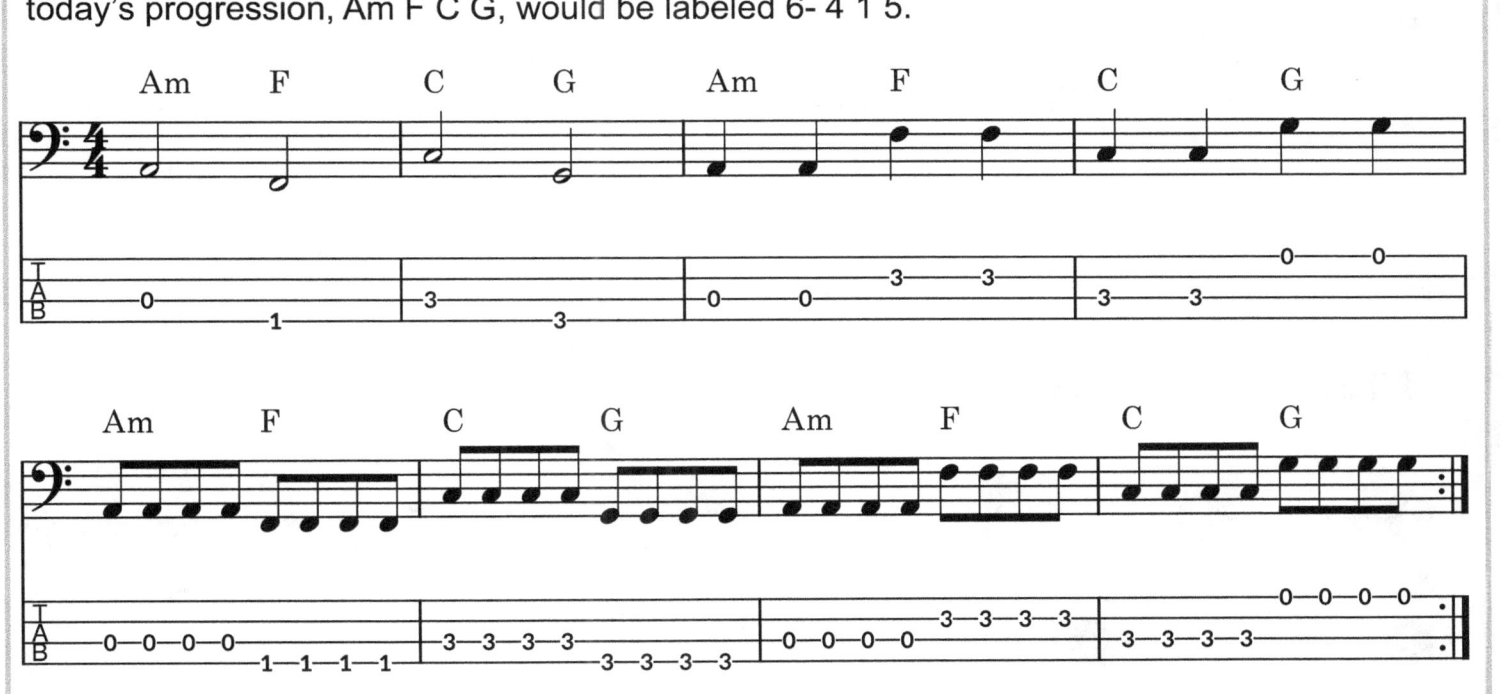

WEEK 3: A MAJOR PENTATONIC

The *major pentatonic scale* is incredibly popular. It shares the same notes as the major scale but the 4th and 7th scale degrees are omitted, making it versatile and suitable for various chords. Let's delve into its construction and how it's laid out across the fretboard.

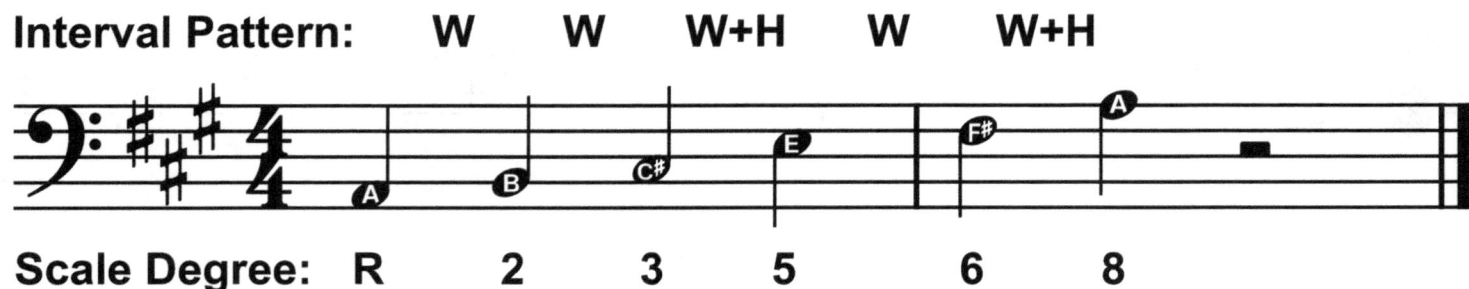

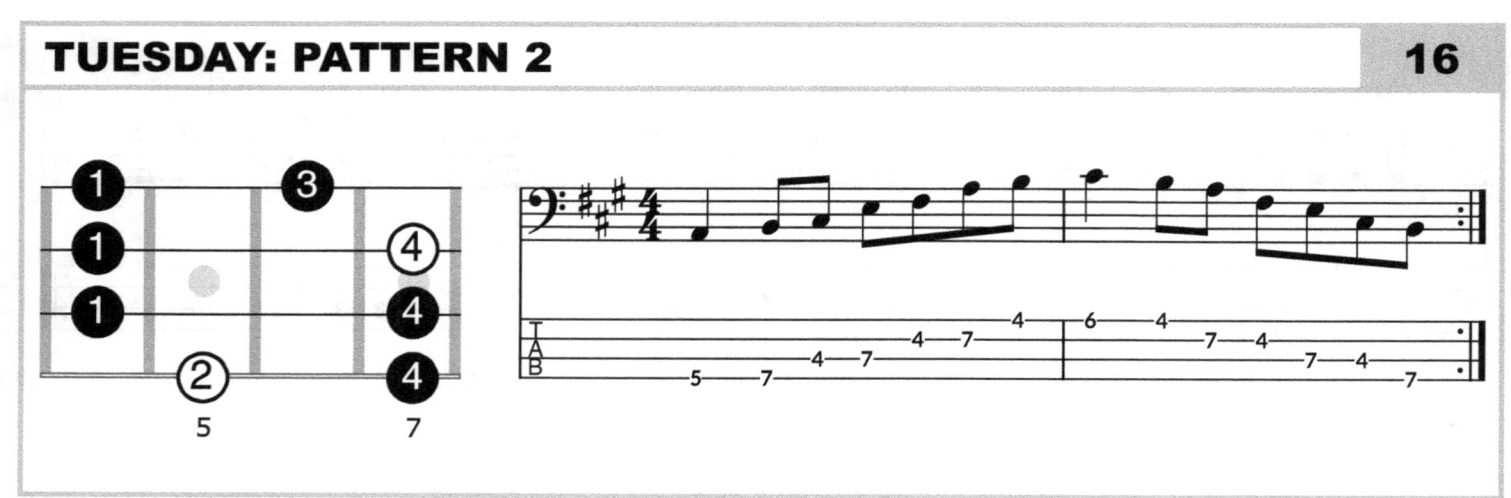

WEDNESDAY: PATTERN 3   17

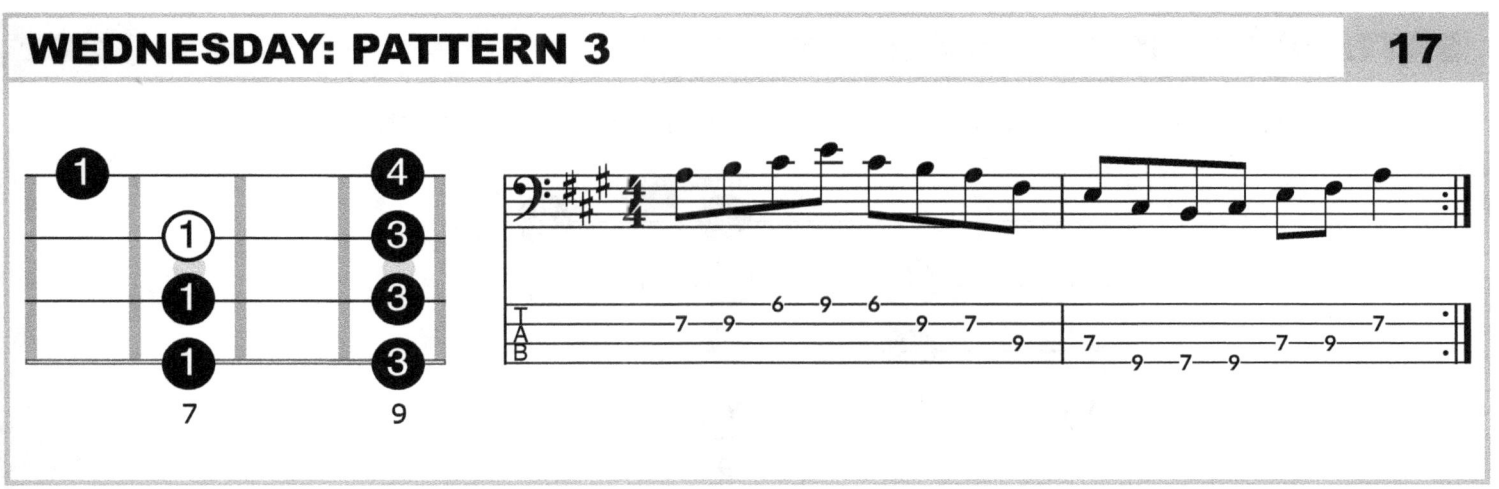

THURSDAY: PATTERN 4   18

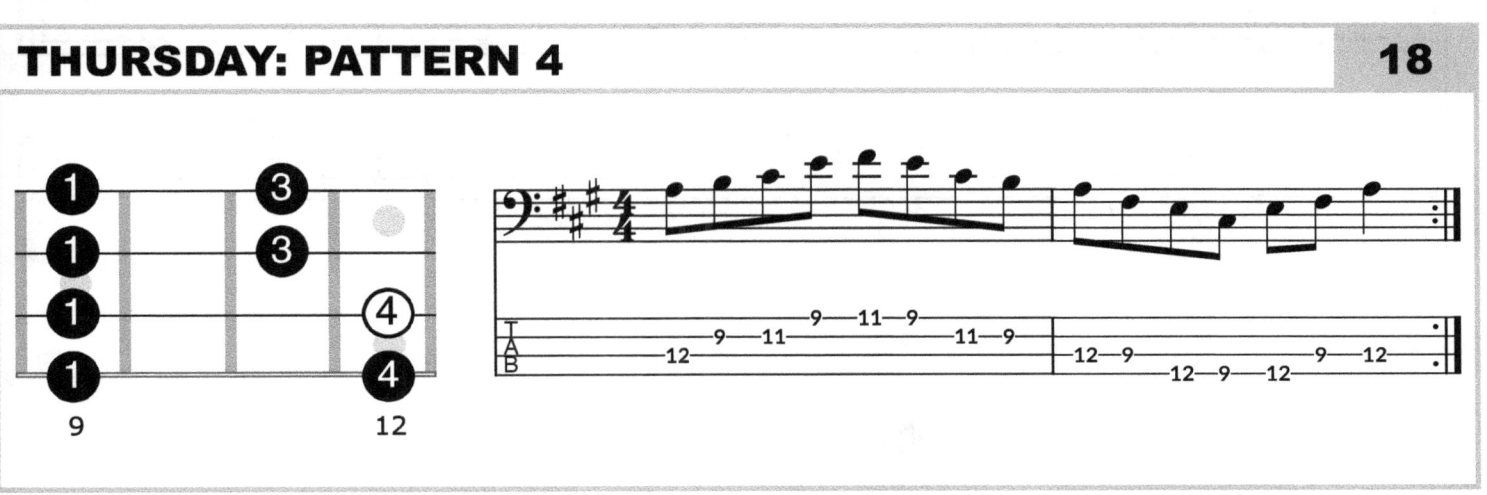

FRIDAY: PATTERN 5   19

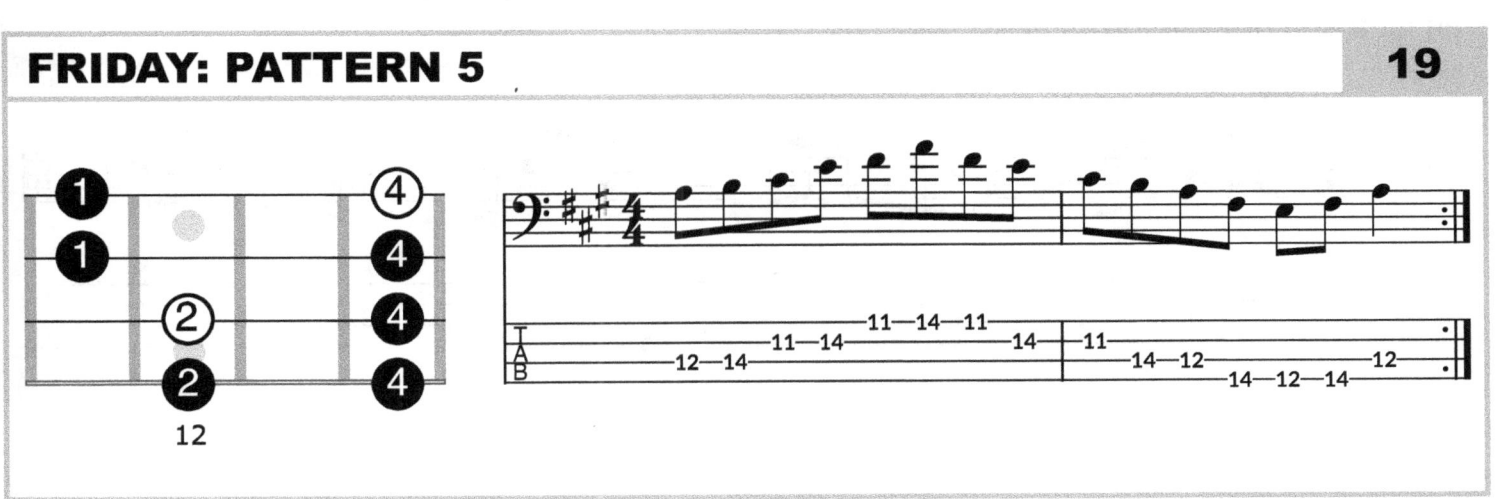

SATURDAY: HORIZONTAL PATTERN   20

Today's scale pattern is a very useful way to move horizontally along the neck.

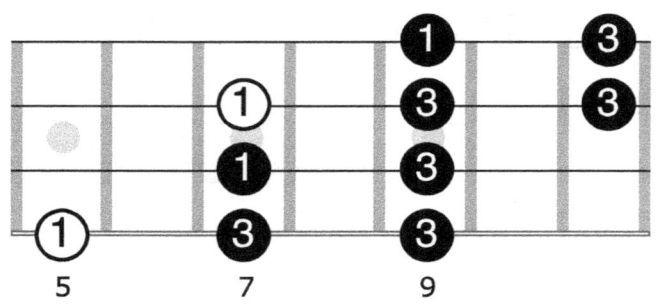

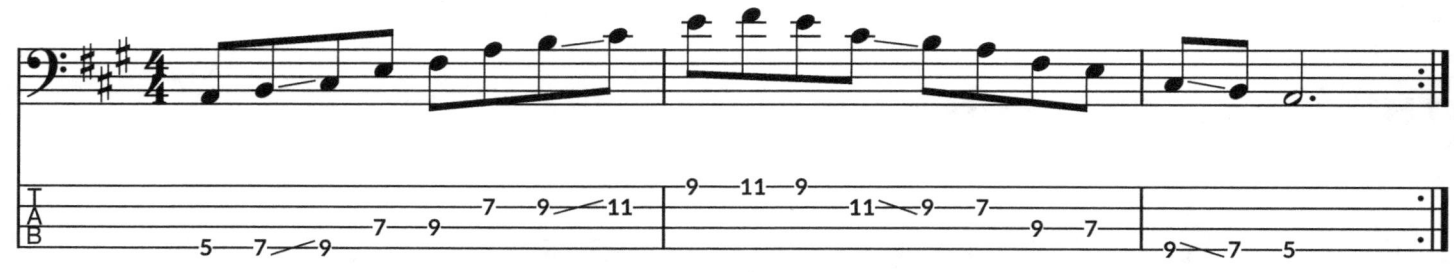

SUNDAY: SCALE APPLICATION   21

Moving from one note of a scale to the next, without skipping any notes, is referred to as "stepwise motion." Bass lines often change direction within a small group of notes while moving stepwise. Adding a rhythm results in excitement, motion, and an element of repetition to build an idea and draw in the listener.

WEEK 4: A MINOR PENTATONIC

Another extremely popular scale is the *minor pentatonic scale*. It shares the same notes as the minor scale but the 2nd and 6th scale degrees are removed, enabling it to be used over many different chords. Let's examine how it's constructed and how it lays across the fretboard.

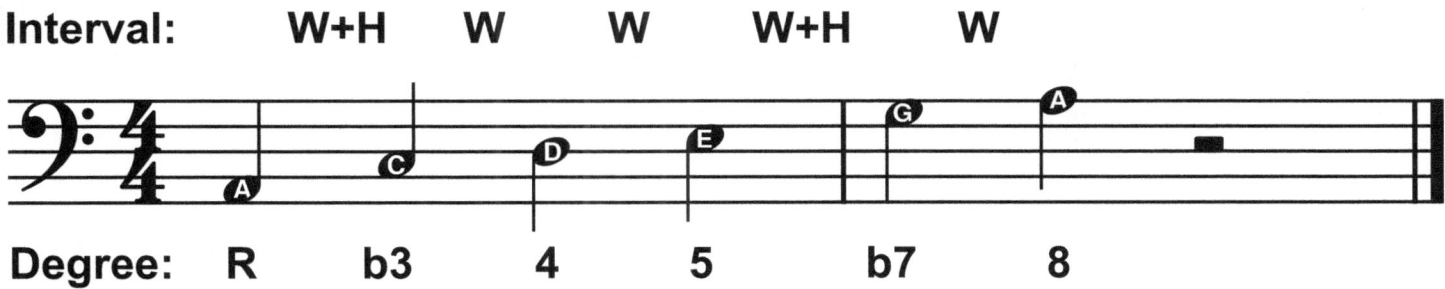

MONDAY: PATTERN 4　　22

TUESDAY: PATTERN 5　　23

WEDNESDAY: PATTERN 1 — 24

THURSDAY: PATTERN 2 — 25

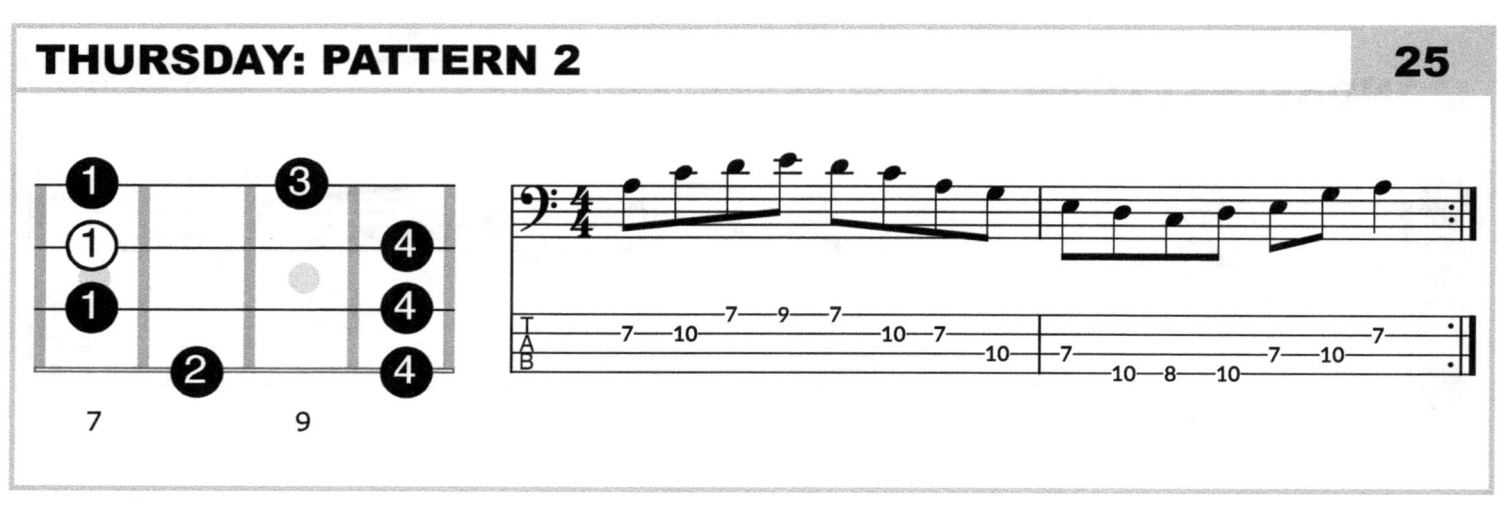

FRIDAY: PATTERN 3 — 26

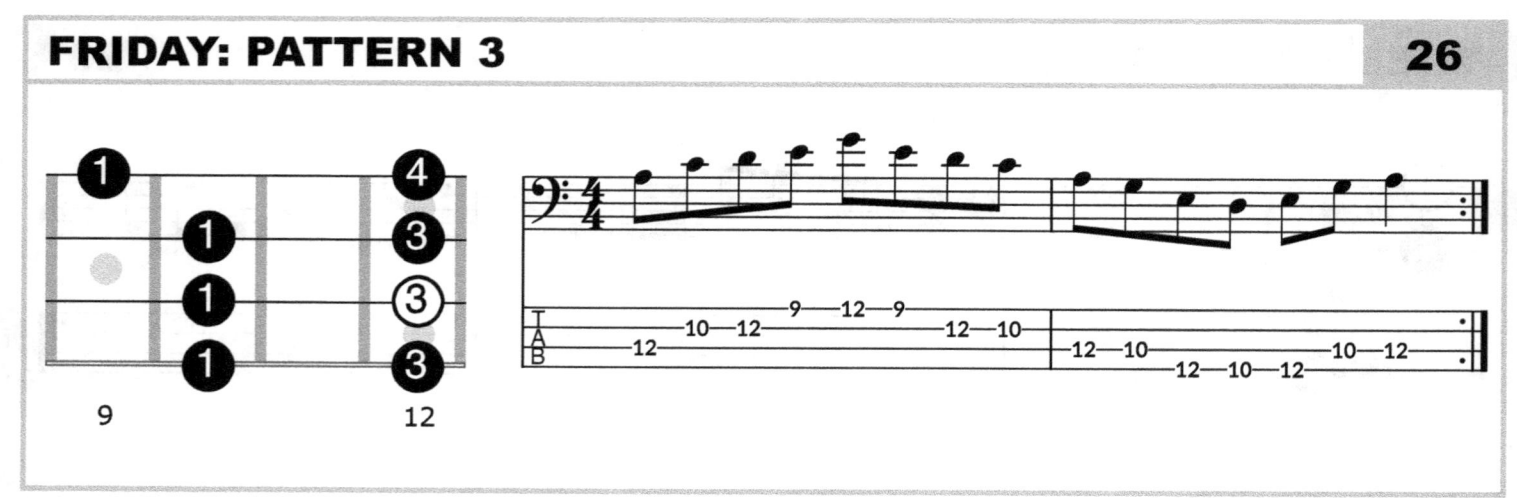

SATURDAY: HORIZONTAL PATTERN   27

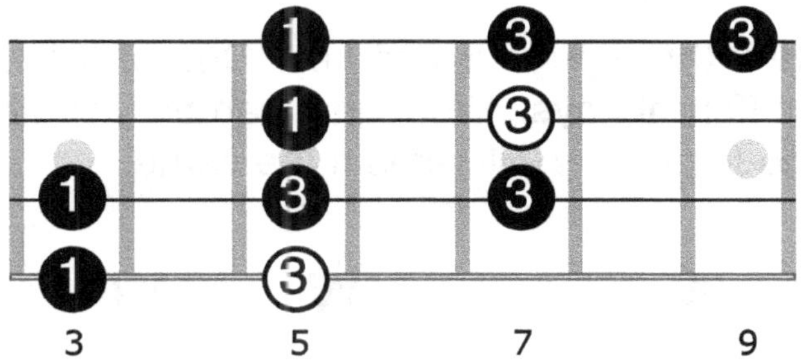

SUNDAY: SCALE APPLICATION   28

Descending stepwise motion is also a common theme in bass lines and melodies. Today's example incorporates descending stepwise motion into Pattern 5. Begin by listening to the accompanying audio while counting aloud "1, 2-and, 3-and, and."

WEEK 5: B♭ MAJOR

Congratulations, you've made it through your first key! One of the challenges of the bass is playing the same patterns in different keys. Although it can be visually awkward when you are on or off the fretboard dots, the fingerings will remain the same.

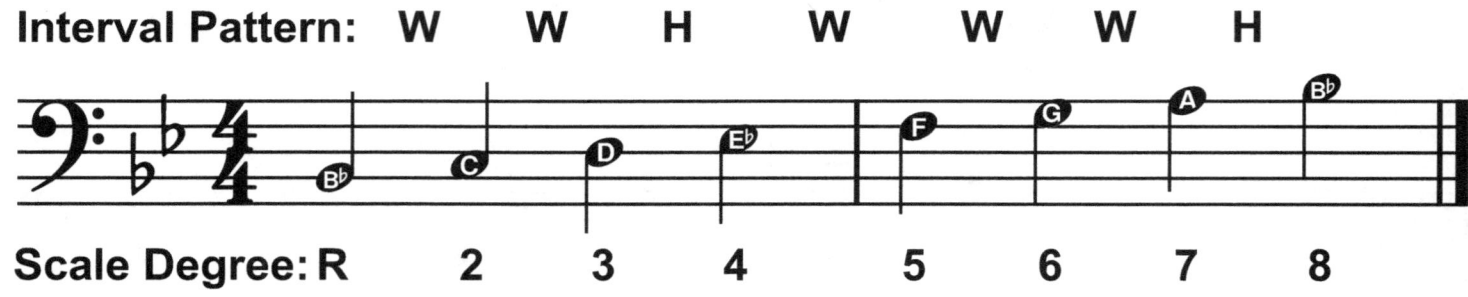

MONDAY: OPEN-STRING PATTERN 5　　29

TUESDAY: PATTERN 1　　30

WEDNESDAY: PATTERN 2

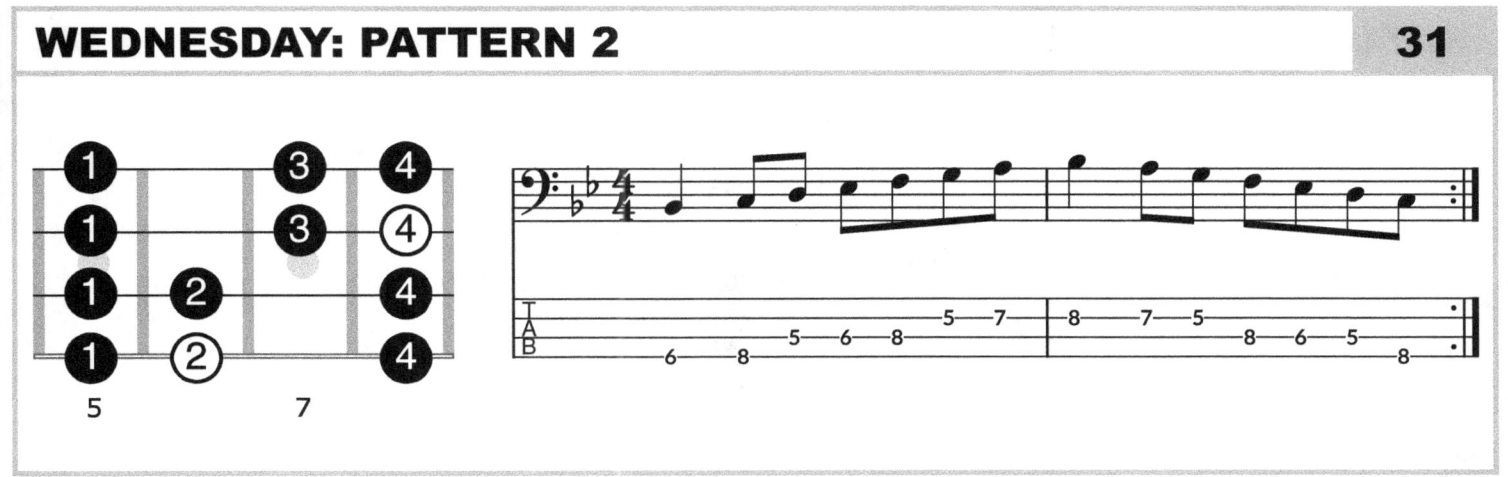

THURSDAY: PATTERN 3

FRIDAY: PATTERN 4

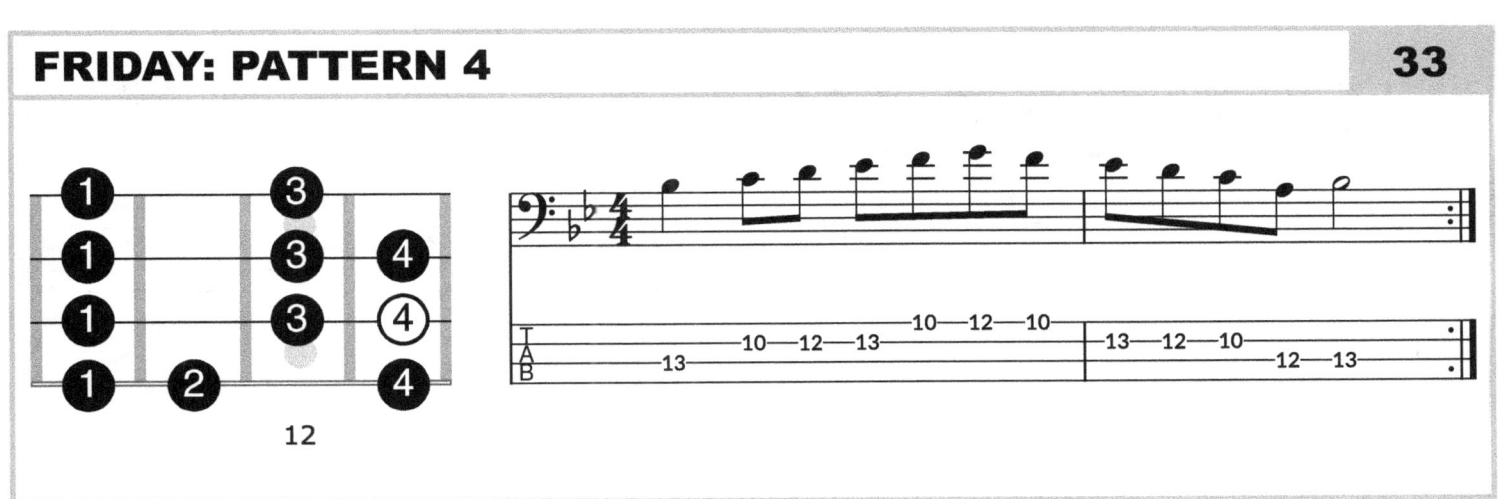

SATURDAY: HORIZONTAL PATTERN — 34

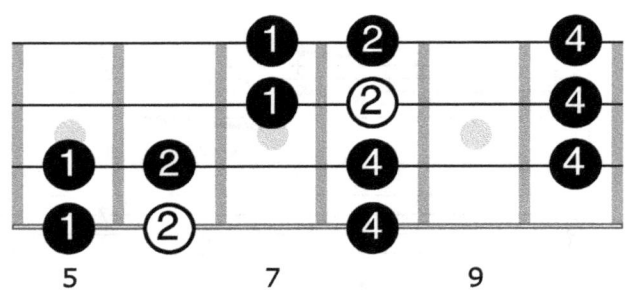
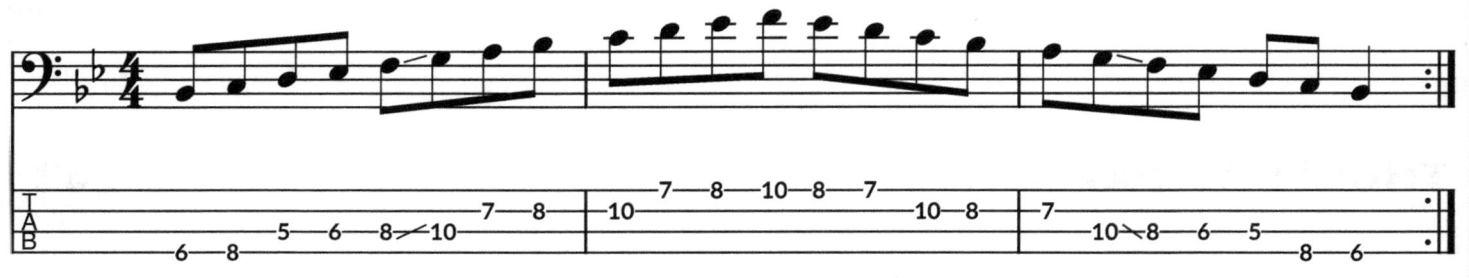

SUNDAY: SCALE APPLICATION — 35

A musical pattern that occurs frequently is stepwise motion is "groups of 3." This pattern can be thought of as ascending three notes, descending one note, and ascending three notes again. You'll find this moves you up the scale a note at a time. Review Wednesday's lesson, as this example uses Pattern 2.

WEEK 6: B♭ MINOR

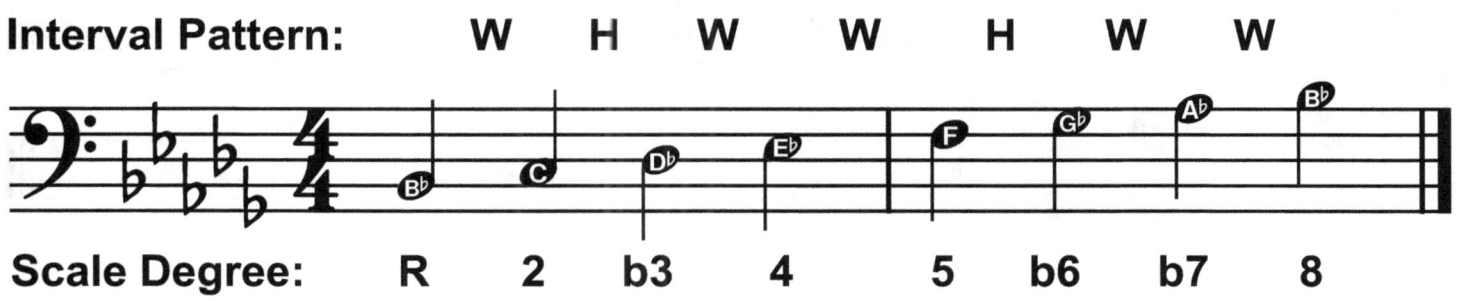

MONDAY: PATTERN 4 — 36

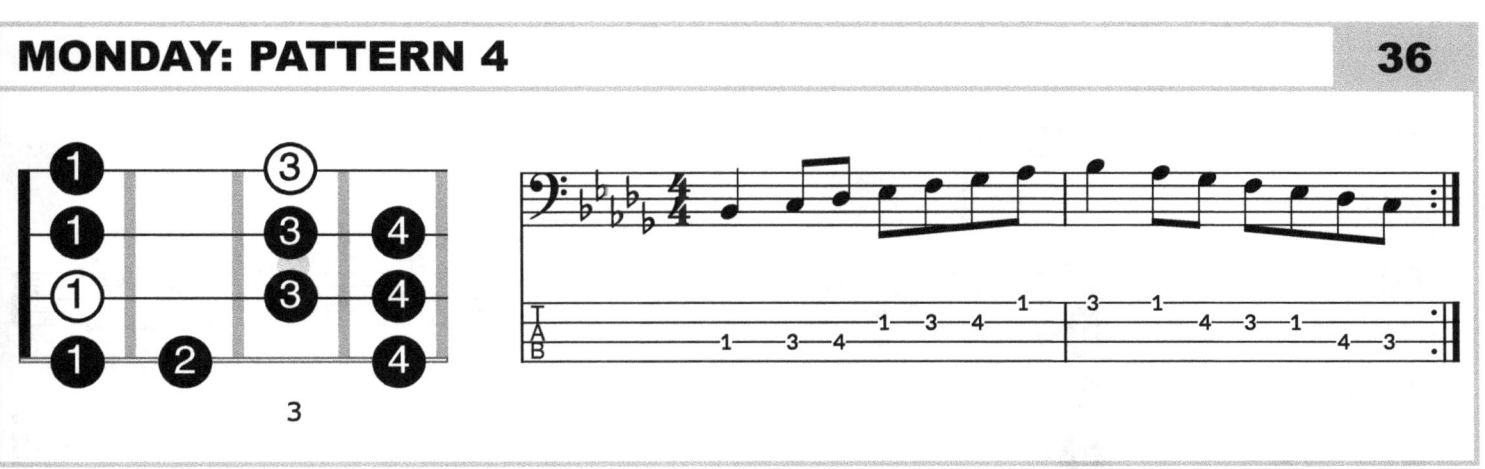

TUESDAY: PATTERN 5 — 37

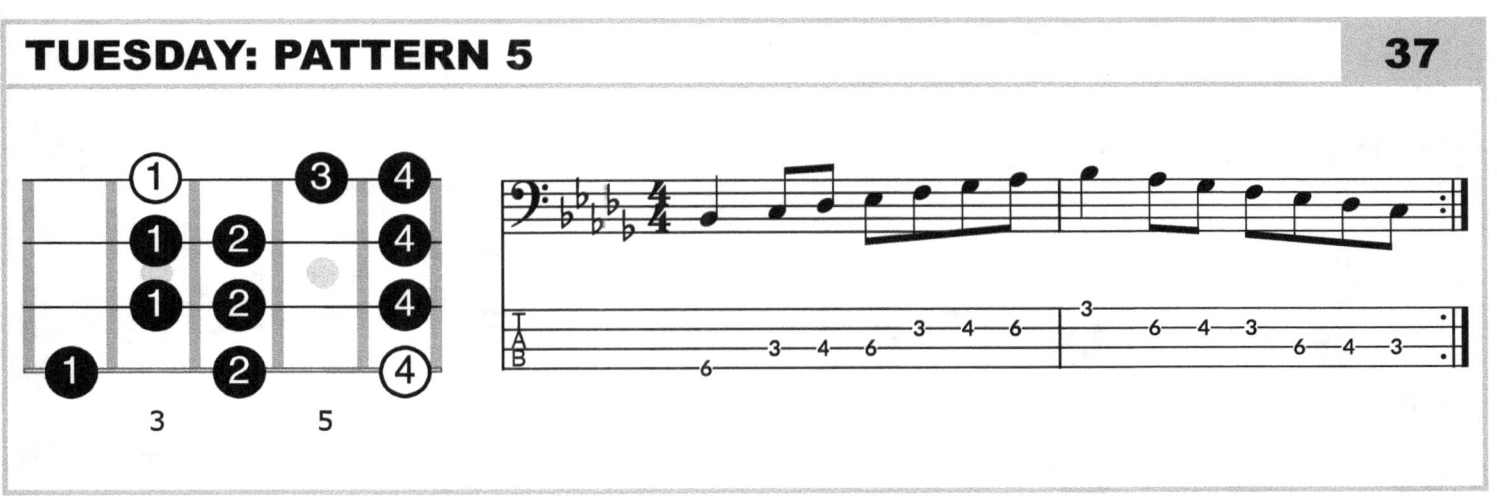

WEDNESDAY: PATTERN 1

THURSDAY: PATTERN 2

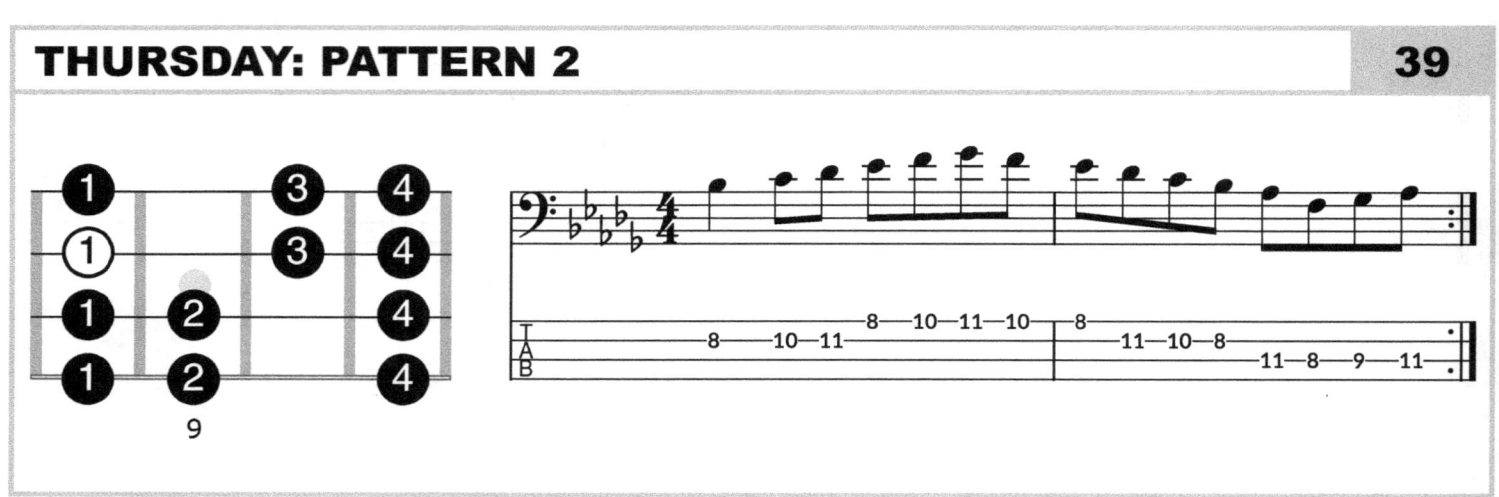

FRIDAY: PATTERN 3

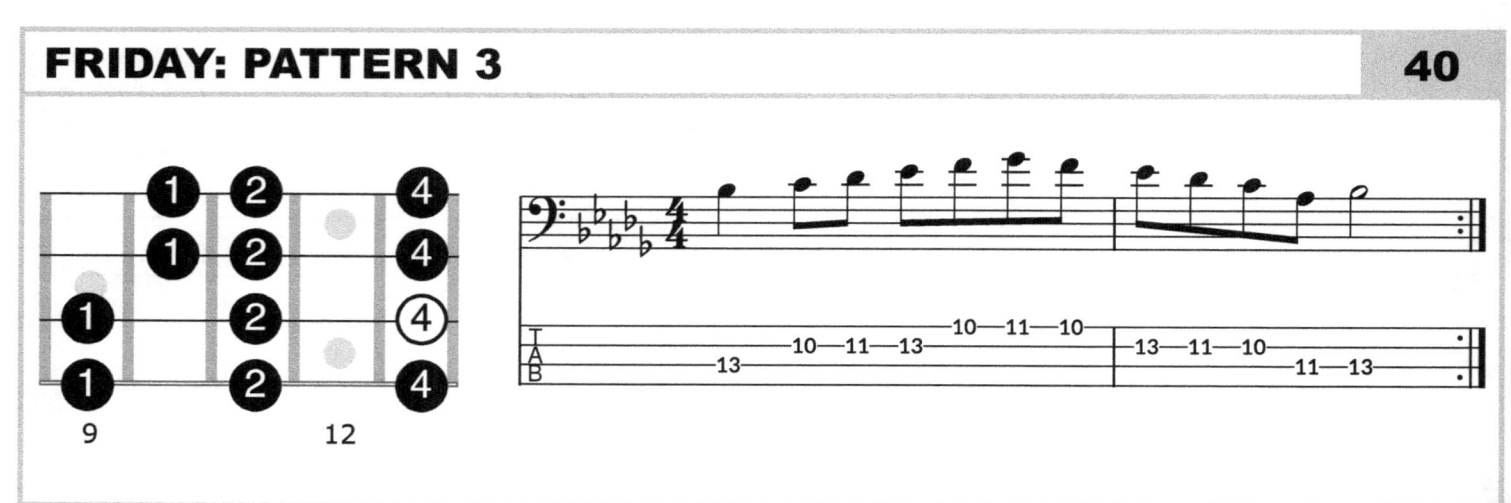

SATURDAY: HORIZONTAL PATTERN 41

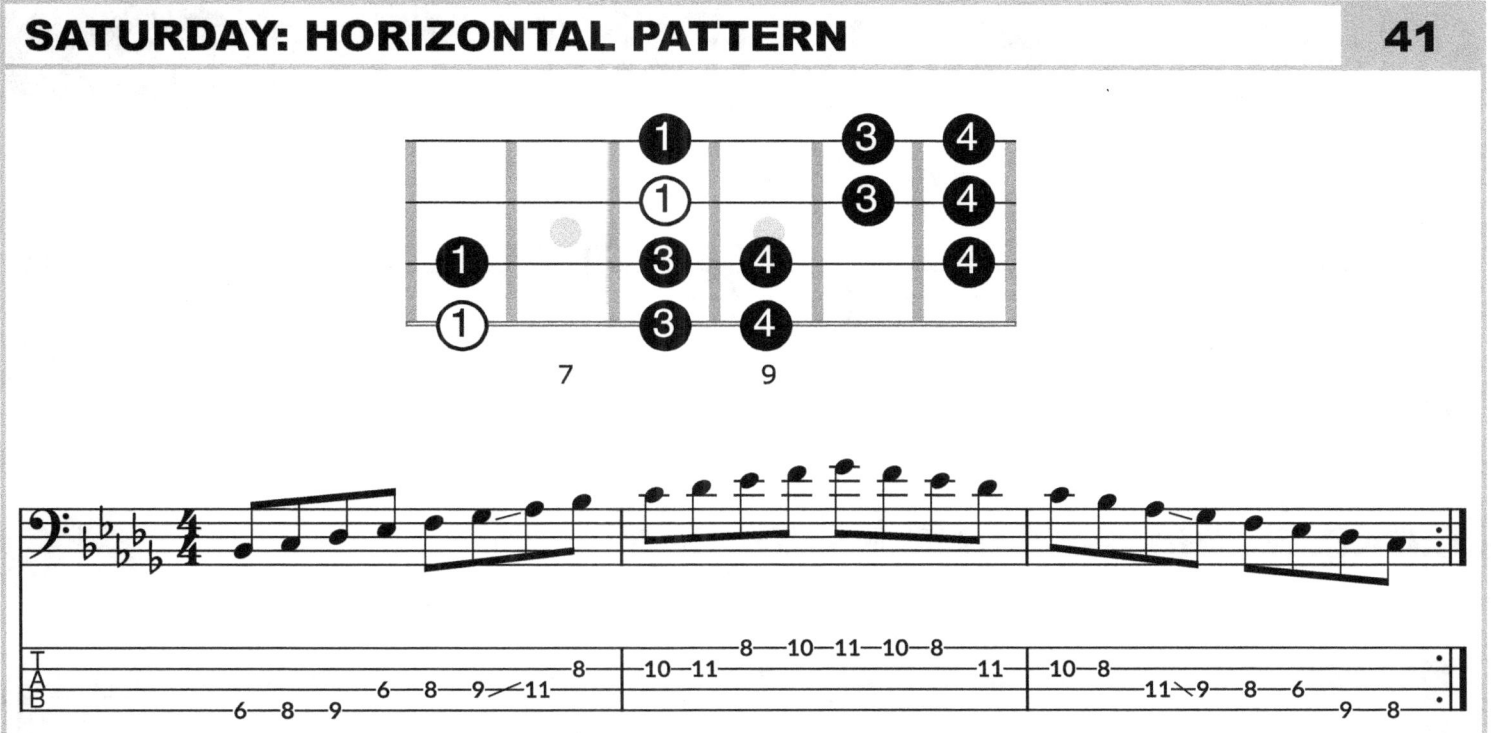

SUNDAY: SCALE APPLICATION 42

A *riff* is usually a lower-voiced, repeated phrase that is typically used as an introduction or refrain in a song. Below is an example riff using Pattern 1. Notice how it incorporates a different resolution in measures 2 and 4, giving it a question-and-answer feel.

WEEK 7: B♭ MAJOR PENTATONIC

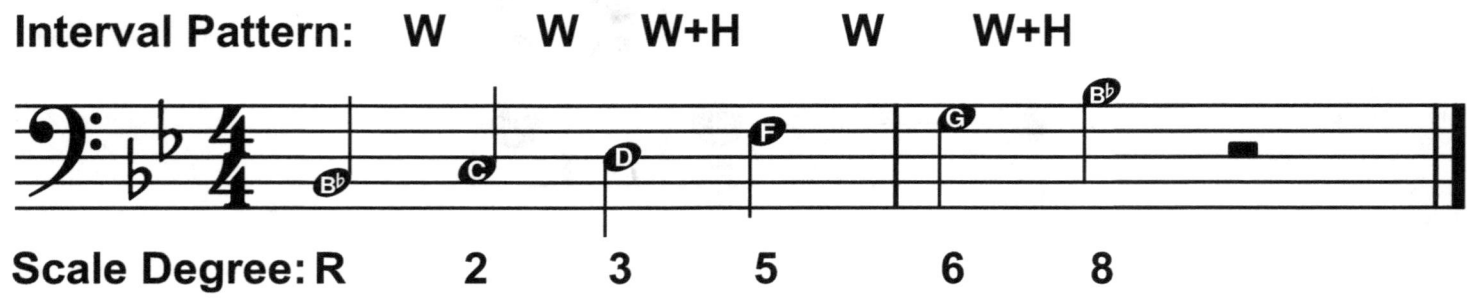

MONDAY: OPEN-STRING PATTERN 5 — 43

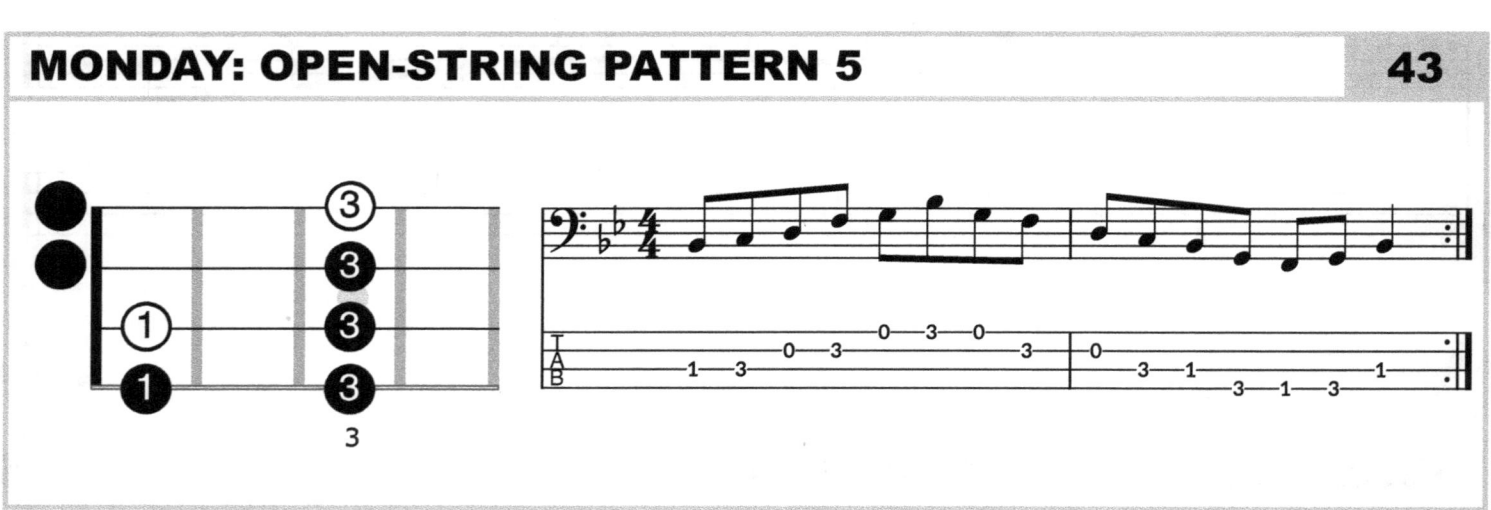

TUESDAY: PATTERN 1 — 44

WEDNESDAY: PATTERN 2

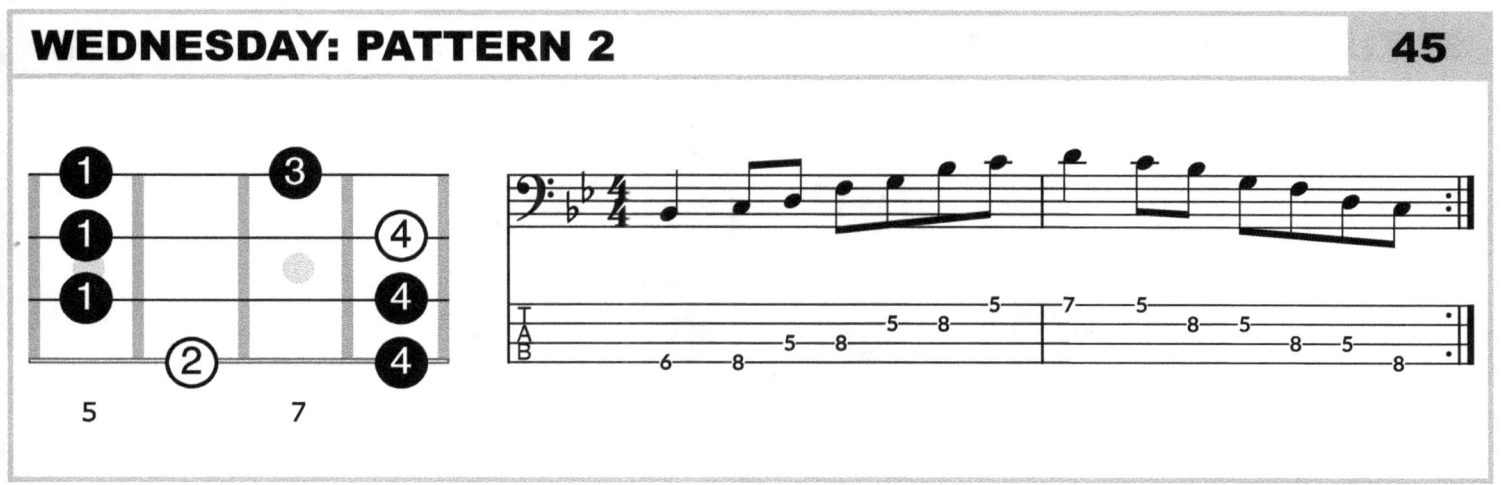

THURSDAY: PATTERN 3

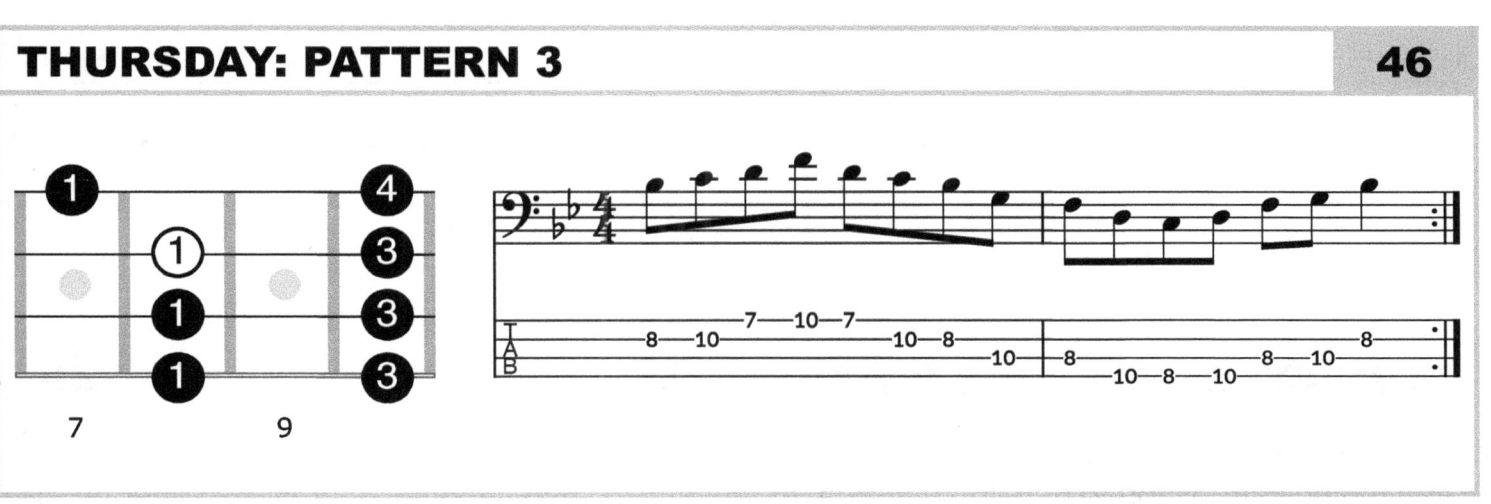

FRIDAY: PATTERN 4

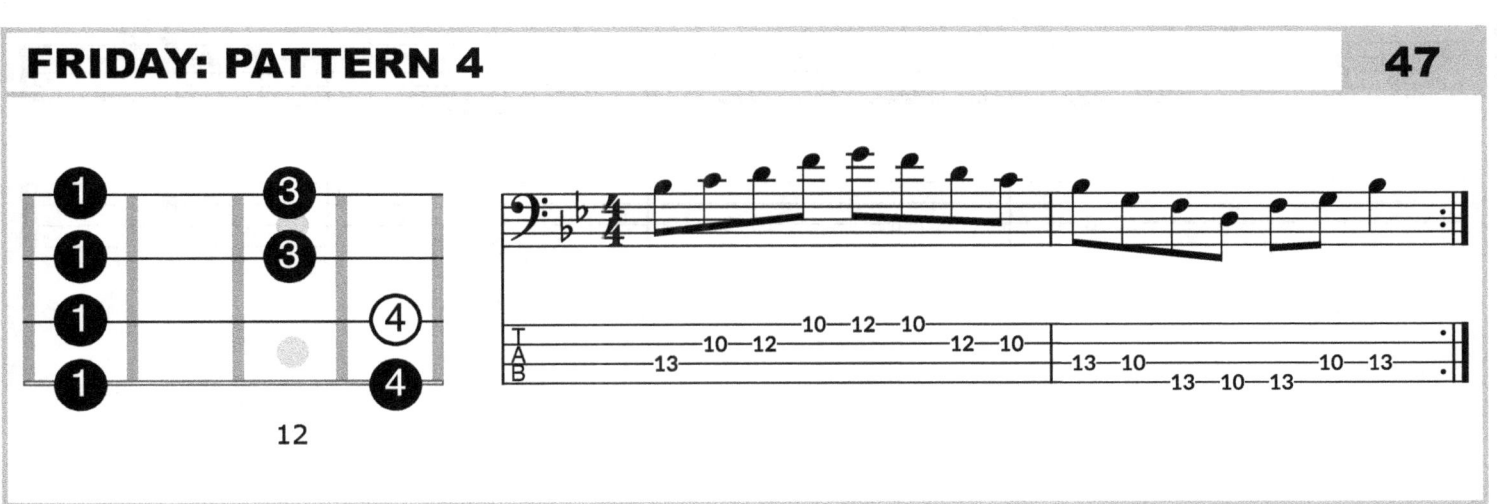

SATURDAY: HORIZONTAL PATTERN 48

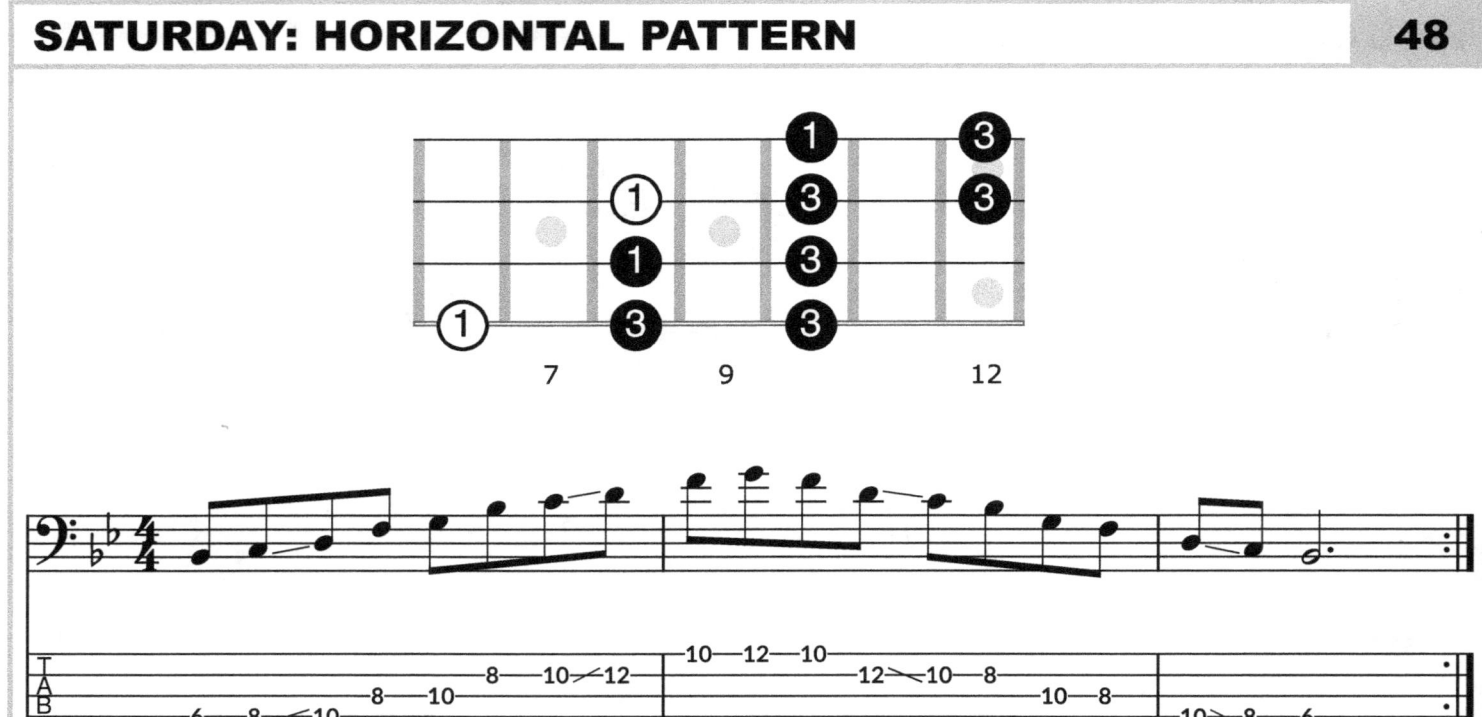

SUNDAY: SCALE APPLICATION 49

The Horizontal Pattern often provides very musical results. Notice how this riff uses rhythmic and melodic repetition to develop a theme. In measure 3, use the tip of your index finger on the 8th fret, string 3 note, then flatten it as you roll to the 2nd-string note on the same fret.

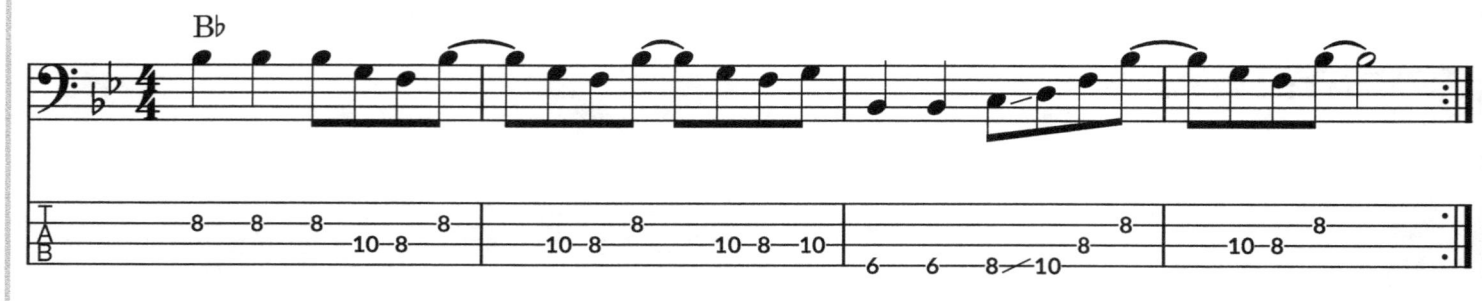

WEEK 8: B♭ MINOR PENTATONIC

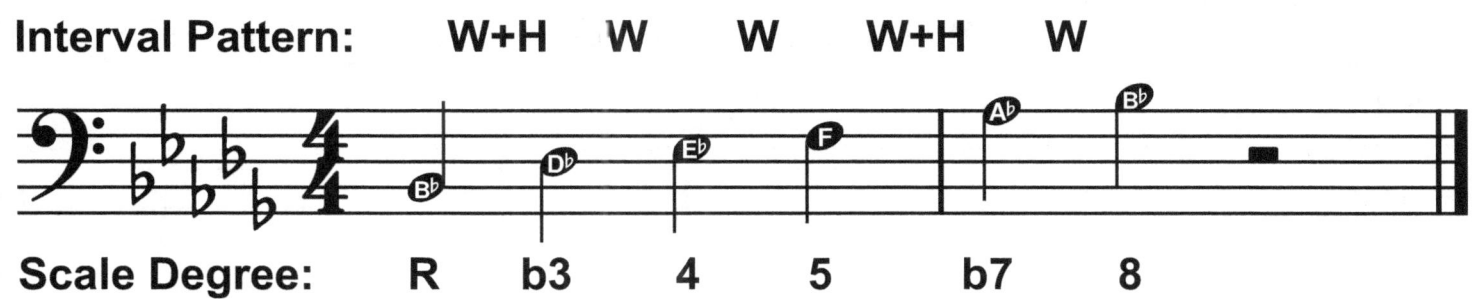

MONDAY: PATTERN 4   50

TUESDAY: PATTERN 5   51

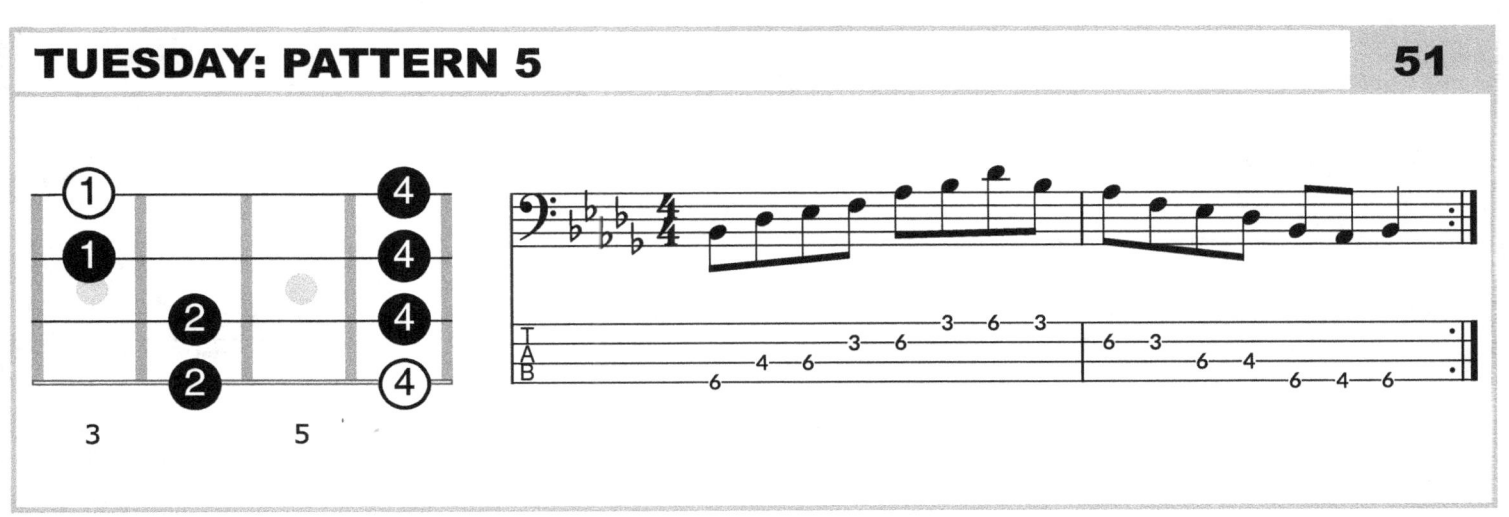

WEDNESDAY: PATTERN 1   52

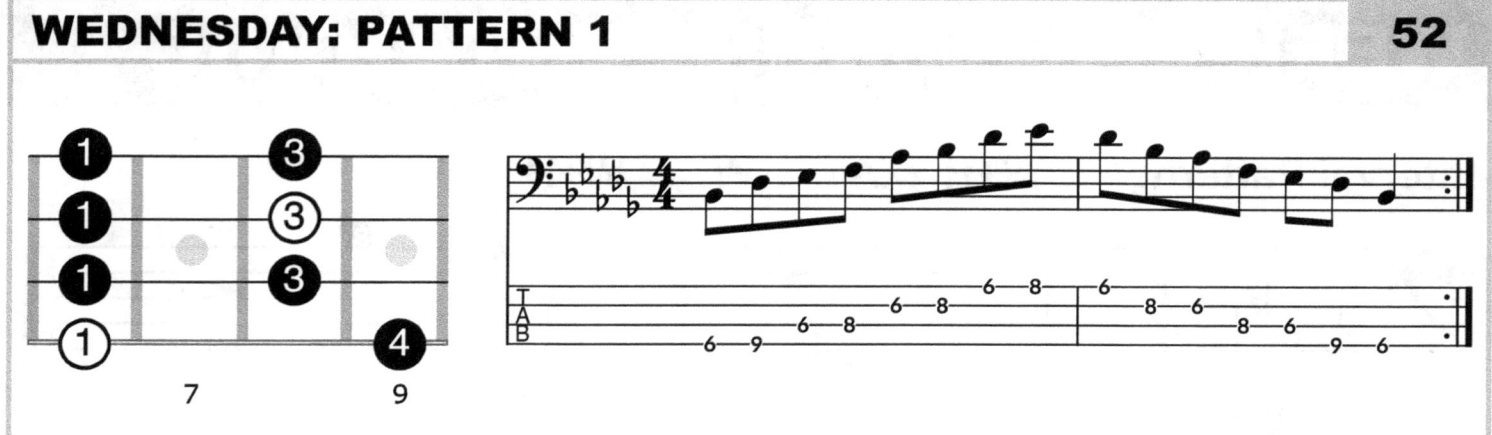

THURSDAY: PATTERN 2   53

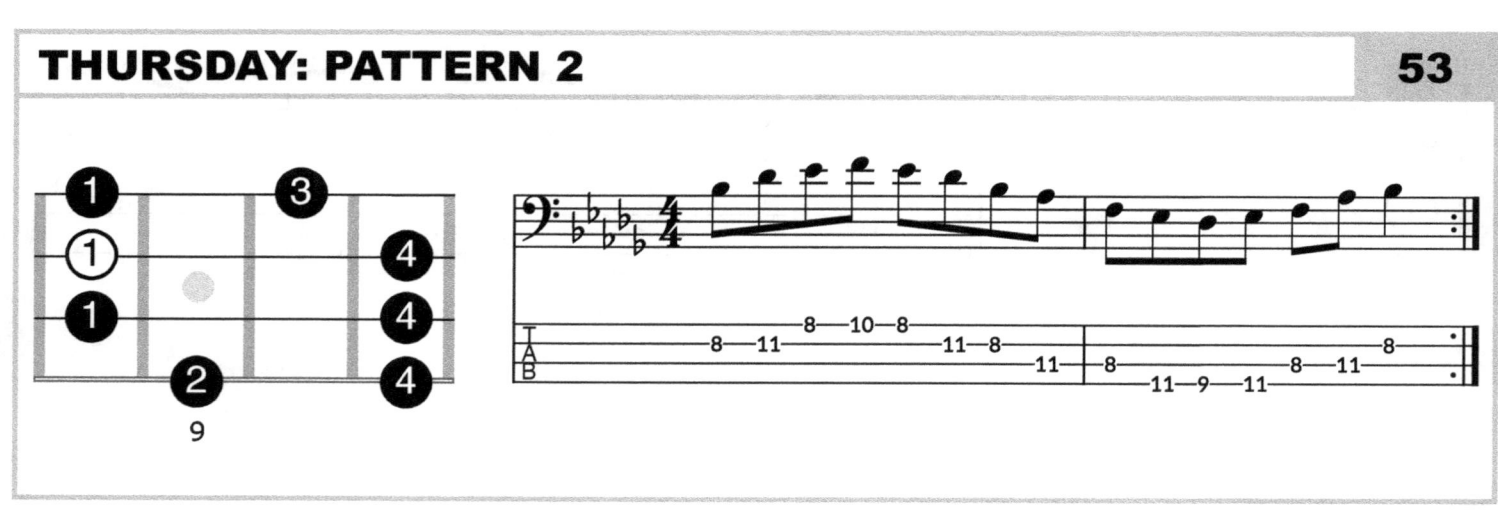

FRIDAY: PATTERN 3   54

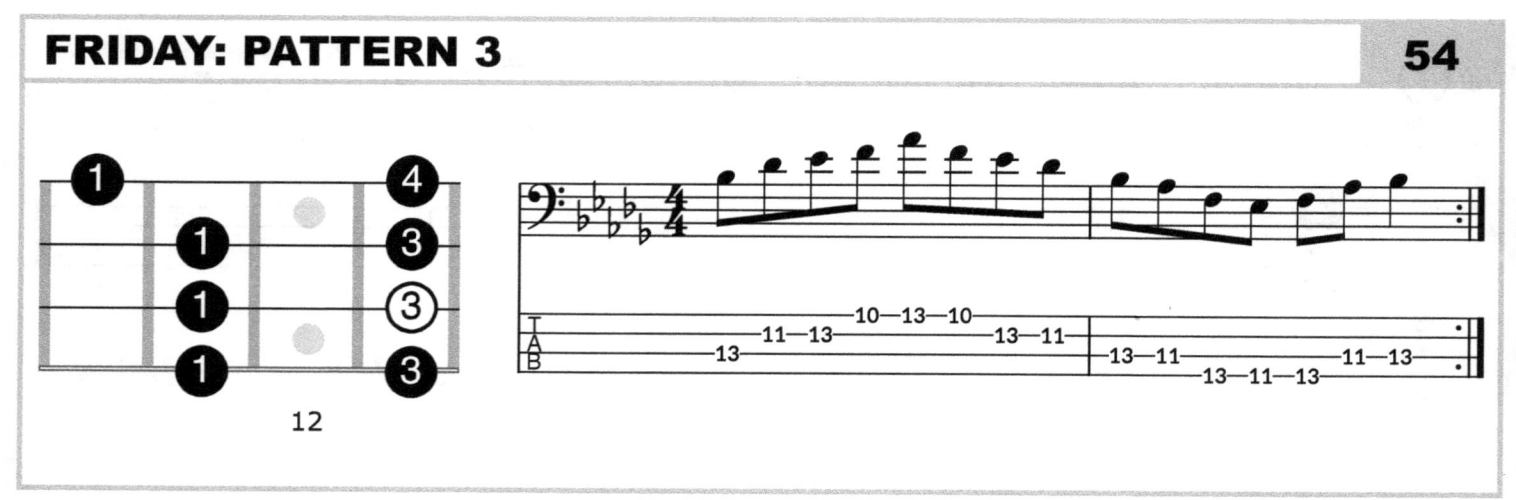

SATURDAY: HORIZONTAL PATTERN 55

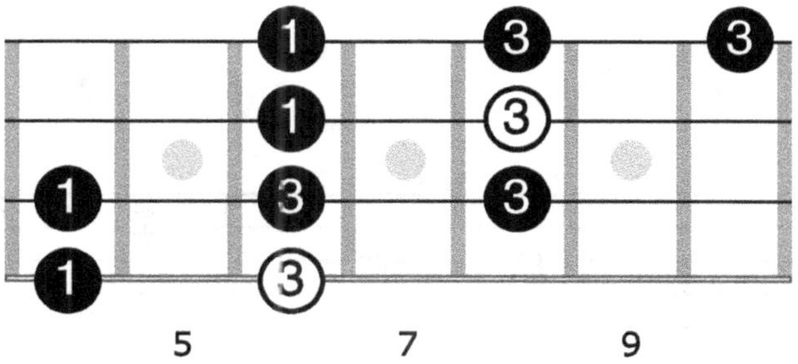

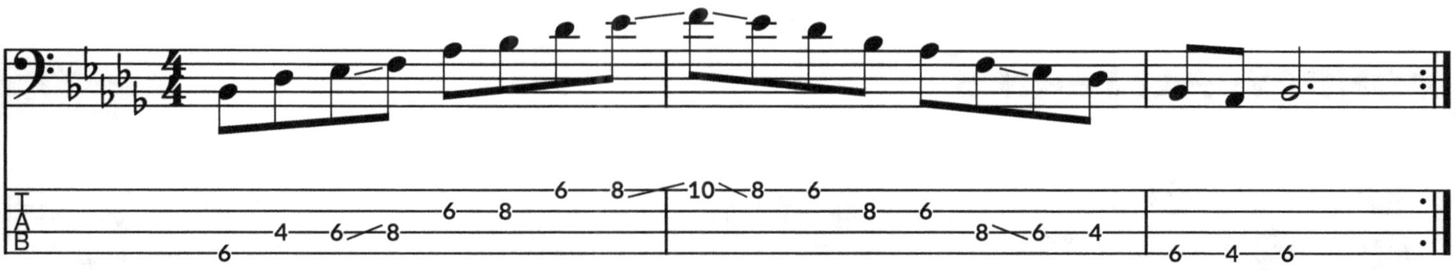

SUNDAY: SCALE APPLICATION 56

Three-note stepwise patterns are also very musical when descending and when used with the pentatonic scale. Review Pattern 1 from Wednesday before playing the example below.

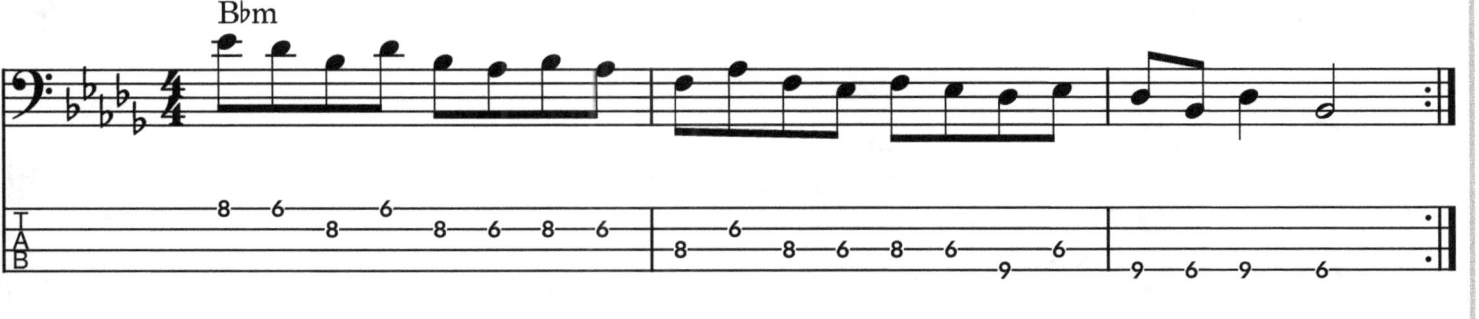

WEEK 9: B MAJOR

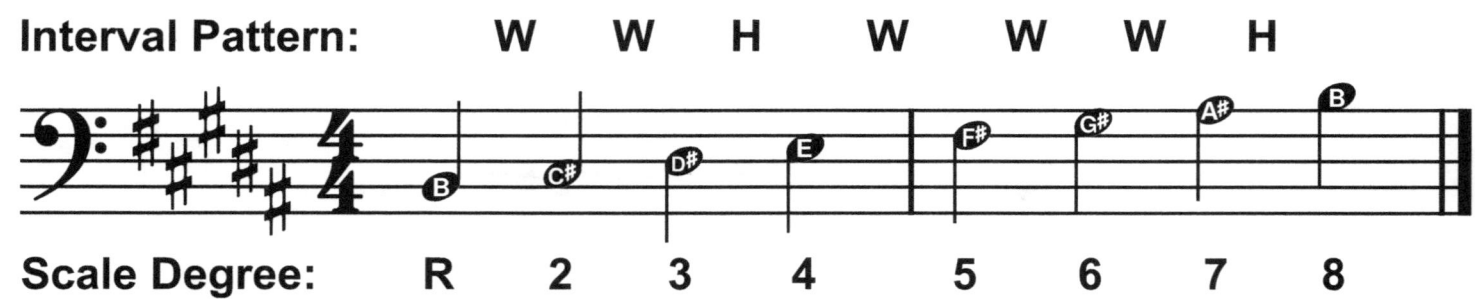

MONDAY: PATTERN 5 — 57

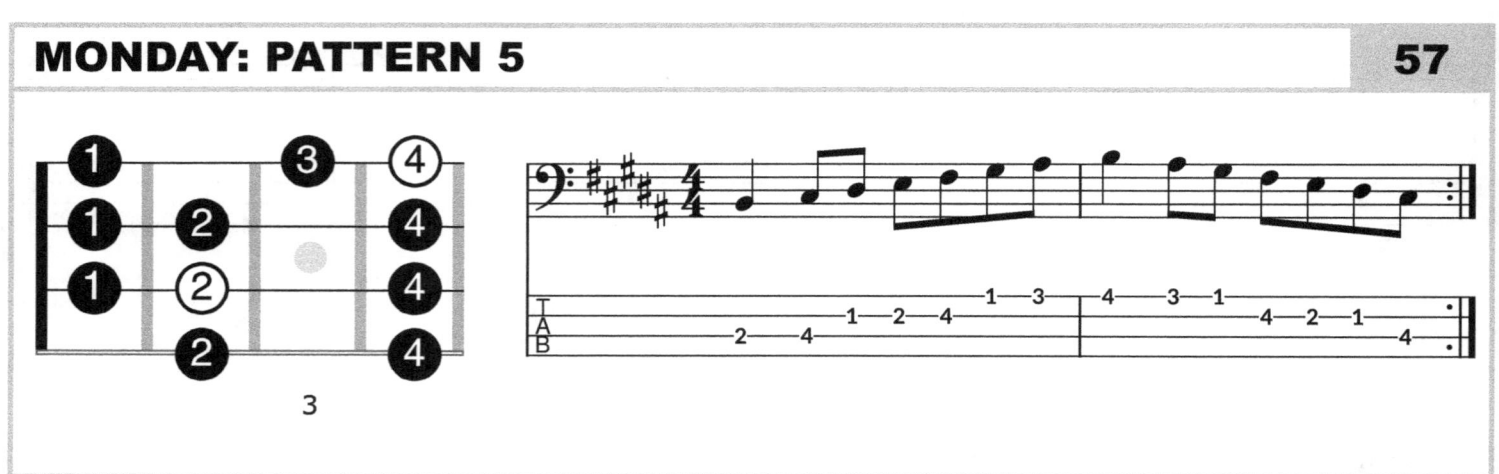

TUESDAY: PATTERN 1 — 58

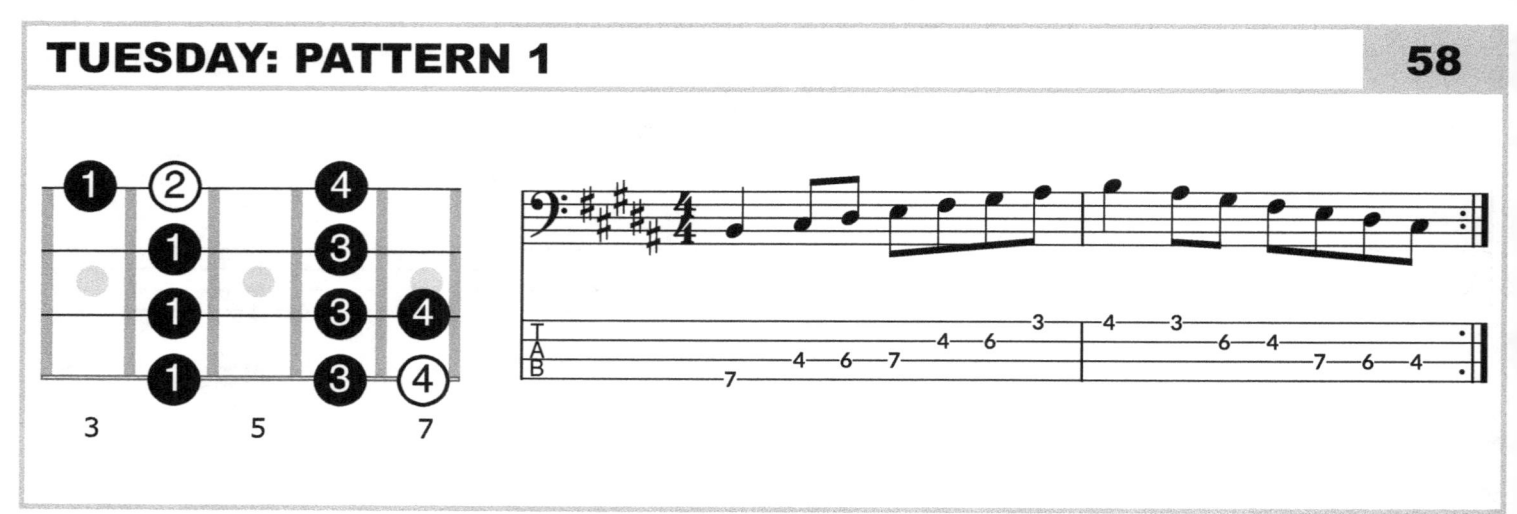

WEDNESDAY: PATTERN 2

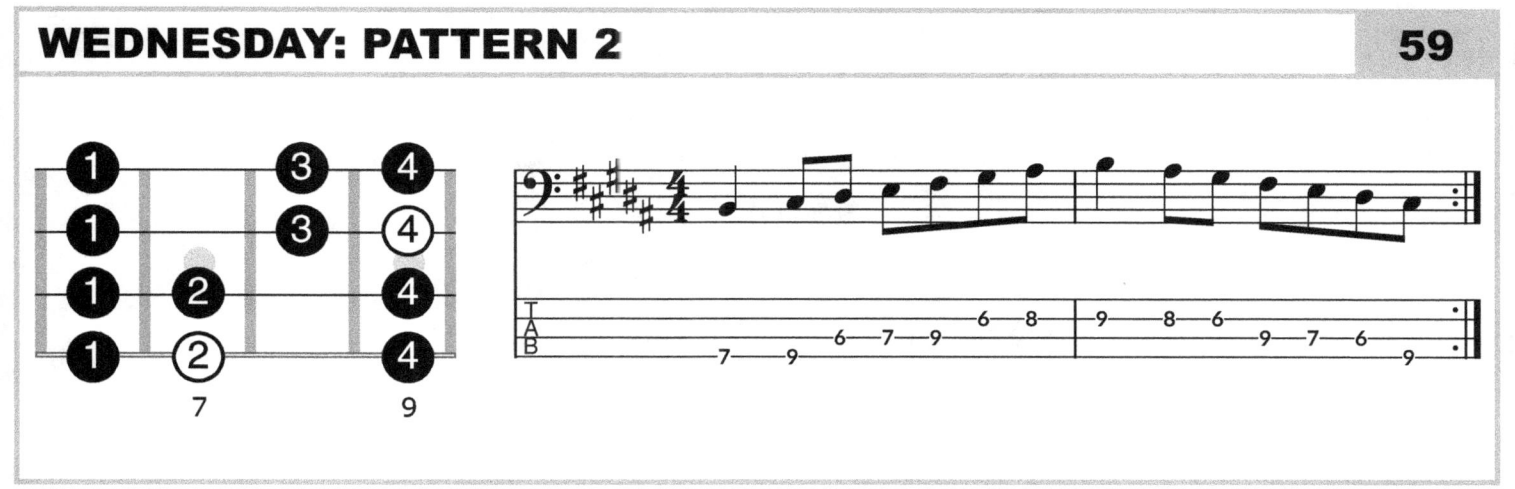

THURSDAY: PATTERN 3

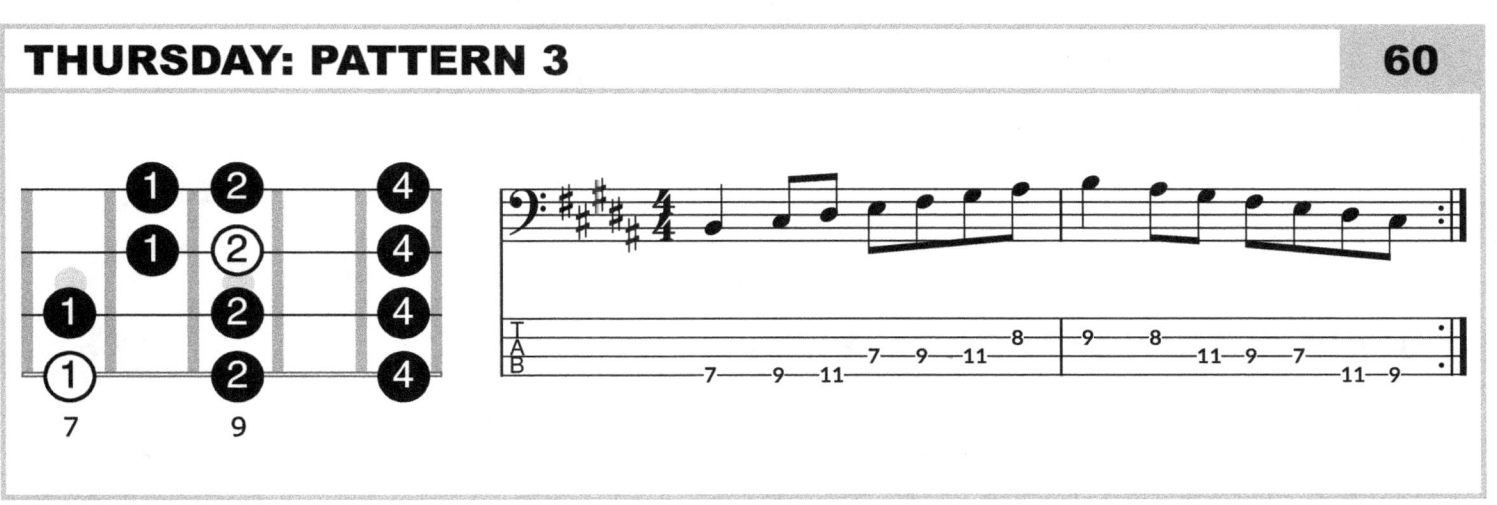

FRIDAY: PATTERN 4

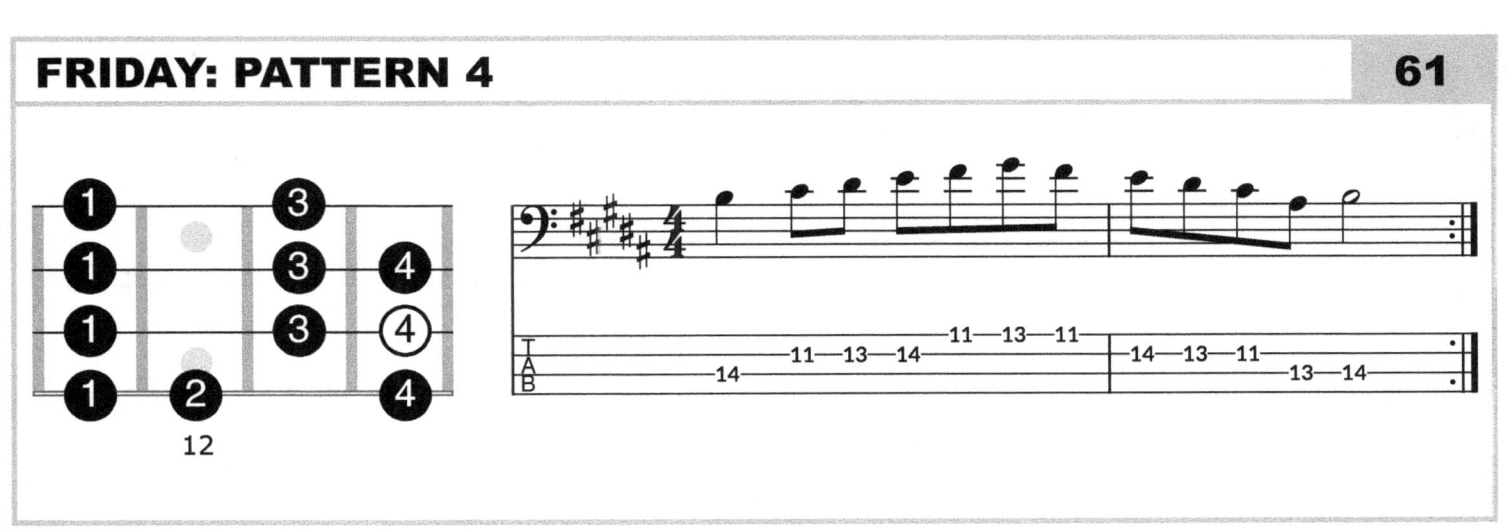

SATURDAY: HORIZONTAL PATTERN 62

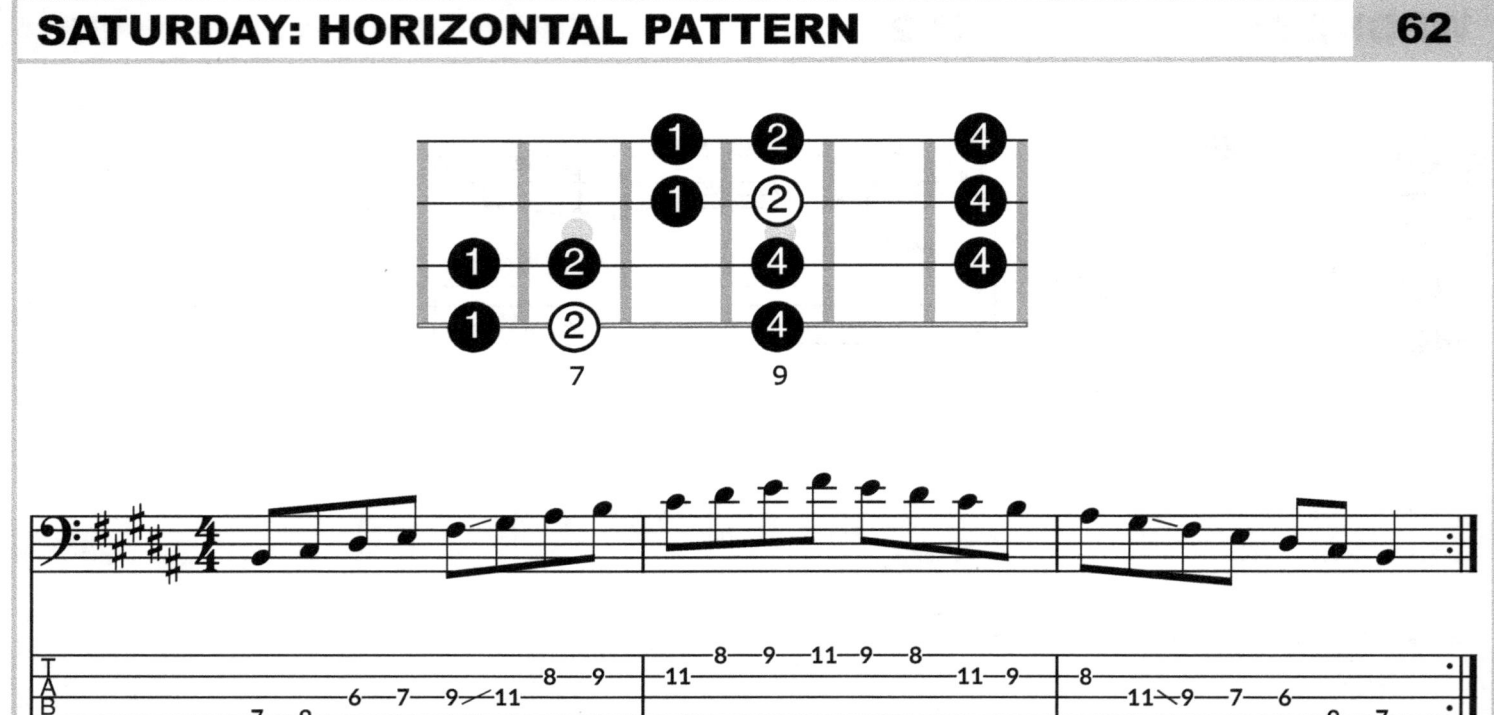

SUNDAY: SCALE APPLICATION 63

One of the most popular rhythms used in bass lines is the dotted quarter note followed by an eighth note. Let's combine this rhythm with one of the most popular chord progressions of all time while using Pattern 5. The chord progression is B G#m E F#, or 1 6- 4 5. Musicians often associate chord progressions with their scale degree, enabling easy transposition to different keys.

WEEK 10: B MINOR

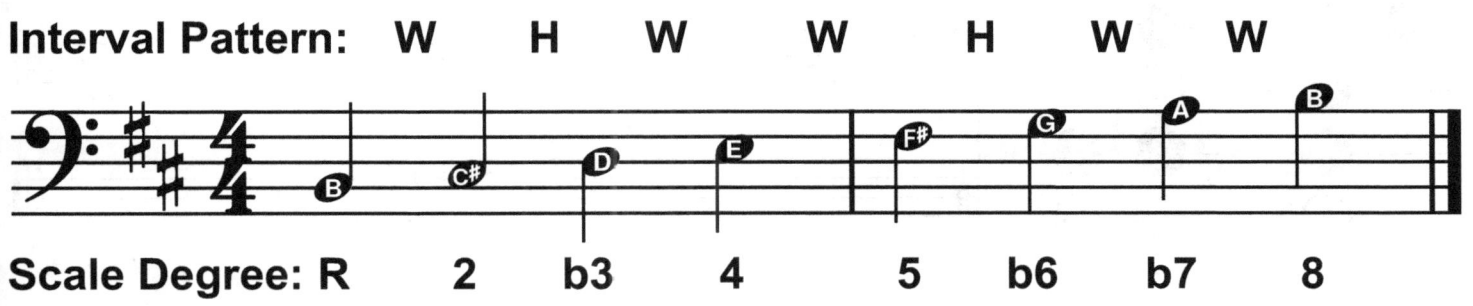

MONDAY: PATTERN 4   64

TUESDAY: PATTERN 5   65

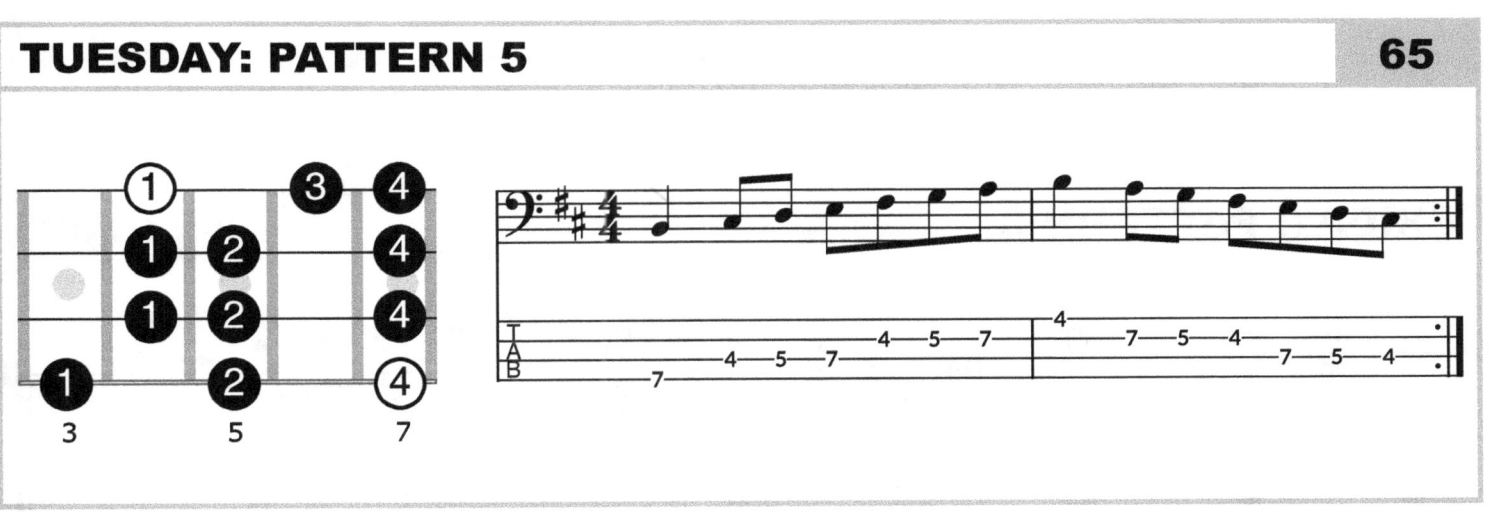

WEDNESDAY: PATTERN 1 — 66

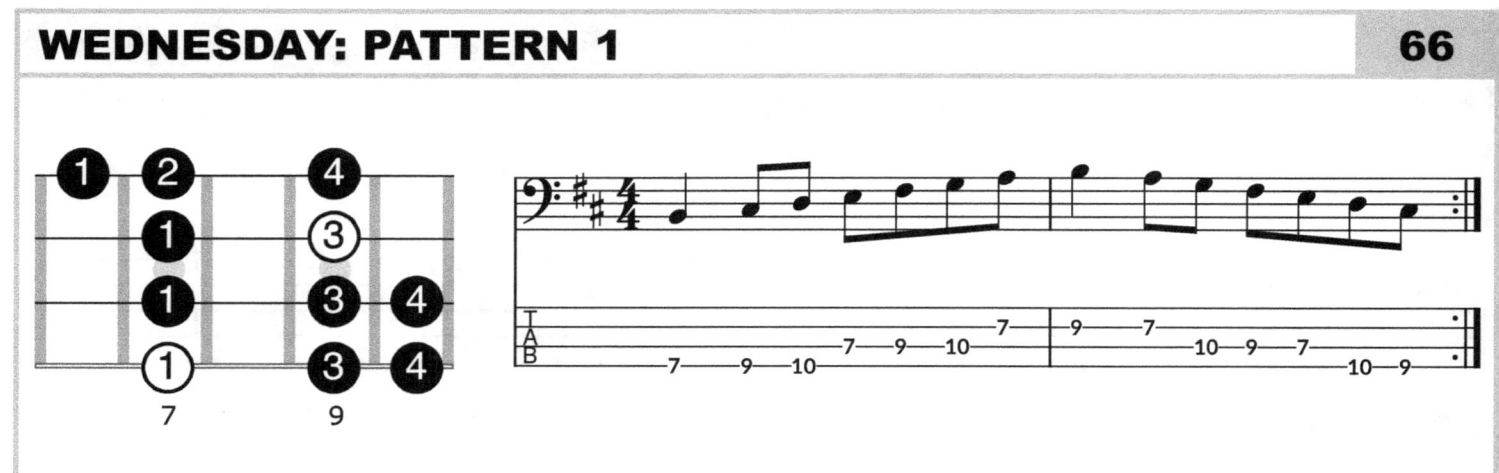

THURSDAY: PATTERN 2 — 67

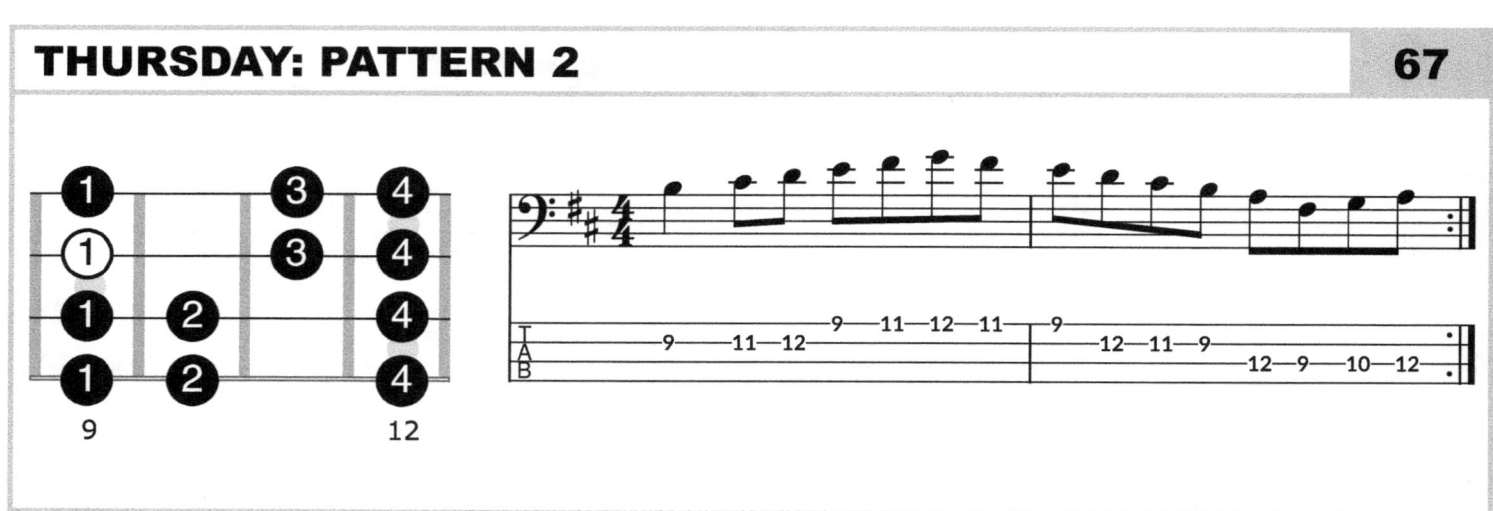

FRIDAY: PATTERN 3 — 68

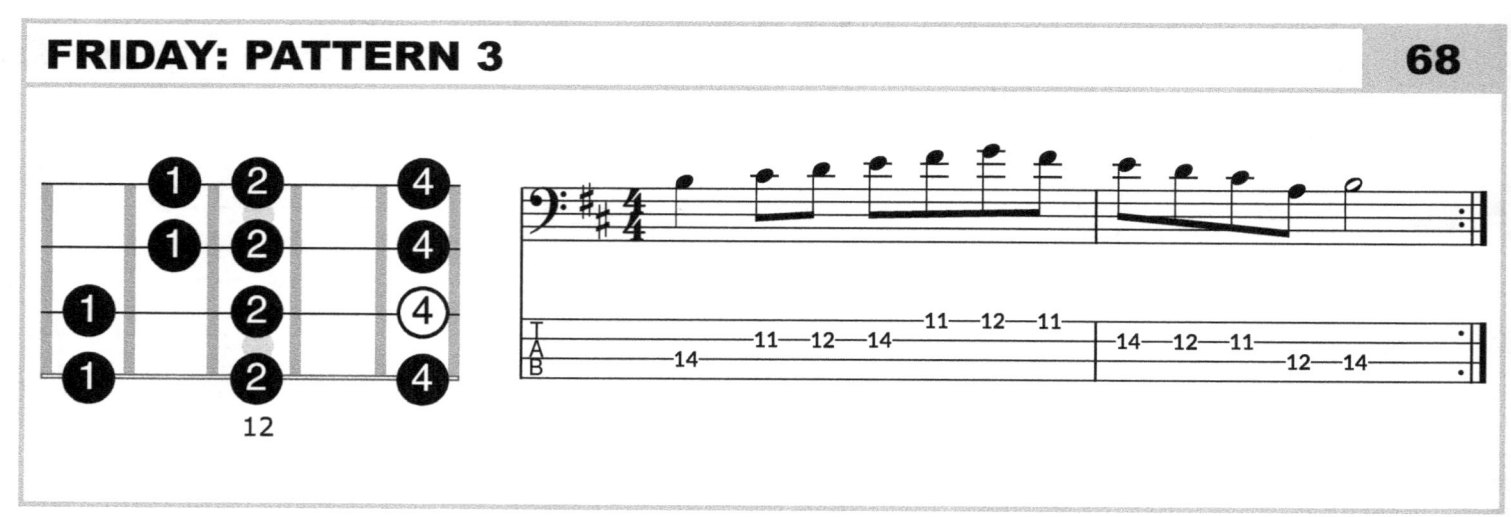

SATURDAY: HORIZONTAL PATTERN 69

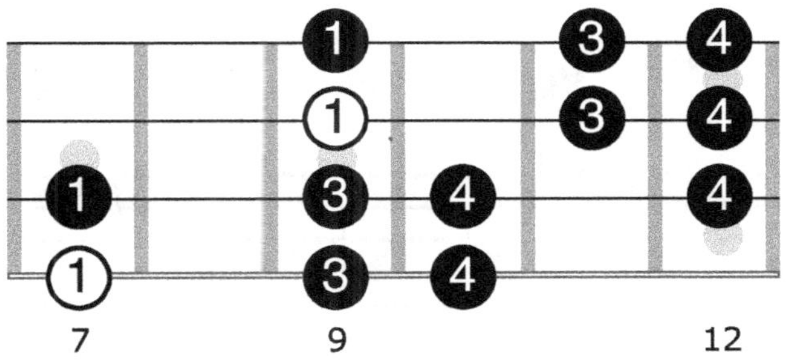

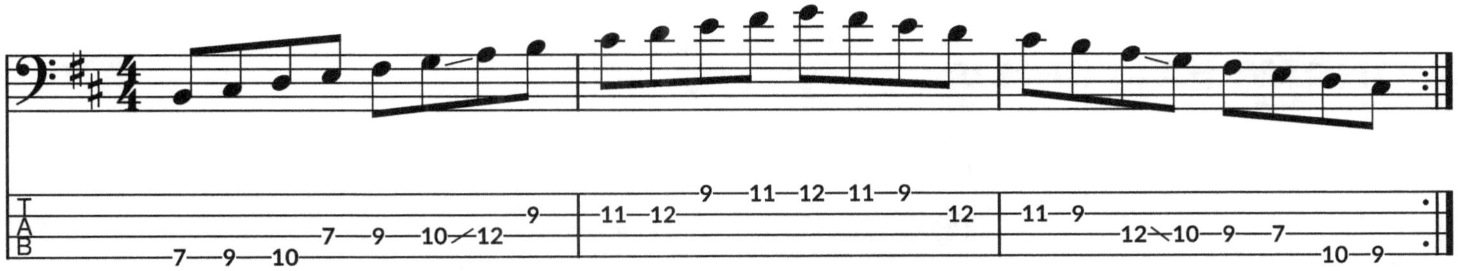

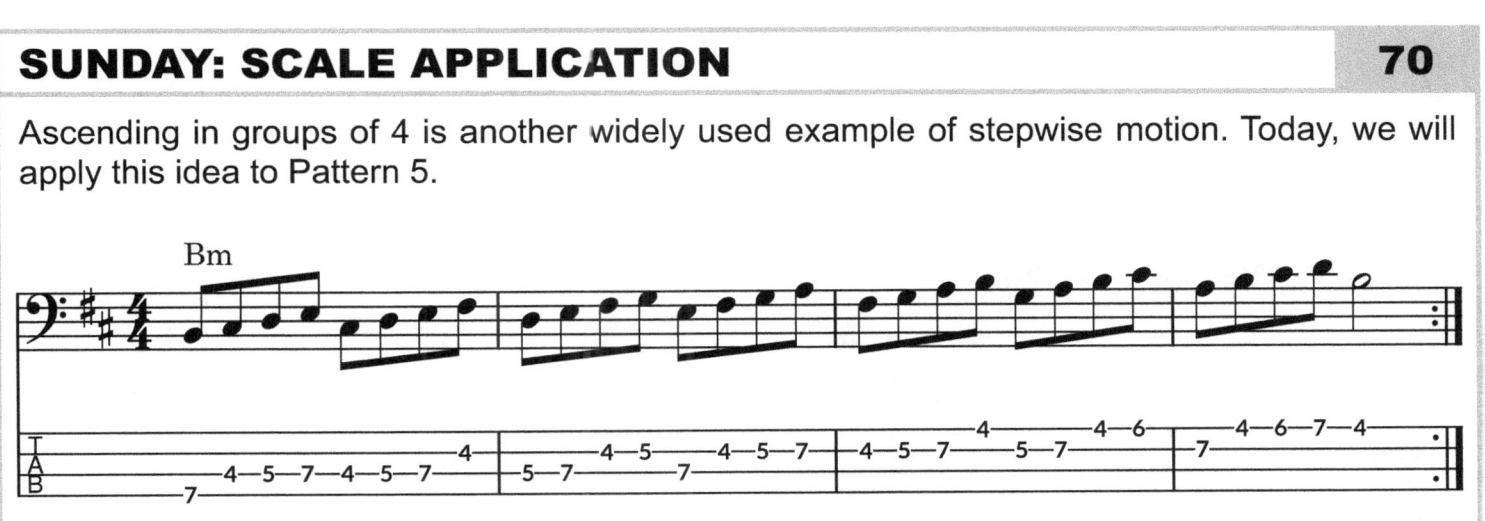

SUNDAY: SCALE APPLICATION 70

Ascending in groups of 4 is another widely used example of stepwise motion. Today, we will apply this idea to Pattern 5.

WEEK 11: B MAJOR PENTATONIC

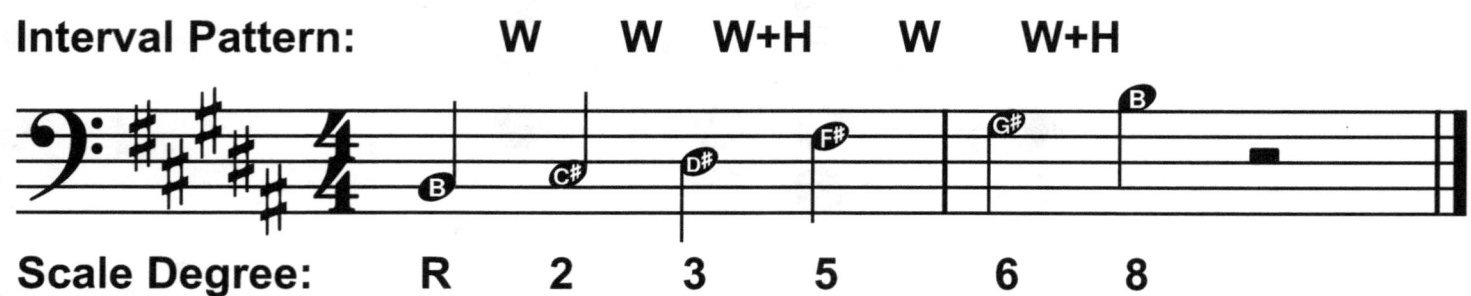

MONDAY: PATTERN 5　　71

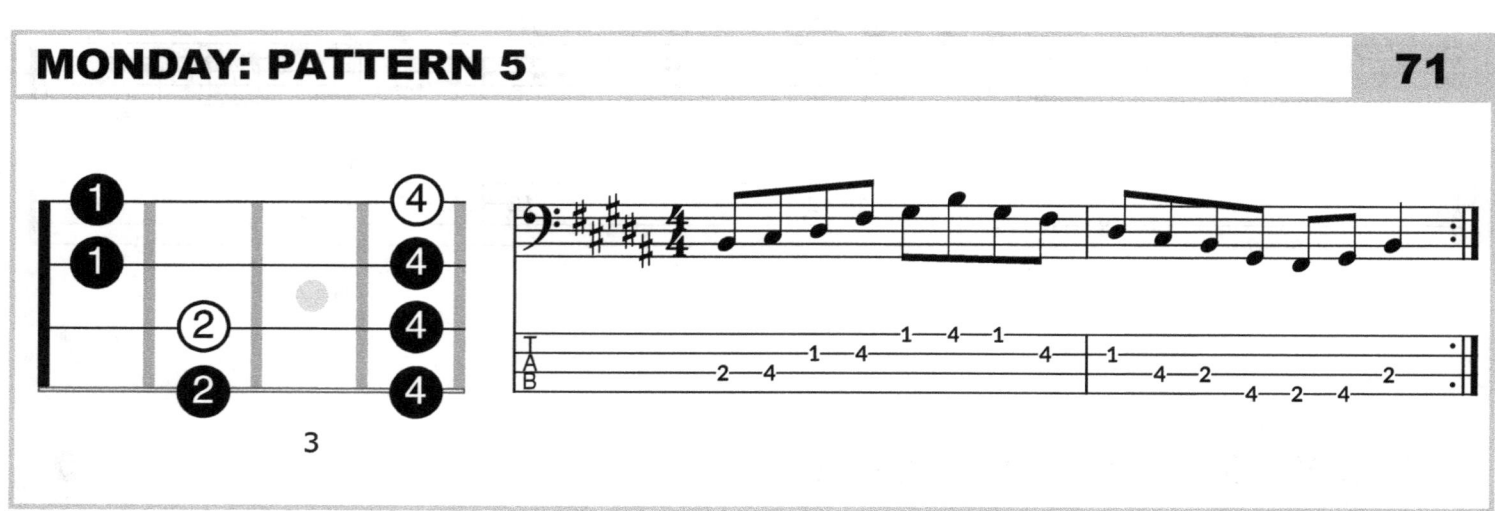

TUESDAY: PATTERN 1　　72

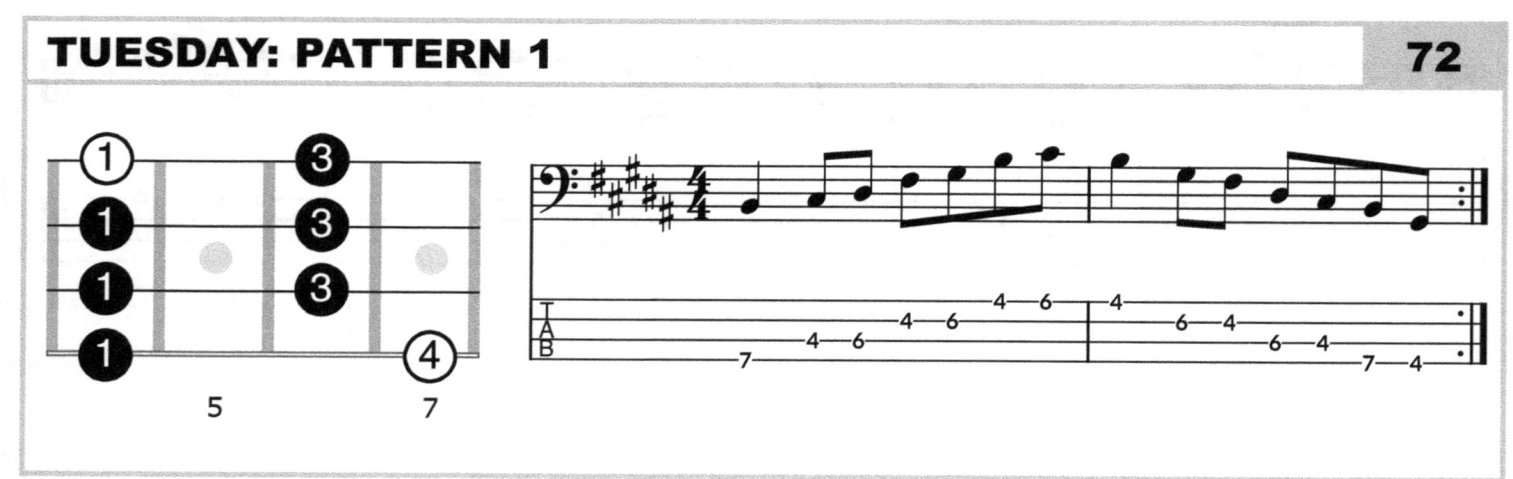

WEDNESDAY: PATTERN 2 — 73

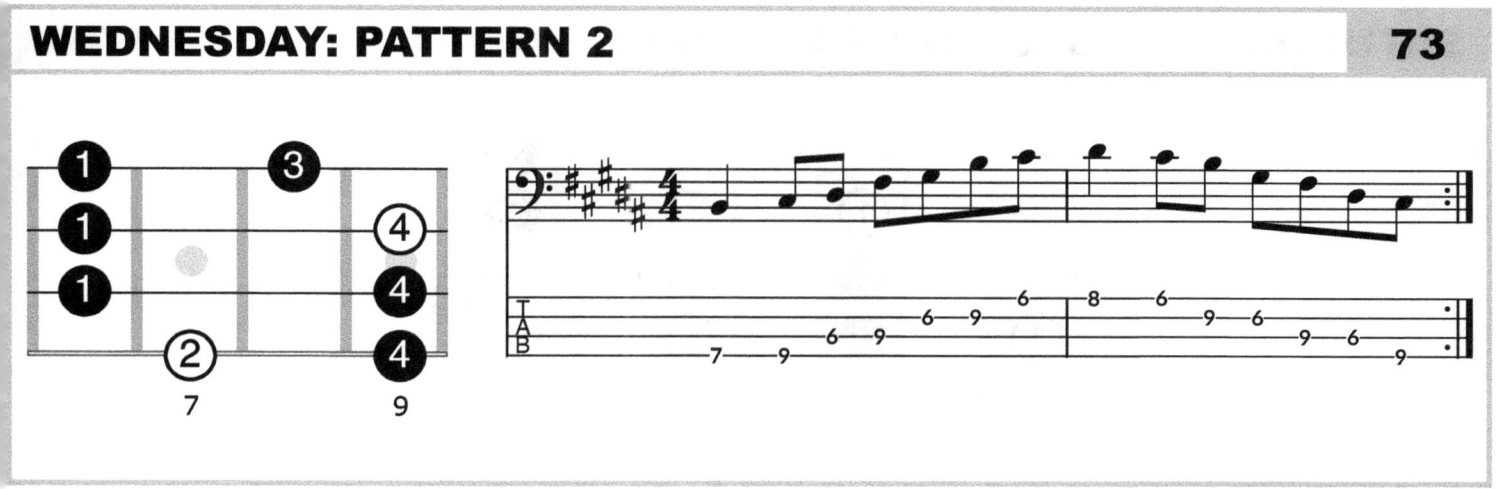

THURSDAY: PATTERN 3 — 74

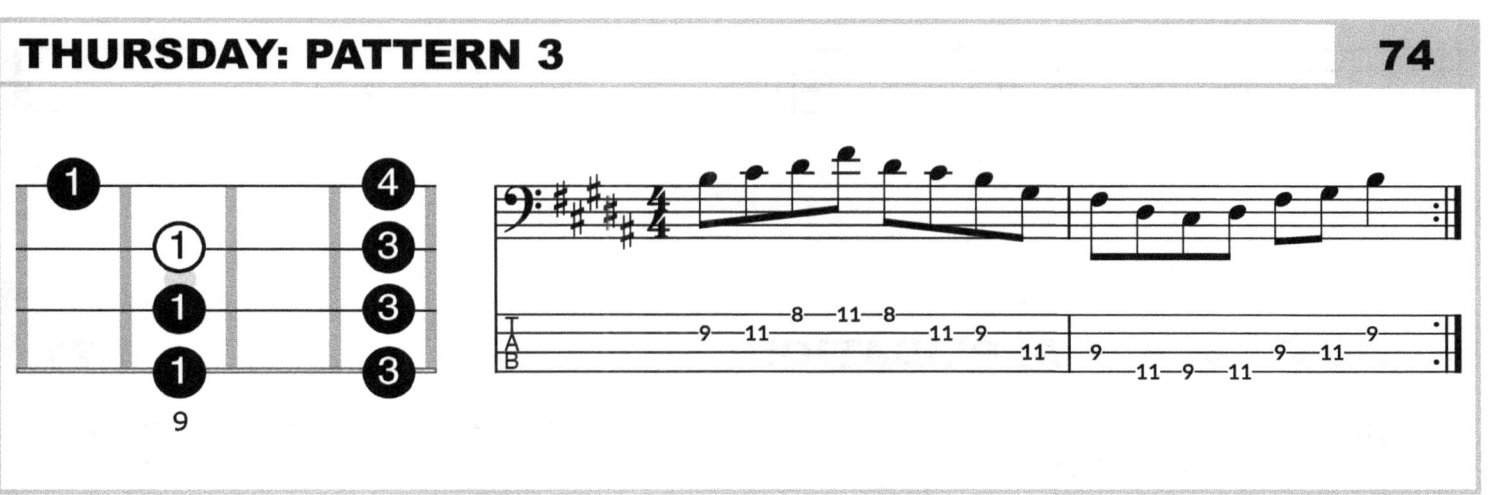

FRIDAY: PATTERN 4 — 75

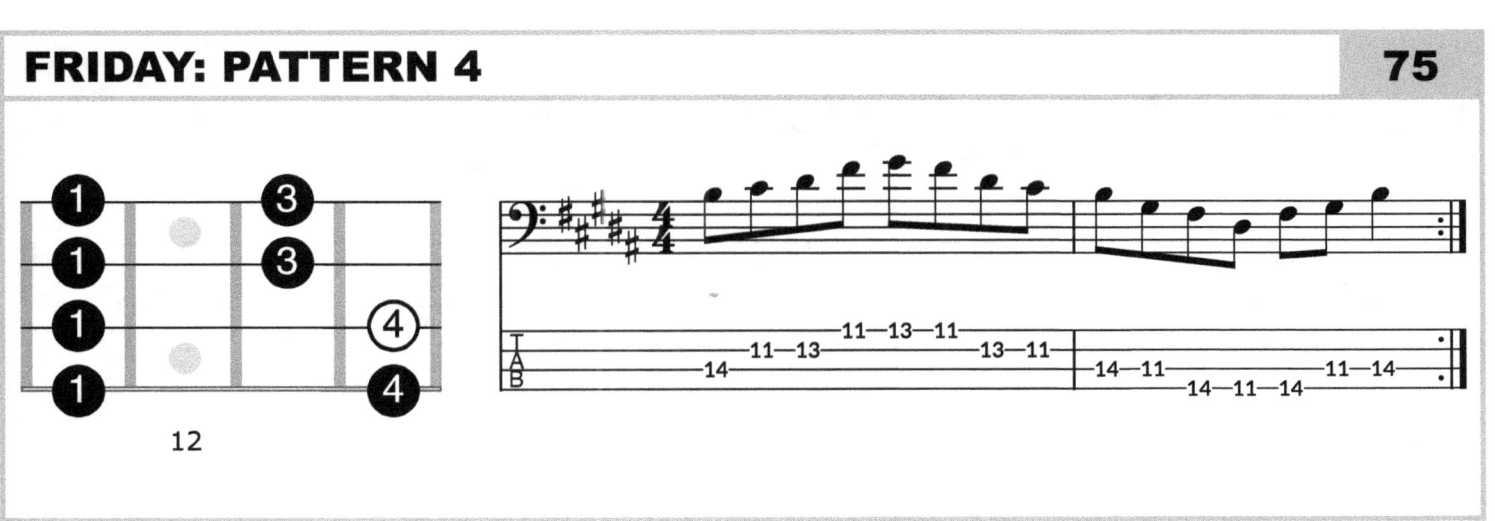

SATURDAY: HORIZONTAL PATTERN 76

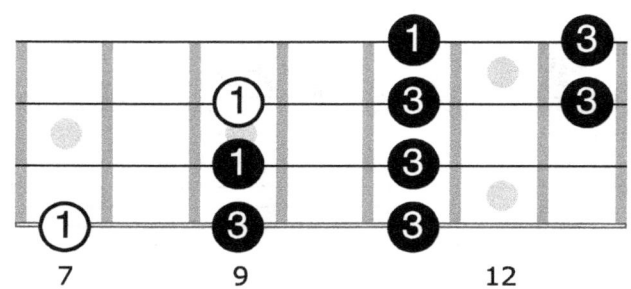
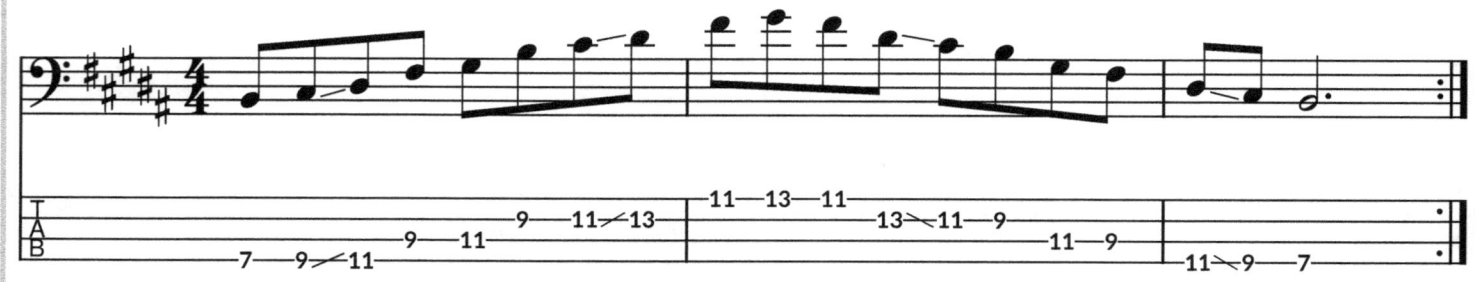

SUNDAY: SCALE APPLICATION 77

A rhythmic idea often combined with the dotted quarter-note rhythm is filling the rest of the measure with eighth notes. Observe how this rhythm transforms going straight up and down Pattern 2 into a musical statement. In measures 3 and 4, an eighth rest replaces the dot and changes the feel of the bass line. You can even tap your hand on the muted string on beat 2 for a percussive effect to help the drummer.

WEEK 12: B MINOR PENTATONIC

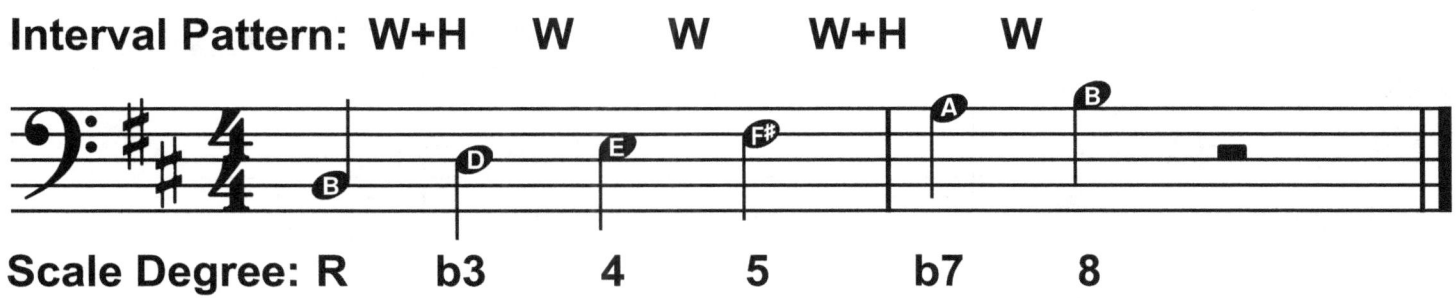

MONDAY: PATTERN 4

TUESDAY: PATTERN 5

WEDNESDAY: PATTERN 1

THURSDAY: PATTERN 2

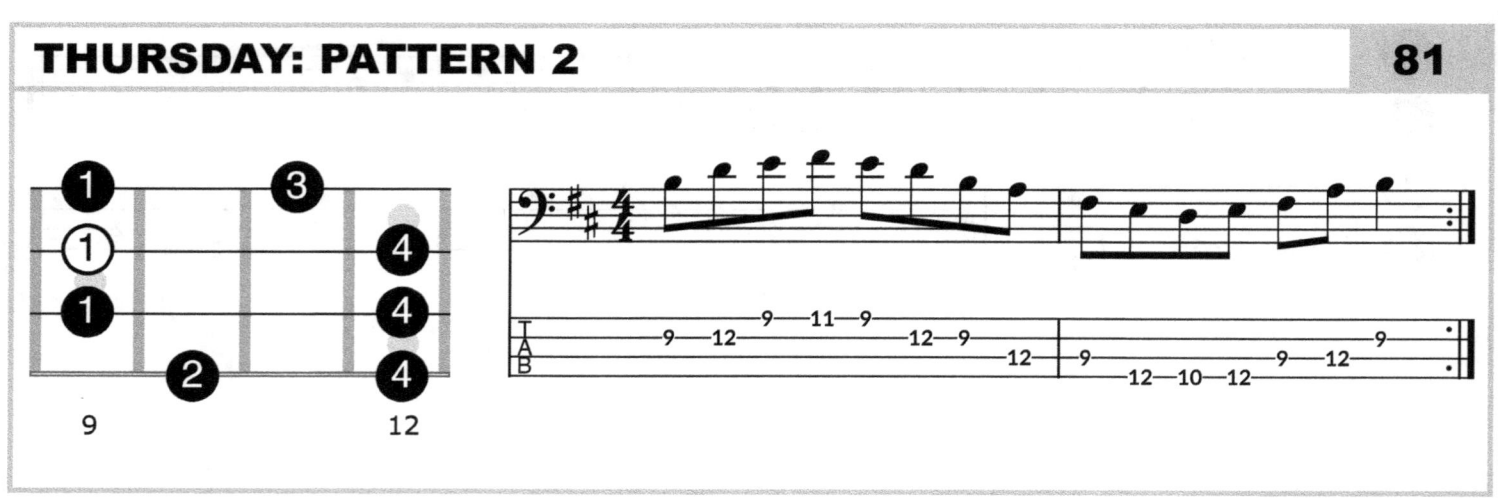

FRIDAY: PATTERN 3

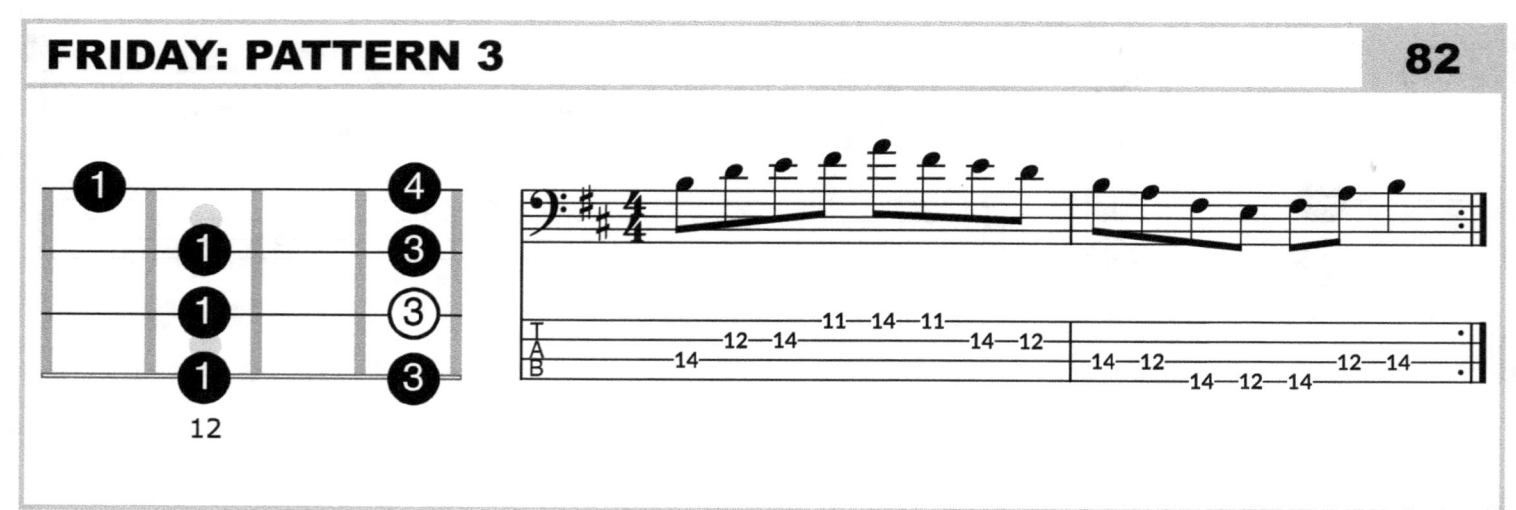

SATURDAY: HORIZONTAL PATTERN 83

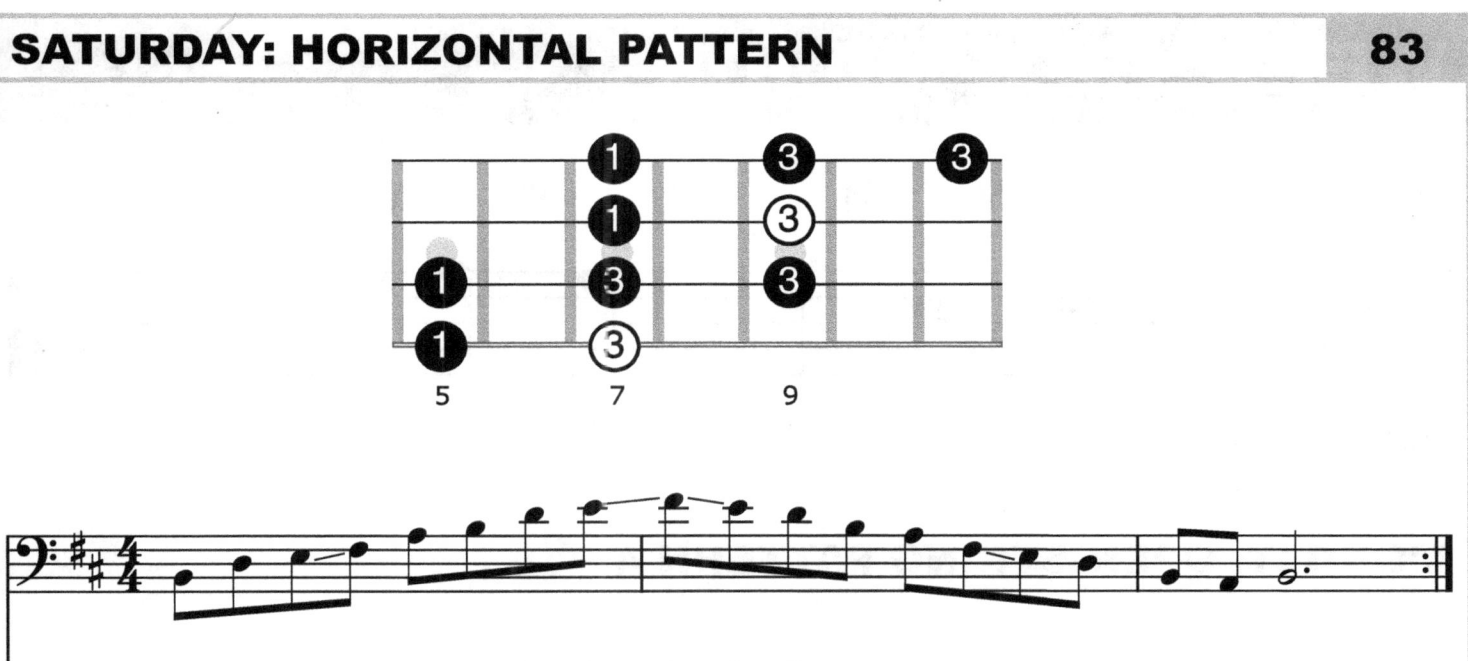

SUNDAY: SCALE APPLICATION 84

The minor pentatonic scale and the blues are historically a perfect fit. This is a popular blues riff that offers an opportunity to practice rolling your 3rd finger. Finger the 2nd string with your 3rd fingertip and roll it down, collapsing your knuckle to play the 1st string. Listen to the audio to get the blues shuffle feel.

WEEK 13: C MAJOR

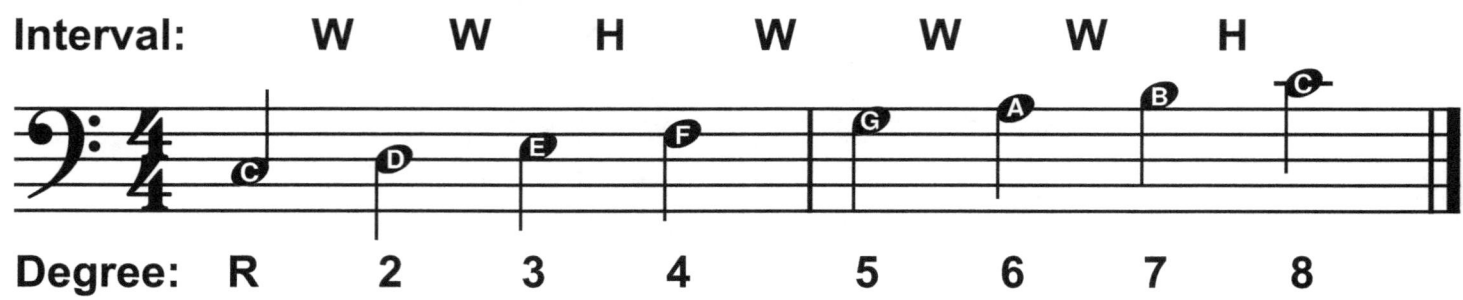

MONDAY: OPEN-STRING PATTERN 4 — 85

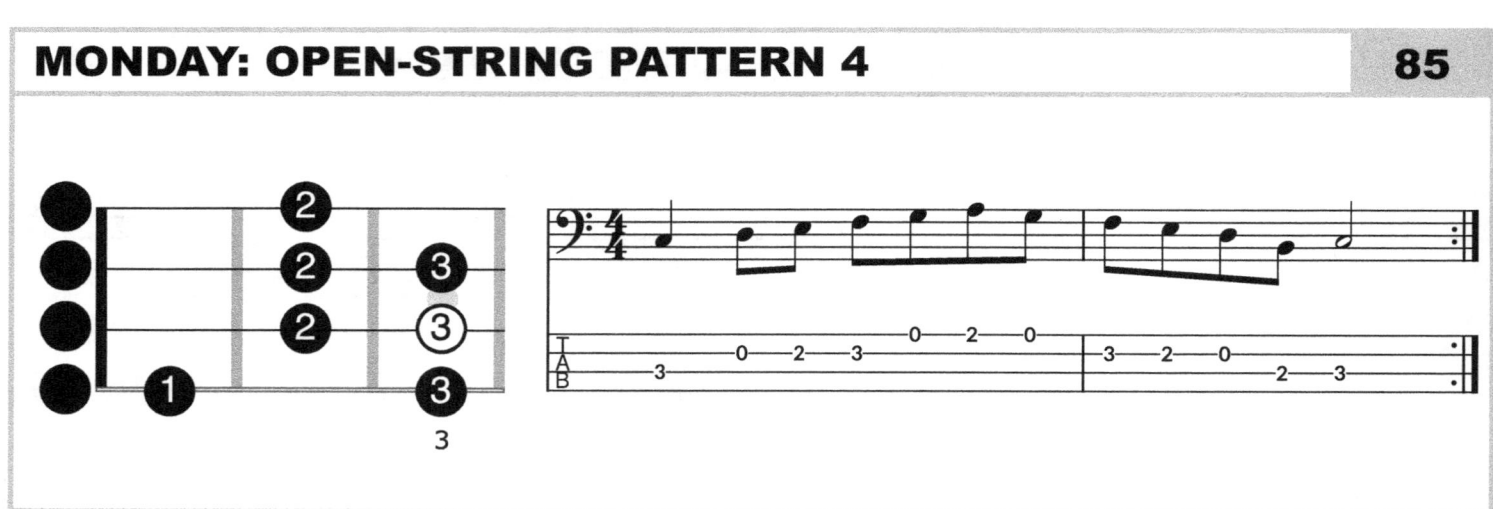

TUESDAY: PATTERN 5 — 86

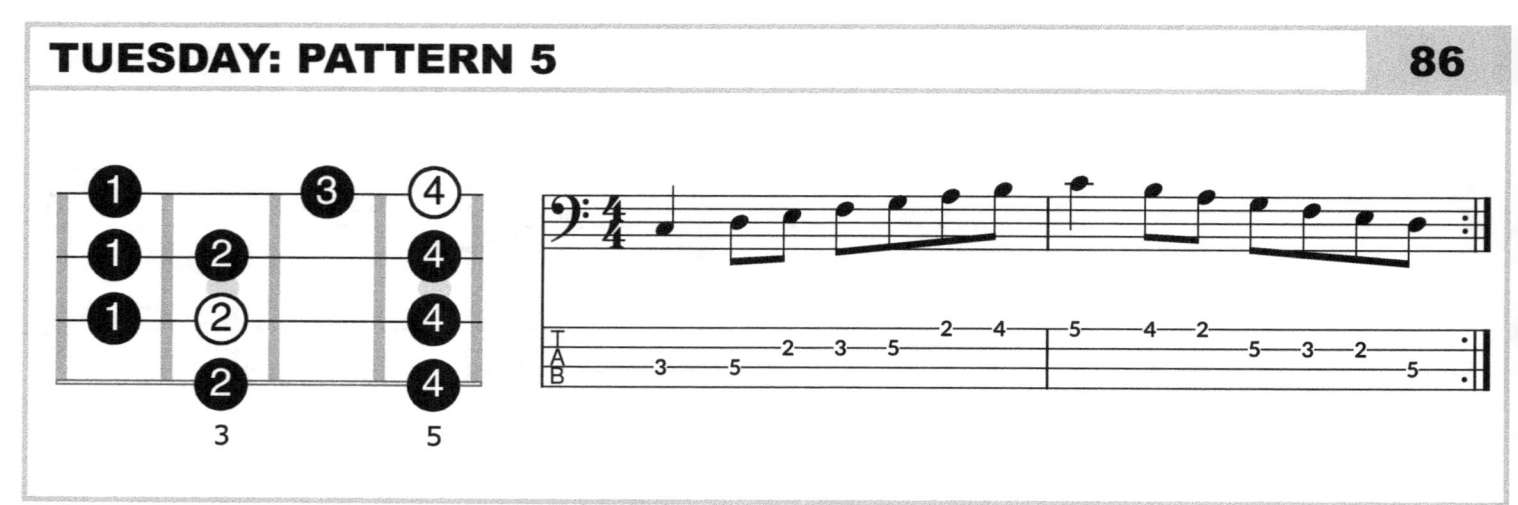

WEDNESDAY: PATTERN 1 — 87

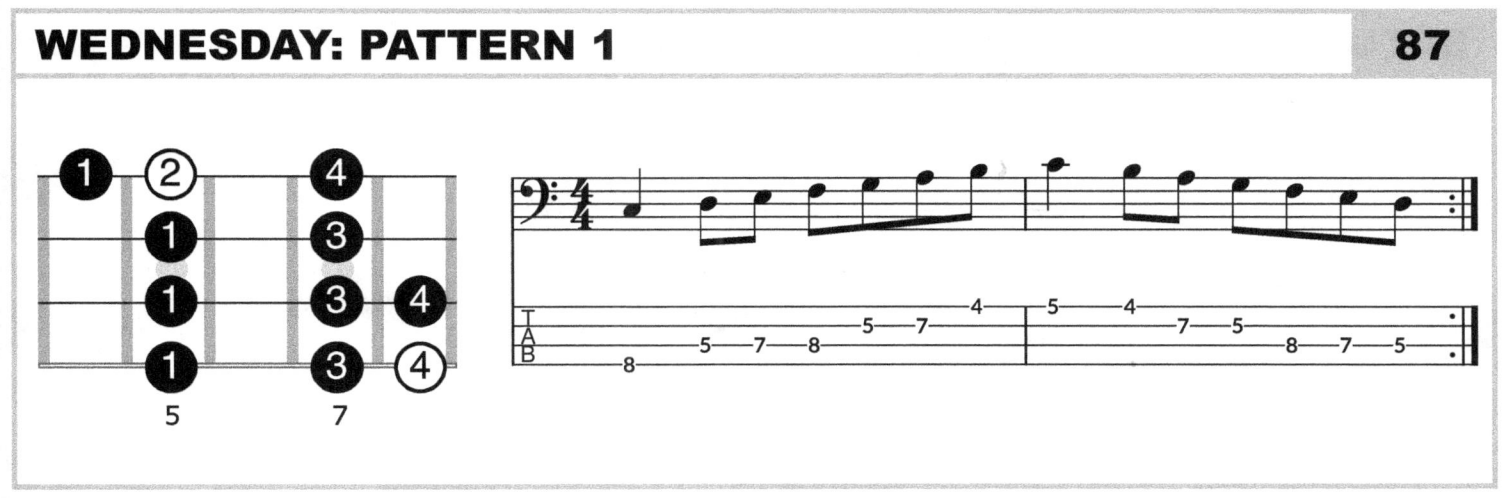

THURSDAY: PATTERN 2 — 88

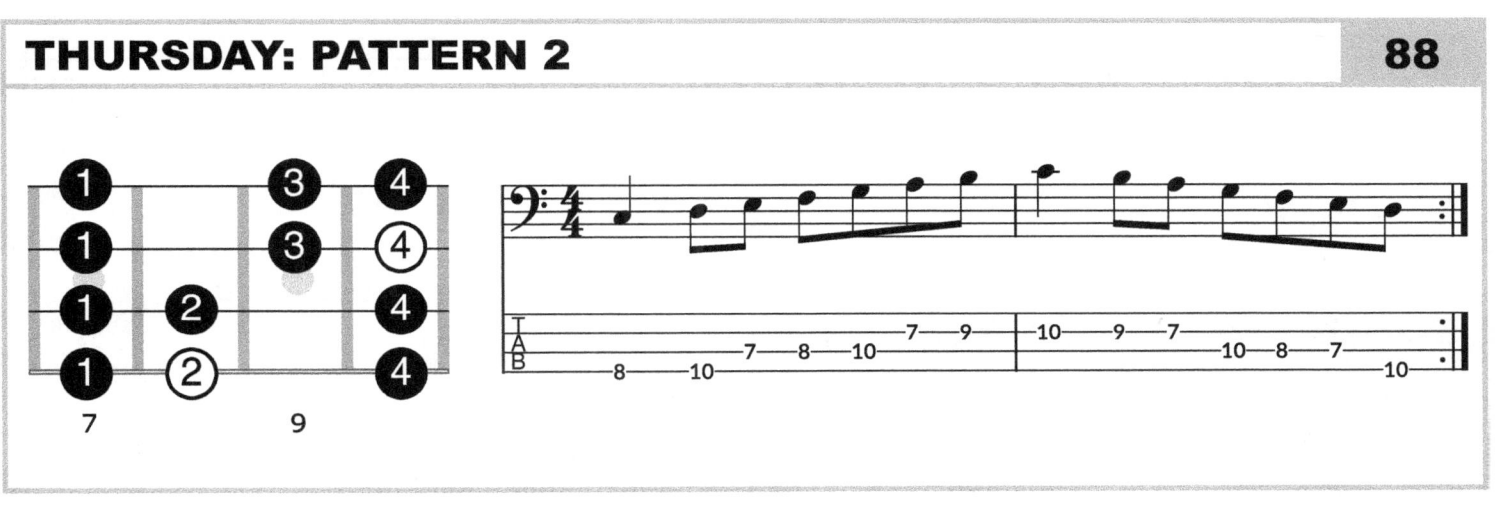

FRIDAY: PATTERN 3 — 89

SATURDAY: HORIZONTAL PATTERN 90

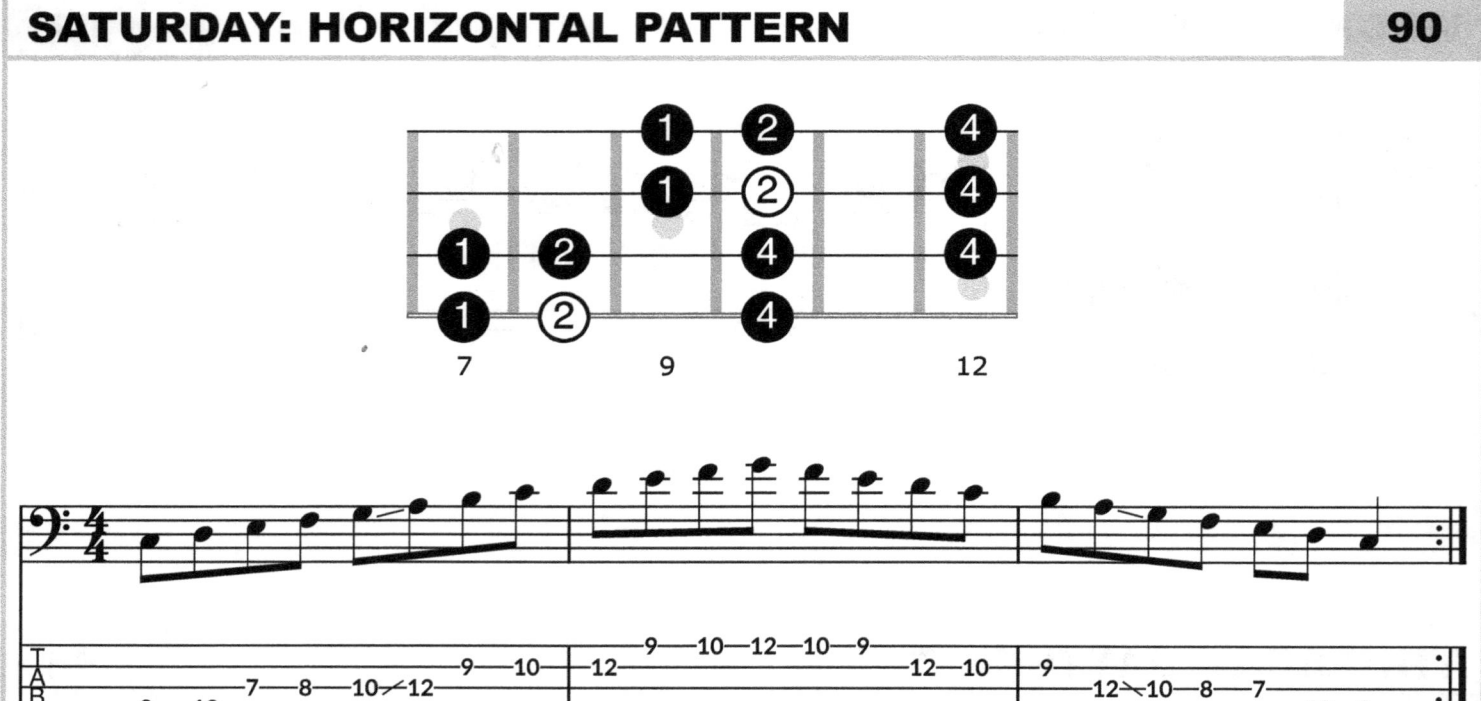

SUNDAY: SCALE APPLICATION 91

Another common stepwise scale sequence is to descend the strings via groups of 4. This example features Pattern 5 and is often used to connect ideas. Practicing this sequence will also help to develop finger dexterity and sync your picking and fretting hands.

WEEK 14: C MINOR

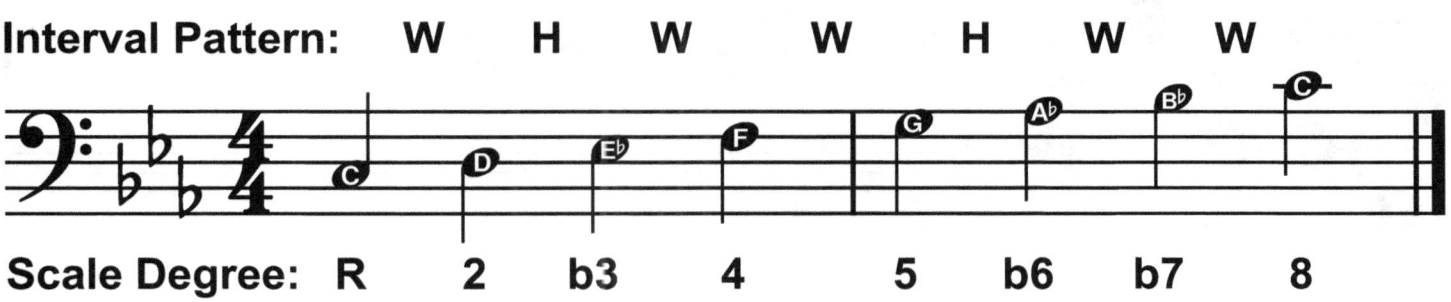

MONDAY: OPEN-STRING PATTERN 3 — 92

To make this pattern fit into open position, we'll play the A♭ note on string 4, fret 4.

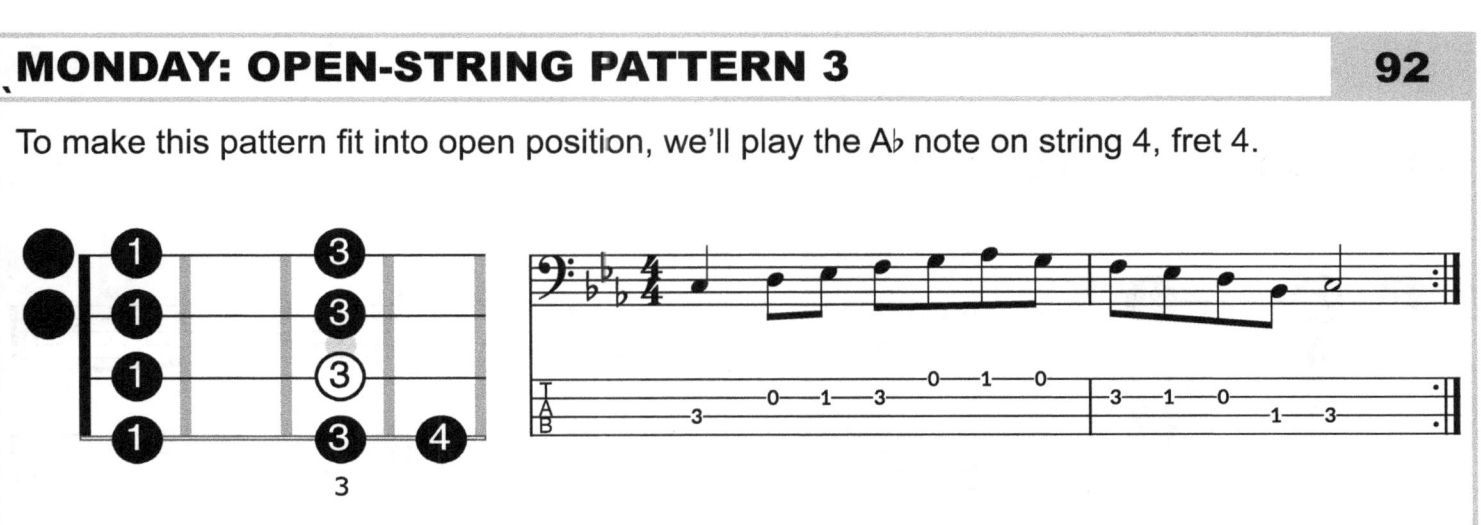

TUESDAY: PATTERN 4 — 93

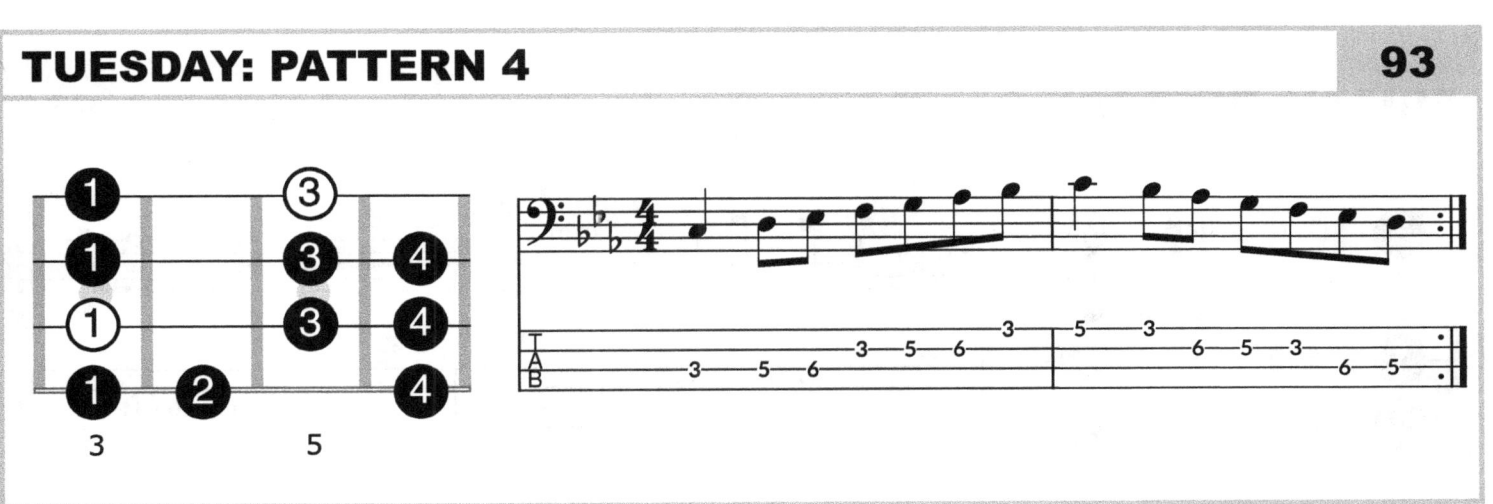

WEDNESDAY: PATTERN 5

THURSDAY: PATTERN 1

FRIDAY: PATTERN 2

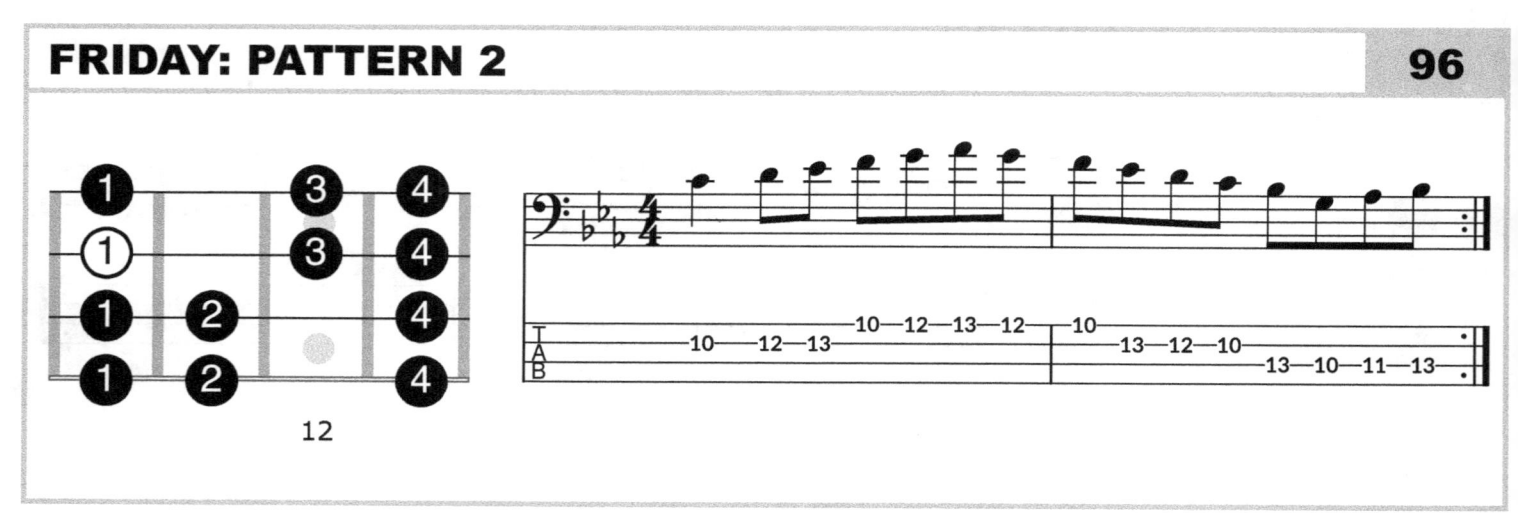

SATURDAY: HORIZONTAL PATTERN 97

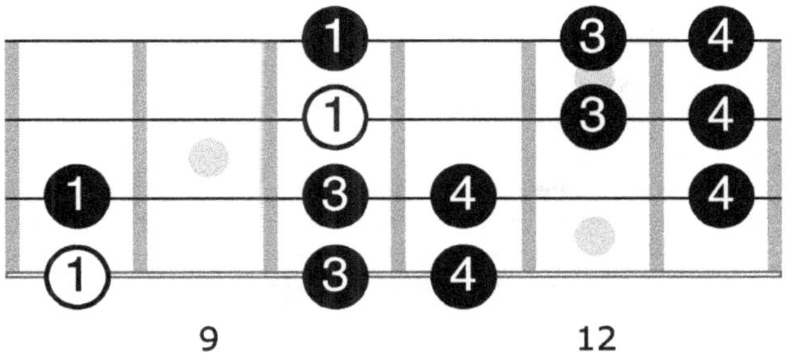

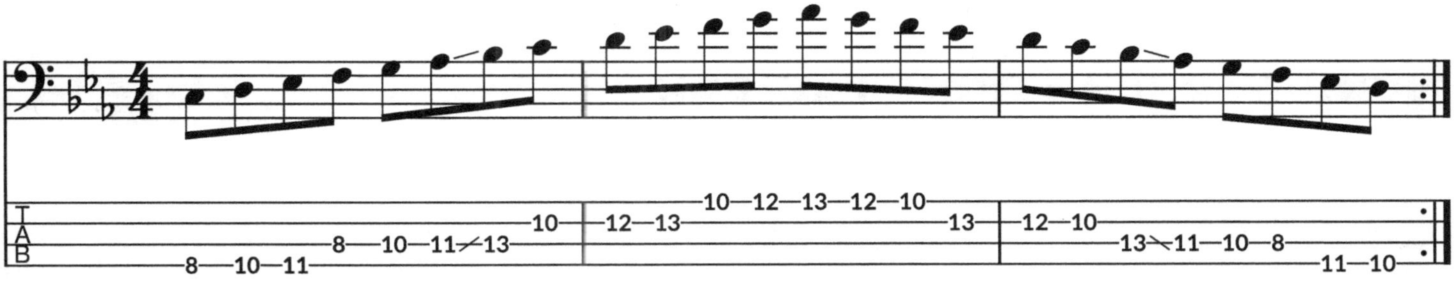

SUNDAY: SCALE APPLICATION 98

Looking to add some spice to your bass line? Octaves are a bass player's best friend when it comes to expanding a simple bass line. Today's example combines octaves with another bass staple, the dotted-quarter rhythm, while staying within Pattern 4. In measure 3, you could try playing the octave on fret 8, string 2 to keep the fretboard shape identical to the others. Learn it both ways!

WEEK 15: C MAJOR PENTATONIC

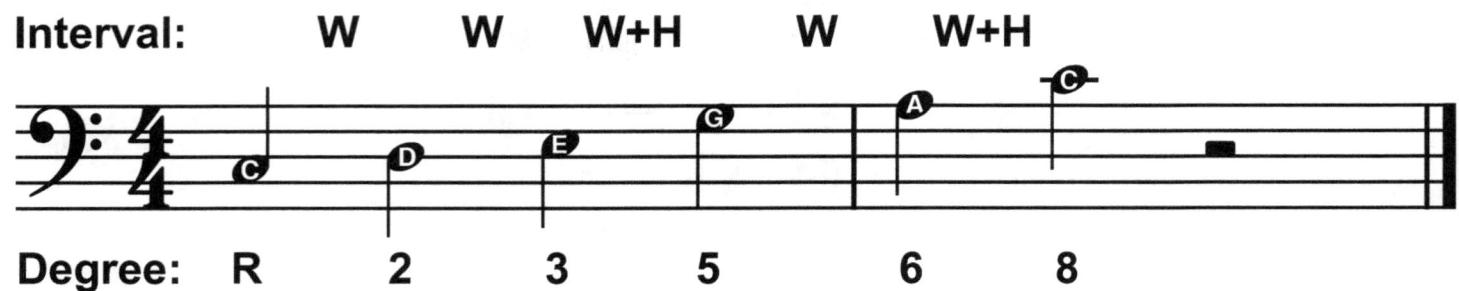

MONDAY: OPEN-STRING PATTERN 4   99

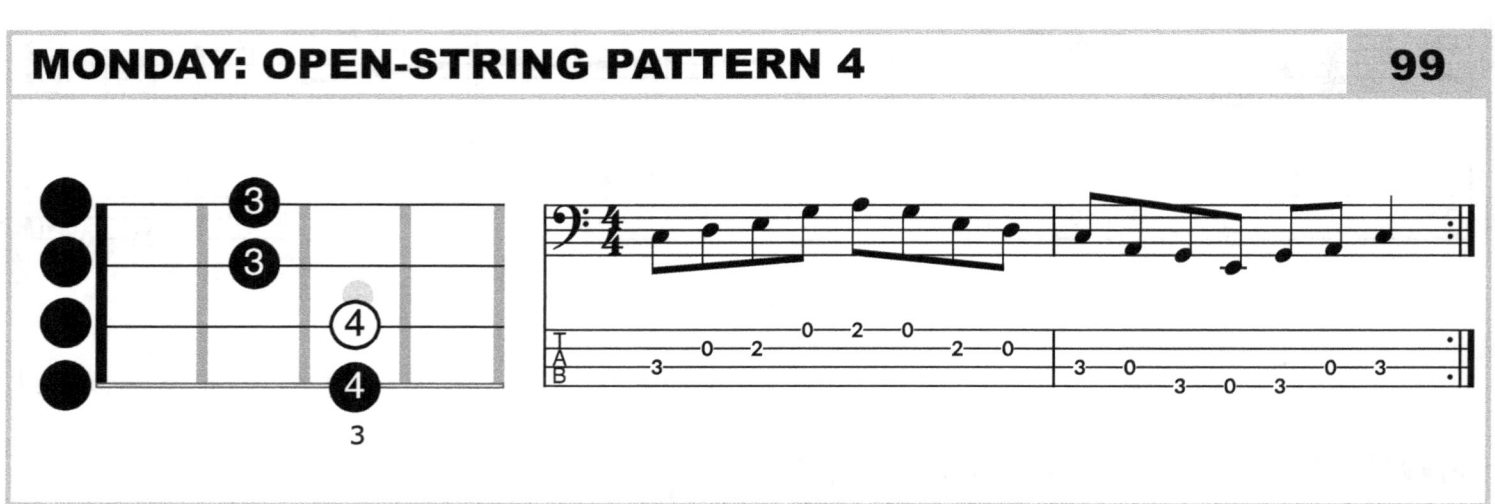

TUESDAY: PATTERN 5   100

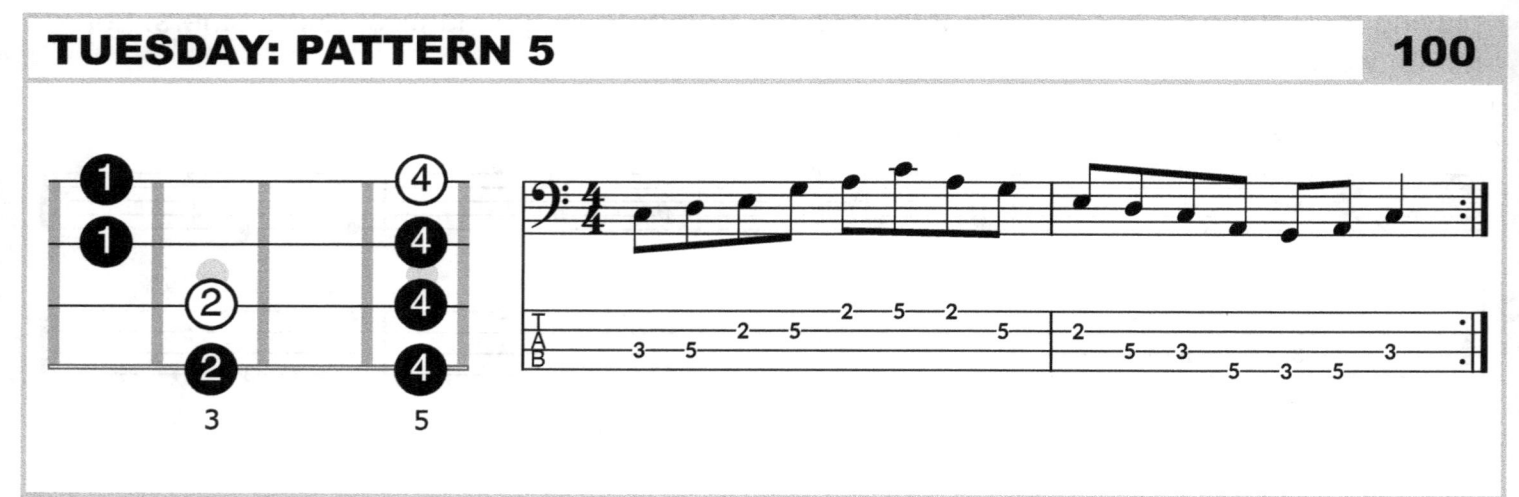

WEDNESDAY: PATTERN 1

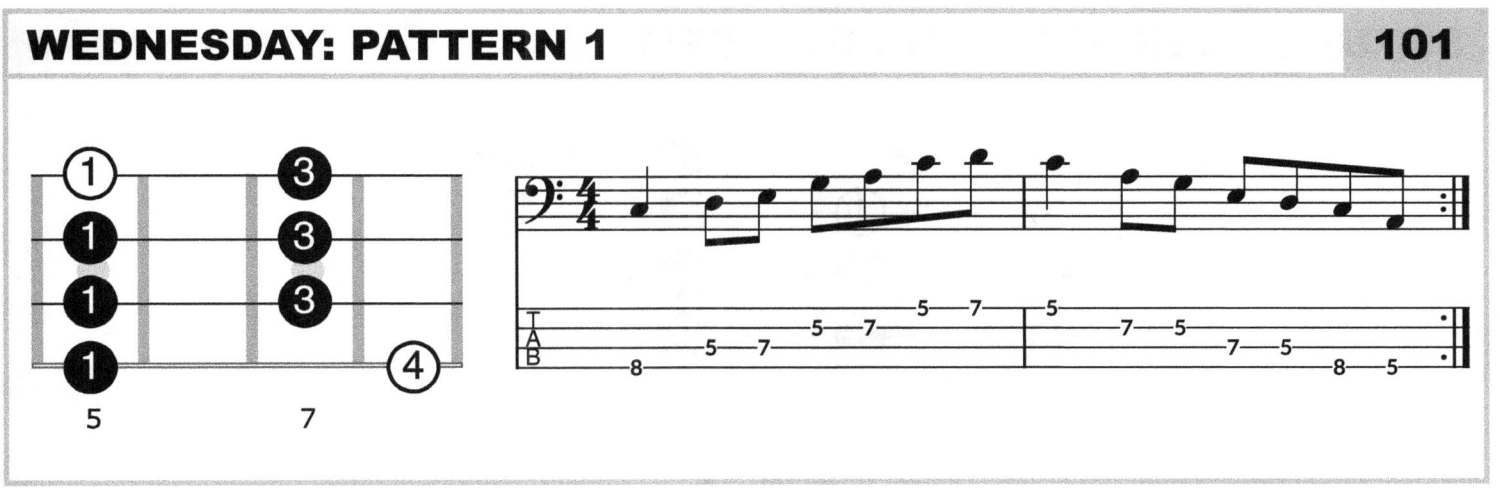

THURSDAY: PATTERN 2

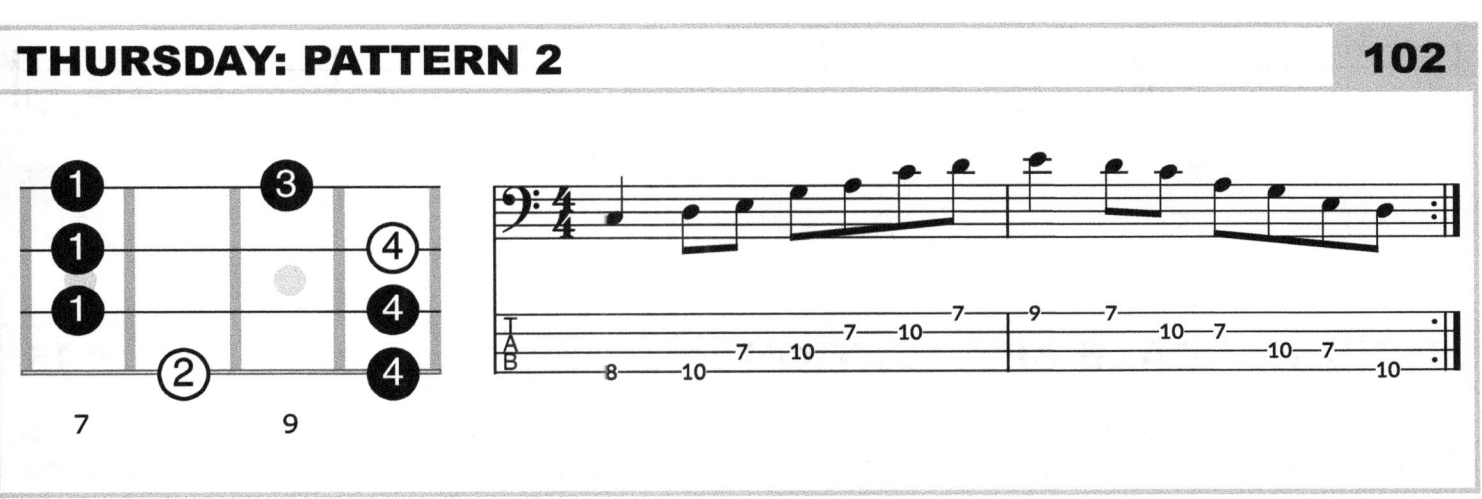

FRIDAY: PATTERN 3

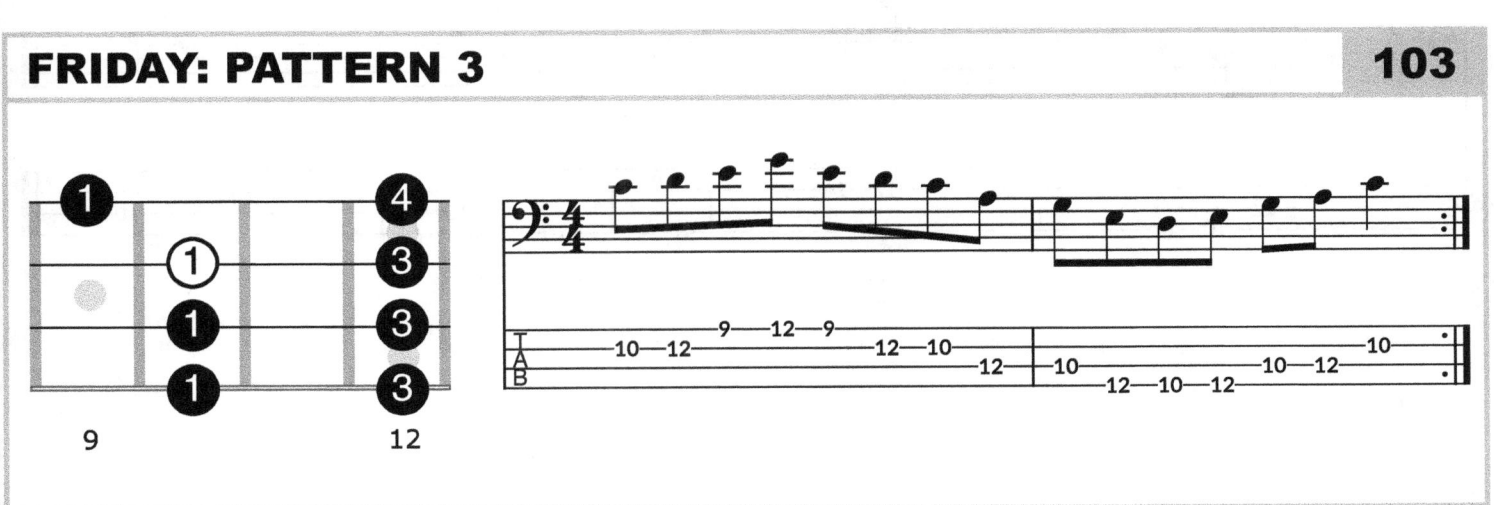

SATURDAY: HORIZONTAL PATTERN   104

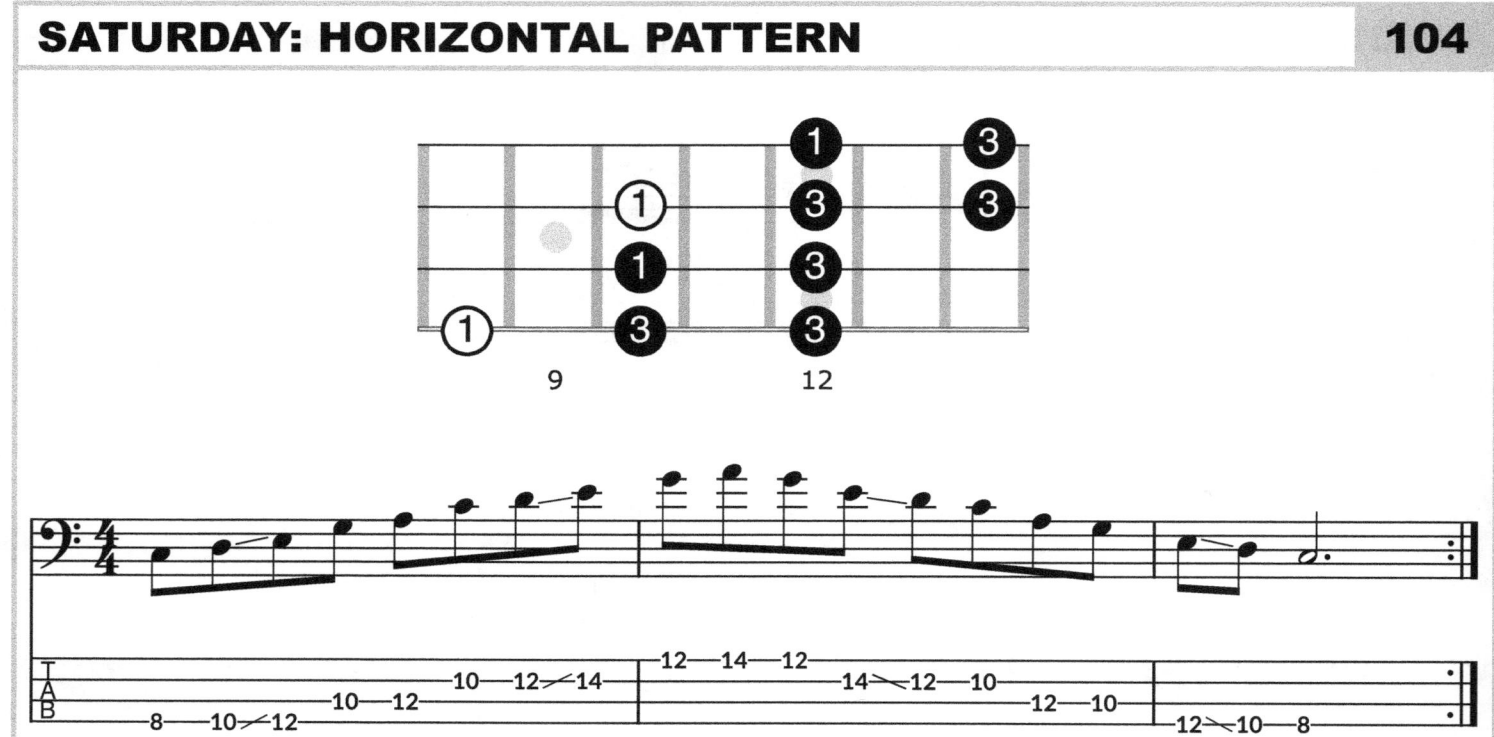

SUNDAY: SCALE APPLICATION   105

A great attribute of the horizontal pentatonic pattern is the two symmetrical groups of five notes. The following phrase demonstrates how to use the same idea in a different octave of the scale to create a theme. Changing the last note brings variety to the phrase by utilizing the octave from last week.

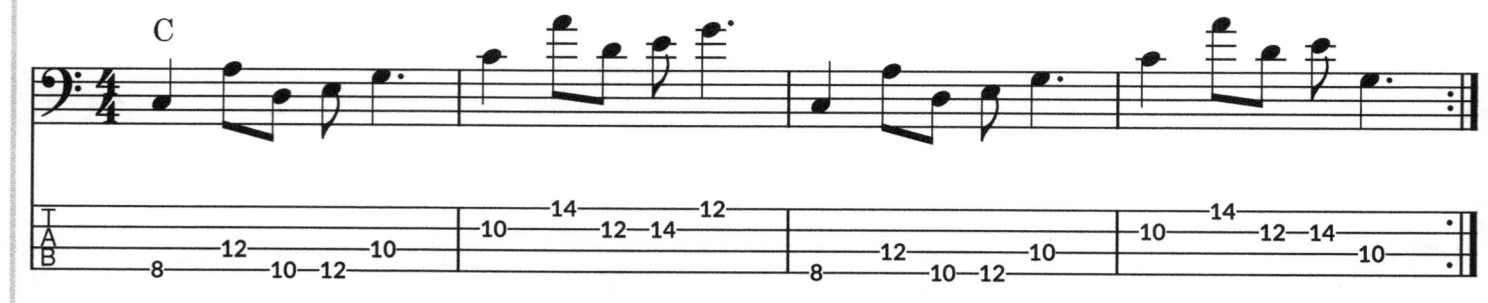

WEEK 16: C MINOR PENTATONIC

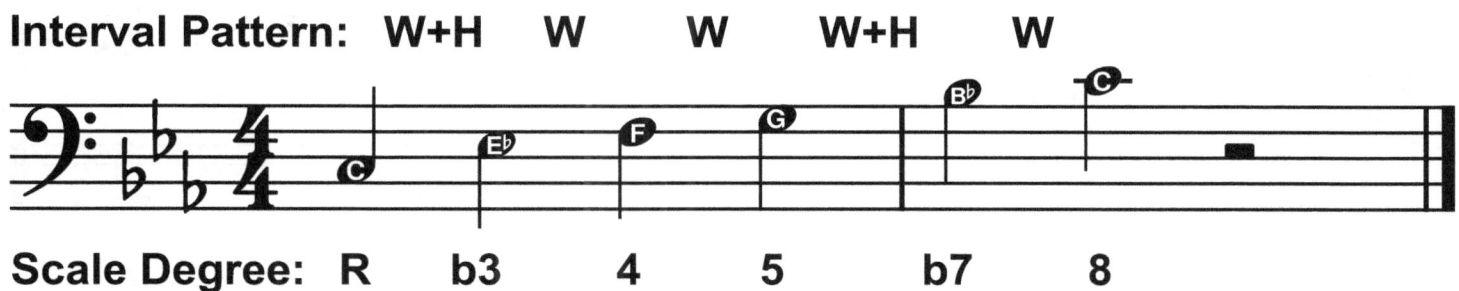

MONDAY: OPEN-STRING PATTERN 3 — 106

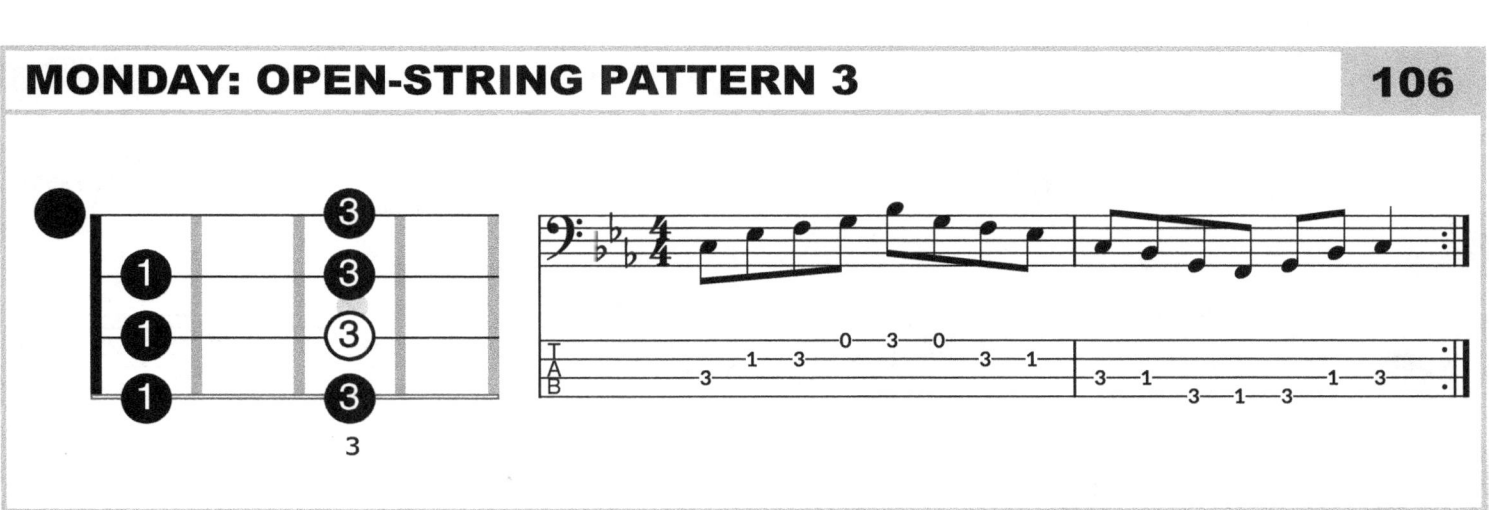

TUESDAY: PATTERN 4 — 107

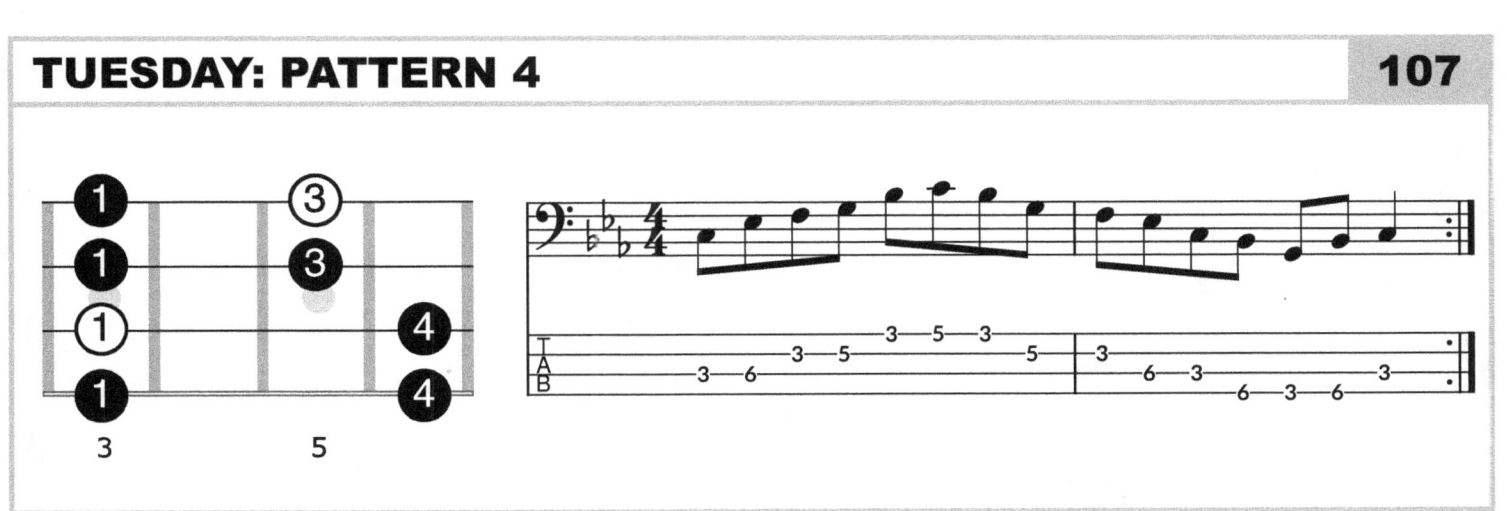

WEDNESDAY: PATTERN 5
108

THURSDAY: PATTERN 1
109
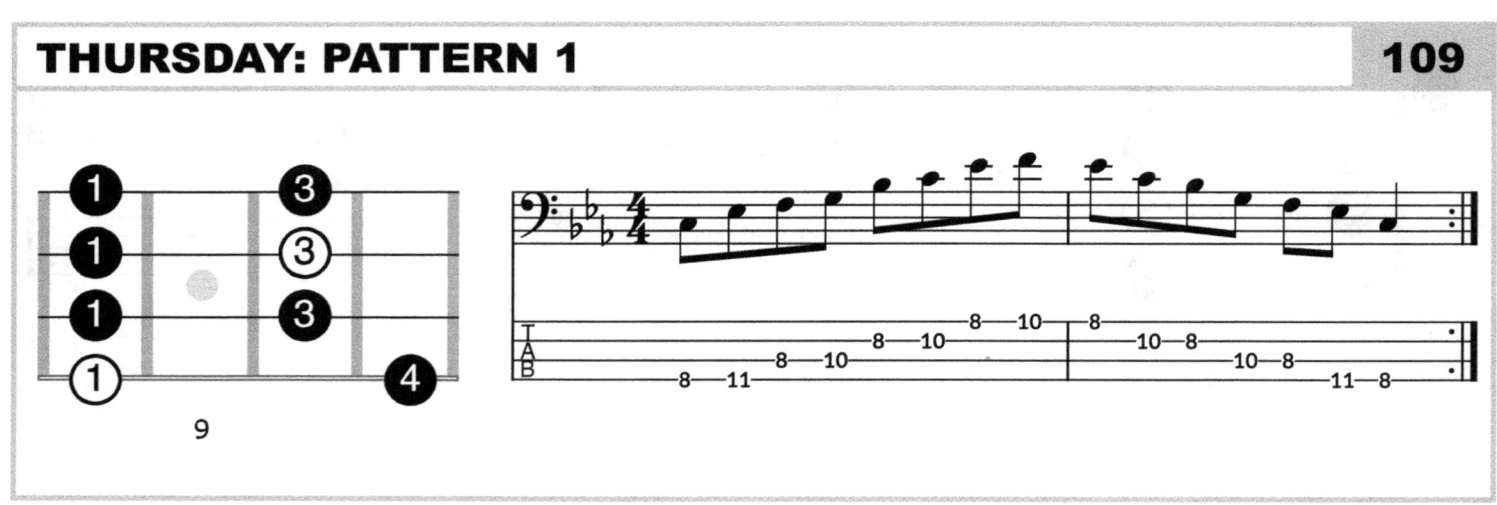

FRIDAY: PATTERN 2
110
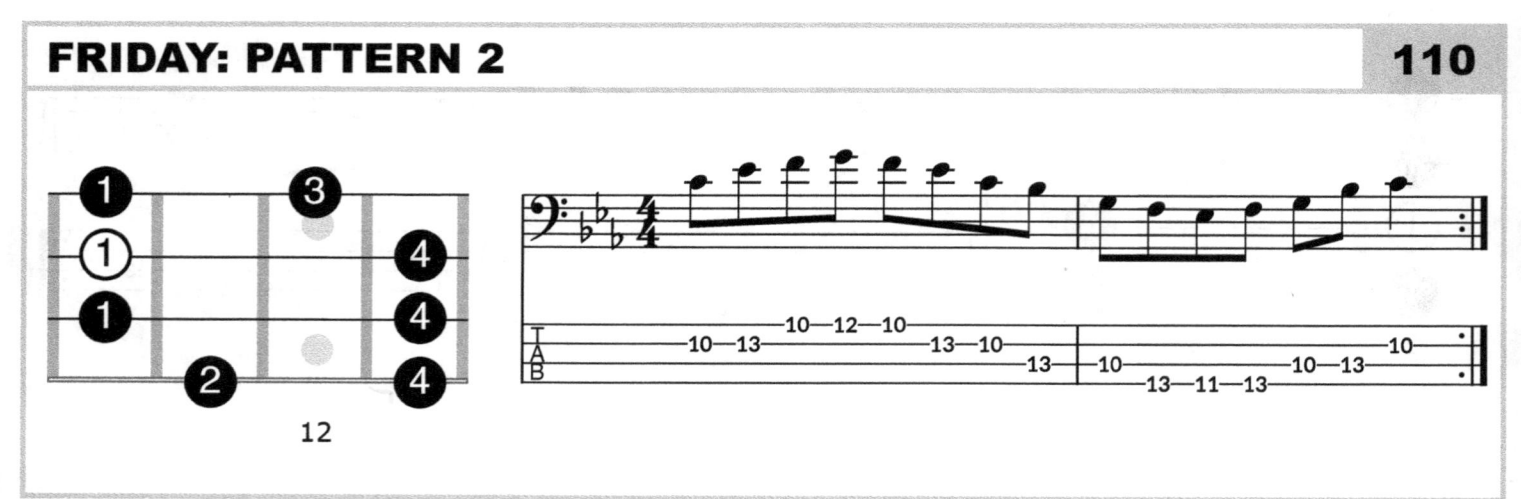

SATURDAY: HORIZONTAL PATTERN

111

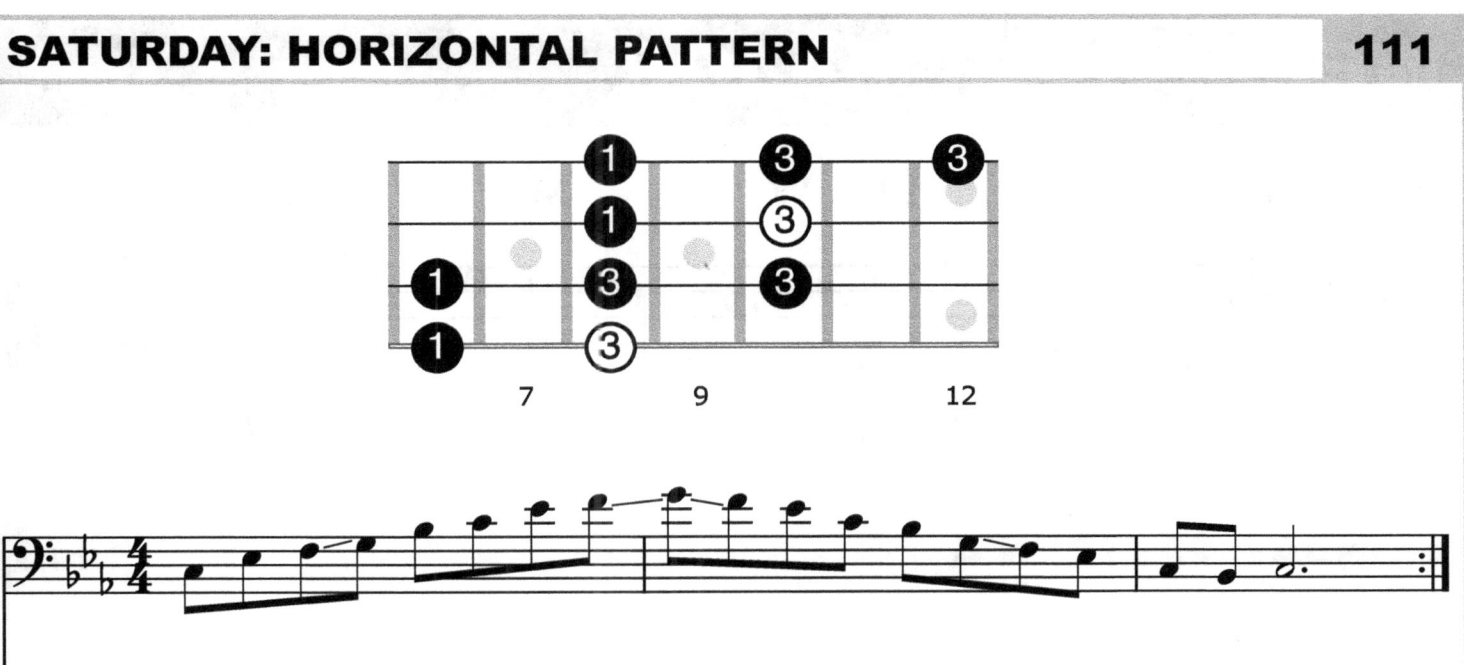

SUNDAY: SCALE APPLICATION

112

The minor horizontal pentatonic pattern also has two symmetrical groups of five notes. Our next phrase combines the down 3, up 1 scale sequence with triplets and spans two octaves. Notice how changing the bass line slightly in measure 4 brings the phrase to a conclusion and sets up the repeat of the phrase, much like a drummer sets up a new group of four measures with a fill.

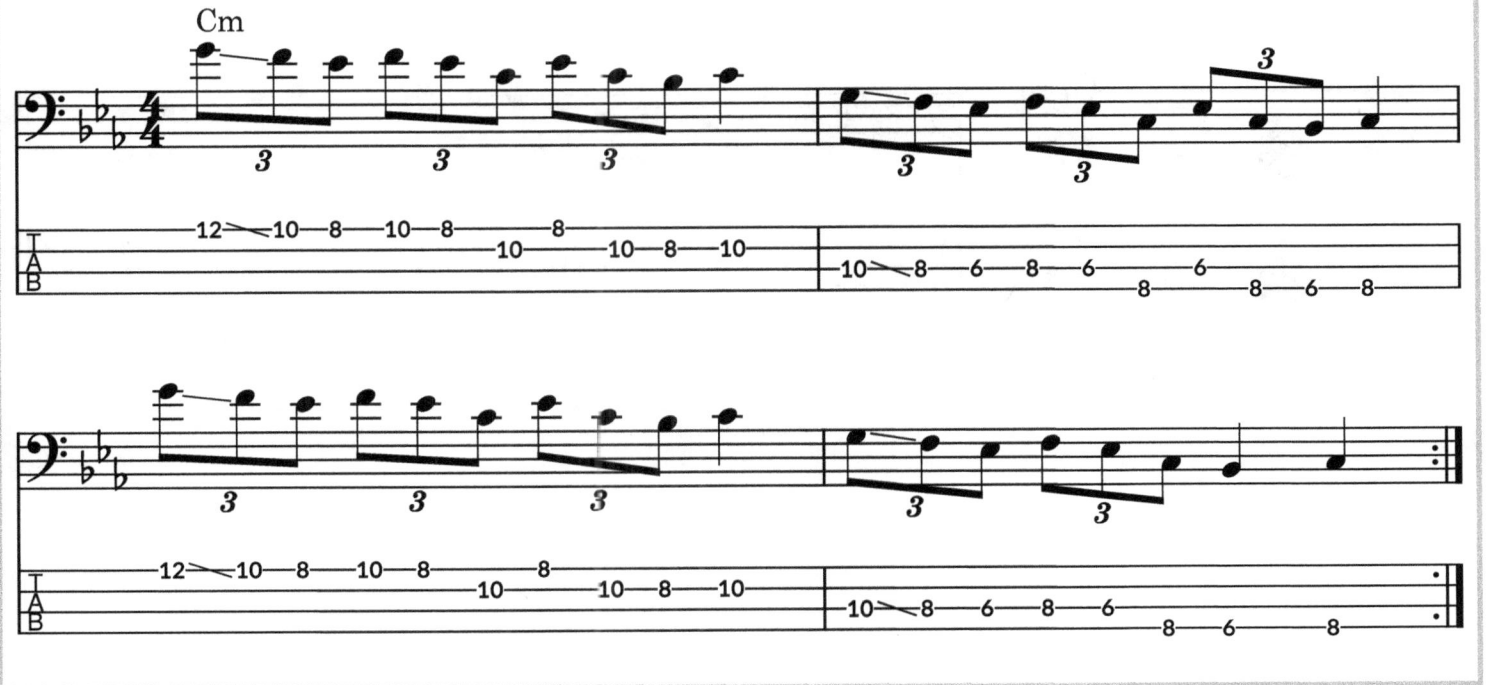

WEEK 17: C♯ MAJOR

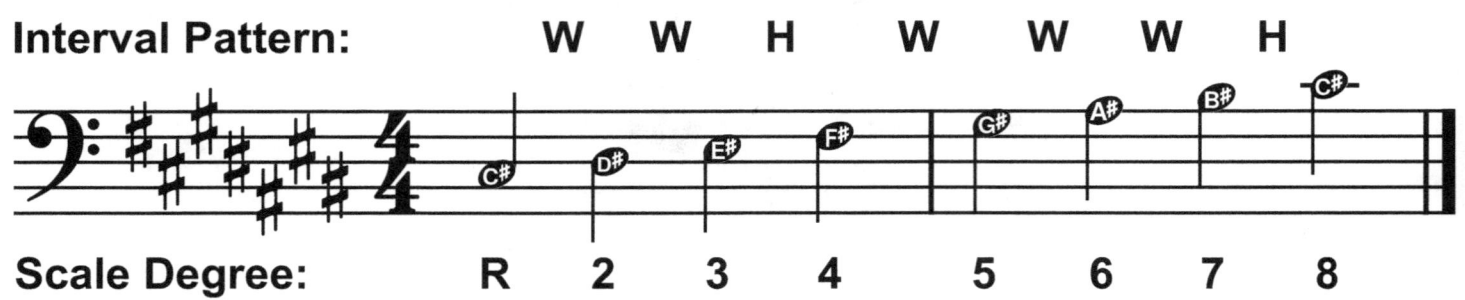

MONDAY: PATTERN 4 — 113

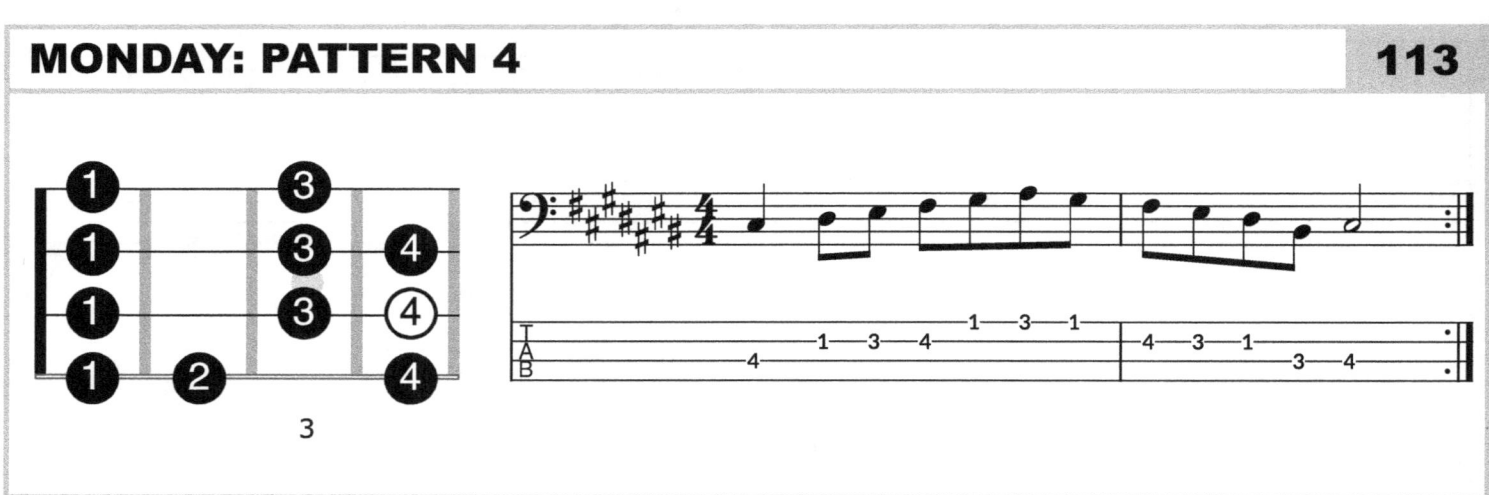

TUESDAY: PATTERN 5 — 114

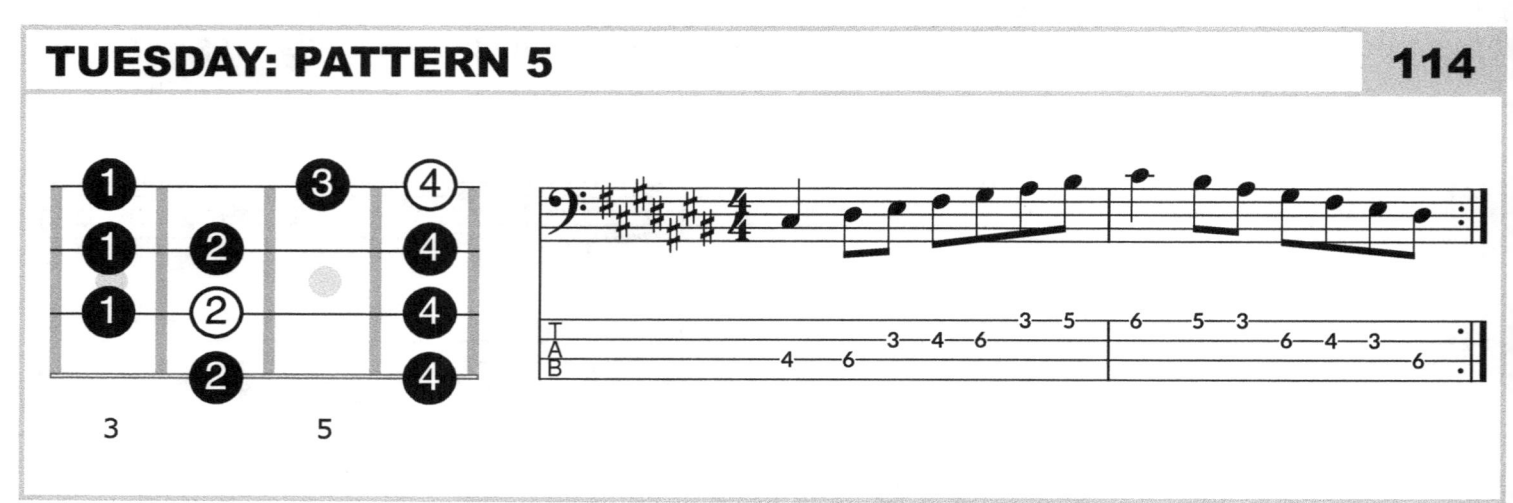

WEDNESDAY: PATTERN 1

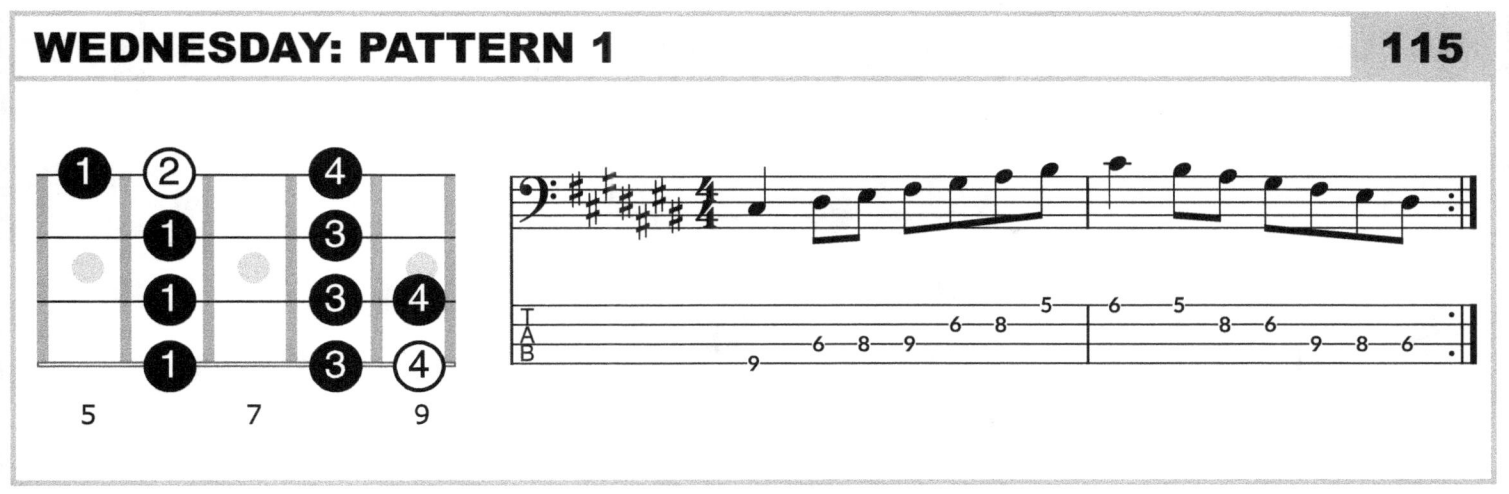

THURSDAY: PATTERN 2

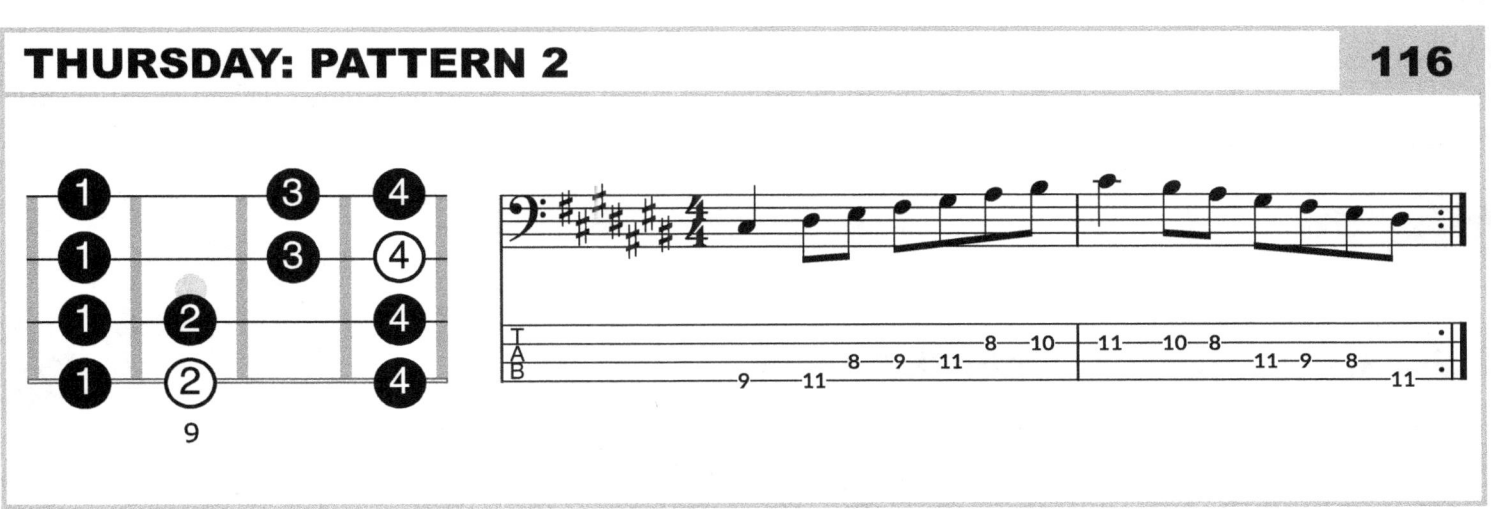

FRIDAY: PATTERN 3

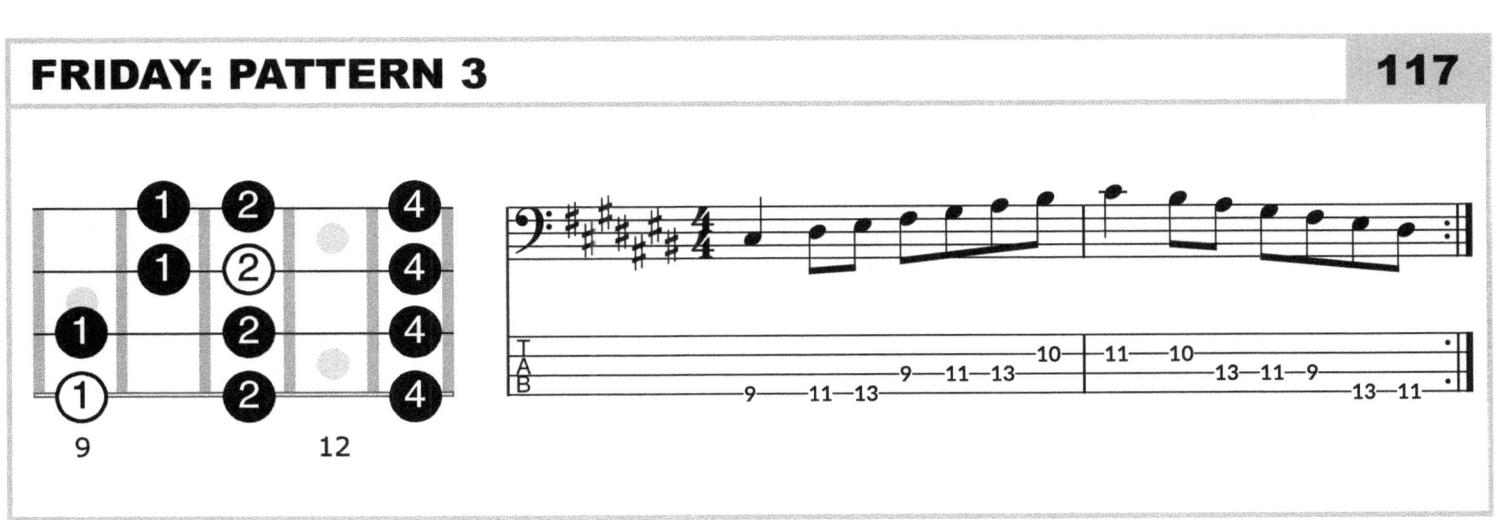

SATURDAY: HORIZONTAL PATTERN   118

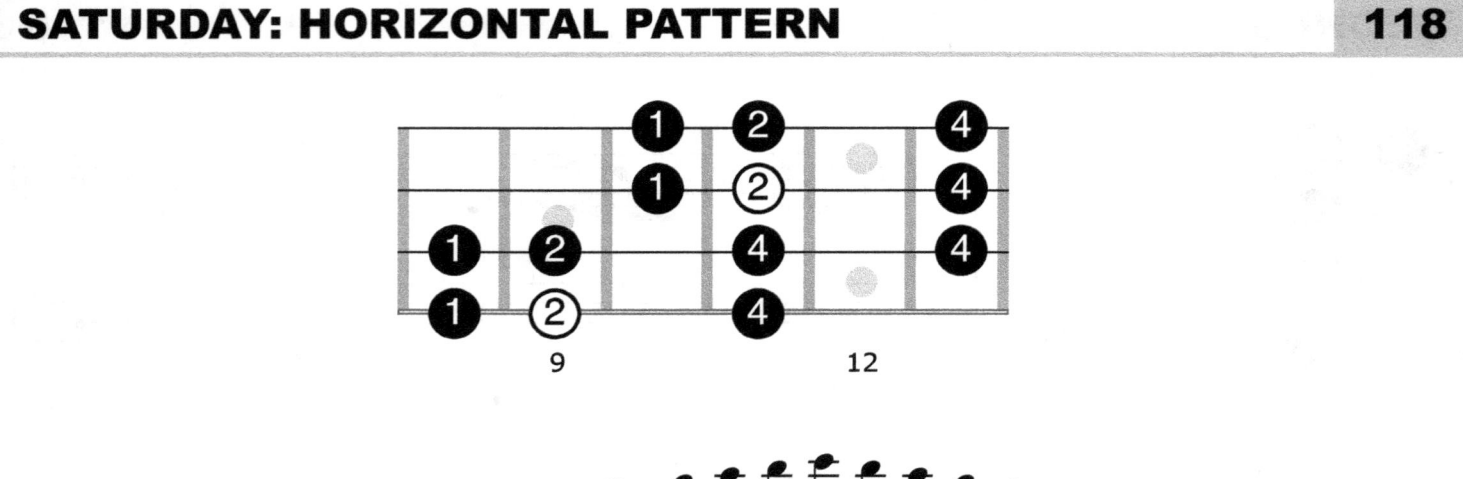

SUNDAY: SCALE APPLICATION   119

A *triad* is a chord built from the root, 3rd, and 5th of a scale. Sometimes these notes are referred to as "chord tones," which are the strongest notes to land on when creating a bass line. Let's practice triad shapes on an extremely popular chord progression, 1 6- 4 5. When using Pattern 5, the major chords share the same fingering.

WEEK 18: C# MINOR

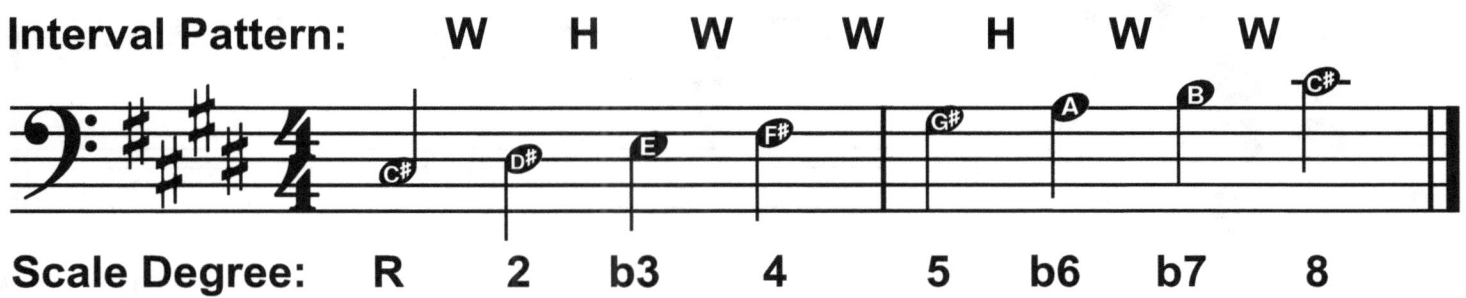

MONDAY: OPEN-STRING PATTERN 3 — 120

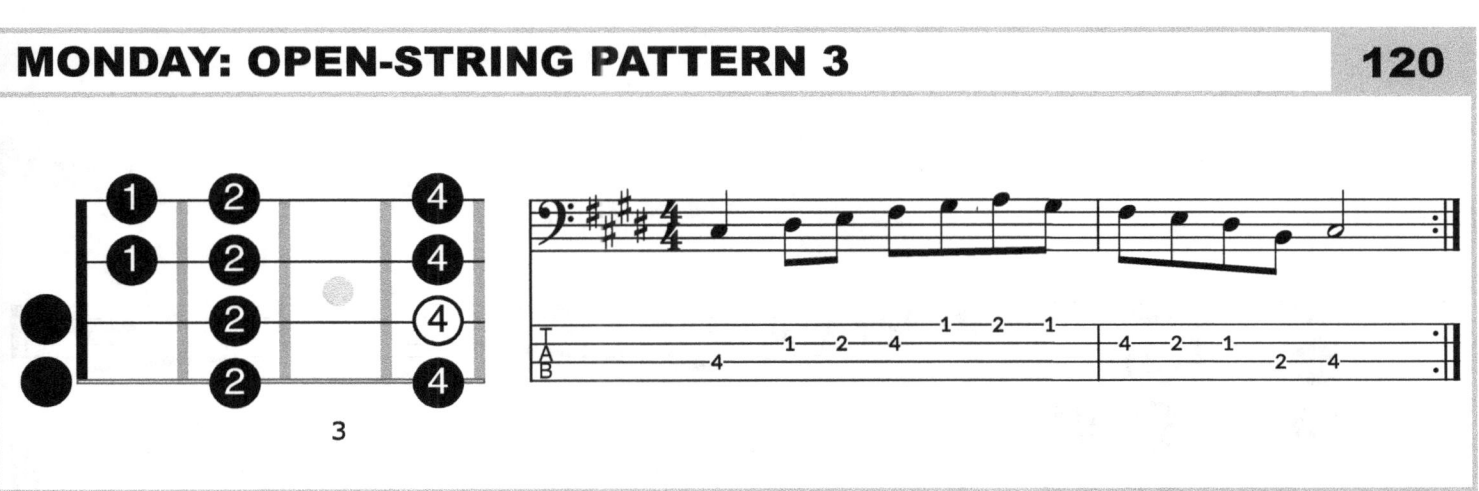

TUESDAY: PATTERN 4 — 121

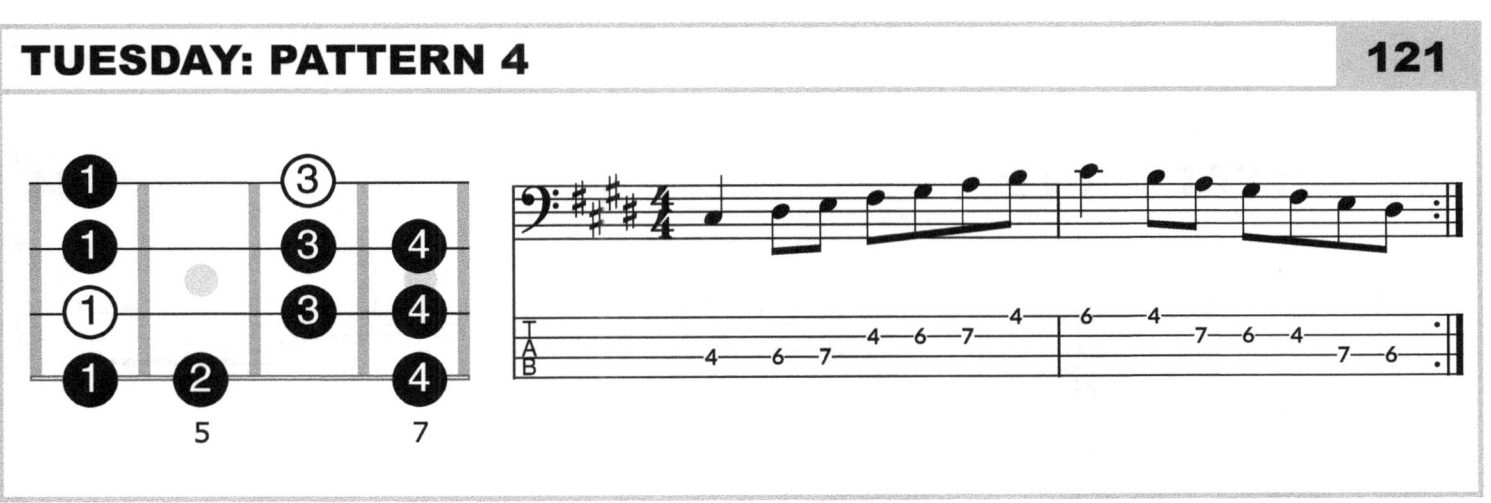

WEDNESDAY: PATTERN 5

THURSDAY: PATTERN 1

FRIDAY: PATTERN 2

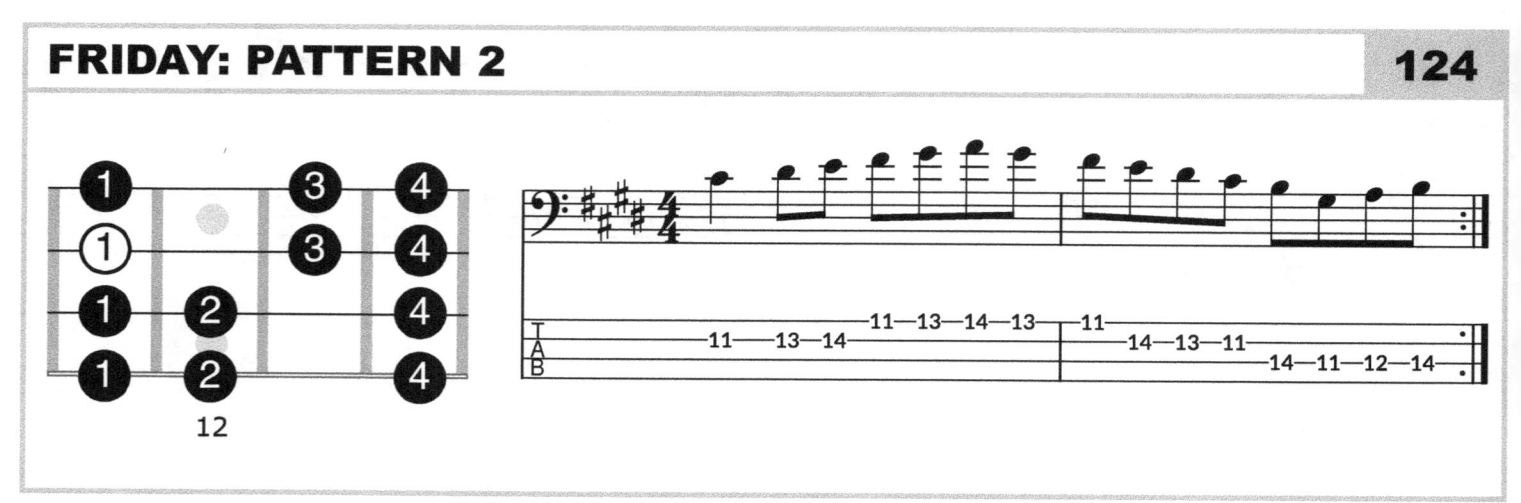

SATURDAY: HORIZONTAL PATTERN 125

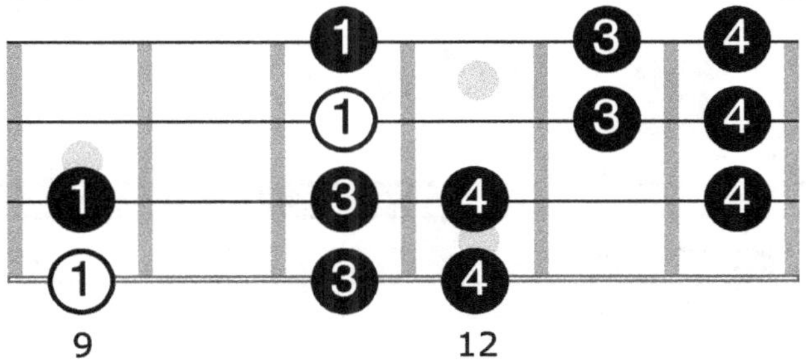

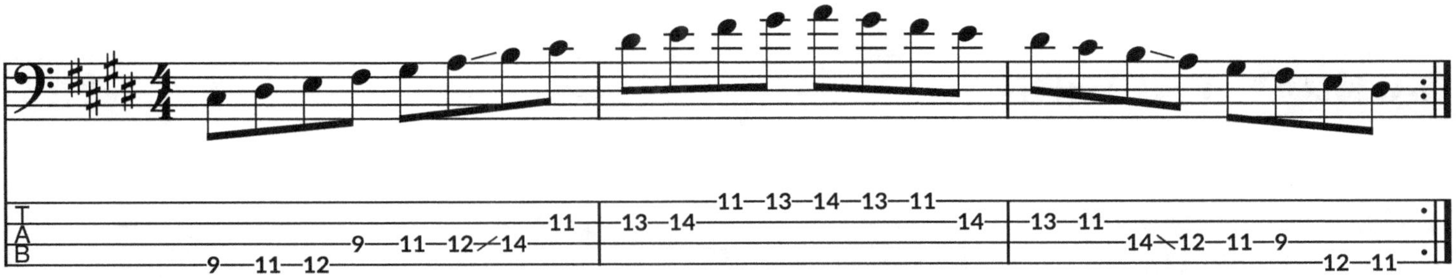

SUNDAY: SCALE APPLICATION 126

A great way to break up stepwise scale motion is to introduce 3rd intervals to your line. When you're on a note of a scale and, while moving stepwise, skip the note immediately next to it, you are playing a 3rd interval. Intervals of a 3rd are either three or four half steps (frets) apart. Get your fingers used to this with our next example.

WEEK 19: C# MAJOR PENTATONIC

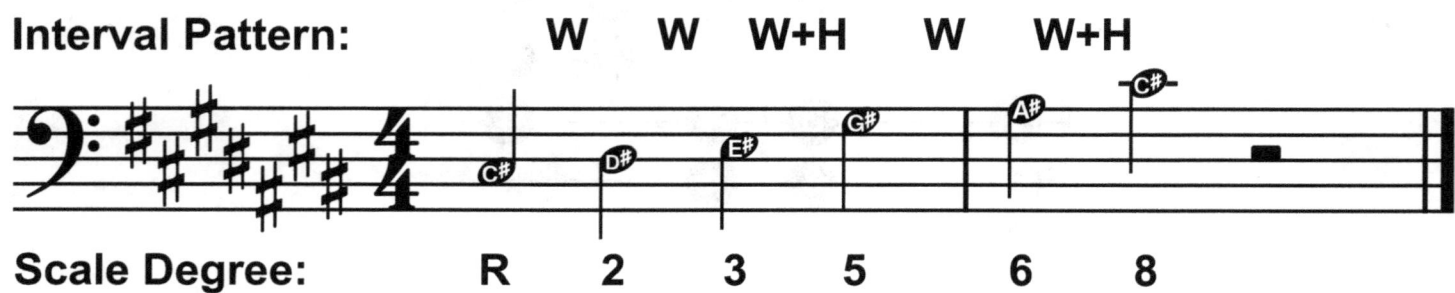

MONDAY: PATTERN 4　　　127

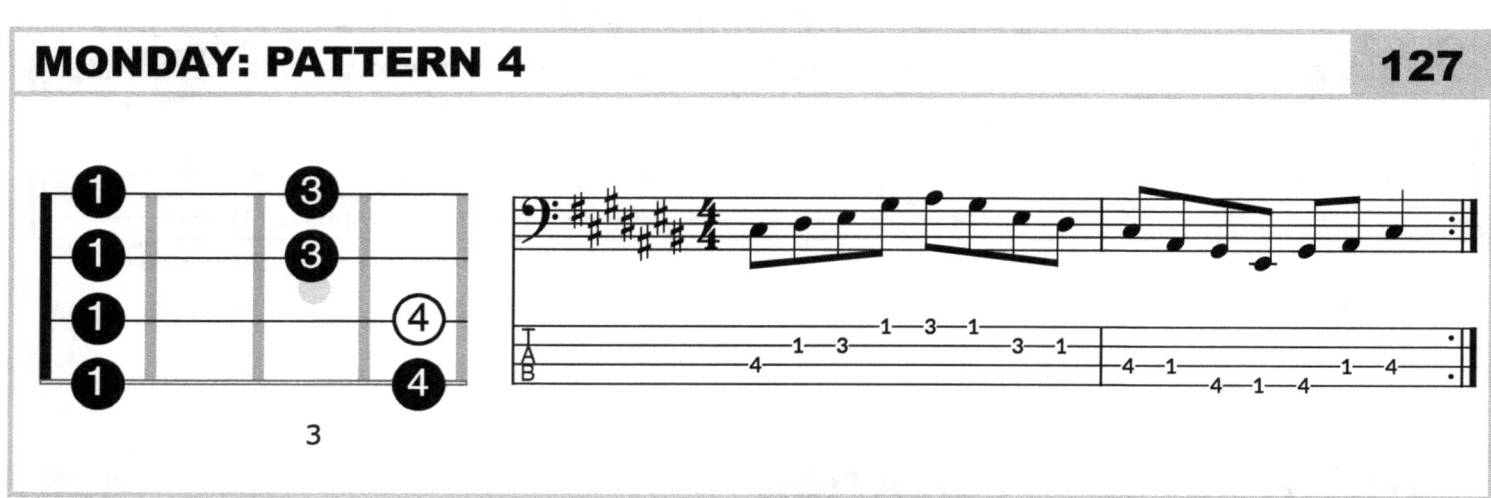

TUESDAY: PATTERN 5　　　128

WEDNESDAY: PATTERN 1 — 129

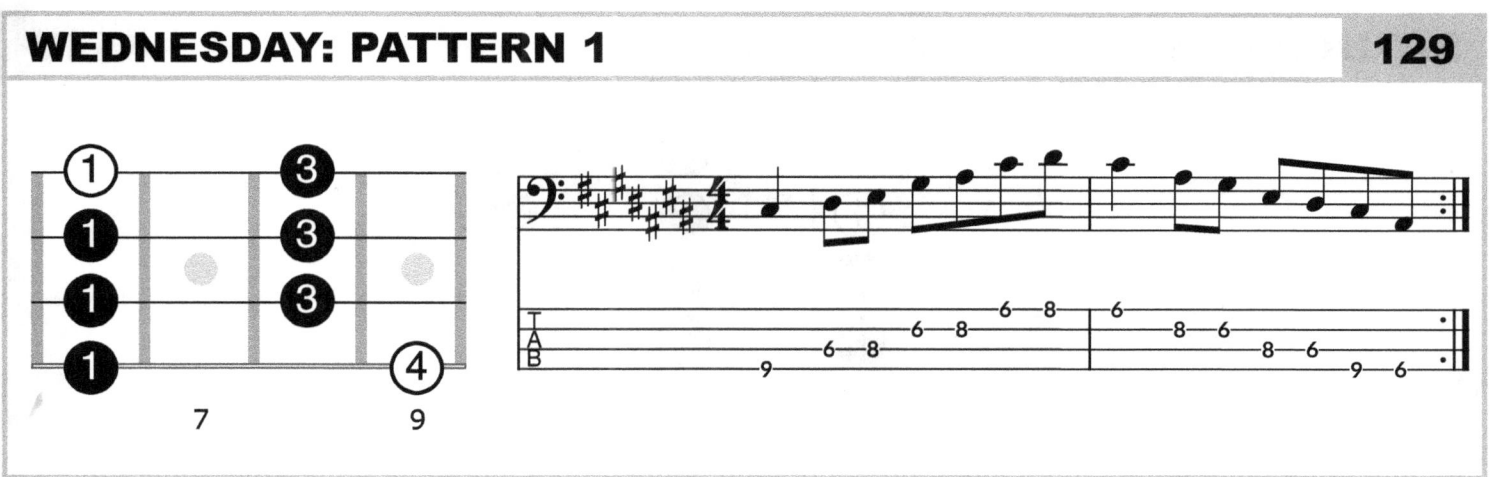

THURSDAY: PATTERN 2 — 130

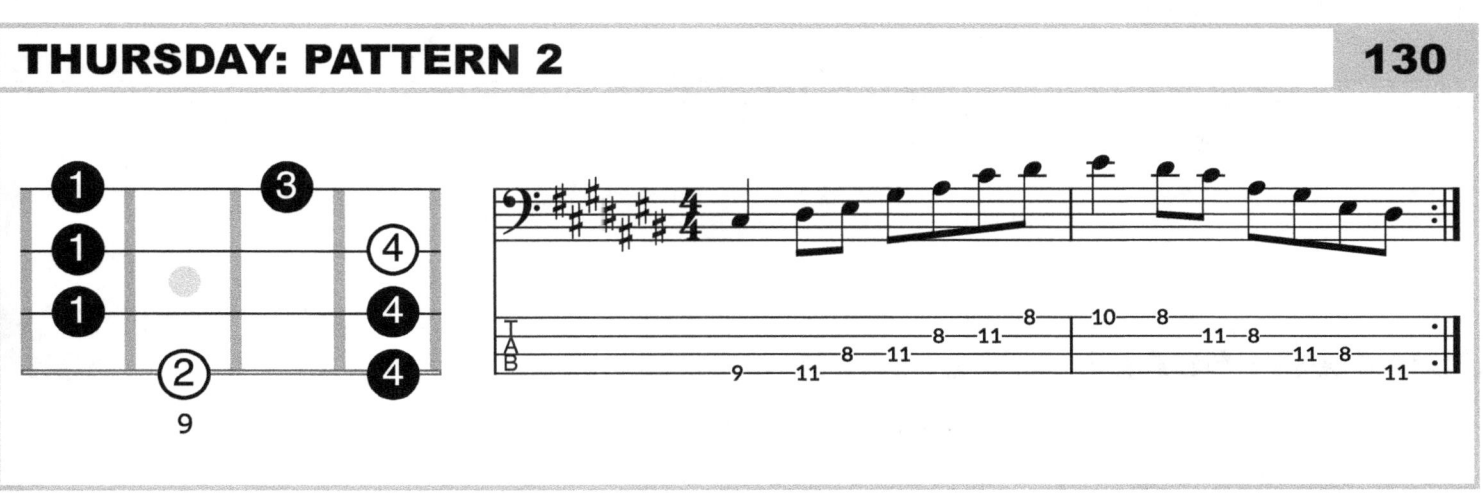

FRIDAY: PATTERN 3 — 131

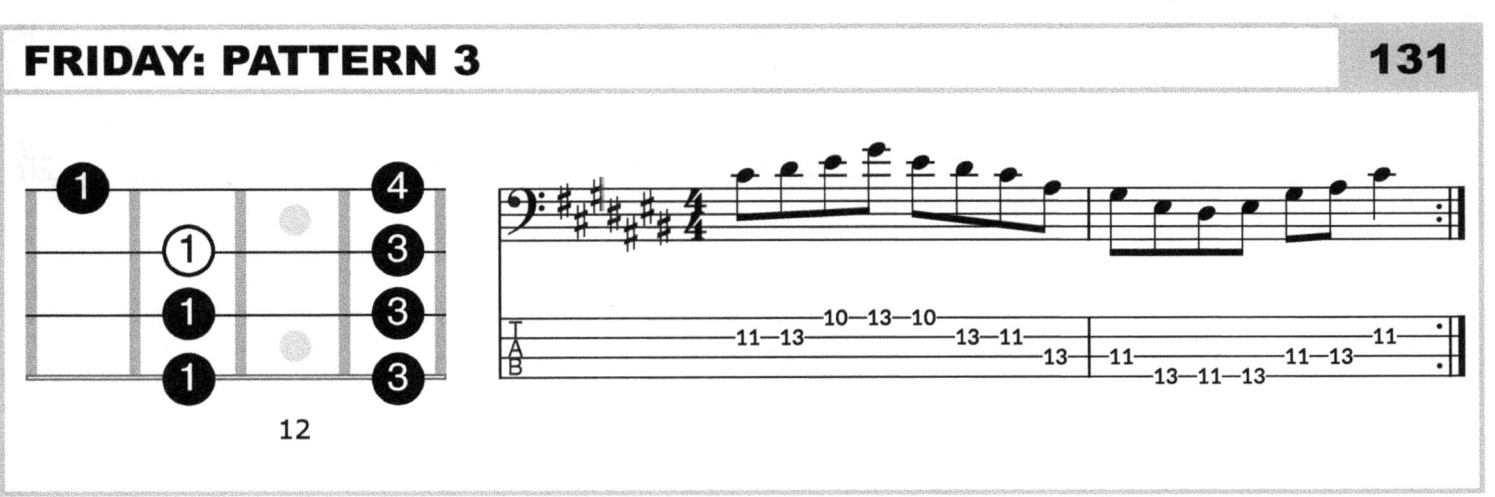

SATURDAY: HORIZONTAL PATTERN   132

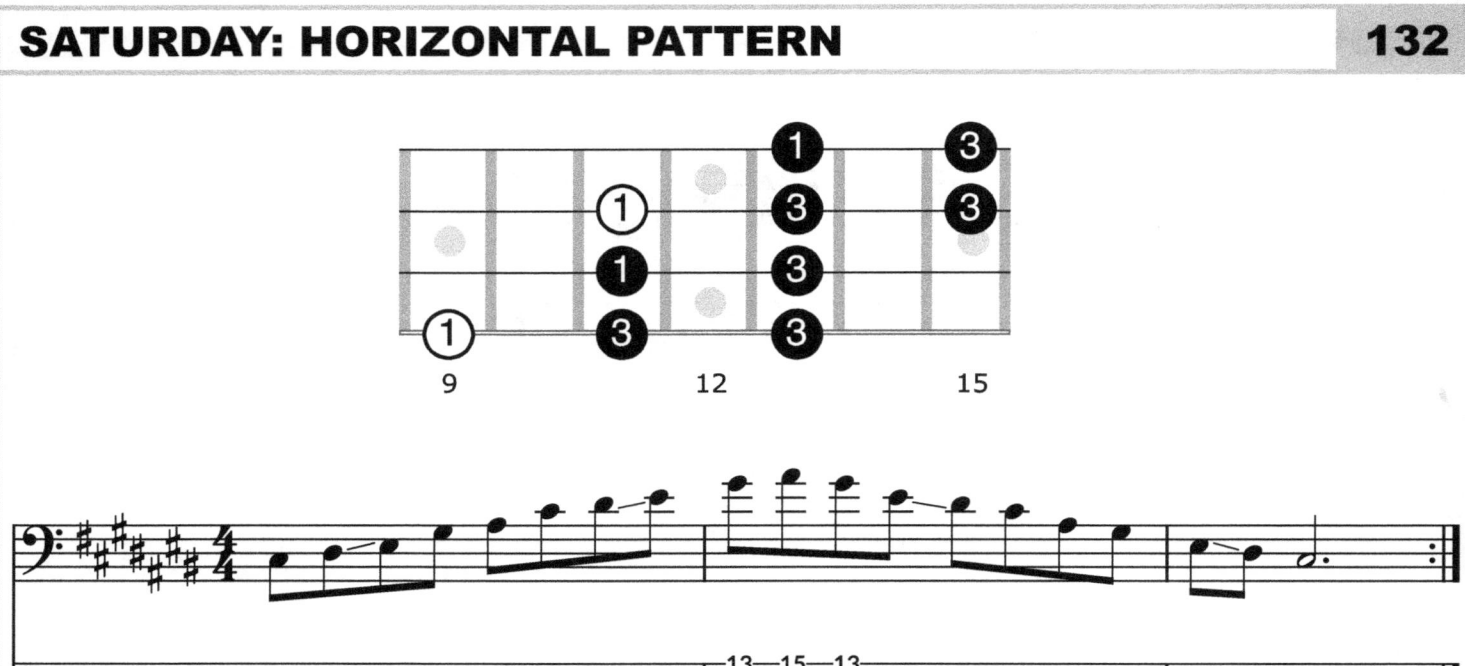

SUNDAY: SCALE APPLICATION   133

Groups of 4 are highly effective in the pentatonic scale, as well. These exercises are great for dexterity and make great phrases for connecting ideas.

WEEK 20: C# MINOR PENTATONIC

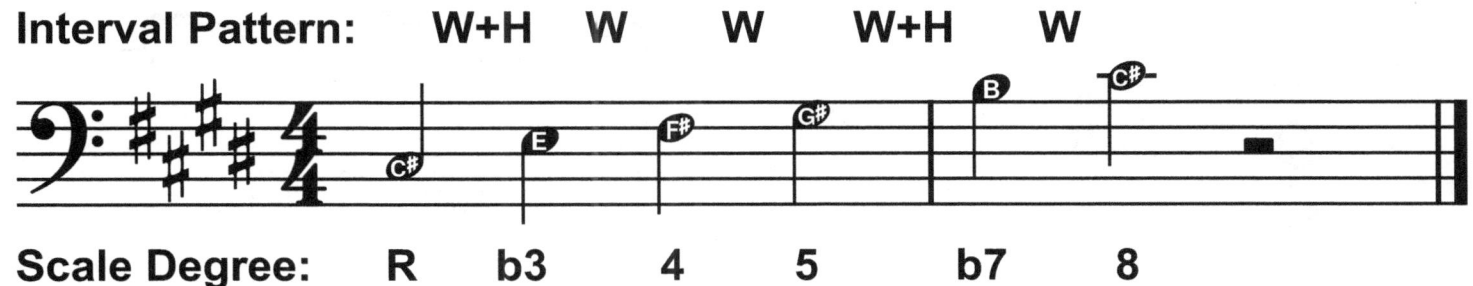

MONDAY: PATTERN 3

TUESDAY: PATTERN 4

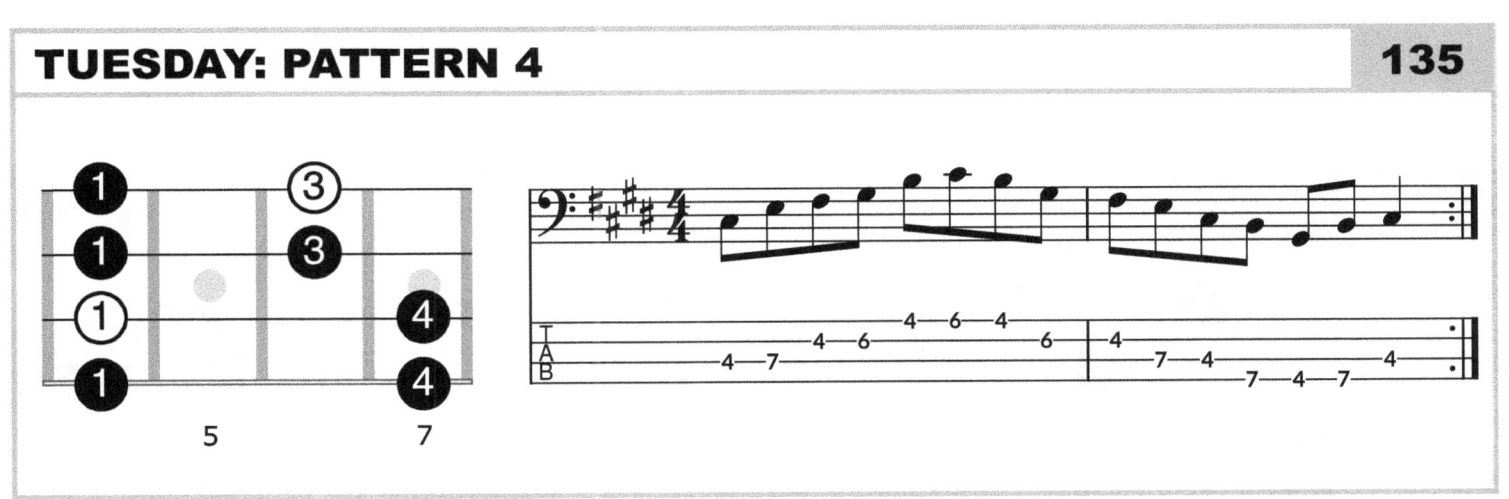

WEDNESDAY: PATTERN 5 — 136

THURSDAY: PATTERN 1 — 137

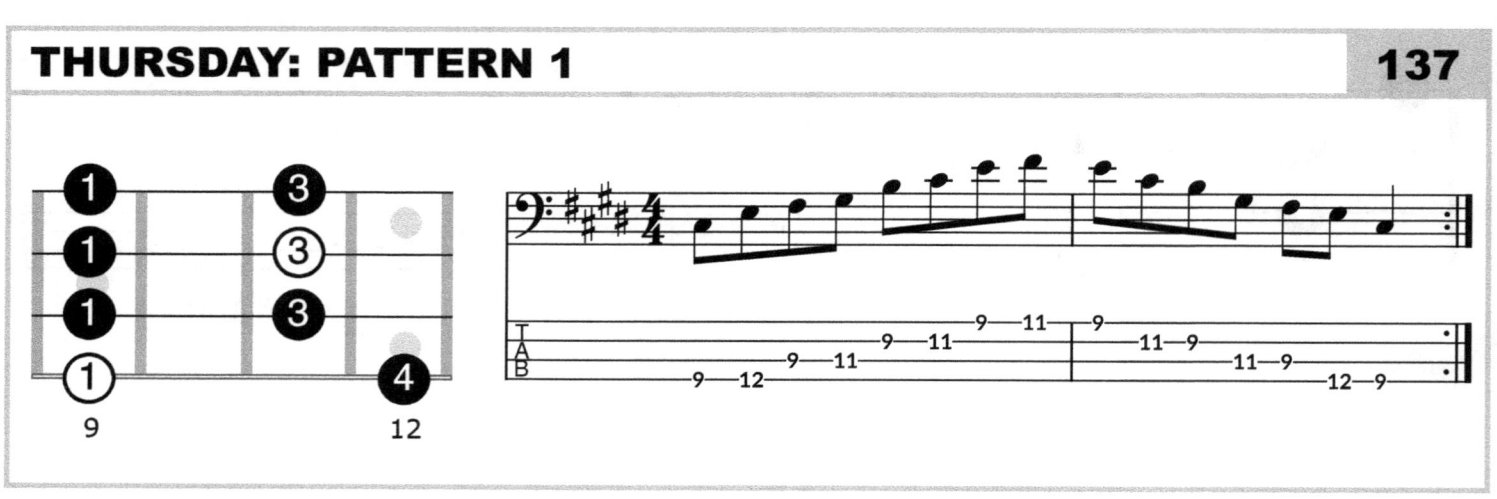

FRIDAY: PATTERN 2 — 138

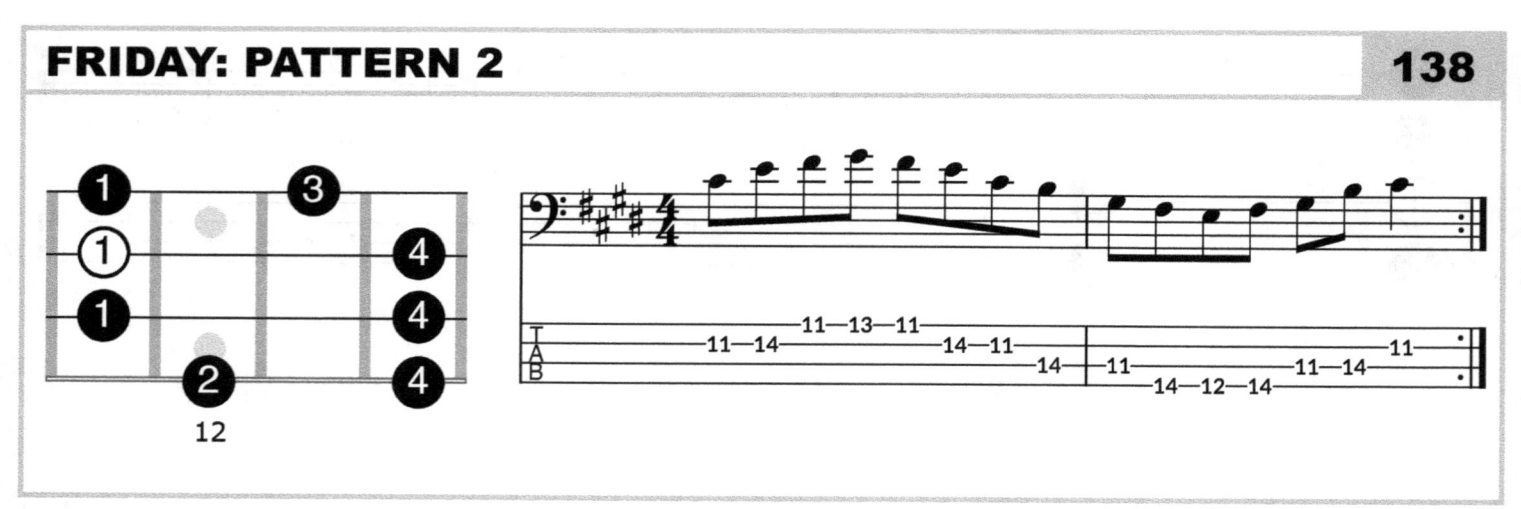

SATURDAY: HORIZONTAL PATTERN   139

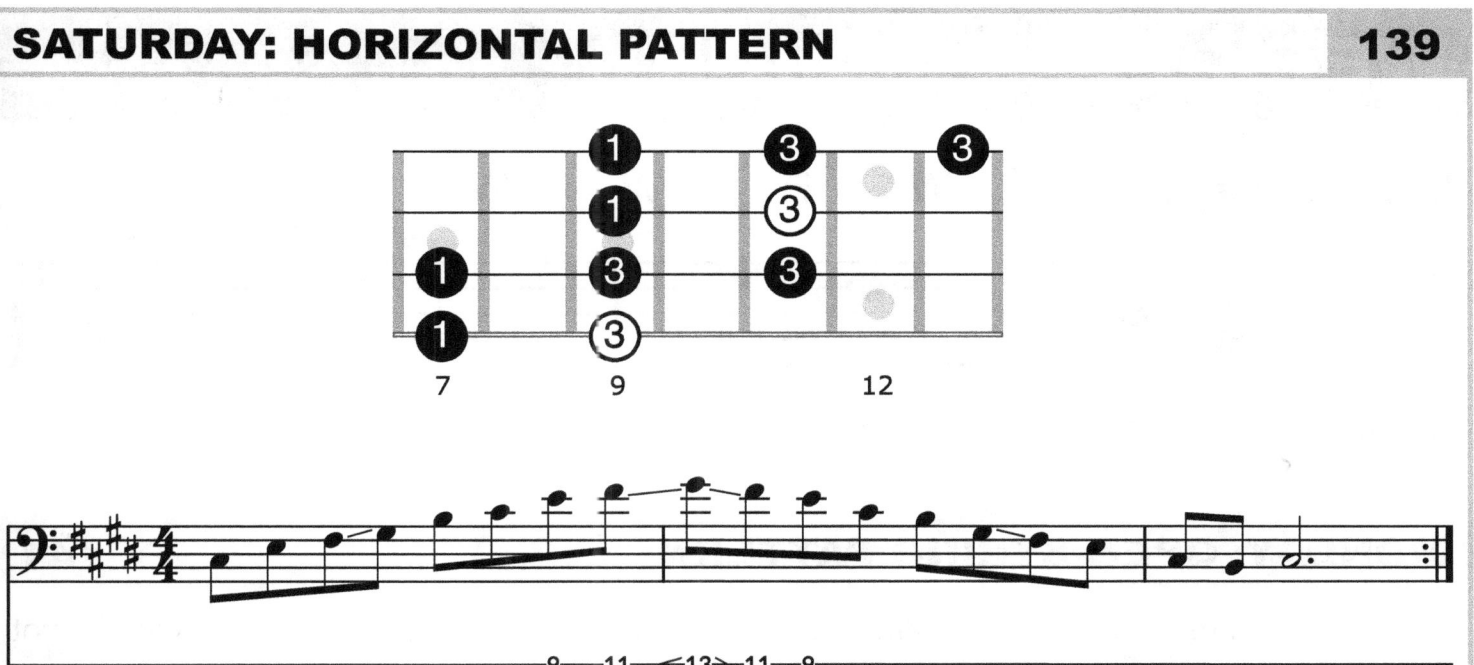

SUNDAY: SCALE APPLICATION   140

Our next example is a very popular blues riff that incorporates a swing feel and a triplet. Having two different endings sets up a question-and-answer feel that is demonstrated often in this book.

WEEK 21: D MAJOR

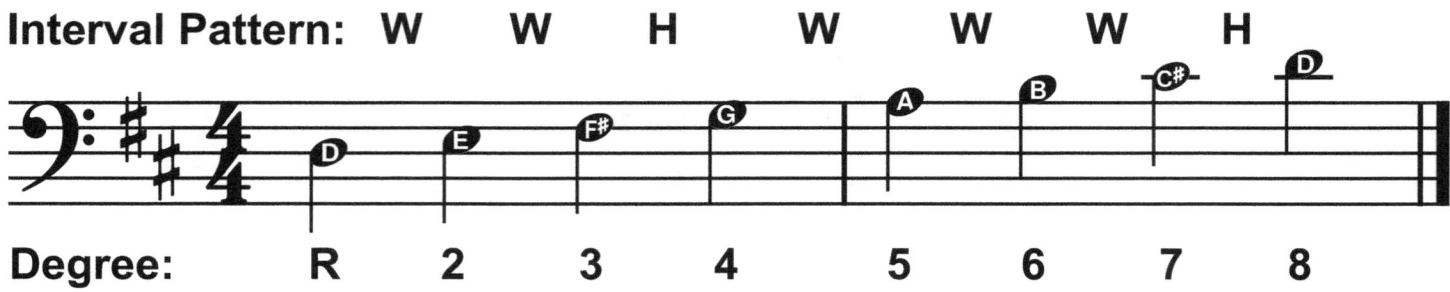

MONDAY: OPEN-STRING PATTERN — 141

The key of D presents us with an interesting situation: a useful open-string pattern that is not one of our standard five. Instead, it's an amalgam of the higher part of Pattern 3 and the lower part of Pattern 4.

TUESDAY: PATTERN 4 — 142

WEDNESDAY: PATTERN 5   143

THURSDAY: PATTERN 1   144

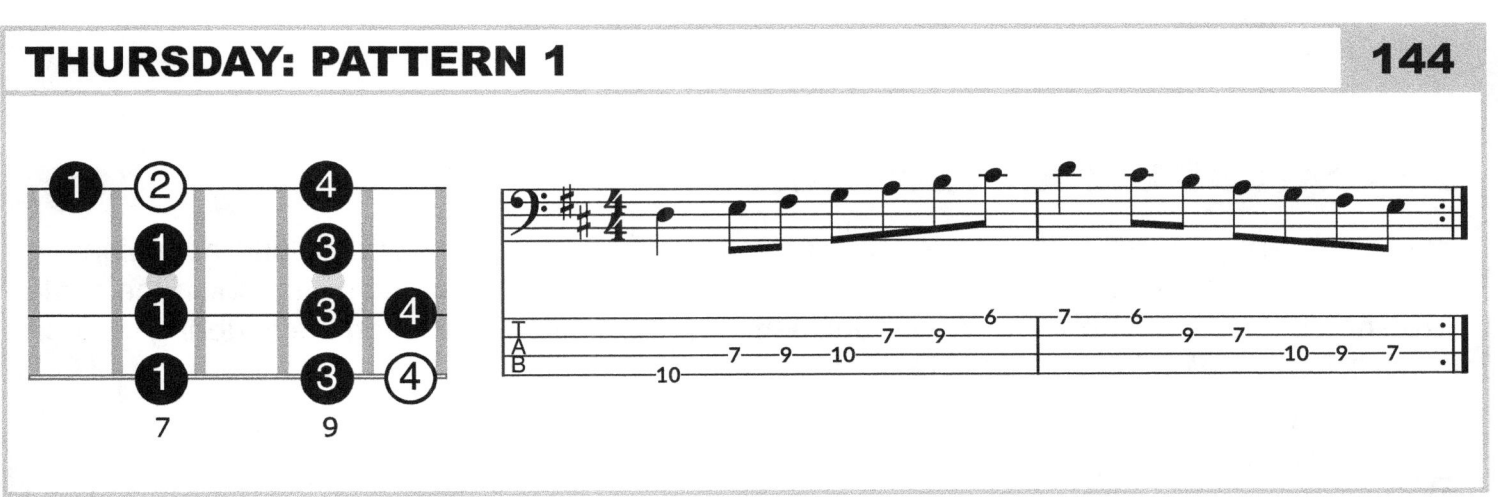

FRIDAY: PATTERN 2   145

SATURDAY: PATTERN 3   146

To allow all our patterns to be represented, we'll demonstrate how Pattern 3 lays higher on the fretboard.

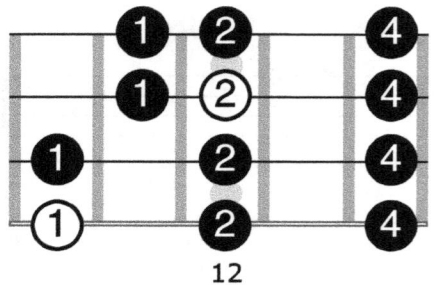
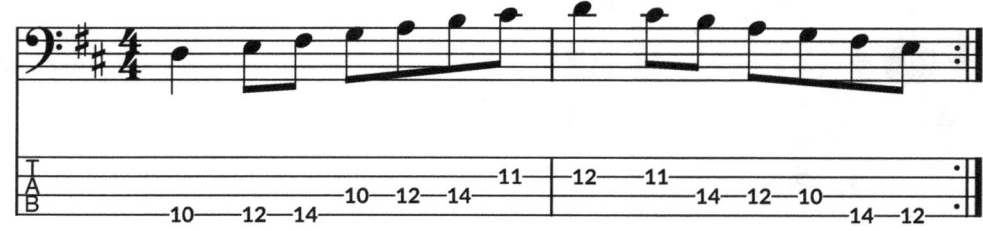

SUNDAY: SCALE APPLICATION   147

Here is a very popular scale sequence that you will find in many melodies and bass lines. It even has a distinctive look on the staff. You can think of it as moving stepwise down the scale three notes, then back up a 3rd. Watch out in measure 2, where navigating the fingering through Pattern 1 can make this one a challenge!

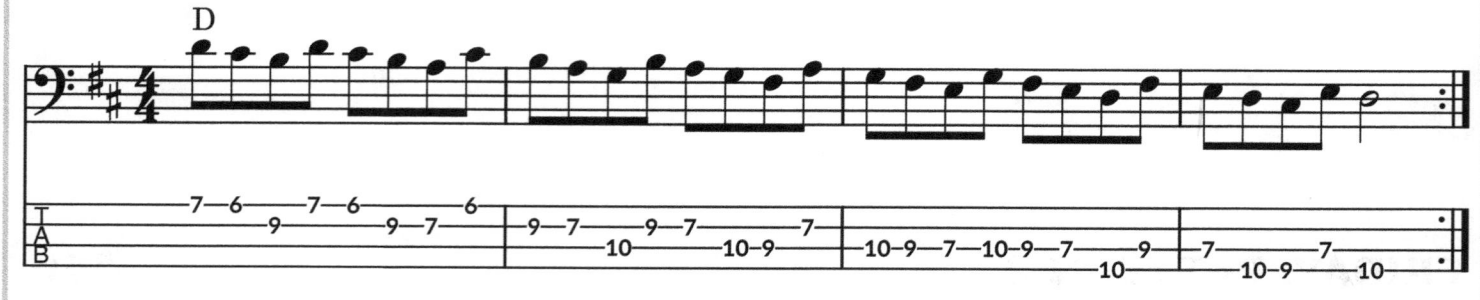

WEEK 22: D MINOR

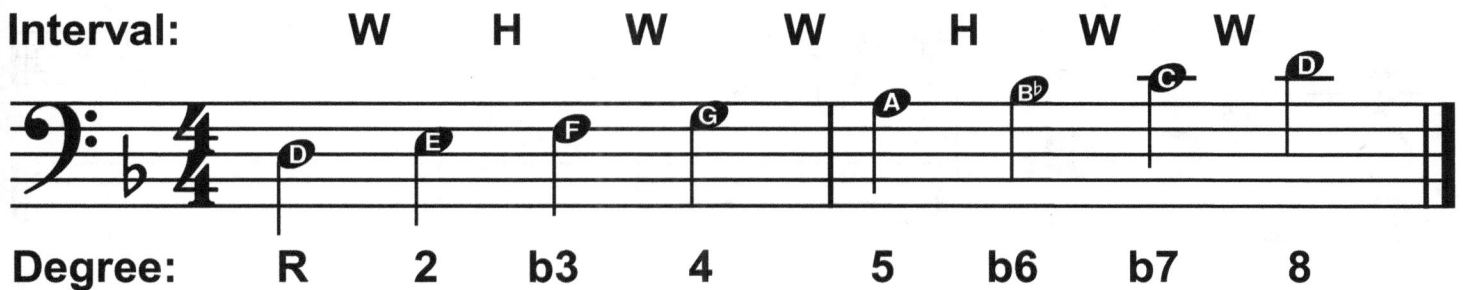

MONDAY: OPEN-STRING PATTERN 2 — 148

Today, we replace the notes closest to the nut in our standard Pattern 2 fingering with open strings.

TUESDAY: PATTERN 3 — 149

WEDNESDAY: PATTERN 4

150

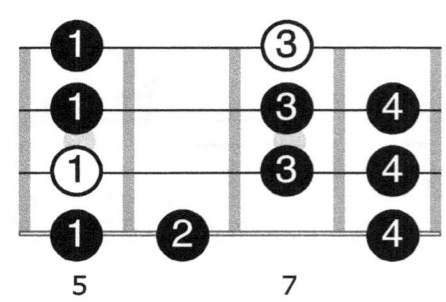

THURSDAY: PATTERN 5

151

FRIDAY: PATTERN 1

152

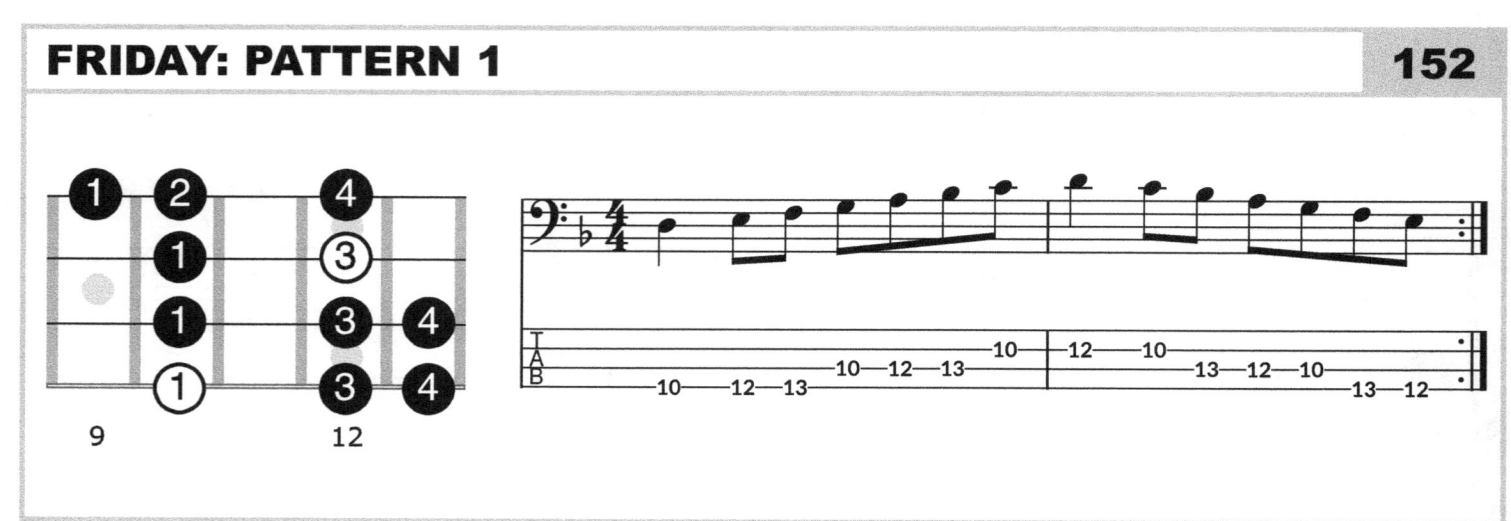

SATURDAY: HORIZONTAL PATTERN   153

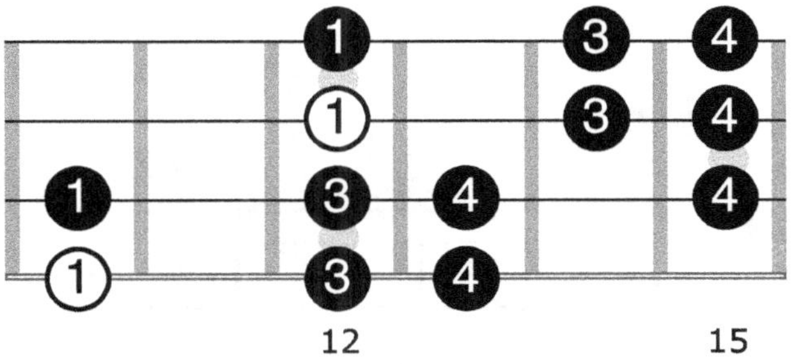

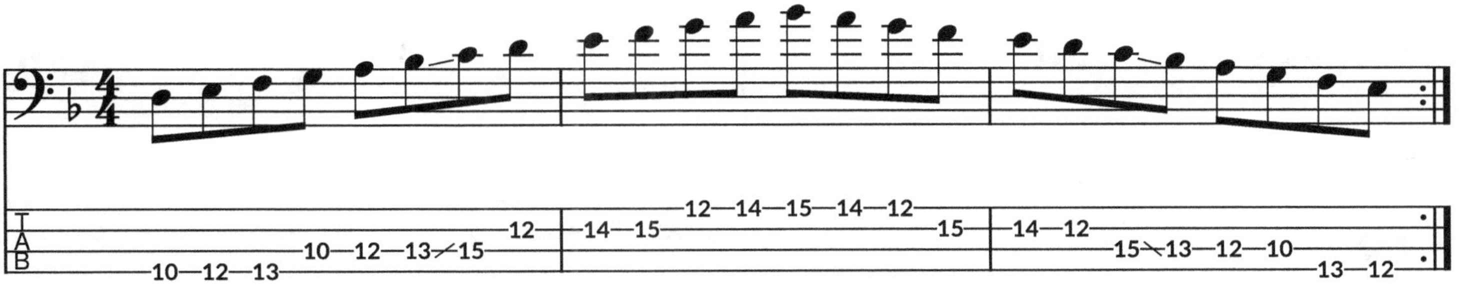

SUNDAY: SCALE APPLICATION   154

Another great device for adding variation to bass lines is using the 5th interval. Notice how today's rhythm pattern utilizes the dotted-quarter rhythm and is two measures long, giving the rhythmic theme its own resolve. This example demonstrates how 5th intervals can use the same general shape: root note with your index finger, 5th with your third finger two frets higher on the adjacent string.

WEEK 23: D MAJOR PENTATONIC

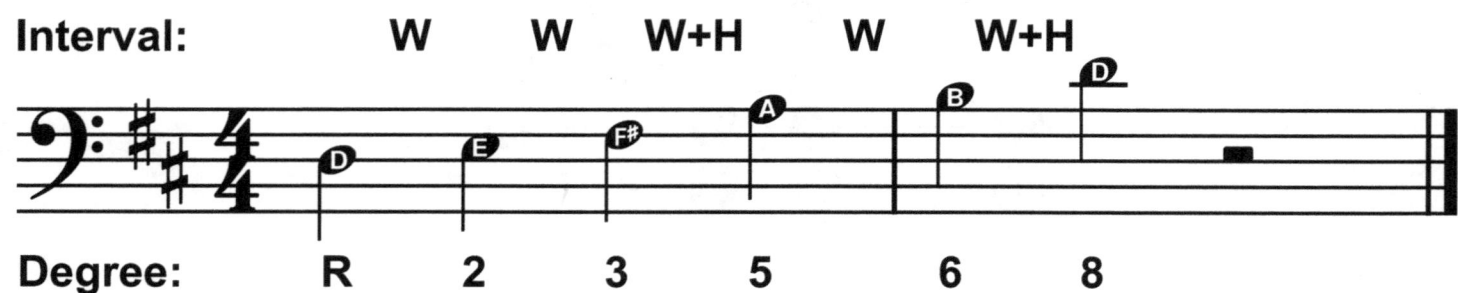

MONDAY: PATTERN 4 — 155

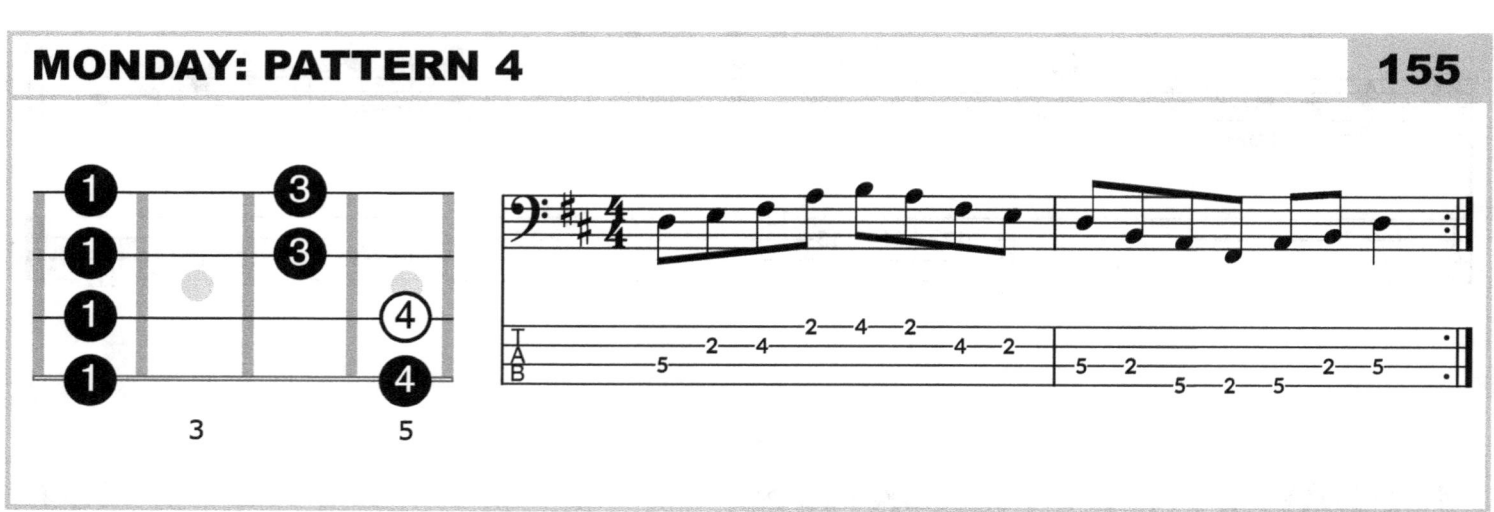

TUESDAY: PATTERN 5 — 156

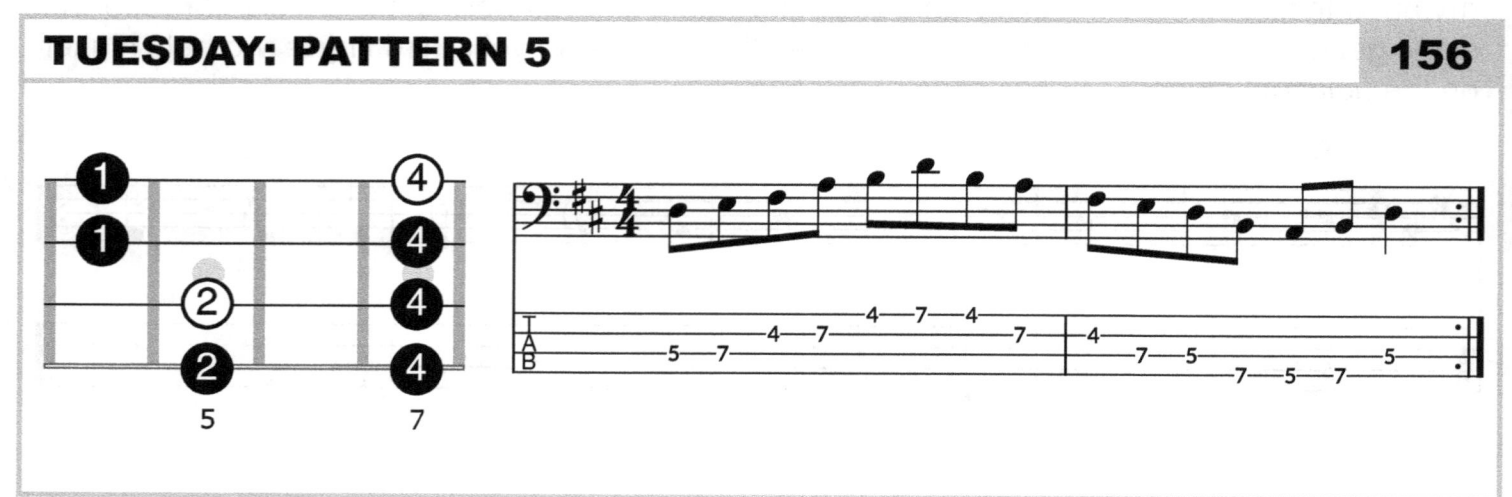

WEDNESDAY: PATTERN 1 — 157

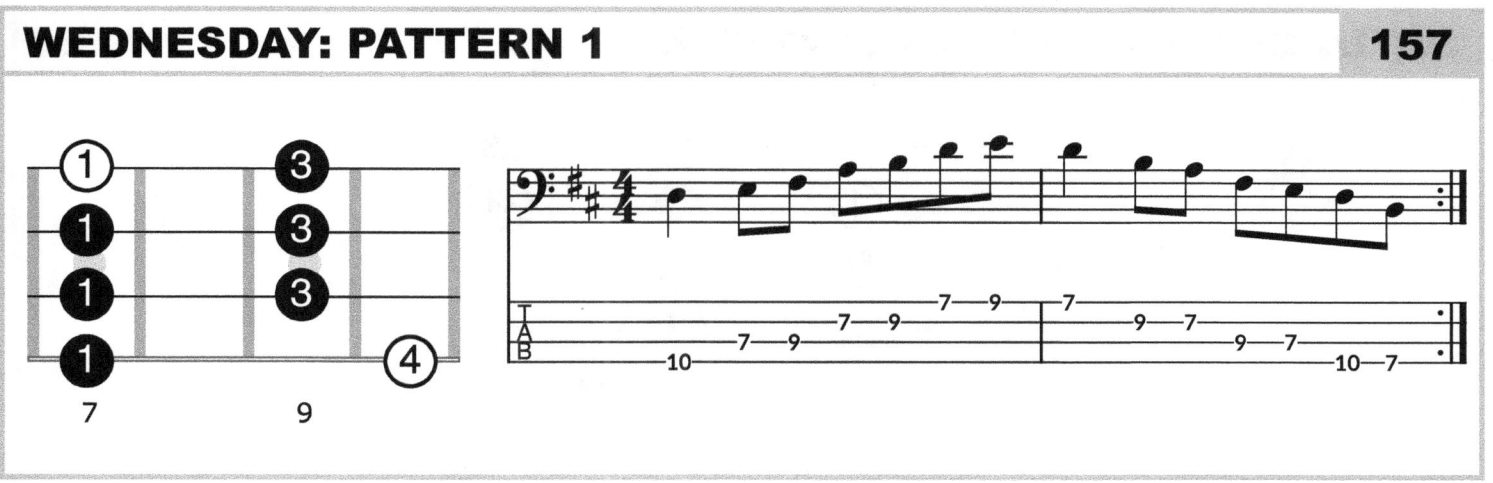

THURSDAY: PATTERN 2 — 158

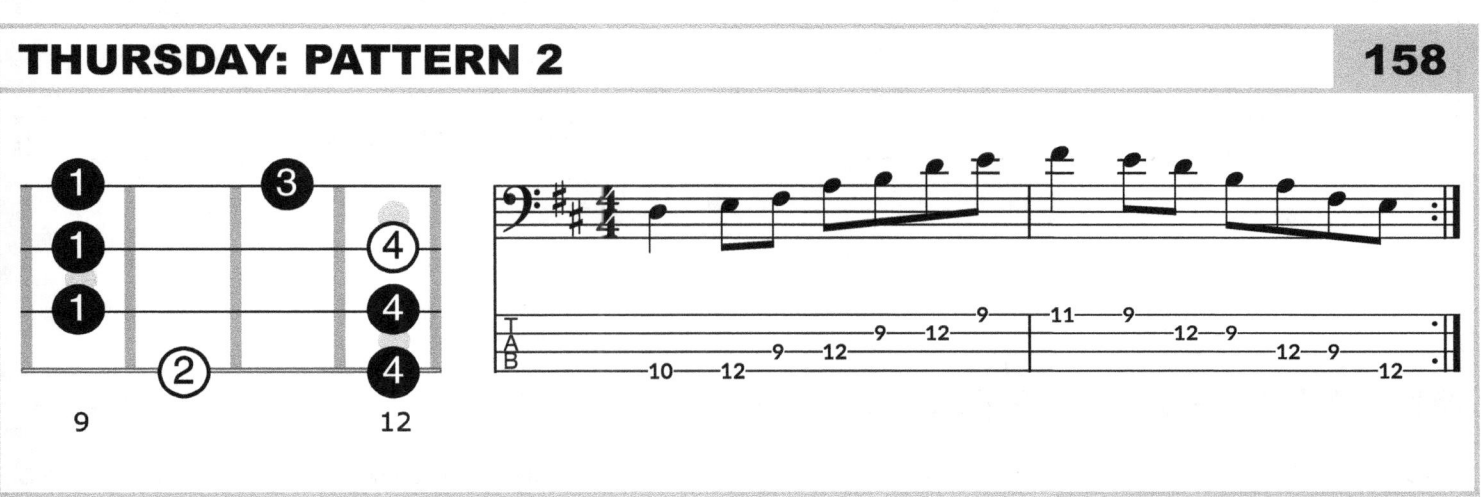

FRIDAY: PATTERN 3 — 159

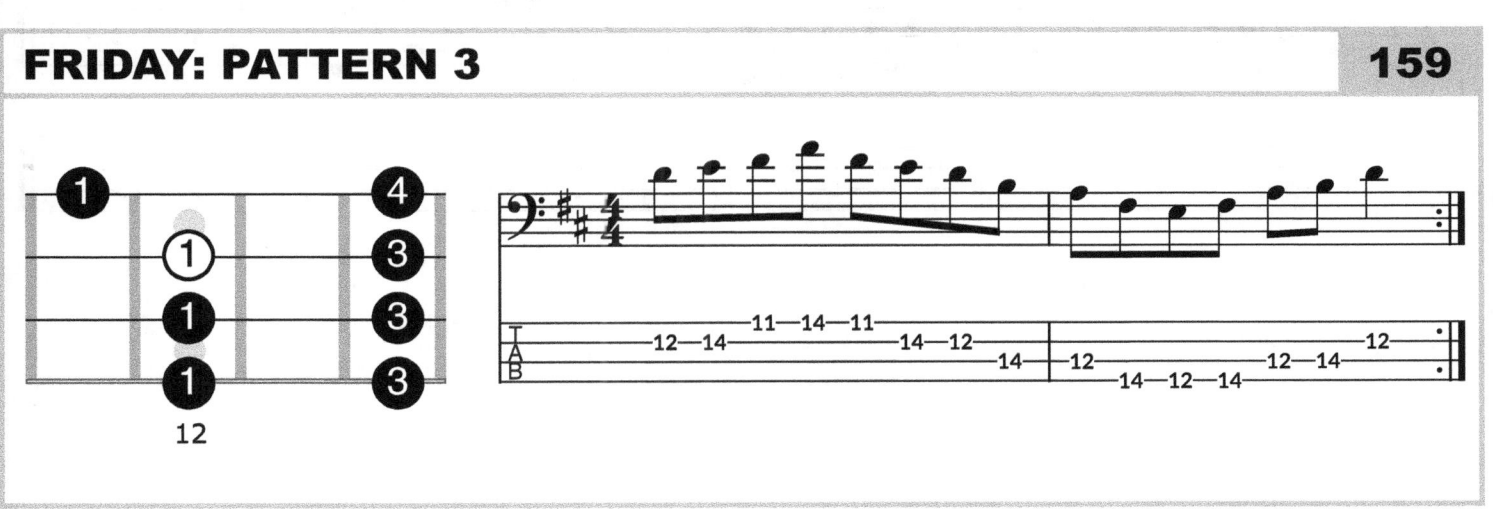

SATURDAY: HORIZONTAL PATTERN 160

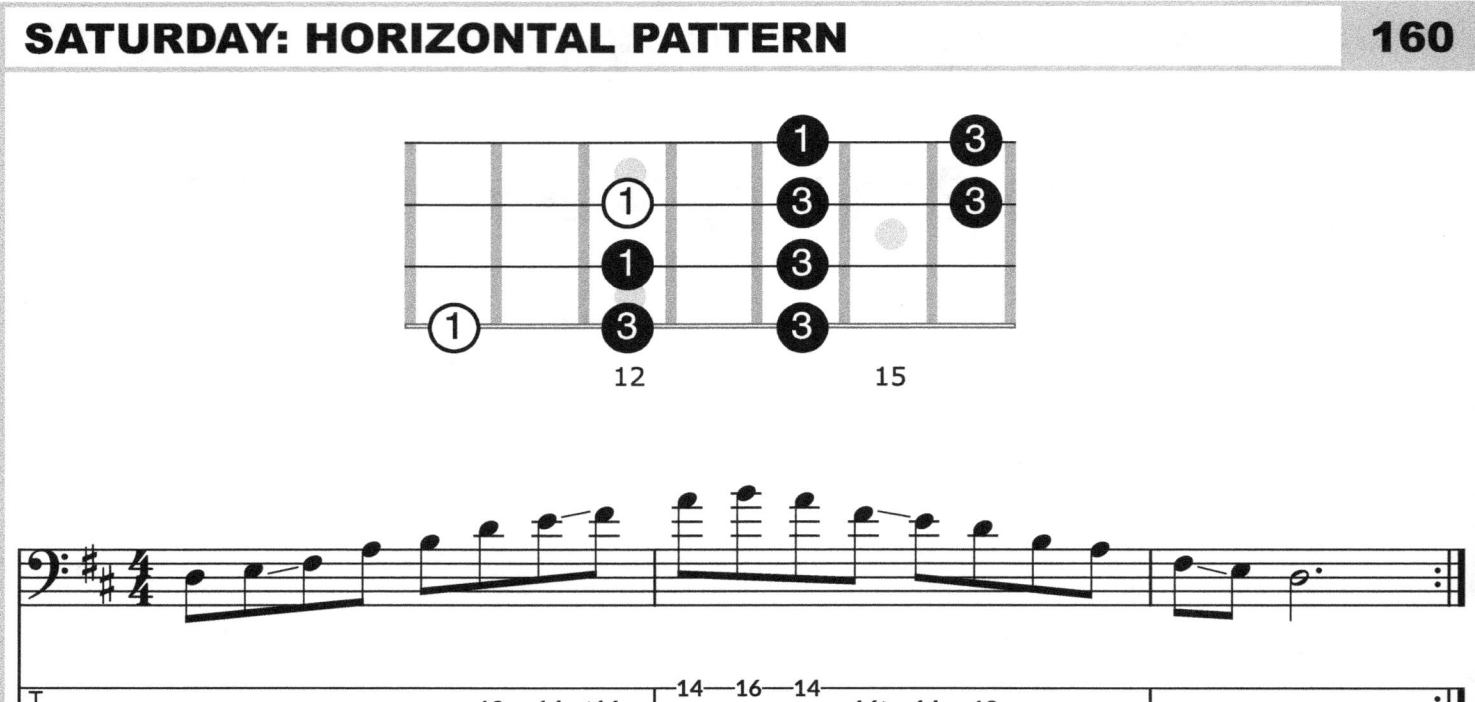

SUNDAY: SCALE APPLICATION 161

Stepwise motion in groups of 4 works well in the pentatonic scale. This example utilizes changes in direction that lead us back to the root.

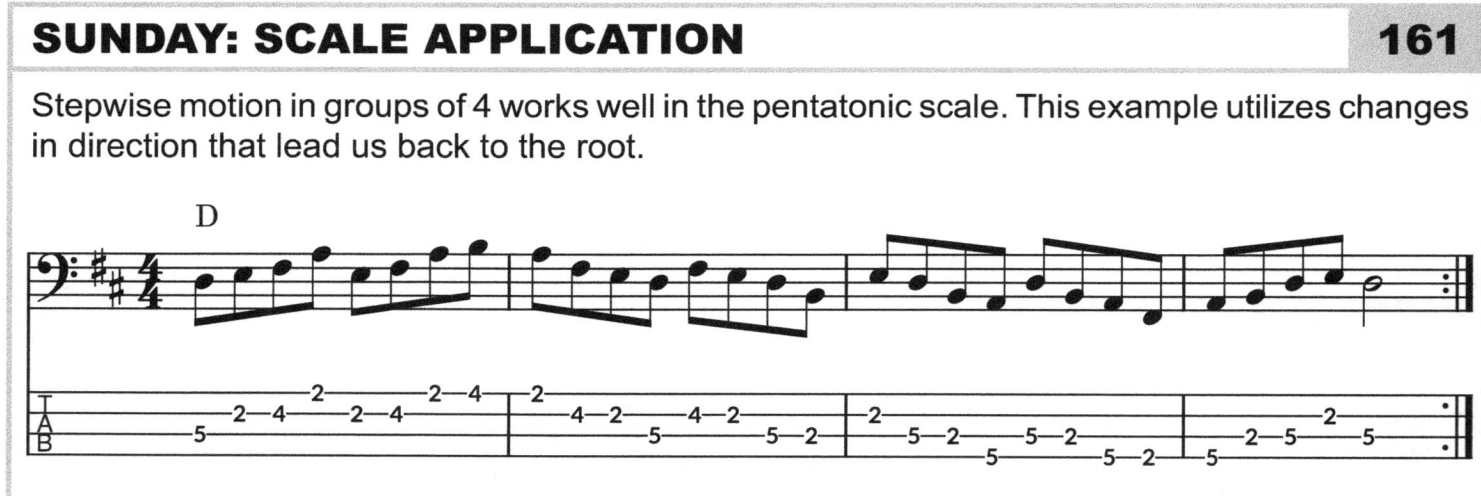

WEEK 24: D MINOR PENTATONIC

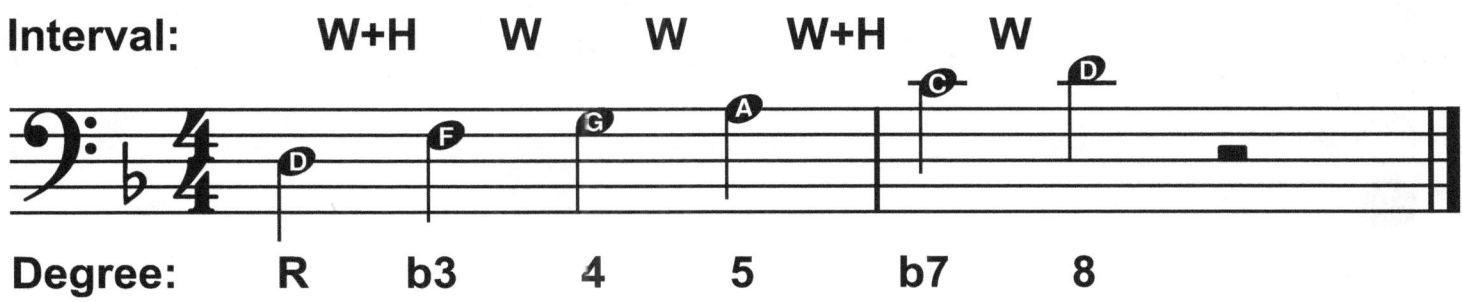

MONDAY: OPEN-STRING PATTERN 2 — 162

Today, we replace the notes closest to the nut in our standard Pattern 2 fingering with open strings.

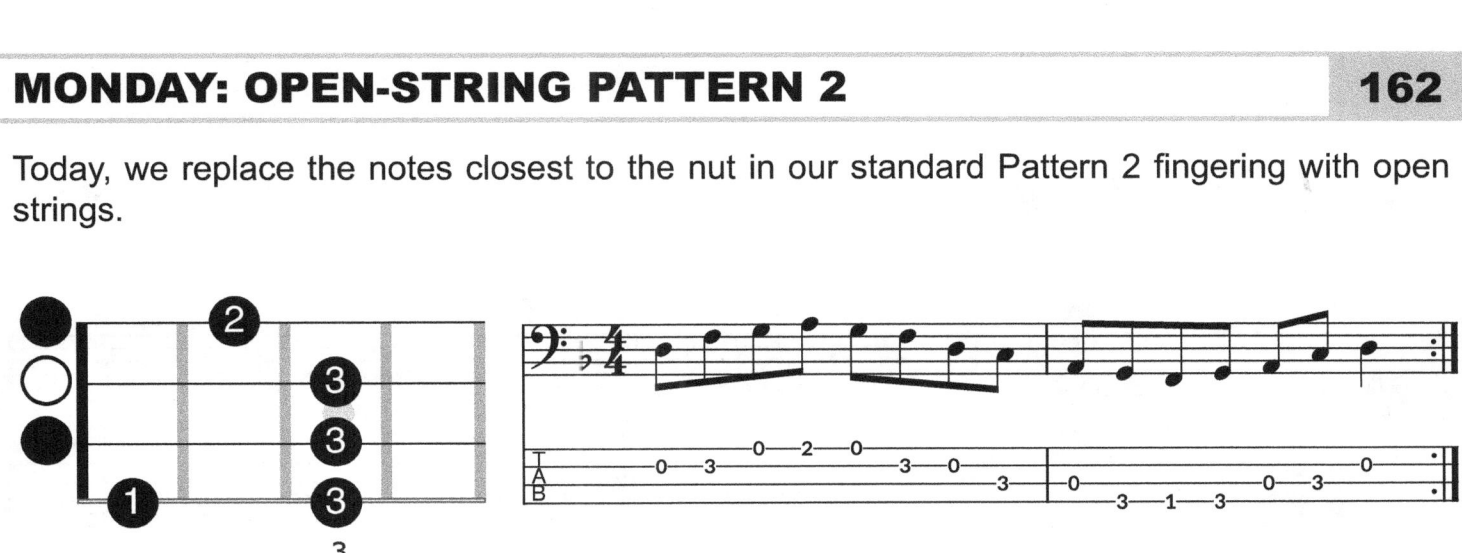

TUESDAY: PATTERN 3 — 163

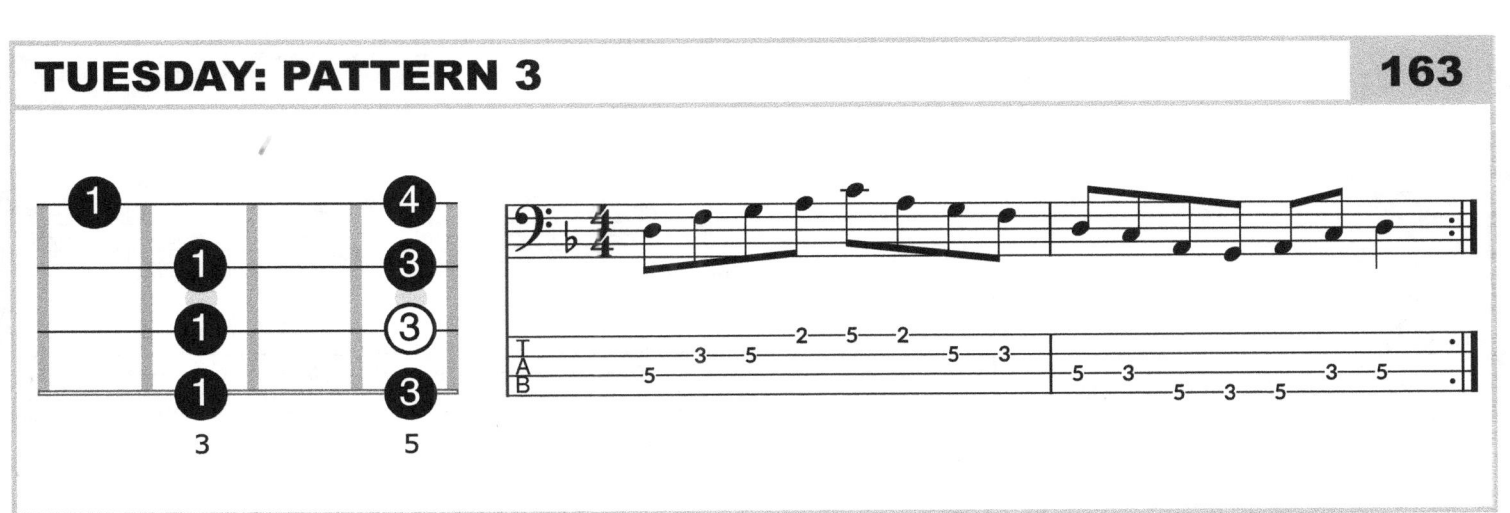

WEDNESDAY: PATTERN 4 — 164

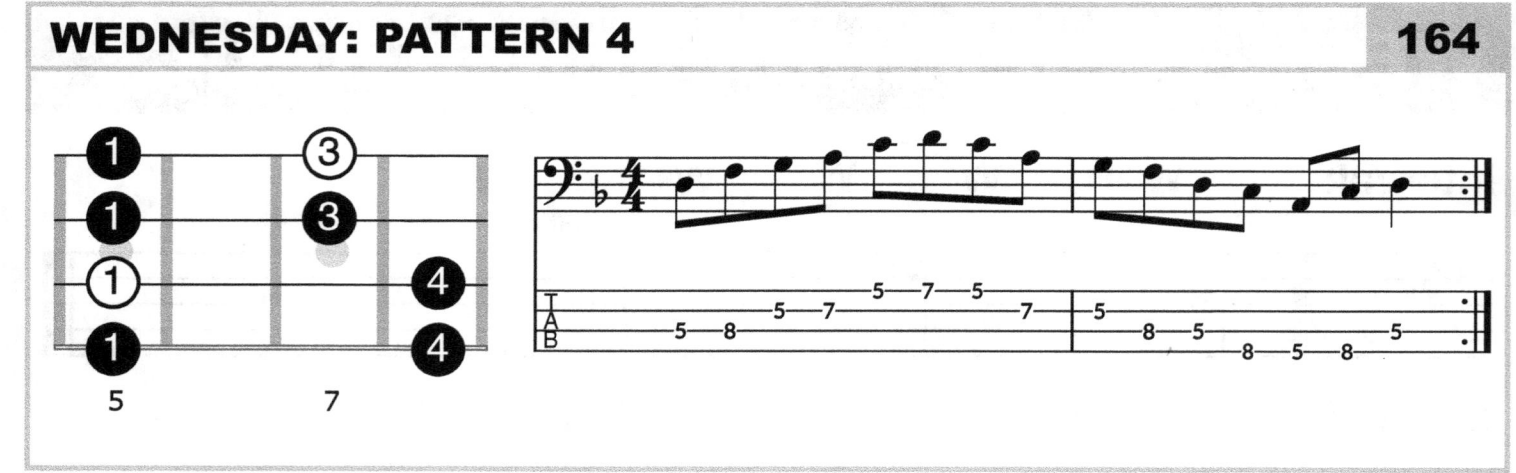

THURSDAY: PATTERN 5 — 165

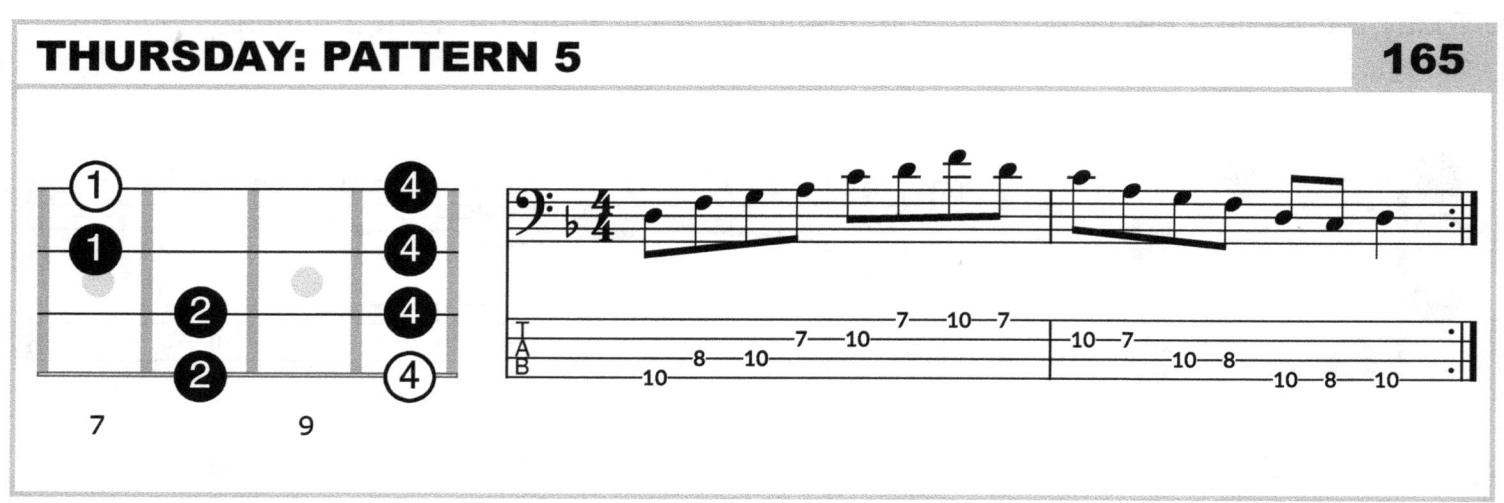

FRIDAY: PATTERN 1 — 166

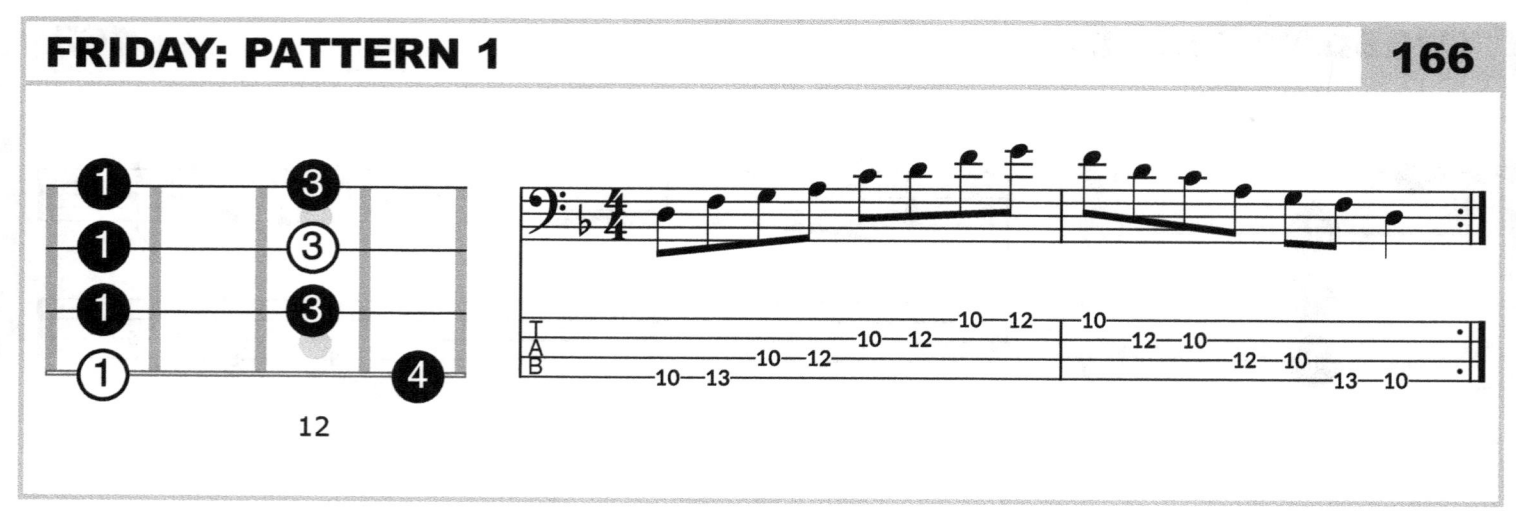

SATURDAY: HORIZONTAL PATTERN 167

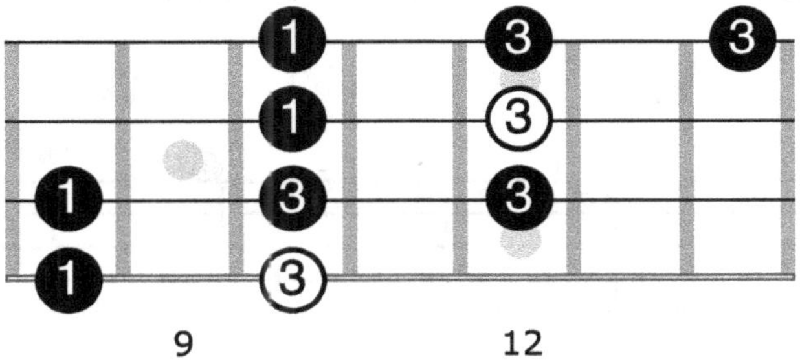

SUNDAY: SCALE APPLICATION 168

Today's example is a blues riff that is sometimes called a "box pattern" due to its fretboard shape. It's also called a "Downtown Blues" because it jumps up an octave, then descends the scale. When labeled as intervals, the riff can be thought of as: root, 8, ♭7, 5.

WEEK 25: E♭ MAJOR

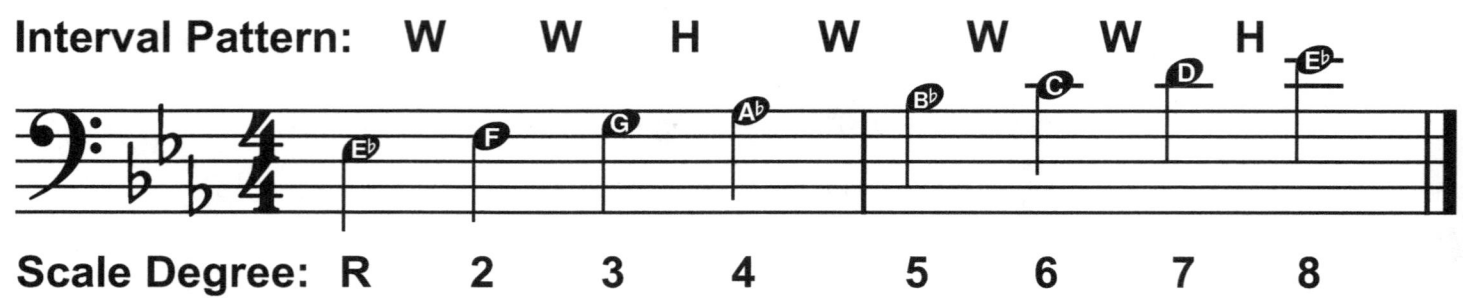

MONDAY: PATTERN 4 — 169

TUESDAY: PATTERN 5 — 170

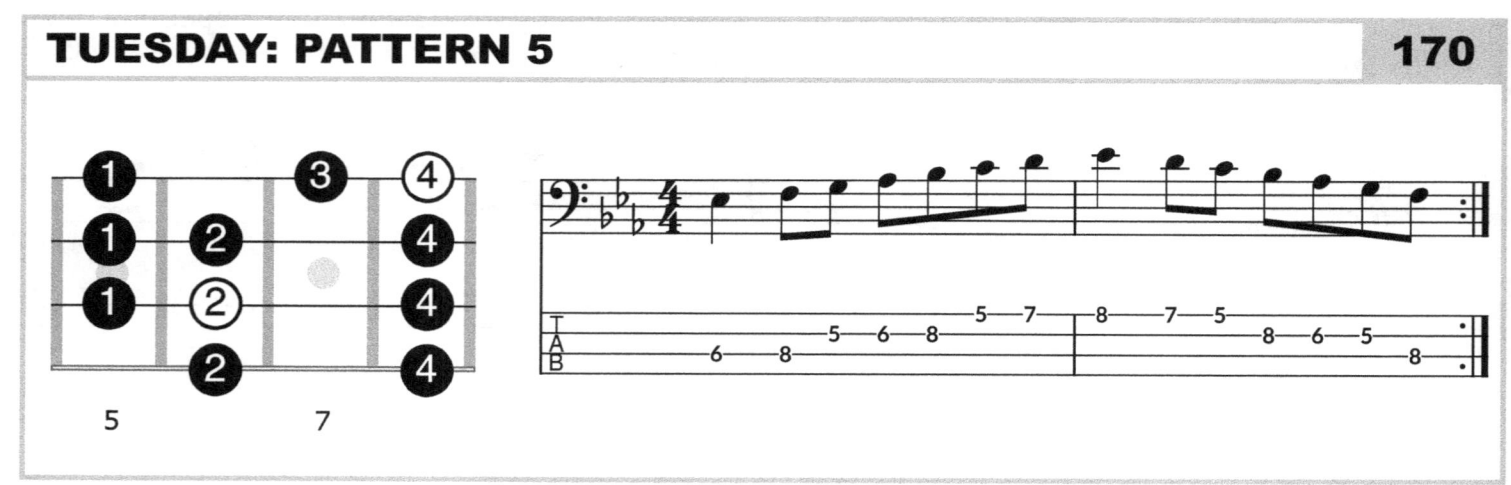

WEDNESDAY: PATTERN 1 — 171

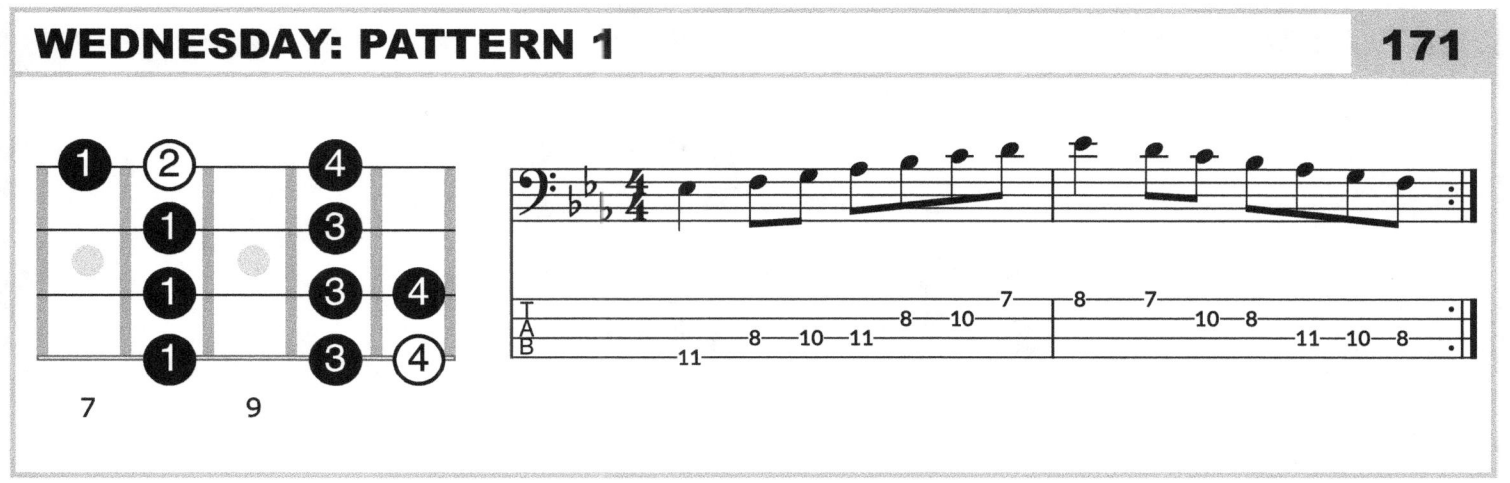

THURSDAY: PATTERN 2 — 172

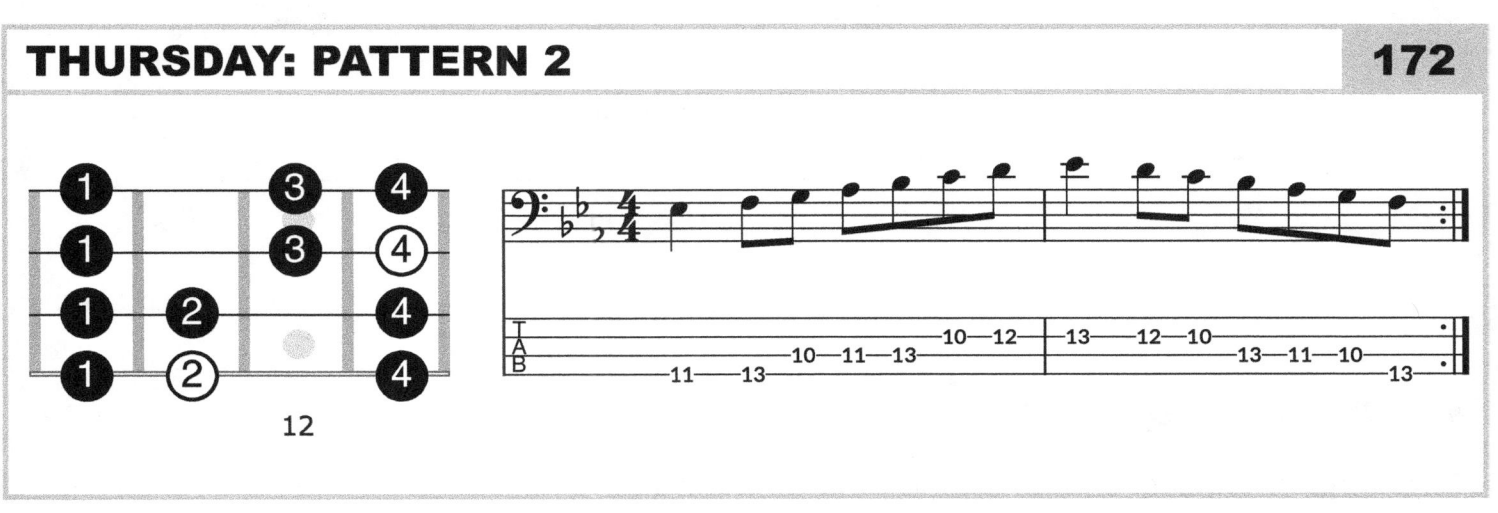

FRIDAY: PATTERN 3 — 173

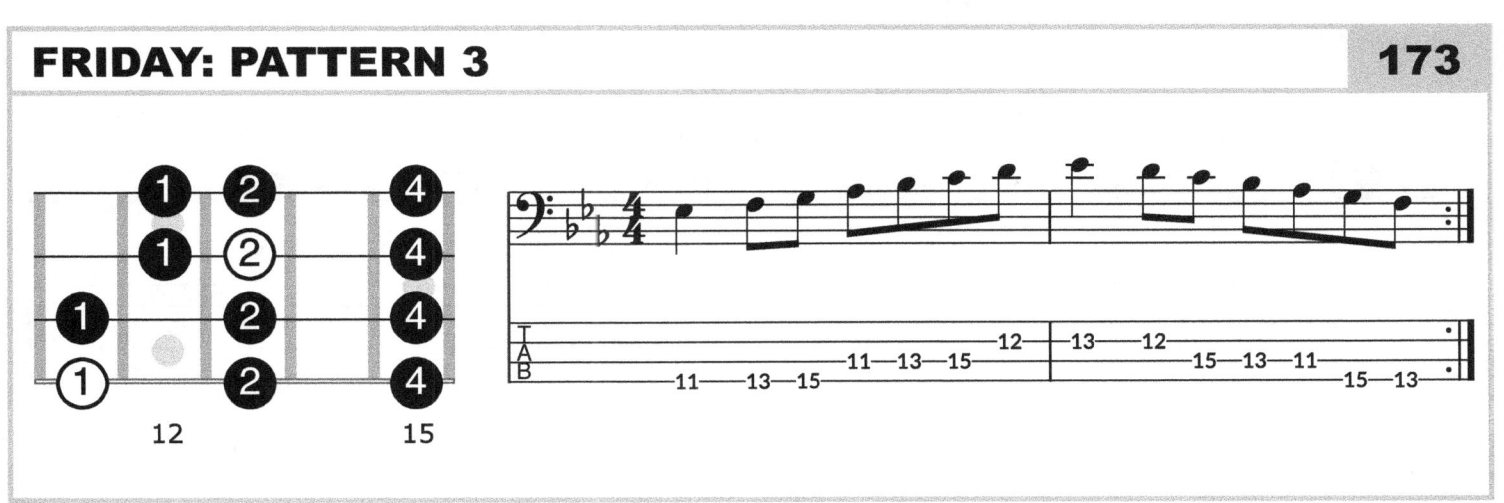

SATURDAY: HORIZONTAL PATTERN 174

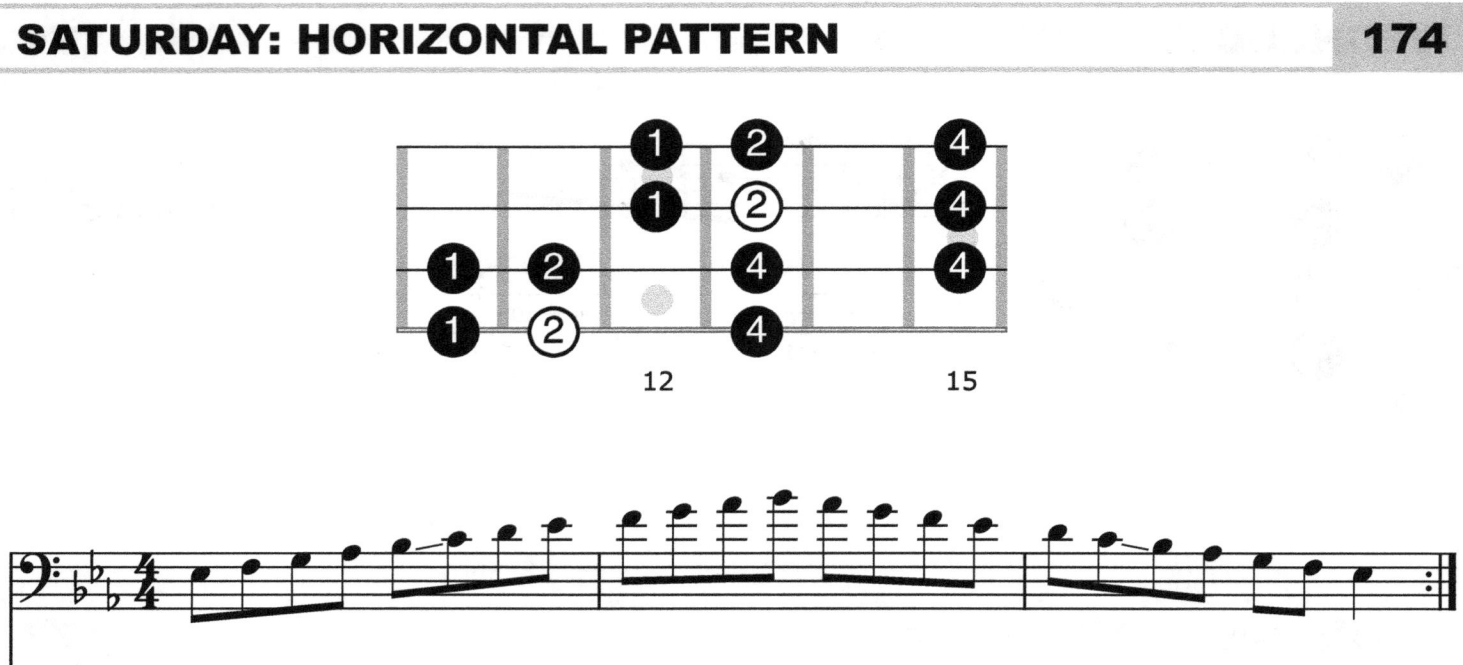

SUNDAY: SCALE APPLICATION 175

The term "chromatic" refers to notes not found in the diatonic scale of the key in which a passage is written. Chromatic notes add flavor to a passage and often provide movement and tension, leading towards resolution on a chord tone. The *chromatic scale* involves ascending or descending in consecutive half steps. Adding a few notes to Pattern 4 makes this line interesting, as well as a great finger exercise.

WEEK 26: E♭ MINOR

Interval Pattern: W H W W H W W

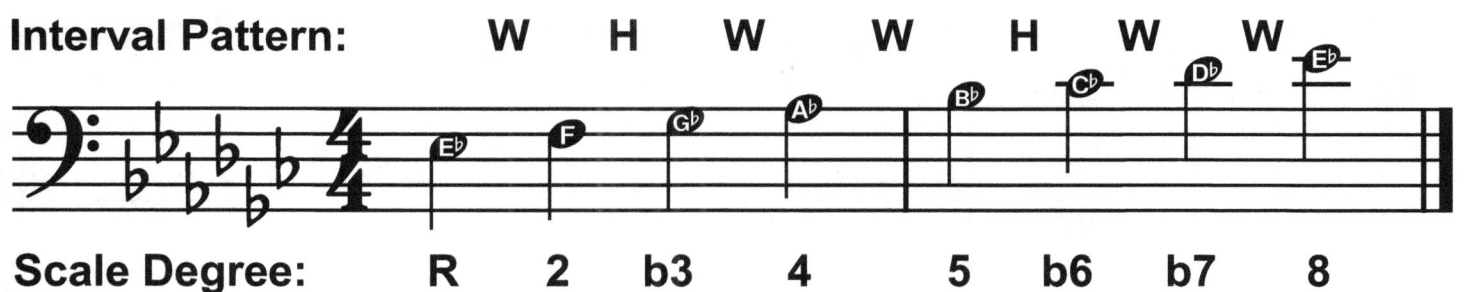

Scale Degree: R 2 b3 4 5 b6 b7 8

MONDAY: PATTERN 2 — 176

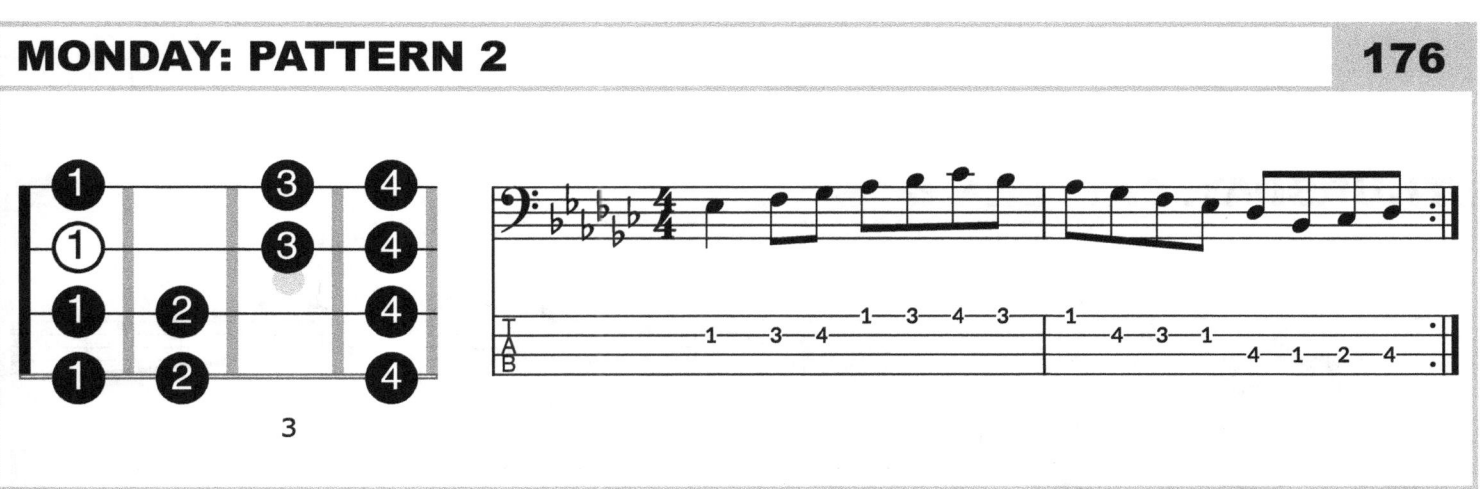

TUESDAY: PATTERN 3 — 177

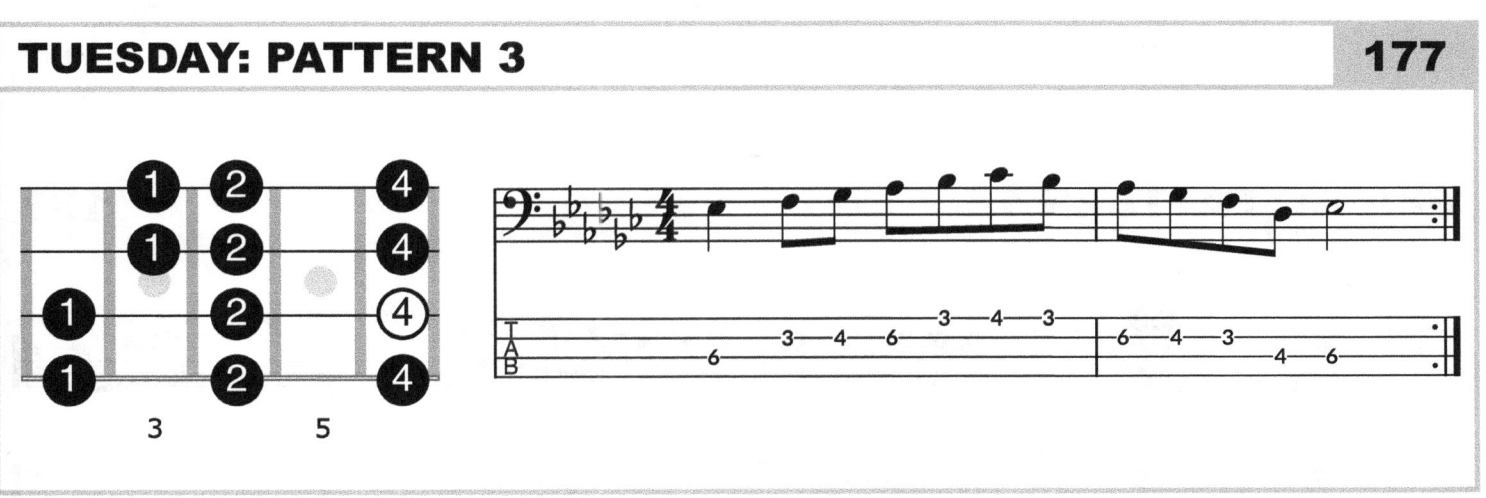

WEDNESDAY: PATTERN 4   178

THURSDAY: PATTERN 5   179

FRIDAY: PATTERN 1   180

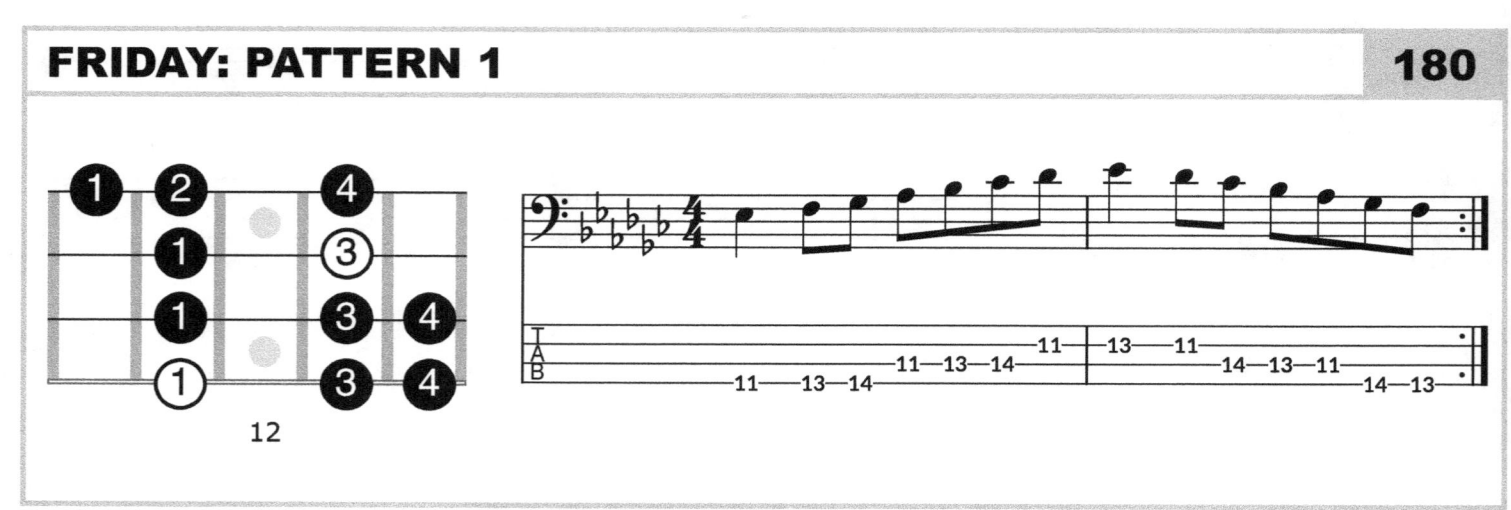

SATURDAY: HORIZONTAL PATTERN 181

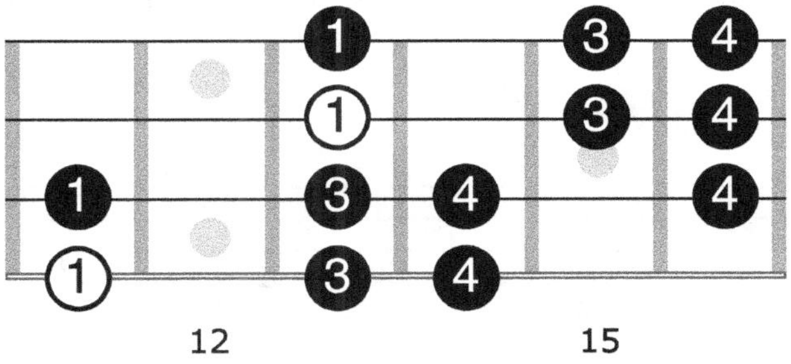

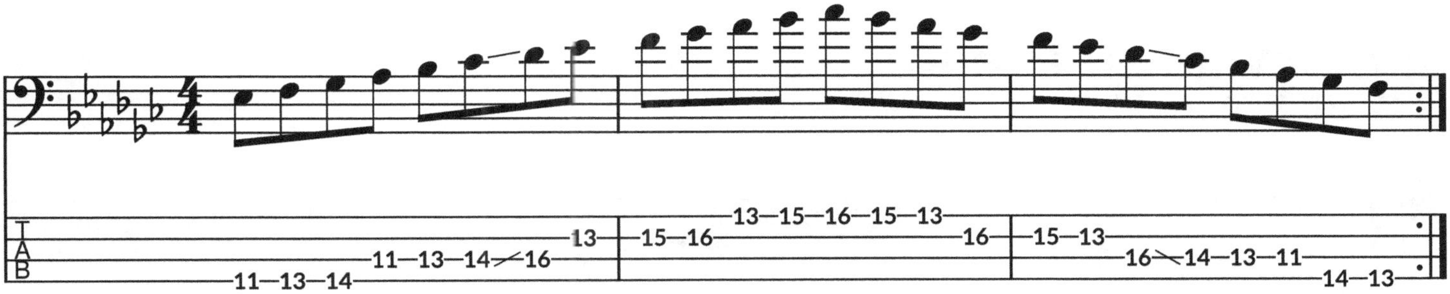

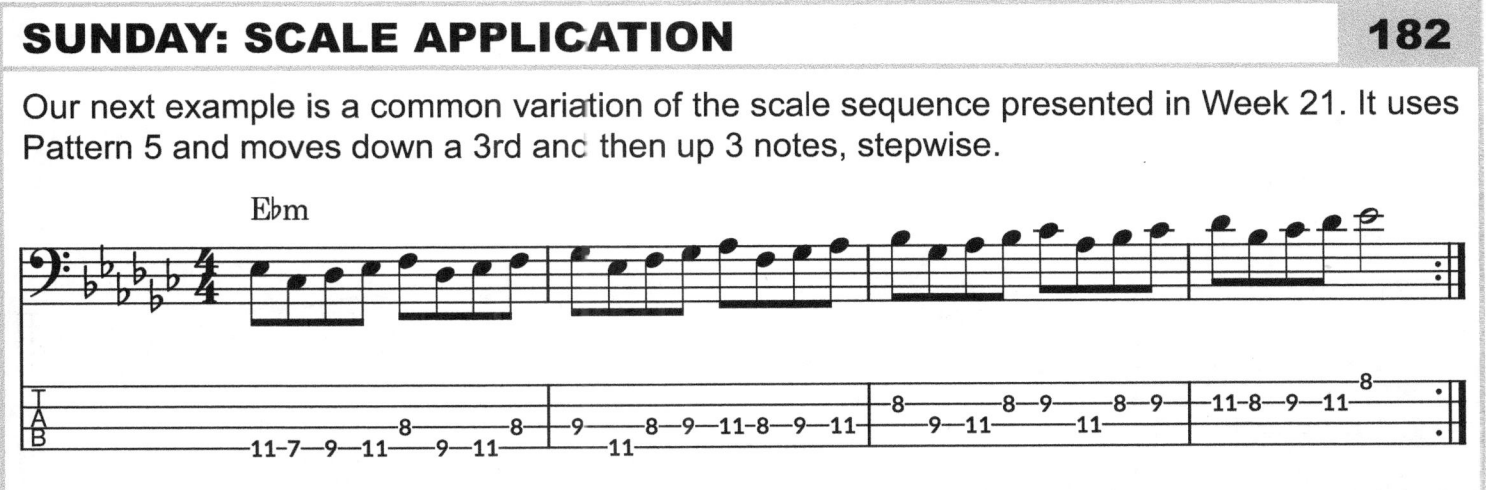

SUNDAY: SCALE APPLICATION 182

Our next example is a common variation of the scale sequence presented in Week 21. It uses Pattern 5 and moves down a 3rd and then up 3 notes, stepwise.

WEEK 27: E♭ MAJOR PENTATONIC

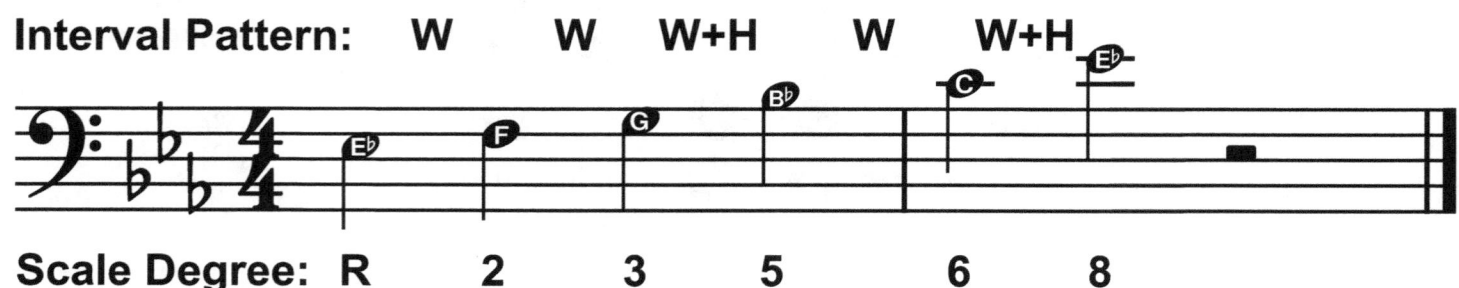

MONDAY: OPEN-STRING PATTERN 3 — 183

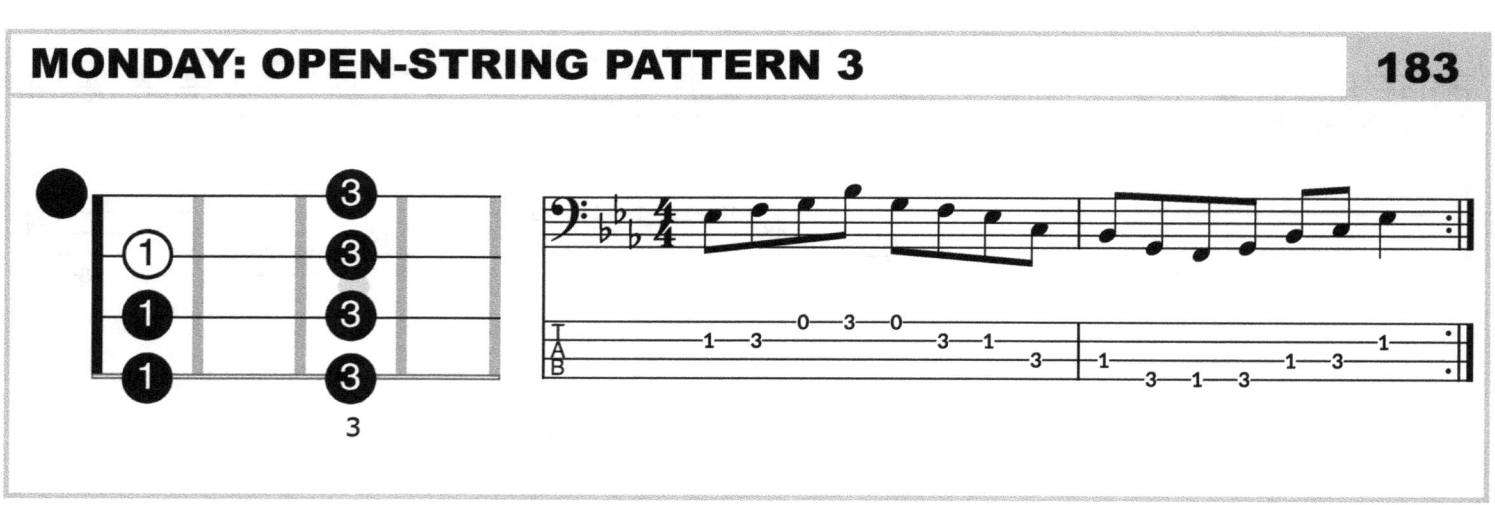

TUESDAY: PATTERN 4 — 184

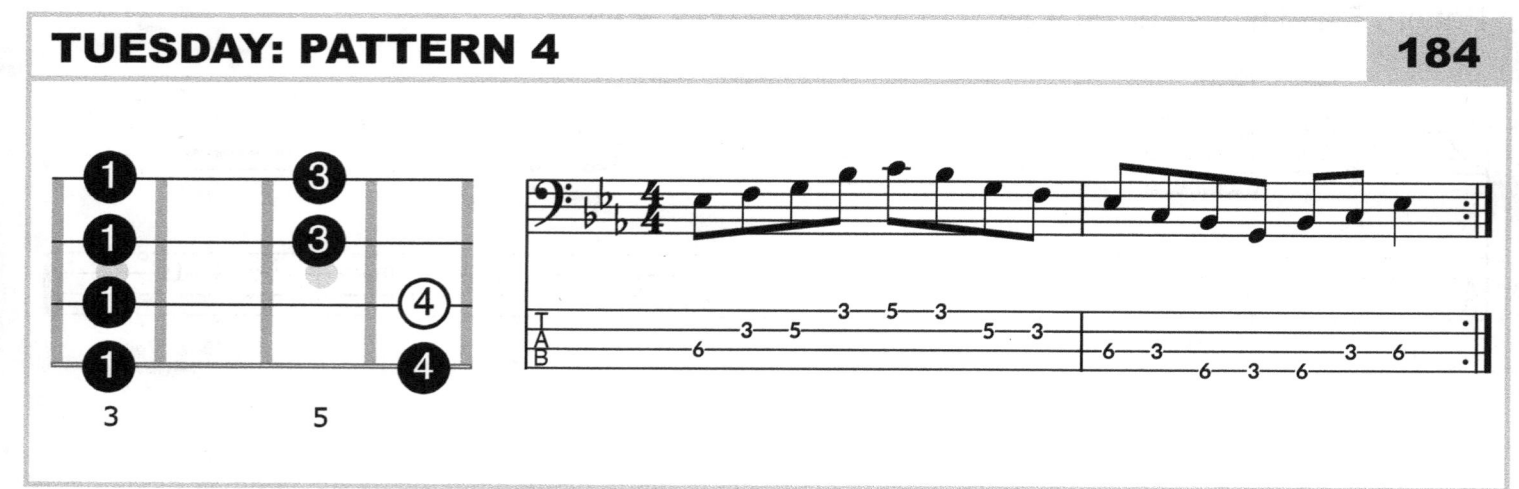

WEDNESDAY: PATTERN 5

185

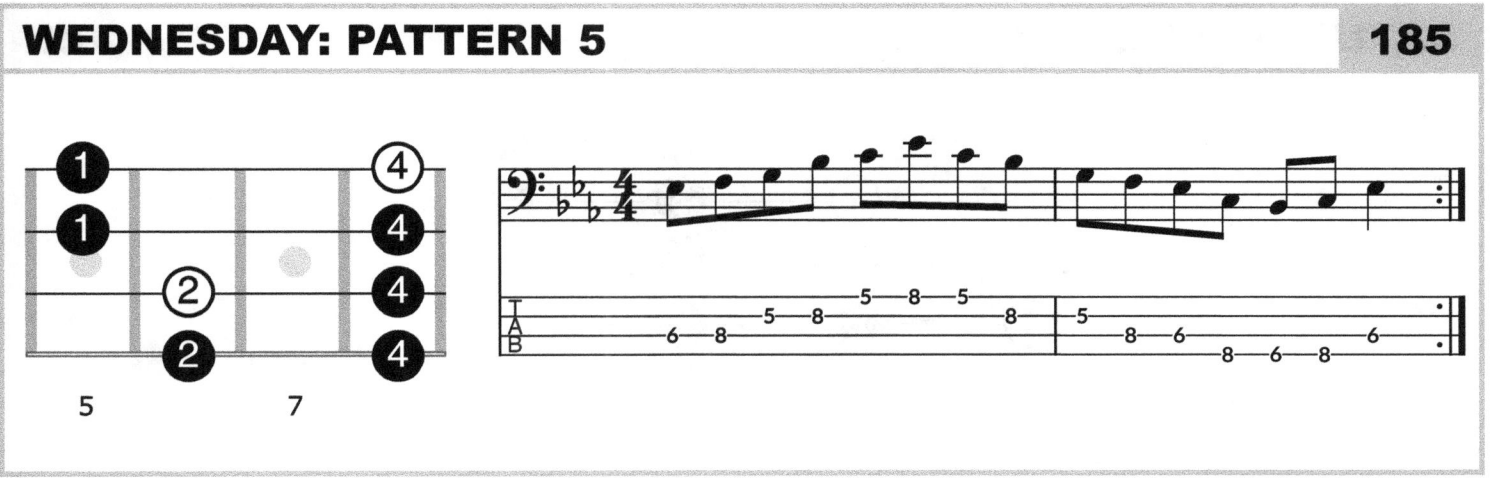

THURSDAY: PATTERN 1

186

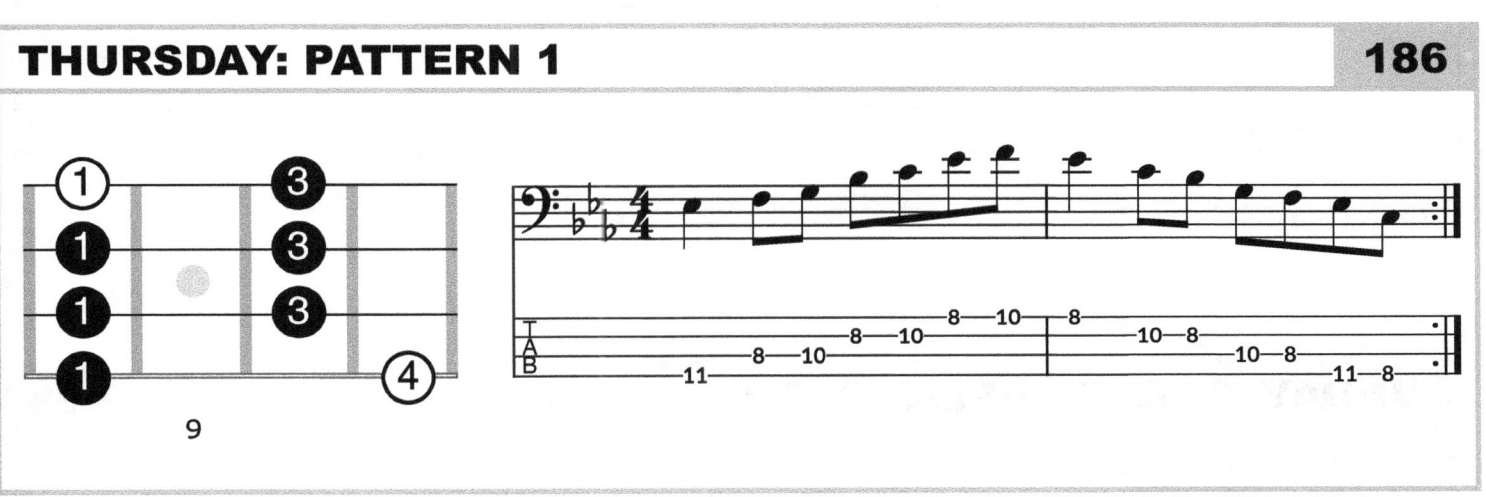

FRIDAY: PATTERN 2

187

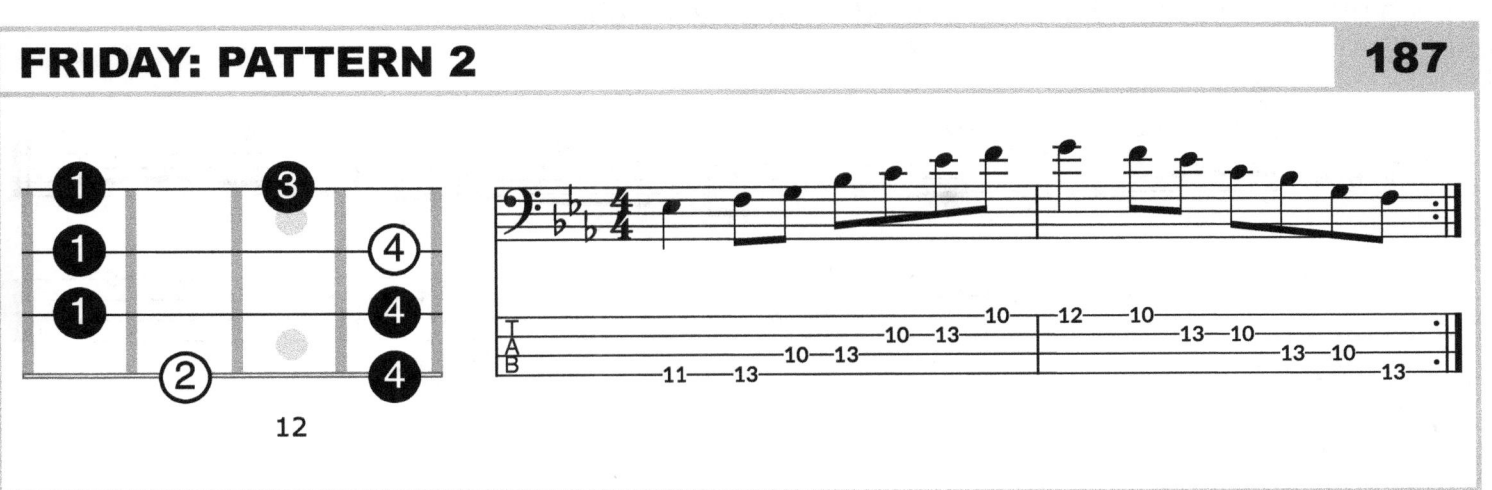

SATURDAY: HORIZONTAL PATTERN   188

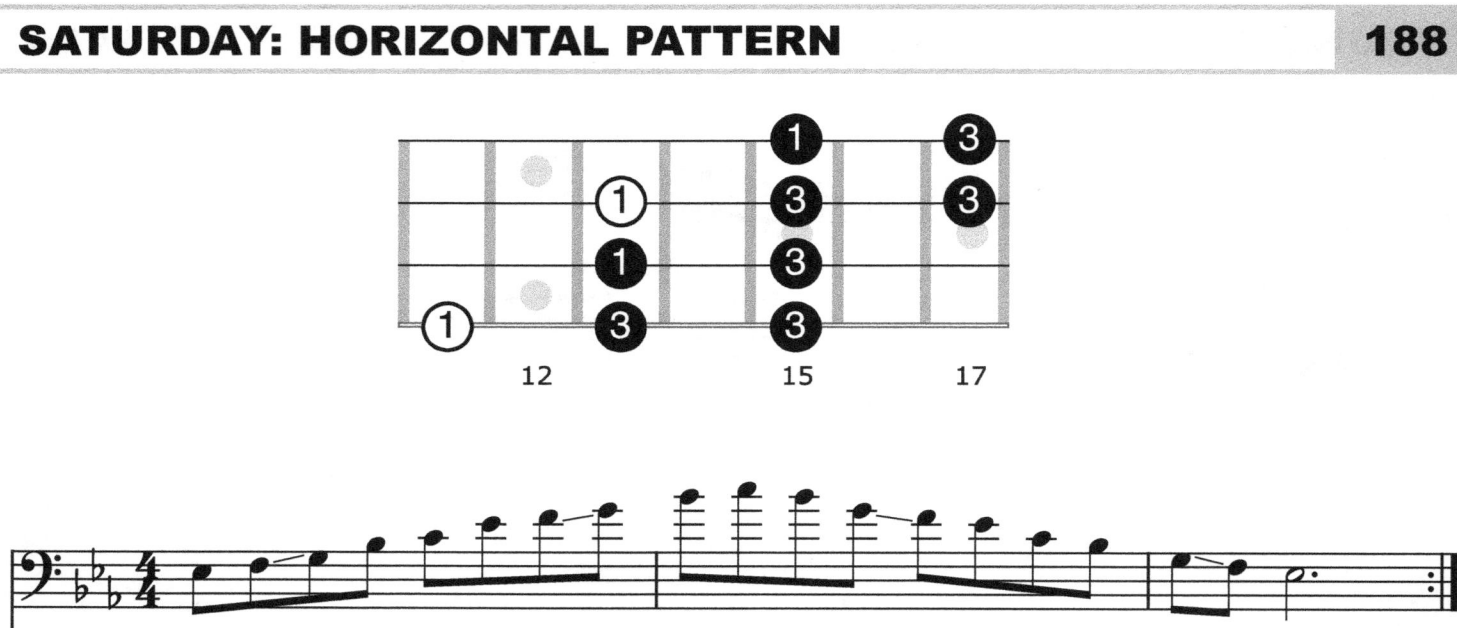

SUNDAY: SCALE APPLICATION   189

New rhythm patterns are a great way to spice up your bass lines. A common rhythmic device is to play a measure of eighth notes grouped as 123–123–12. The phrase below uses Pattern 5 and descends twice in groups of 3 before ascending stepwise with two notes at the end. Notice how the sequence reverses on the way back up. It also moves the pattern across strings. Try each measure separately to get started, then play the entire pattern.

WEEK 28: E♭ MINOR PENTATONIC

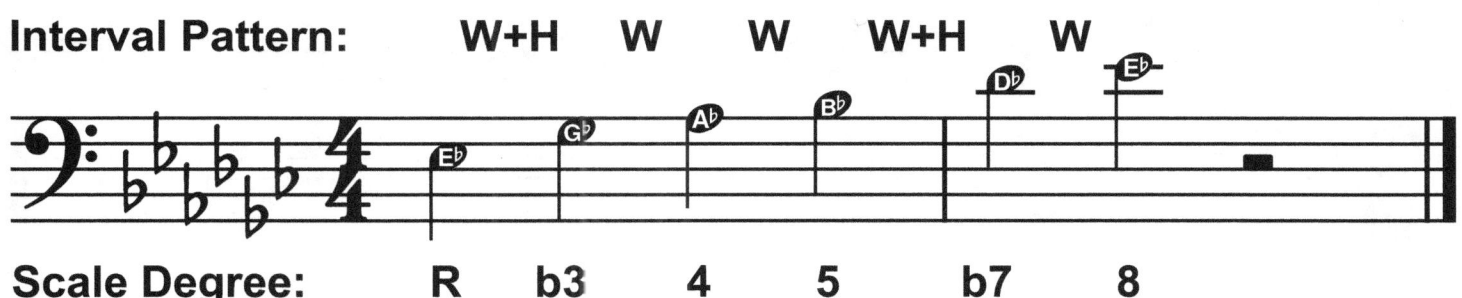

MONDAY: PATTERN 2   190

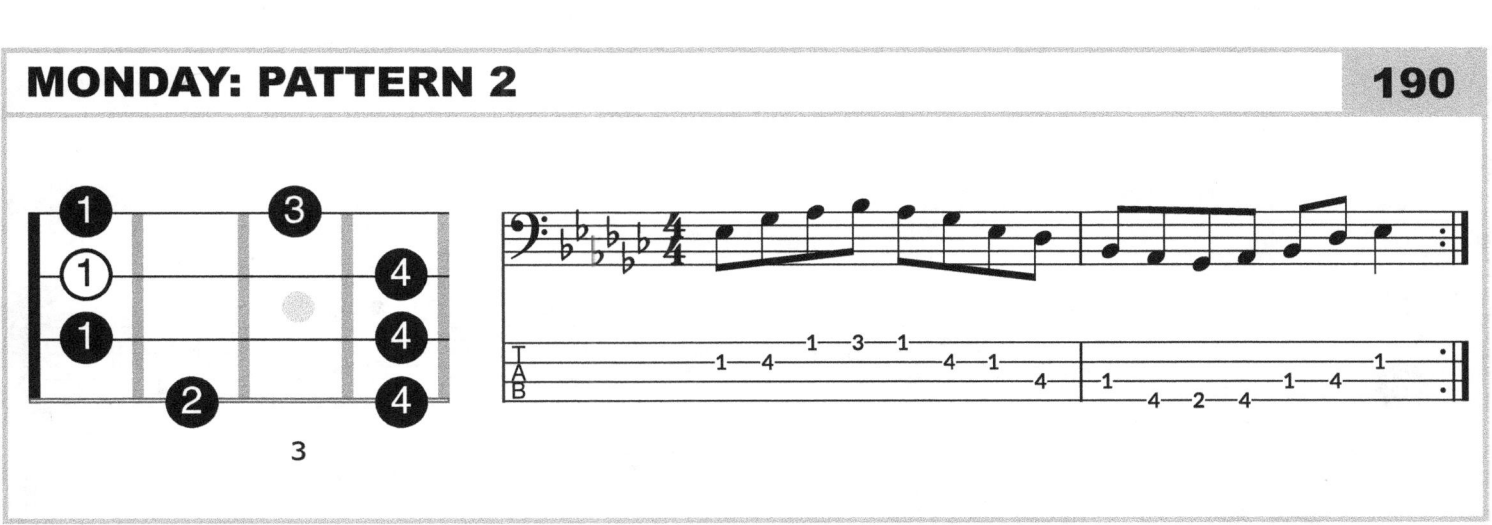

TUESDAY: PATTERN 3   191

WEDNESDAY: PATTERN 4 — 192

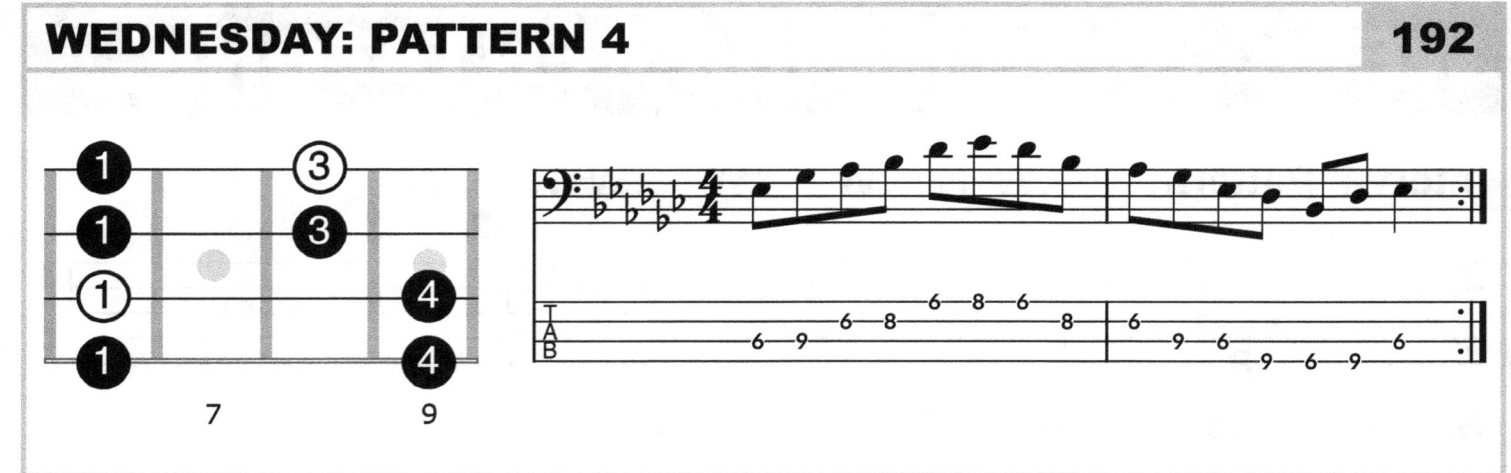

THURSDAY: PATTERN 5 — 193

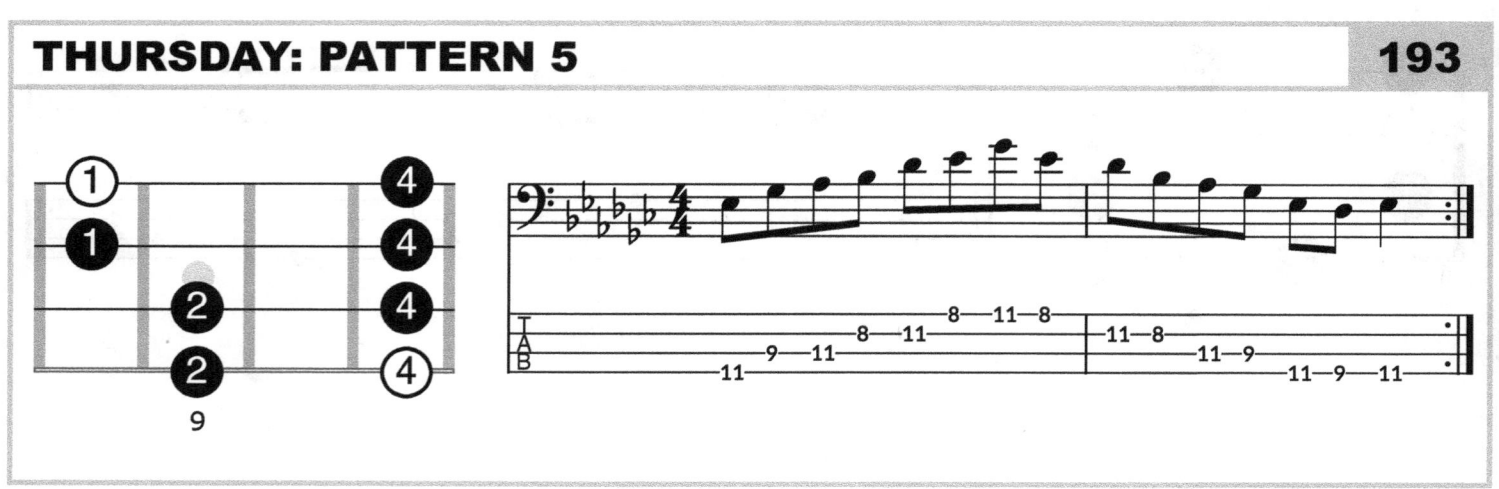

FRIDAY: PATTERN 1 — 194

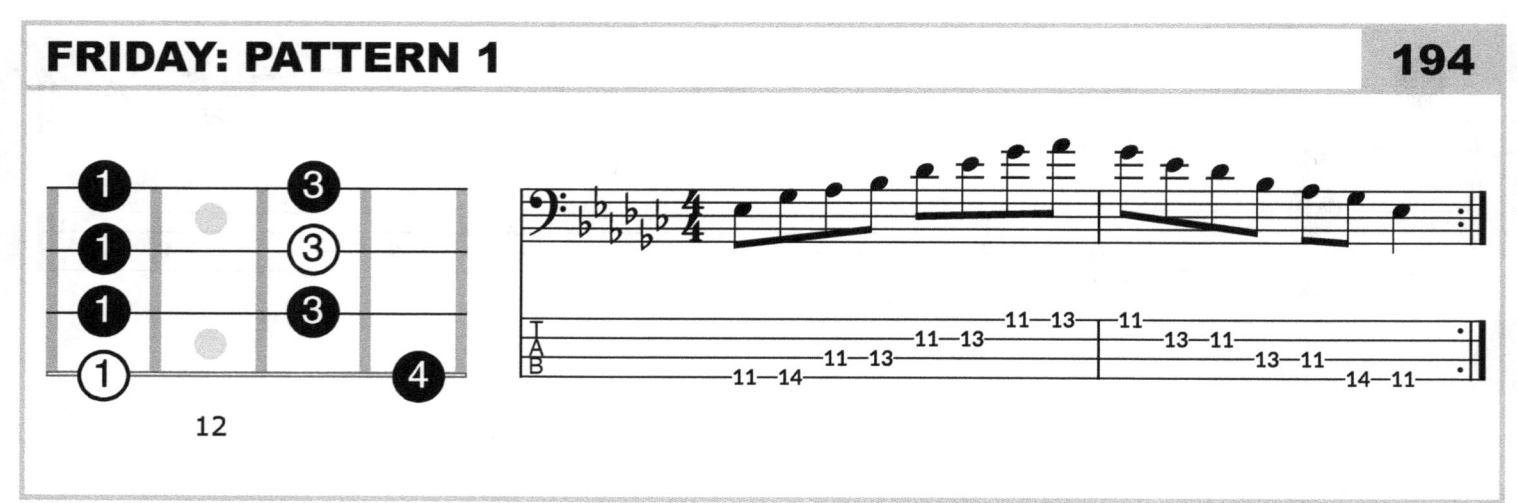

SATURDAY: HORIZONTAL PATTERN   195

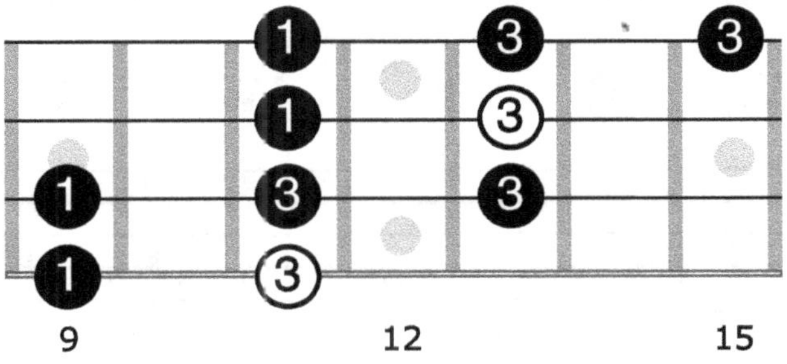

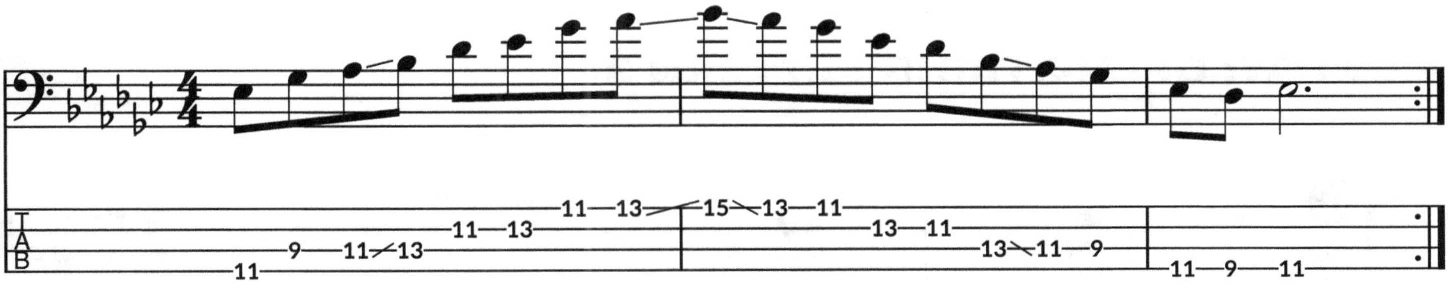

SUNDAY: SCALE APPLICATION   196

Staying with the theme of new rhythms, the riff below utilizes the eighth rest and Pattern 2. It's a two-measure phrase that is counted similarly to the dotted quarter with the exception or resting on beat 2. This rhythmic theme is continued over the bar line, giving lots of forward motion towards measures 1 and 3. Changing the ending of the riff in bar 4 gives it a question-and-answer feel. Use this concept in your own riffs.

WEEK 29: E MAJOR

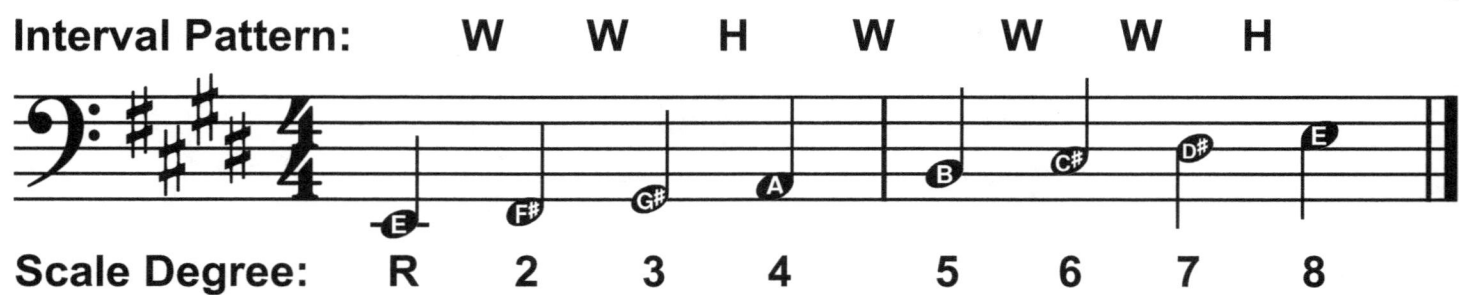

MONDAY: OPEN-STRING PATTERN 3 — 197

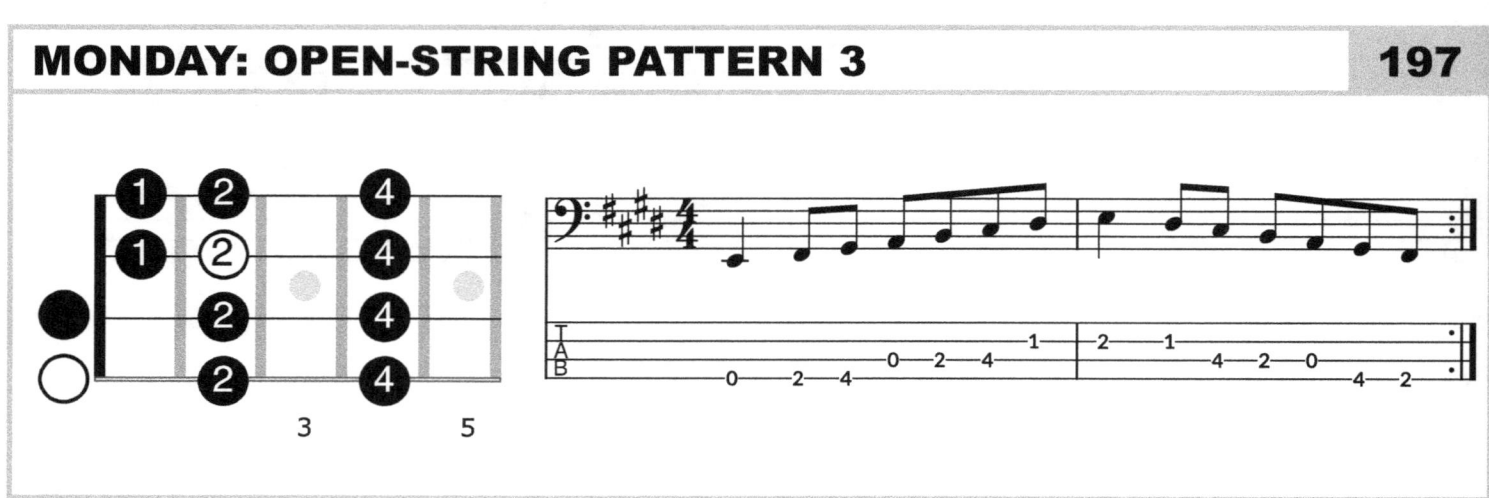

TUESDAY: PATTERN 4 — 198

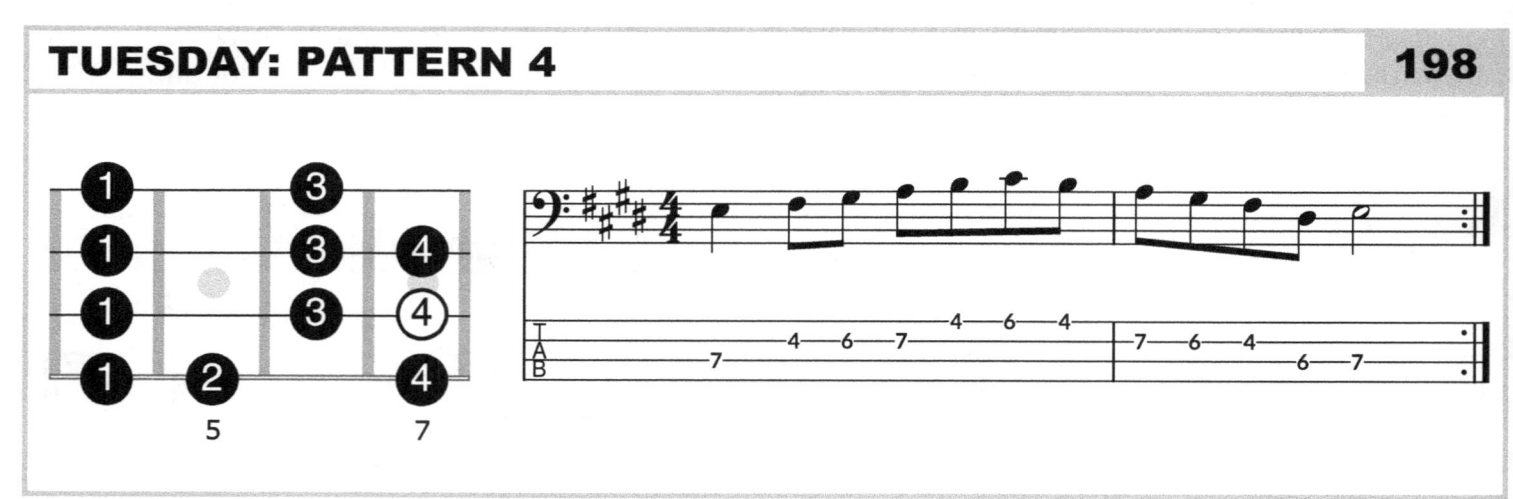

WEDNESDAY: PATTERN 5

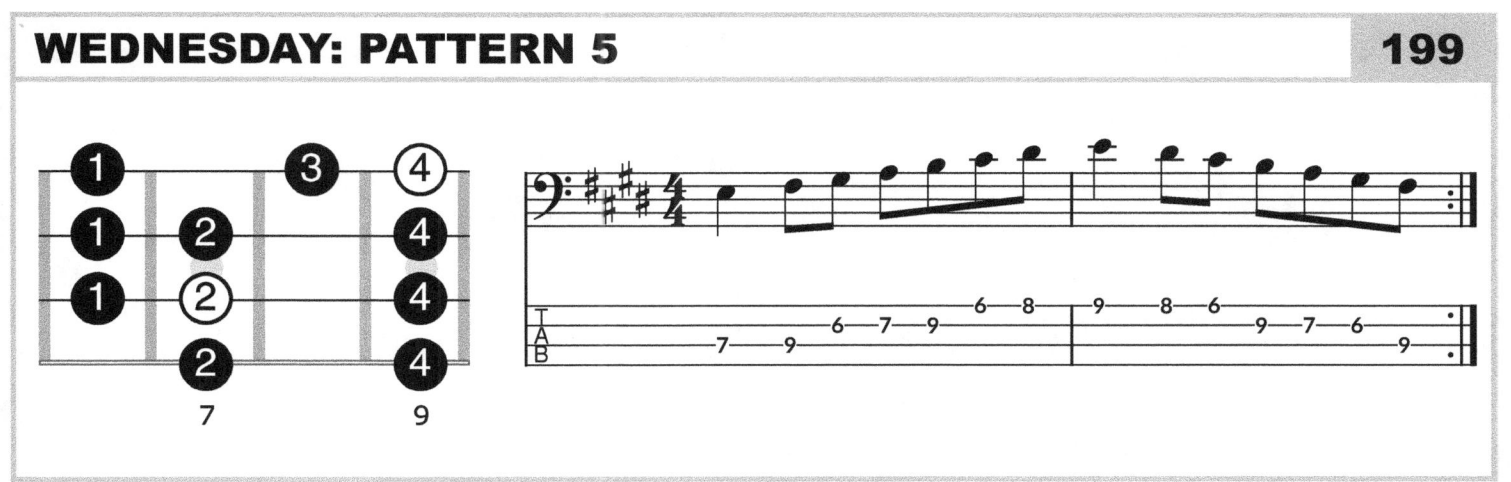

THURSDAY: PATTERN 1

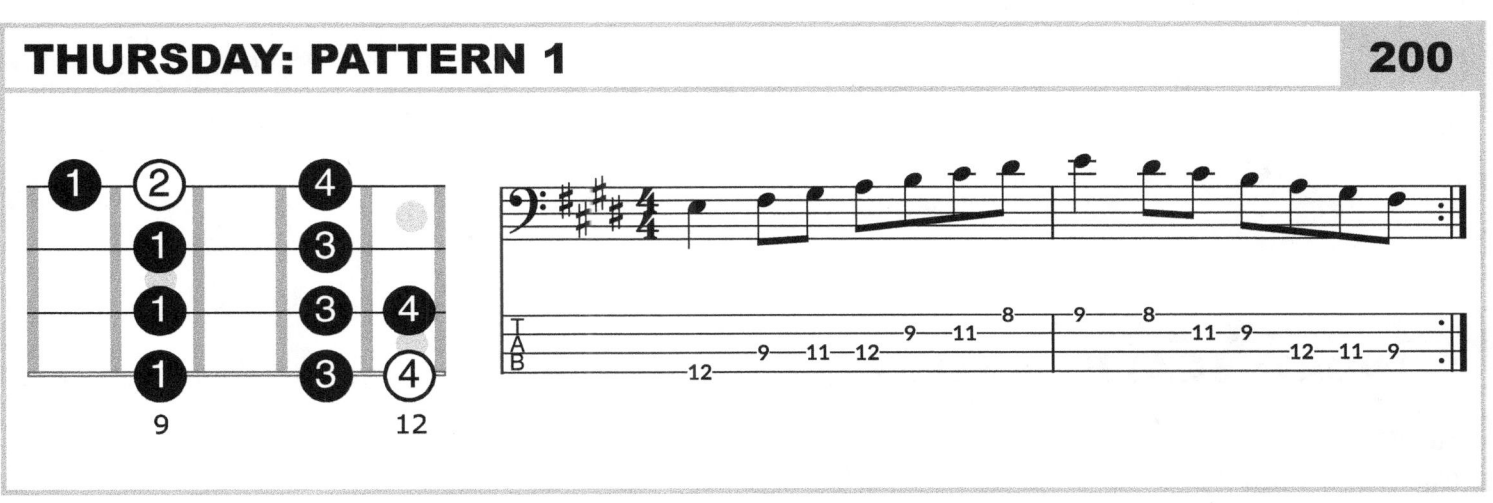

FRIDAY: PATTERN 2

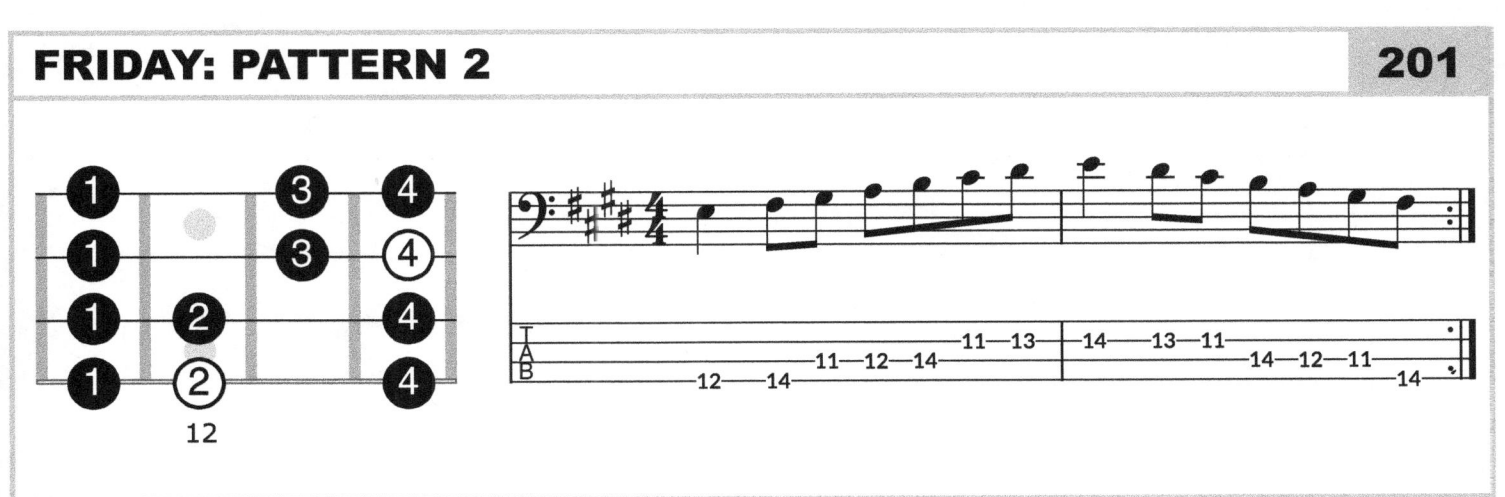

SATURDAY: HORIZONTAL PATTERN 202

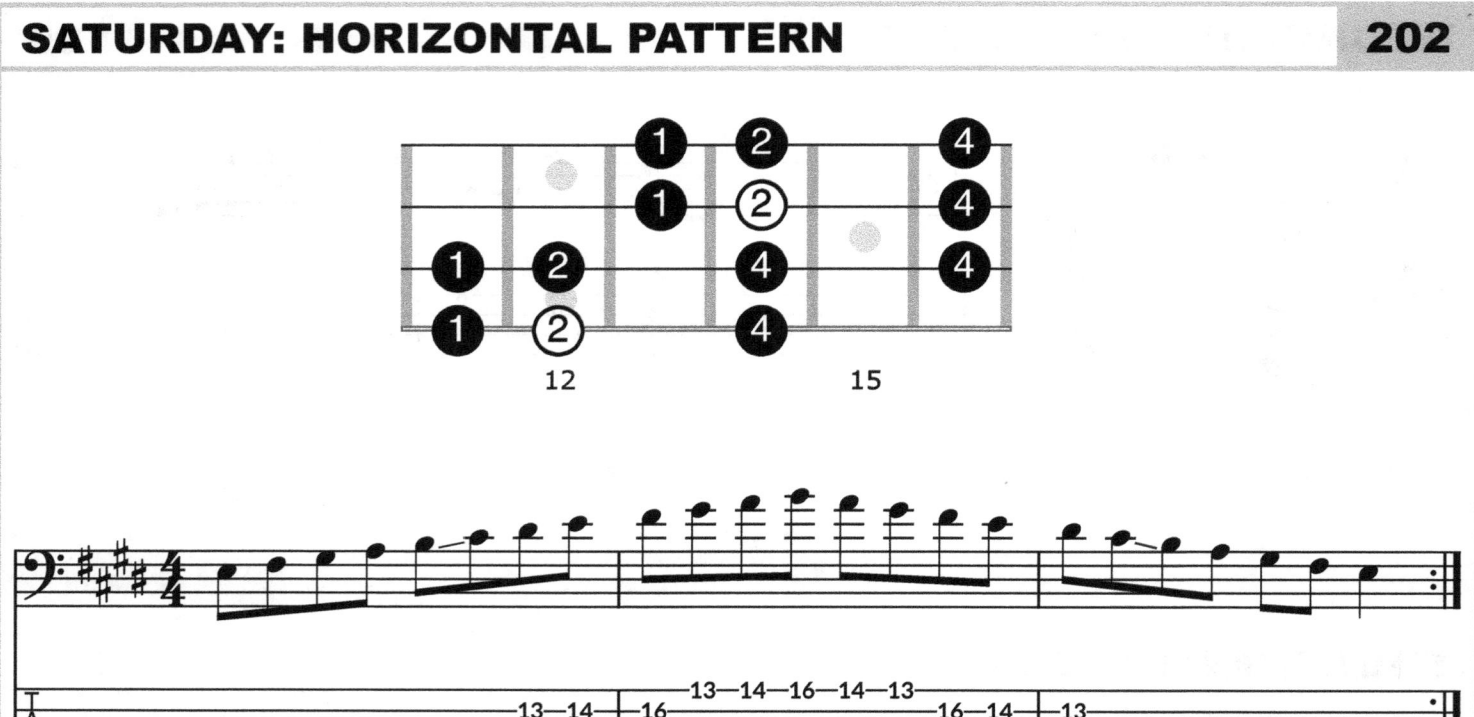

SUNDAY: SCALE APPLICATION 203

Another scale sequence you'll find in many melodies is a variation of Week 26. You can think of this pattern as ascending 3 notes stepwise and then down a 3rd.

WEEK 30: E MINOR

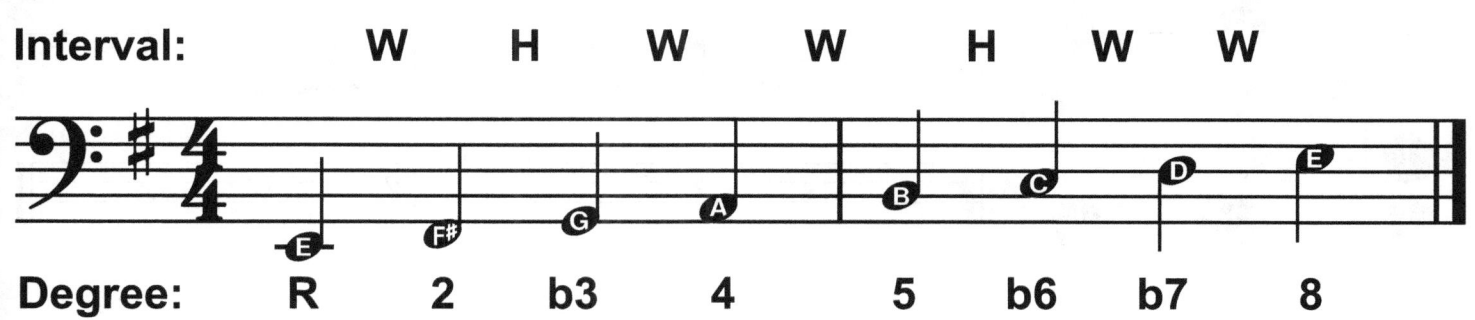

MONDAY: OPEN-STRING PATTERN 204

To make this pattern fit into the open position, we'll move the F# note from string 1 to string 2.

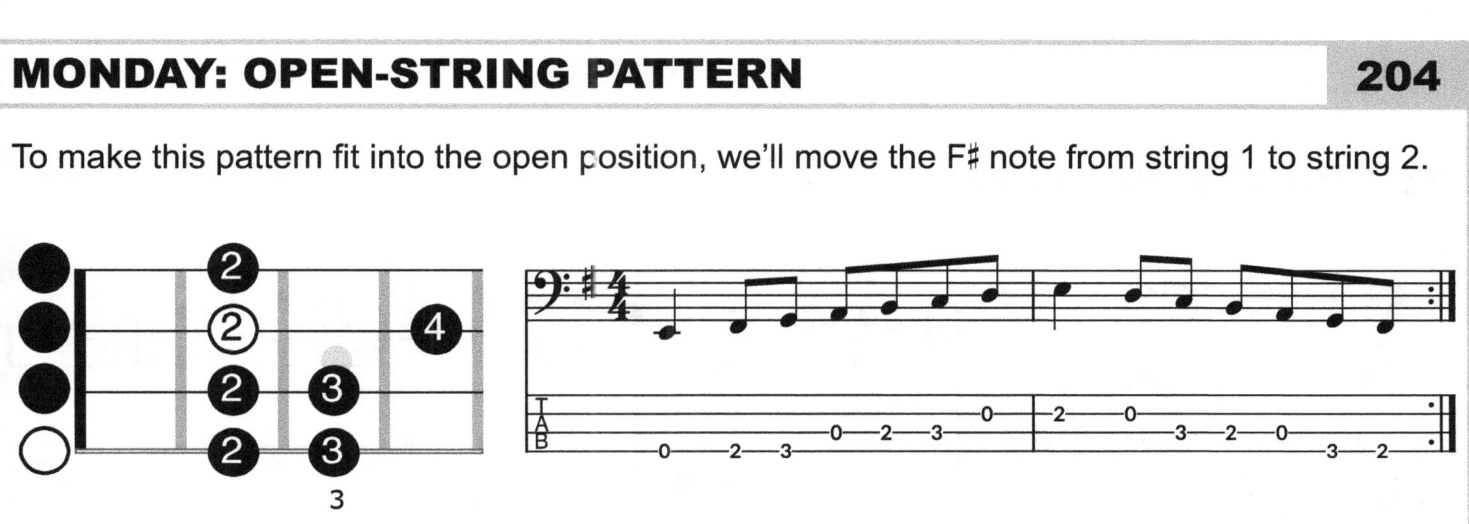

TUESDAY: PATTERN 2 205

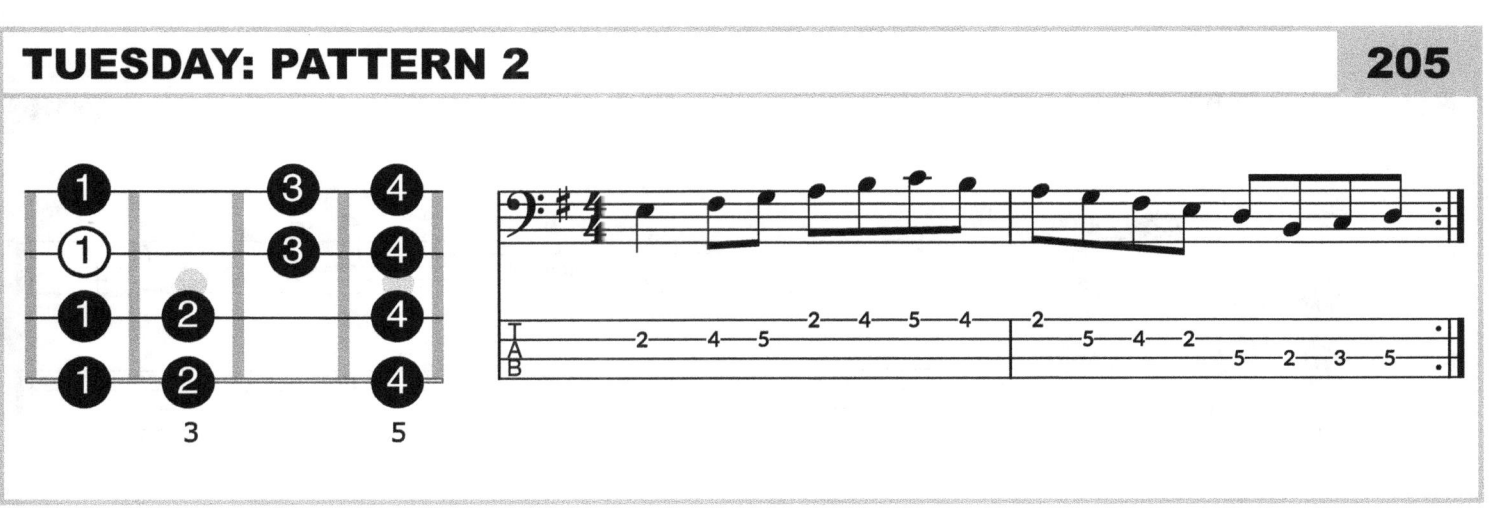

WEDNESDAY: PATTERN 3

206

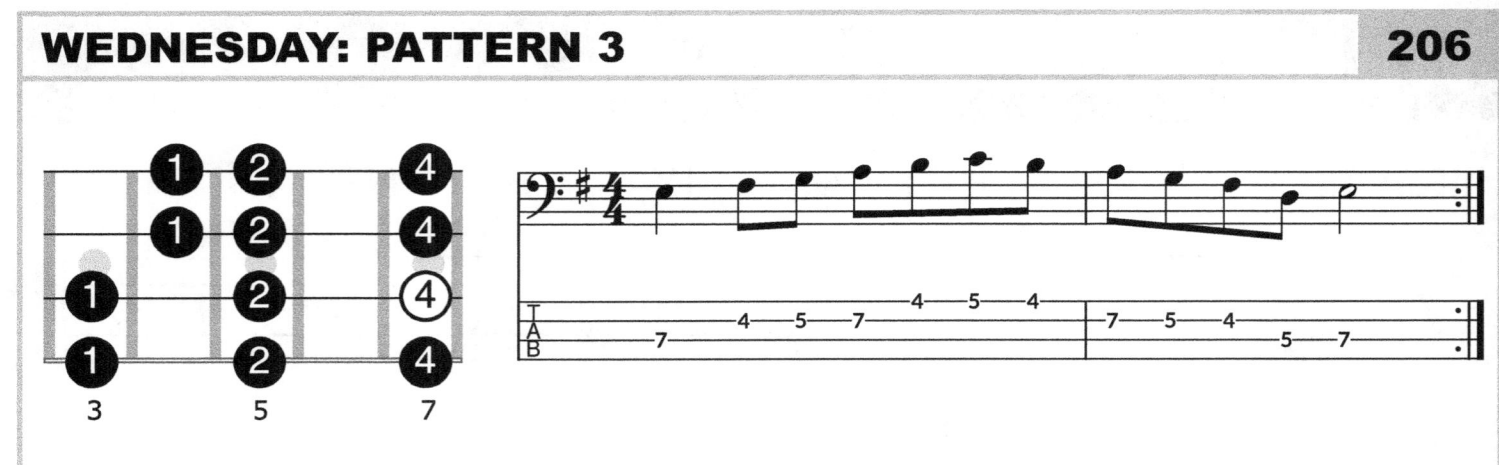

THURSDAY: PATTERN 4

207

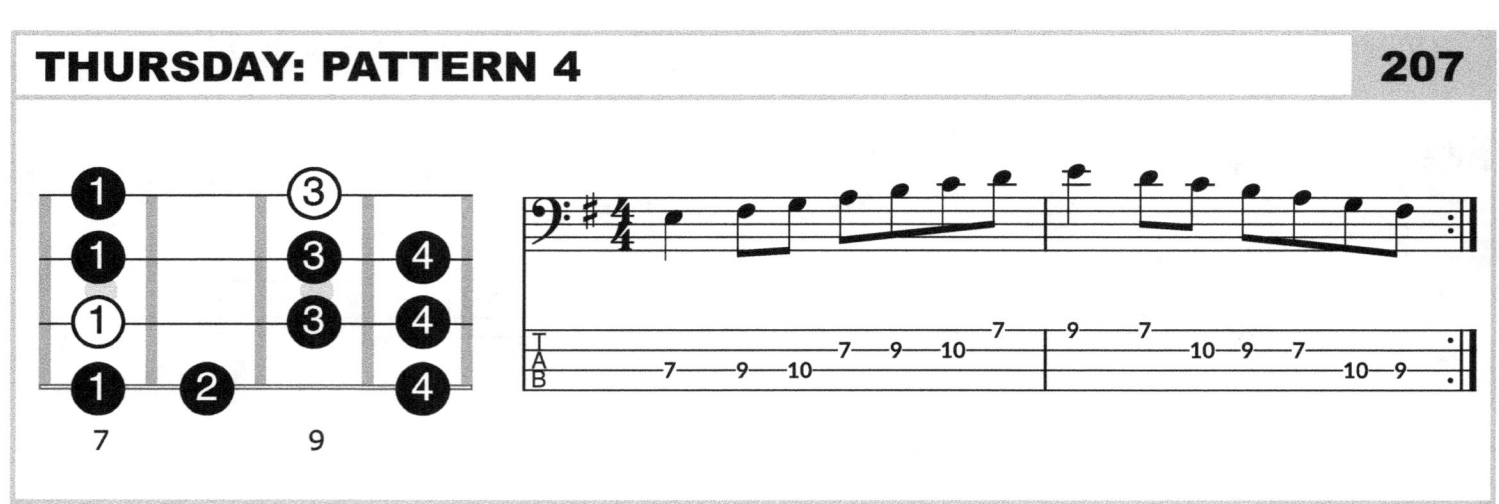

FRIDAY: PATTERN 5

208

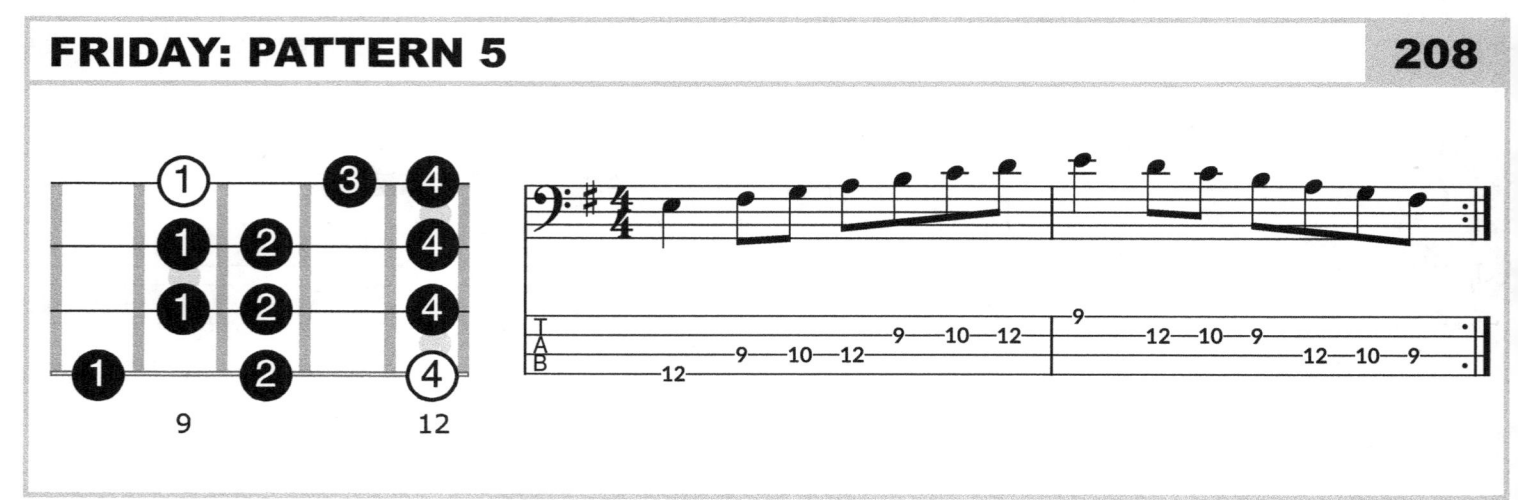

SATURDAY: OPEN-STRING HORIZONTAL PATTERN   209

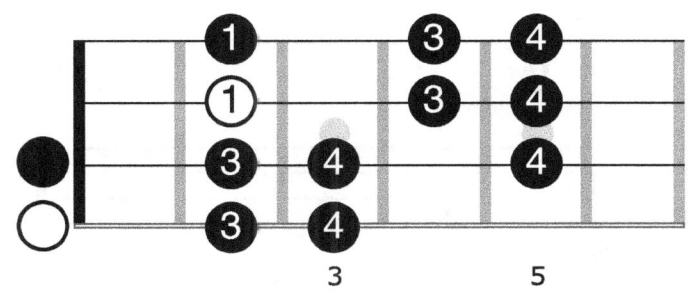

SUNDAY: SCALE APPLICATION   210

This scale sequence uses the open-string pattern (variation of Pattern 1) and is a descending version of last week's application. You can think of it as up a 3rd and down 3 notes, stepwise.

WEEK 31: E MAJOR PENTATONIC

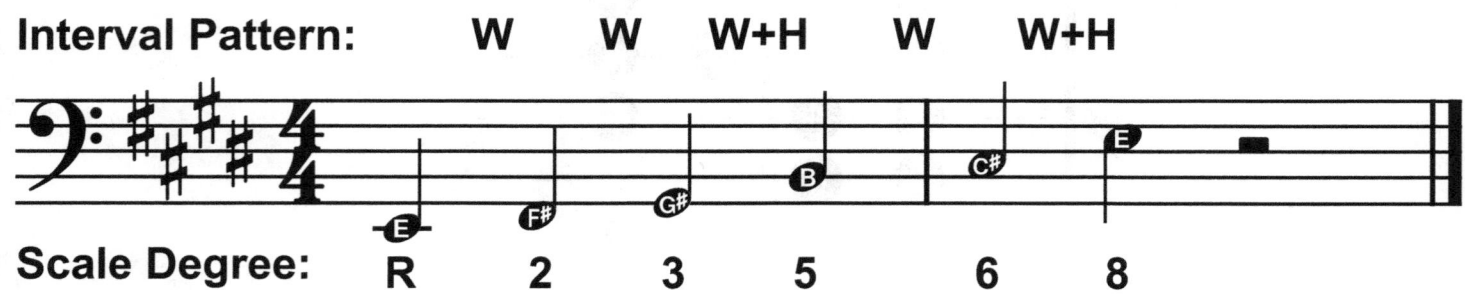

MONDAY: OPEN-STRING PATTERN 3 — 211

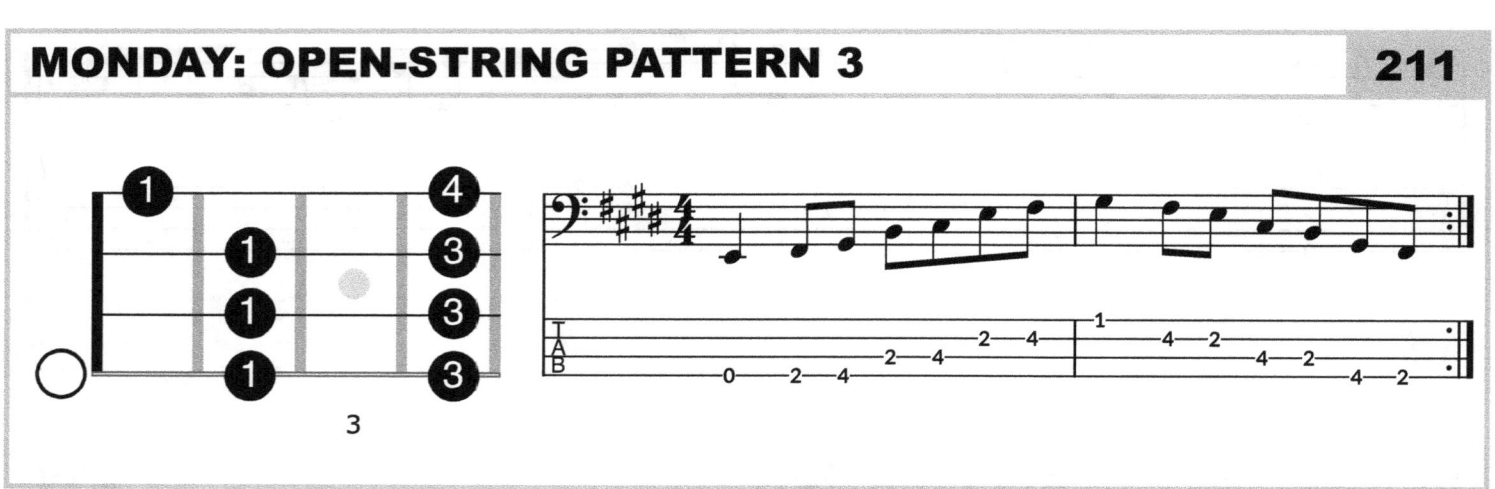

TUESDAY: PATTERN 4 — 212

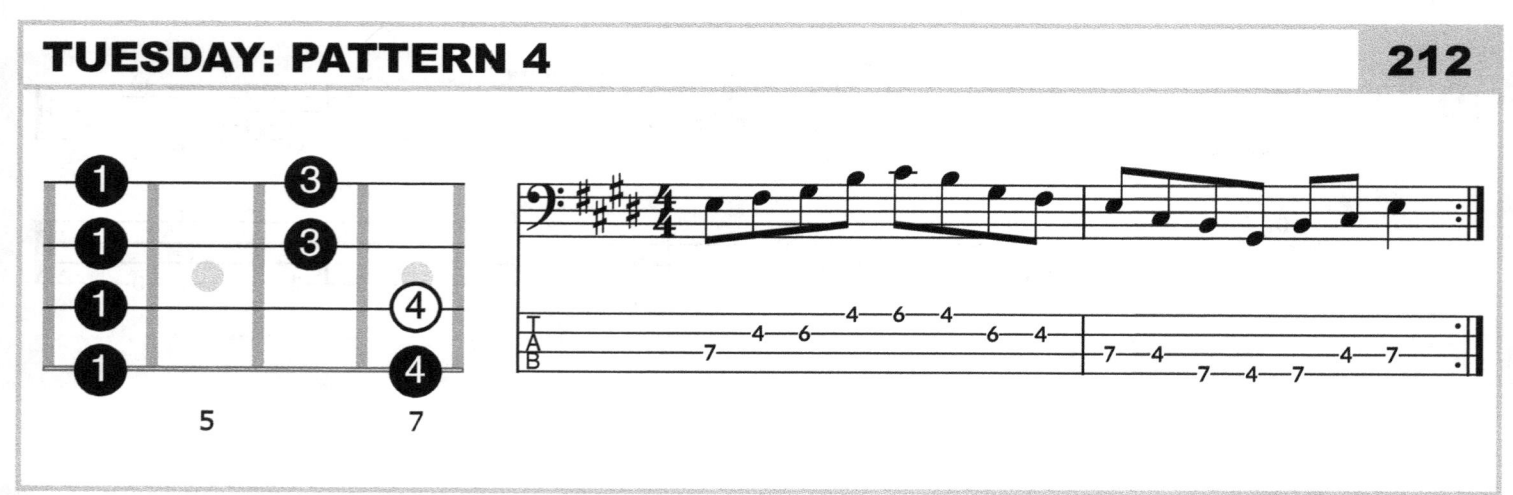

WEDNESDAY: PATTERN 5 — 213

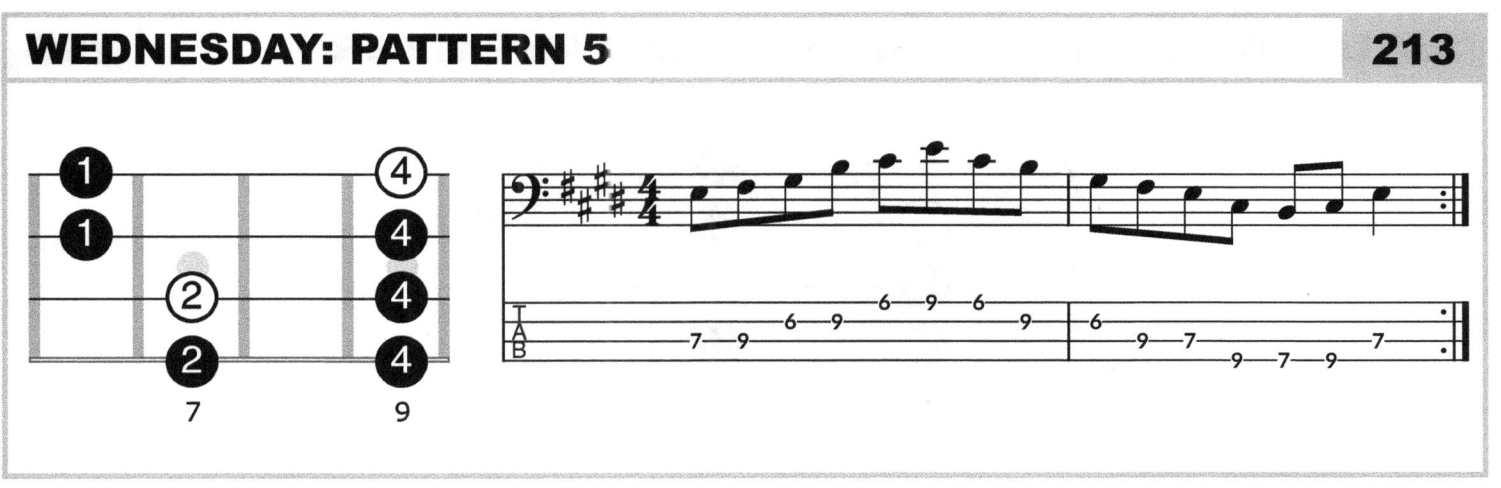

THURSDAY: PATTERN 1 — 214

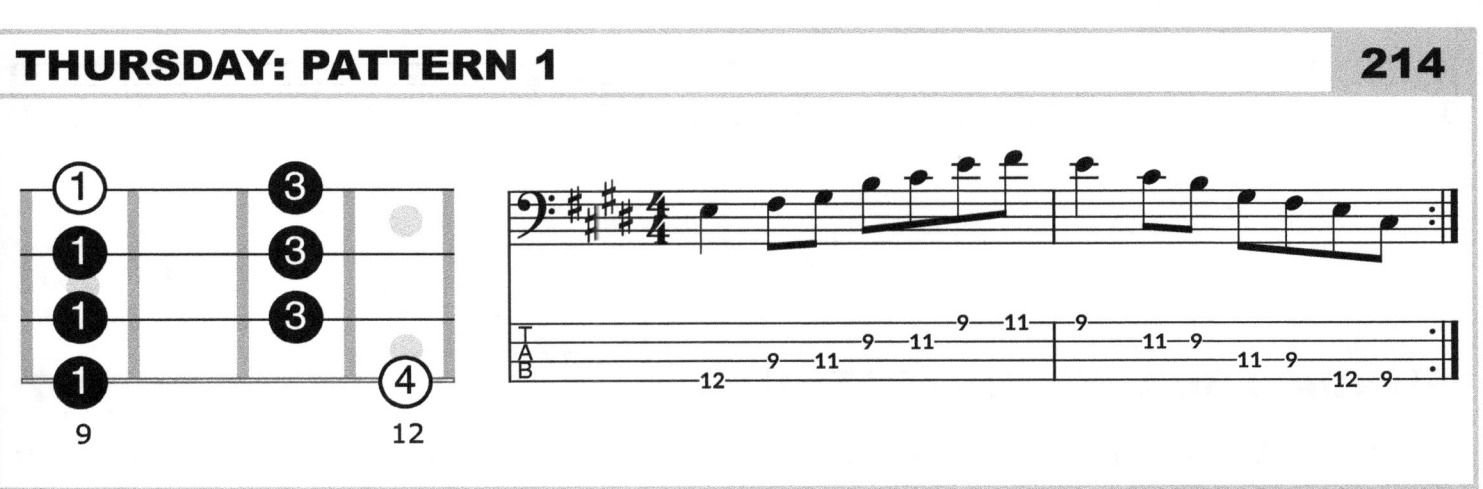

FRIDAY: PATTERN 2 — 215

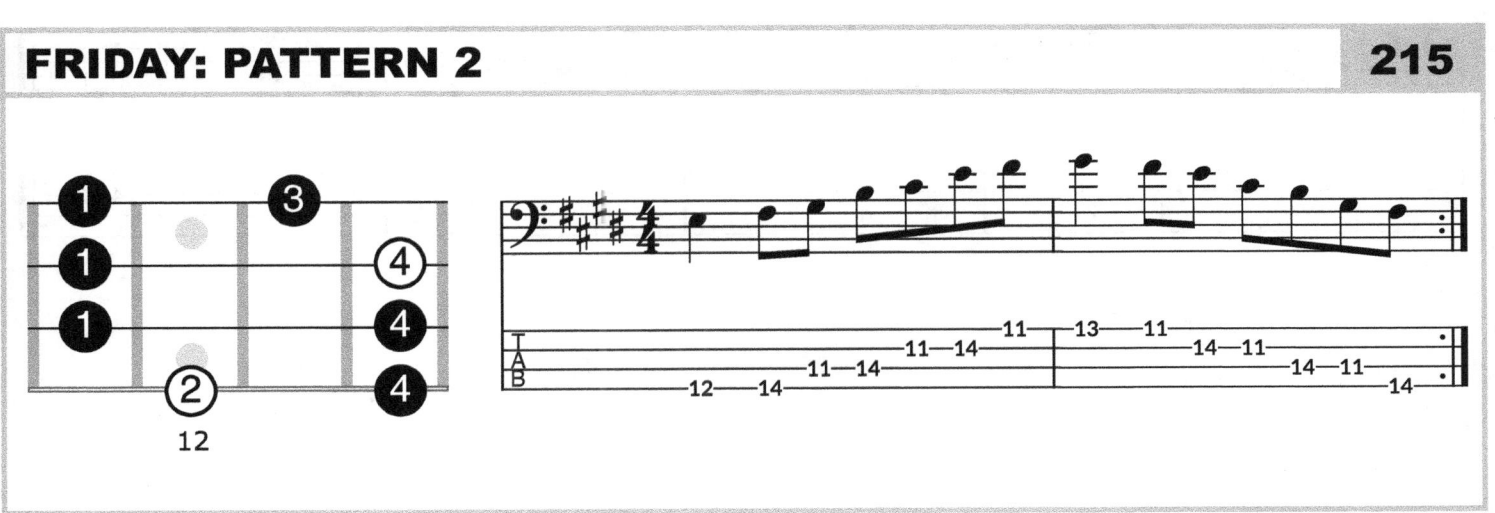

SATURDAY: OPEN-STRING HORIZONTAL PATTERN — 216

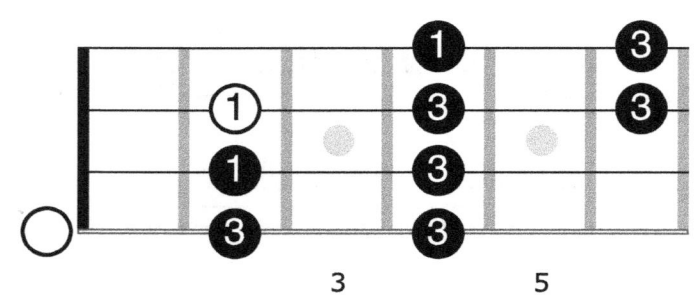

SUNDAY: SCALE APPLICATION — 217

The melody below is an example of combining phrases and sequences you've already learned. It involves descending 4s, rolling a finger, and moving an idea across strings to continue a musical idea.

WEEK 32: E MINOR PENTATONIC

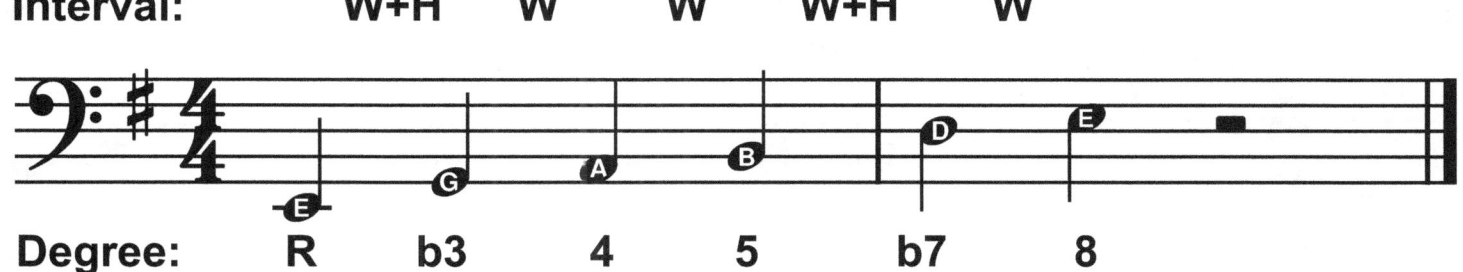

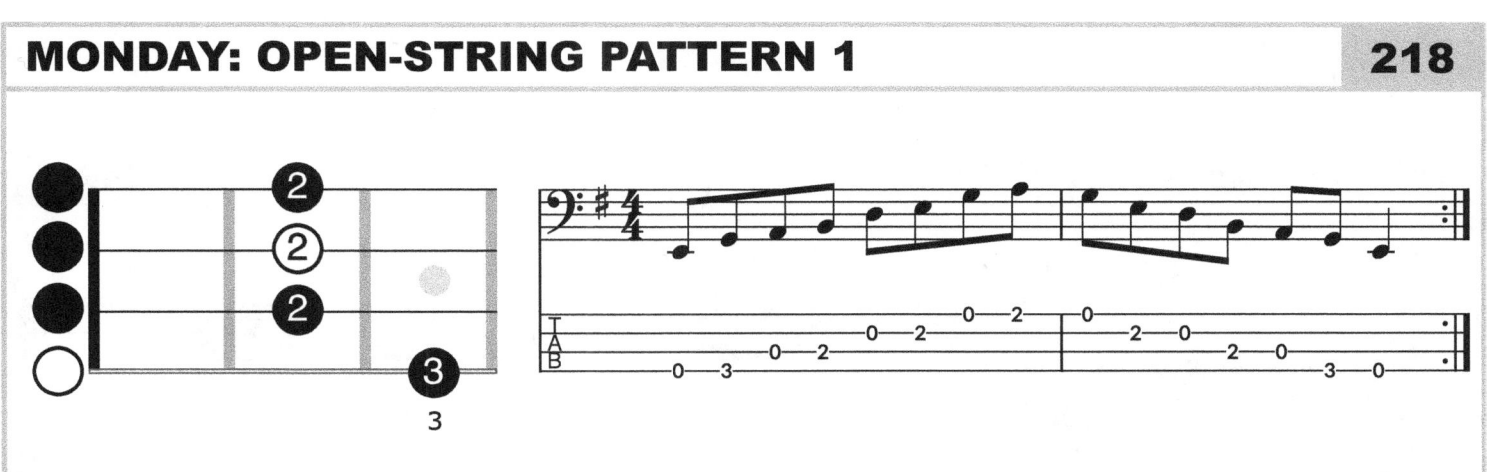

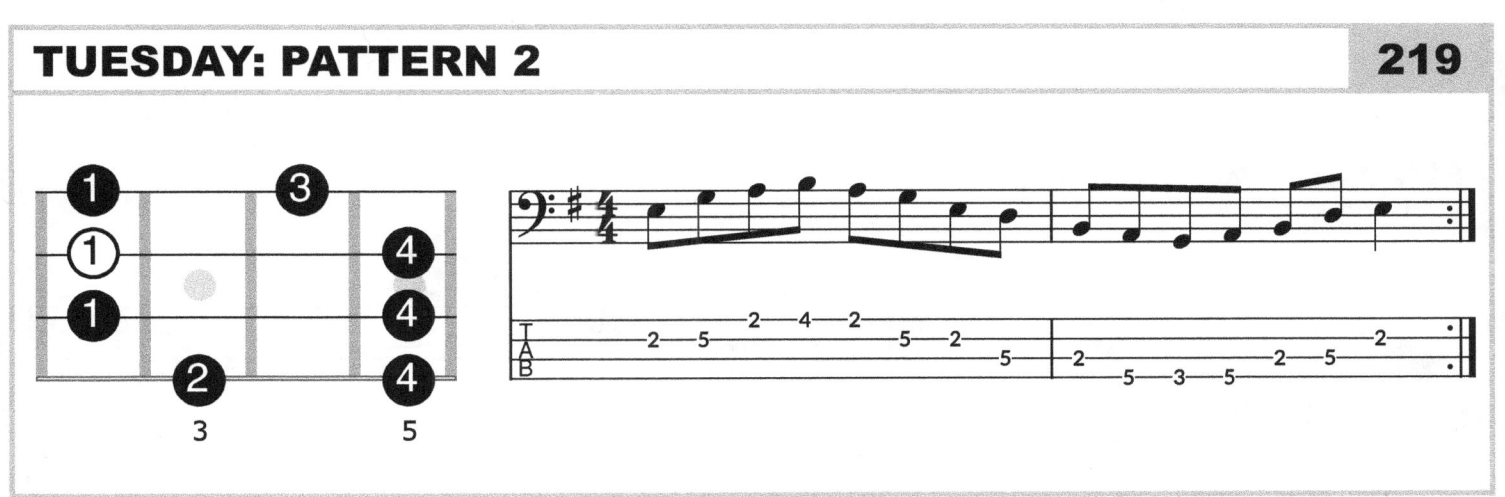

WEDNESDAY: PATTERN 3

220

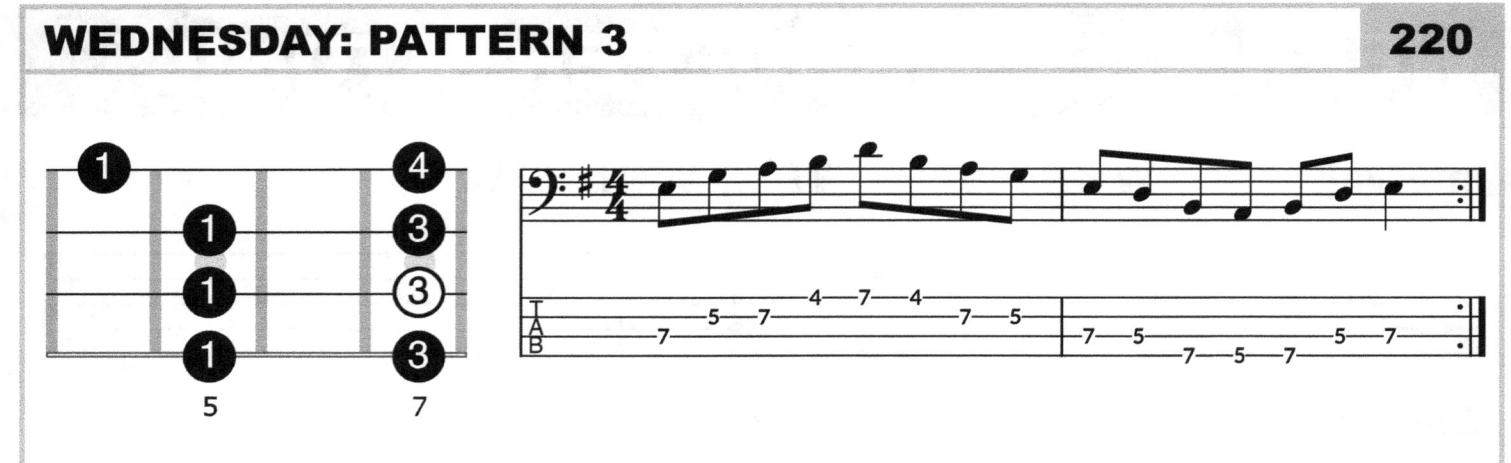

THURSDAY: PATTERN 4

221

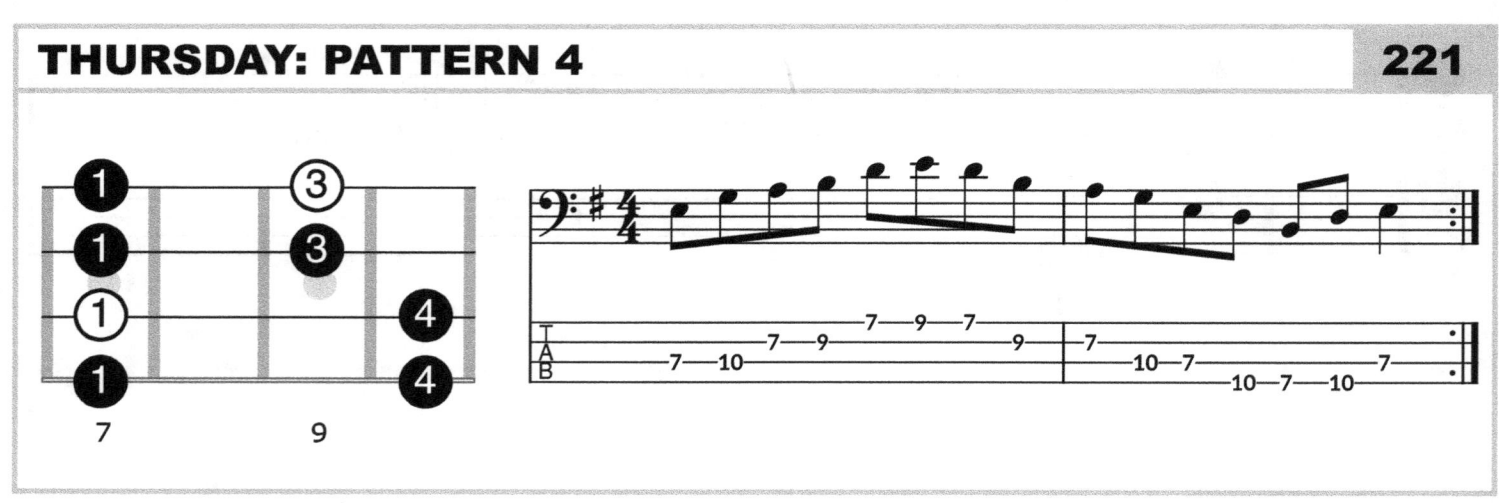

FRIDAY: PATTERN 5

222

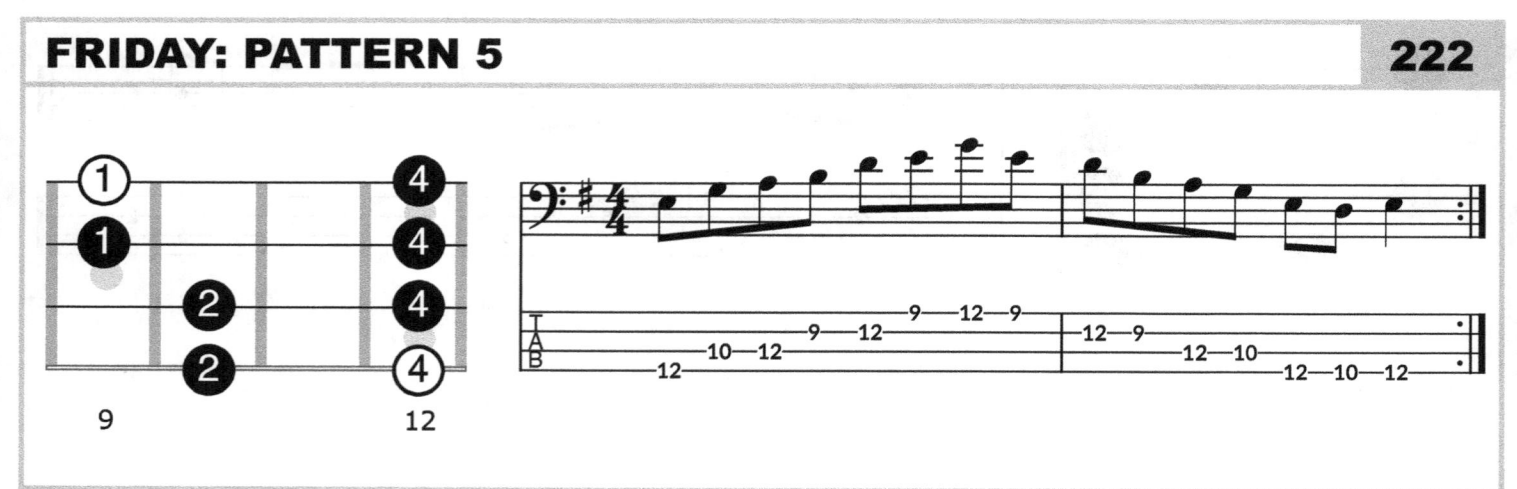

SATURDAY: HORIZONTAL PATTERN 223

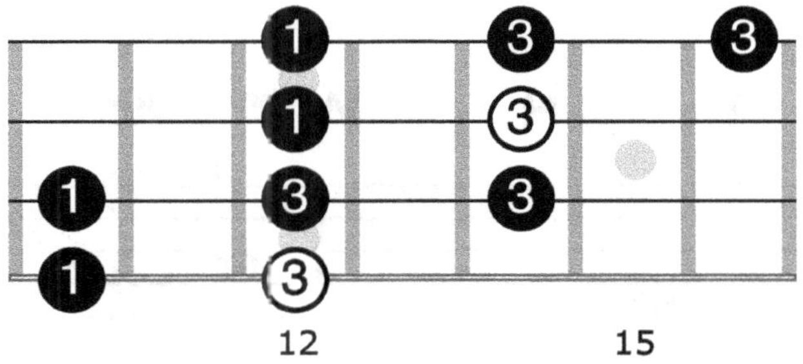

SUNDAY: SCALE APPLICATION 224

This example combines ascending and descending groups of 3 in a strict triplet rhythm. It uses Pattern 5 and makes for a great connecting phrase, as well as a standalone musical idea.

WEEK 33: F MAJOR

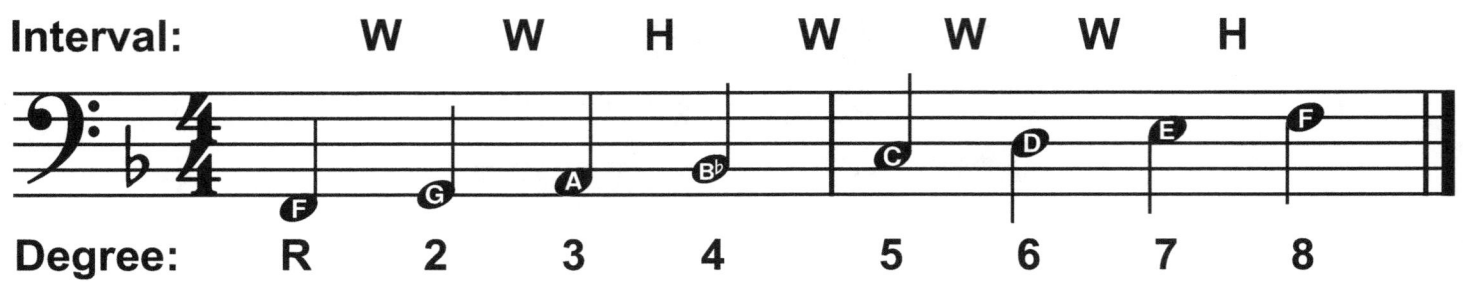

MONDAY: OPEN-STRING PATTERN 2 — 225

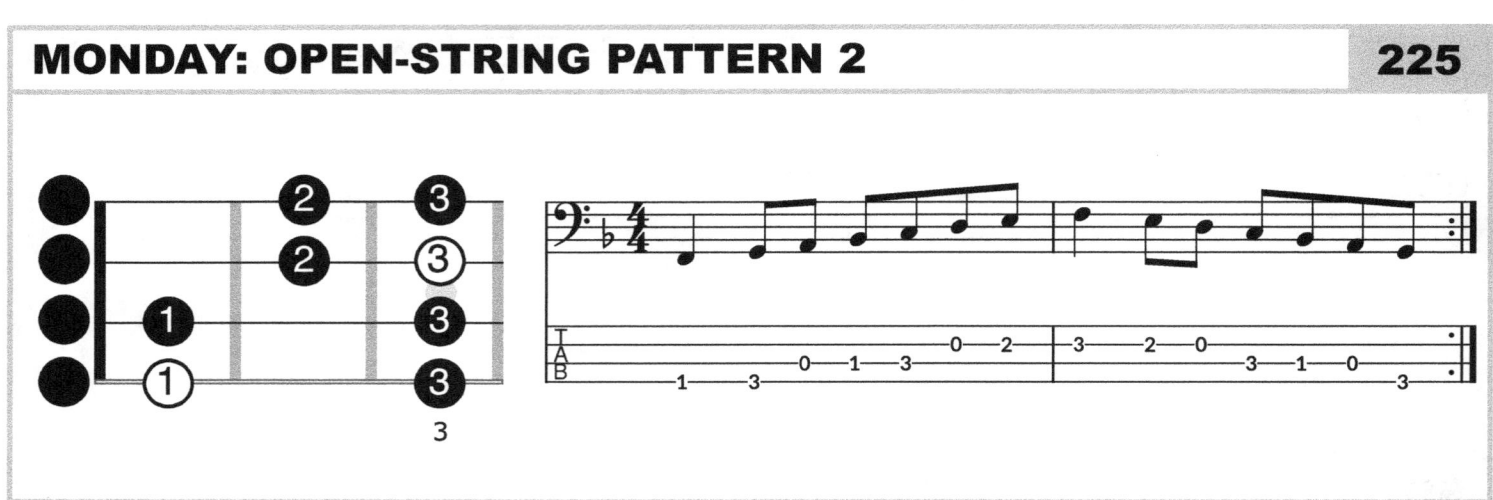

TUESDAY: PATTERN 3 — 226

WEDNESDAY: PATTERN 4
227

THURSDAY: PATTERN 5
228
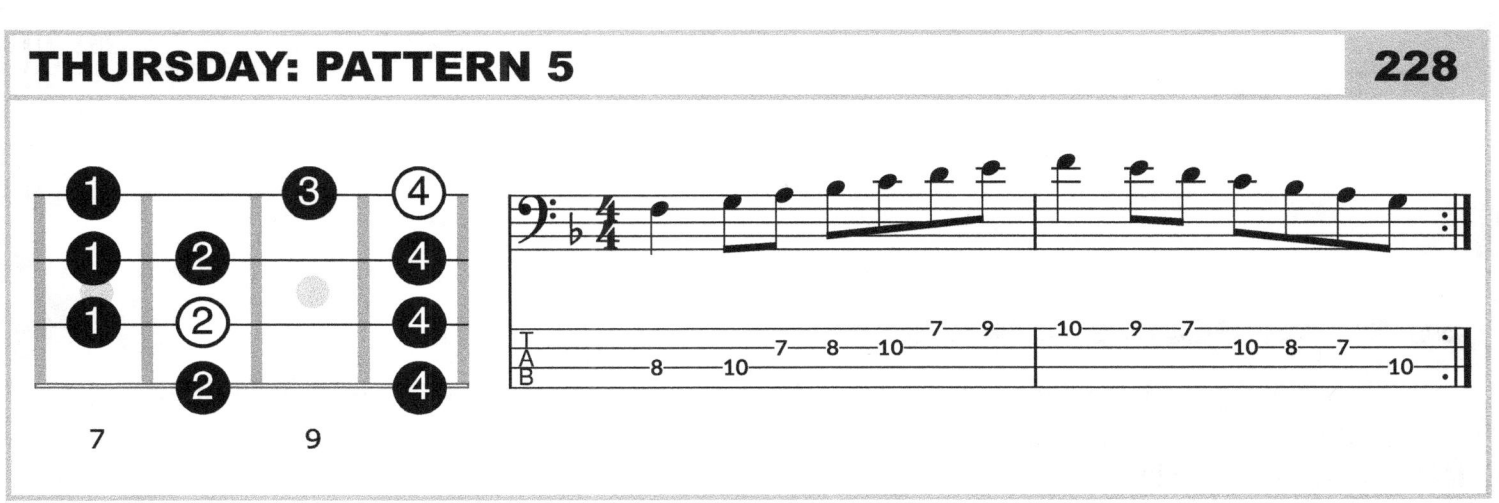

FRIDAY: PATTERN 1
229
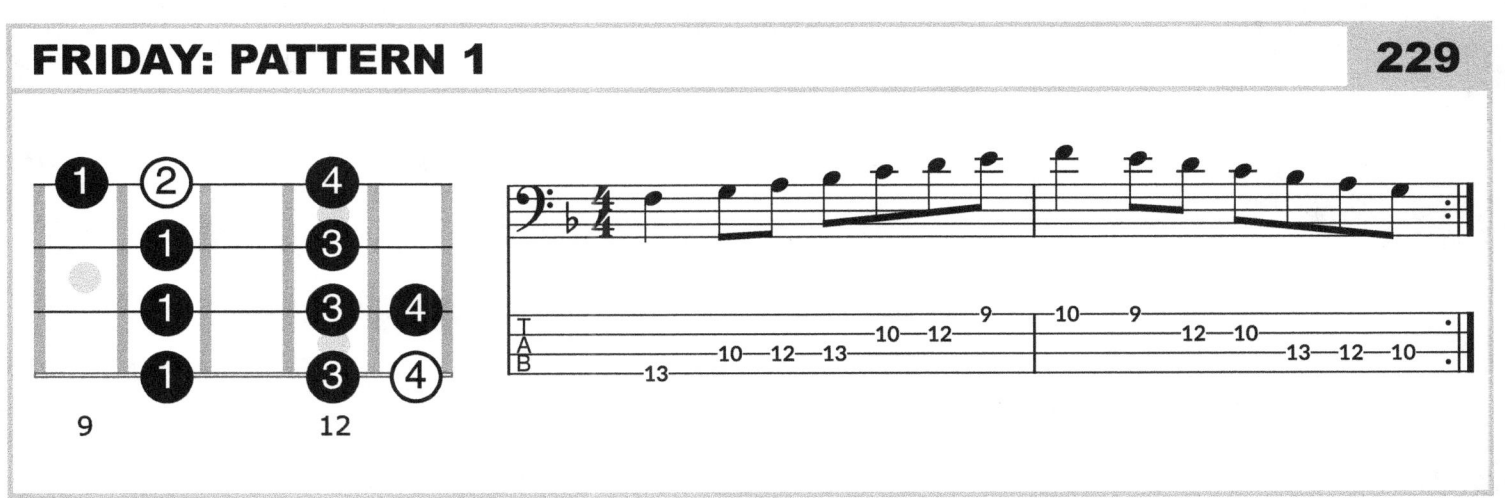

SATURDAY: OPEN-STRING HORIZONTAL PATTERN   230

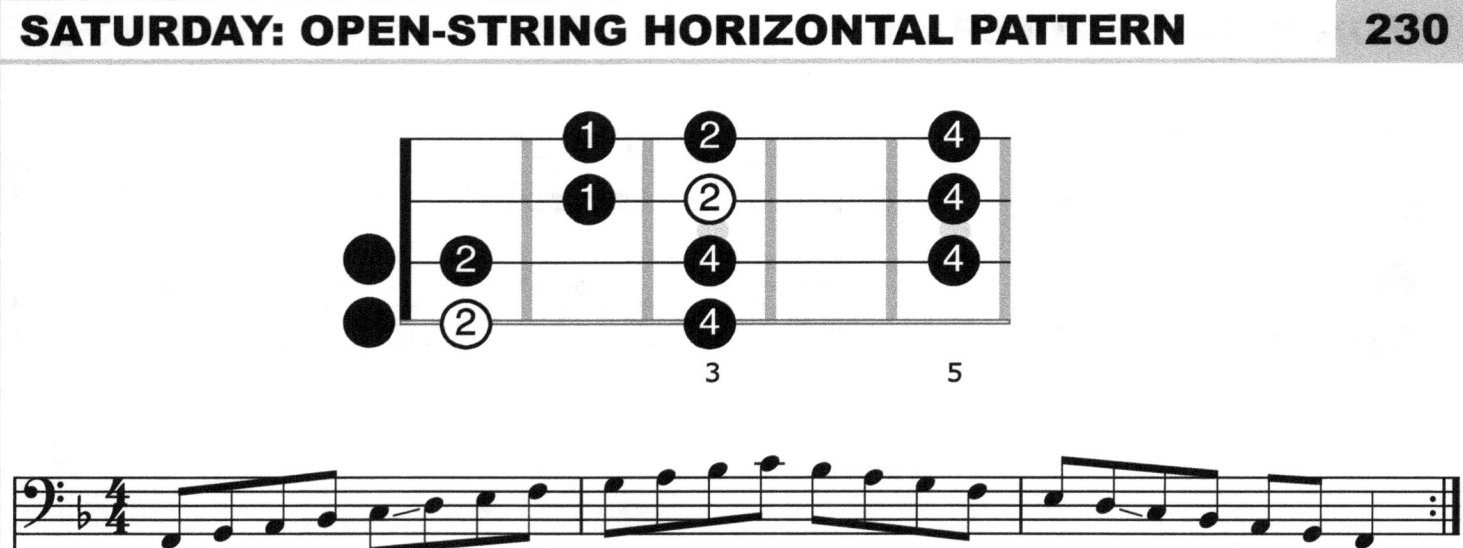

SUNDAY: SCALE APPLICATION   231

This example uses chromatic notes and is a variation of Week 25. Review Pattern 4 and watch out for the leap from the low F on fret 1 to the 5th position. Take note of how the rhythm adds interest to the bass line.

WEEK 34: F MINOR

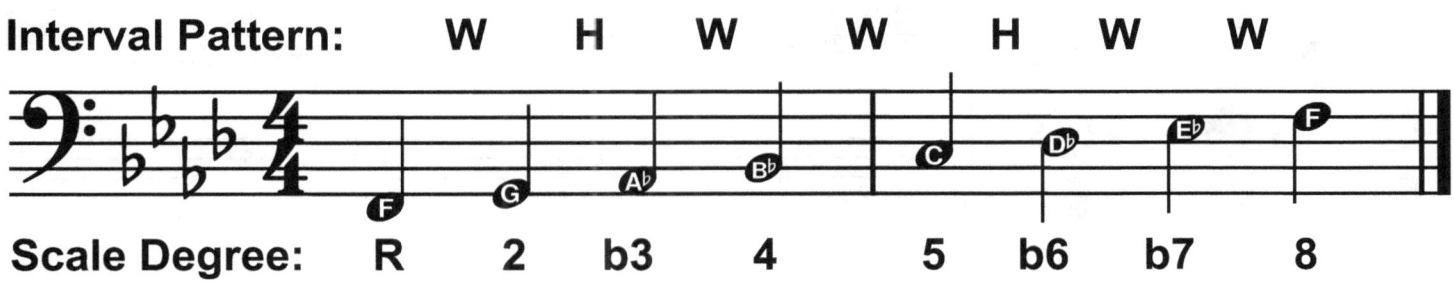

MONDAY: OPEN-STRING PATTERN 1 — 232

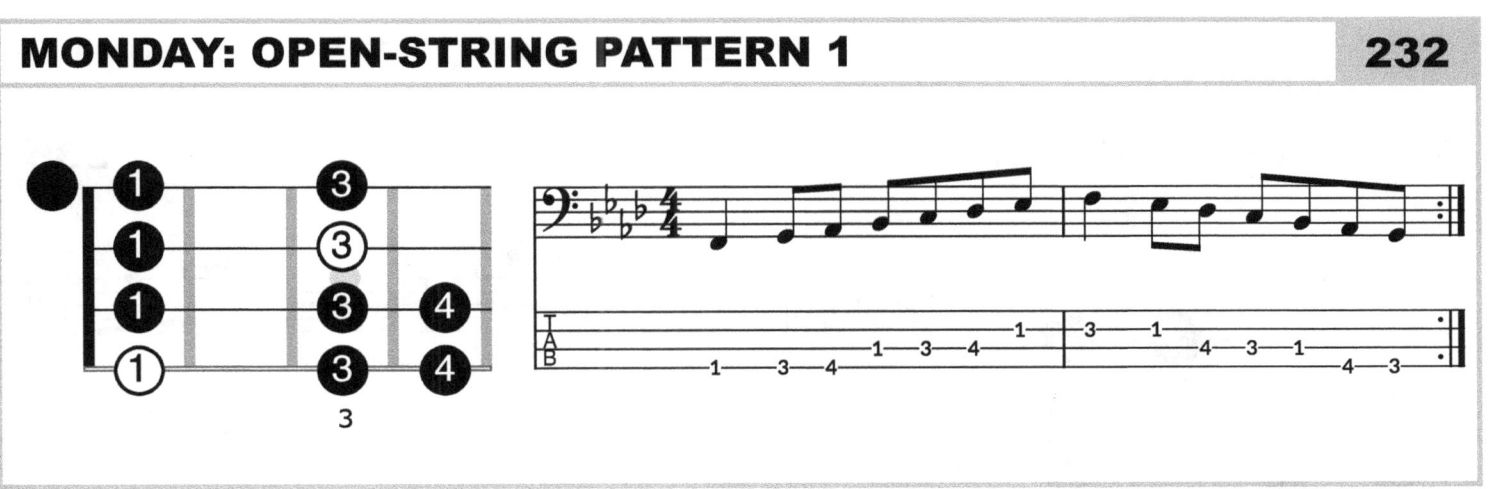

TUESDAY: PATTERN 2 — 233

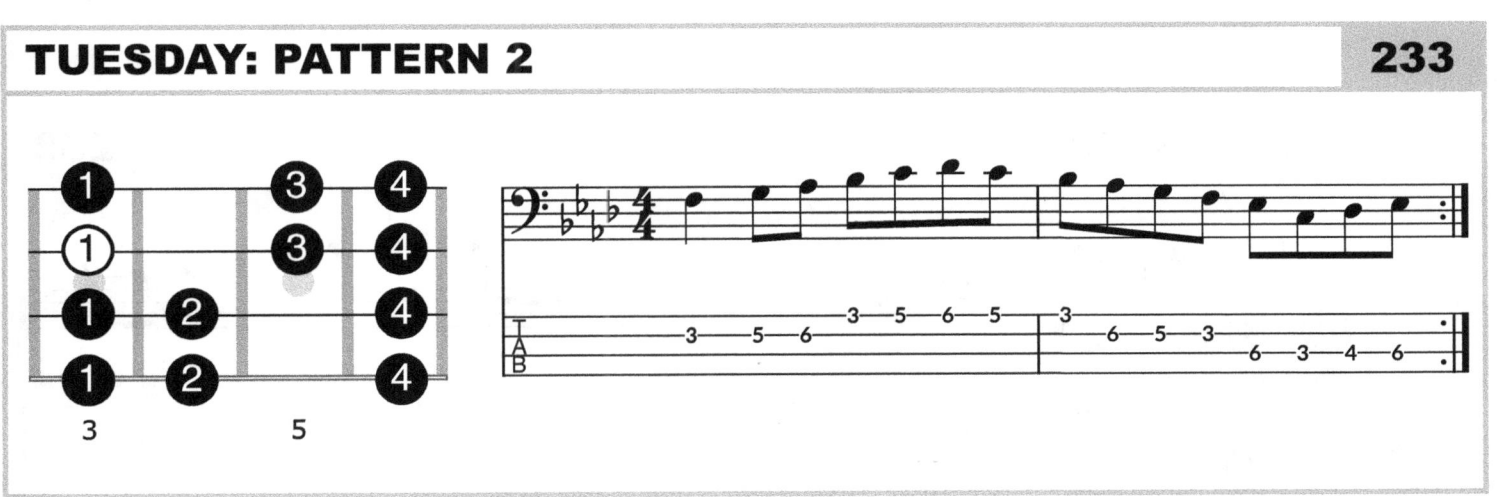

WEDNESDAY: PATTERN 3

THURSDAY: PATTERN 4

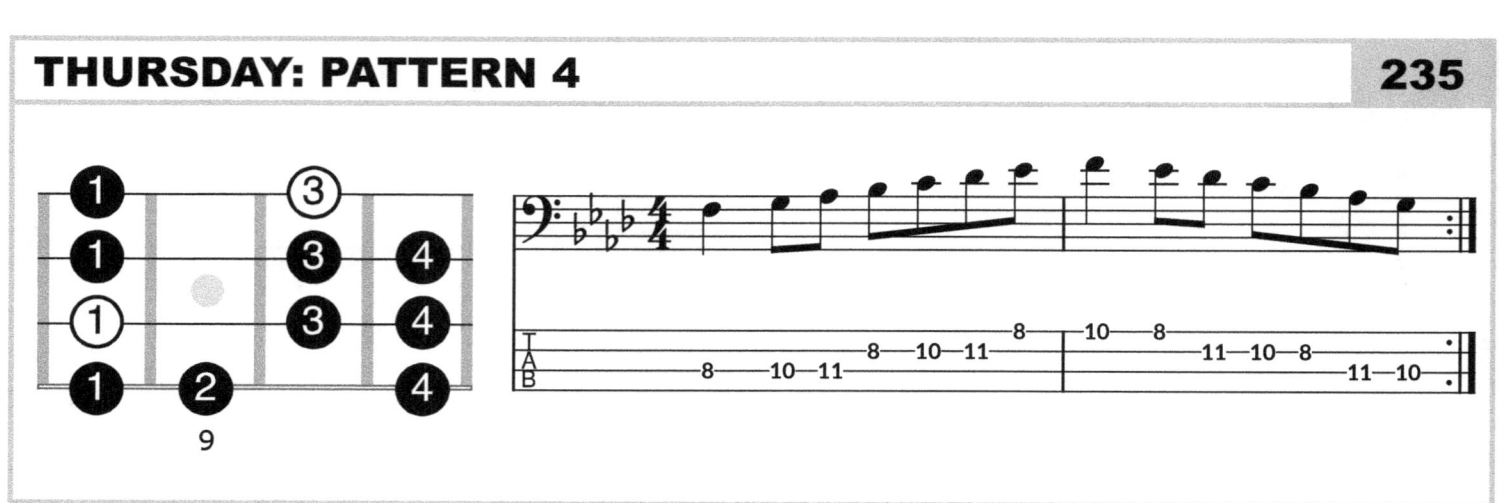

FRIDAY: PATTERN 5

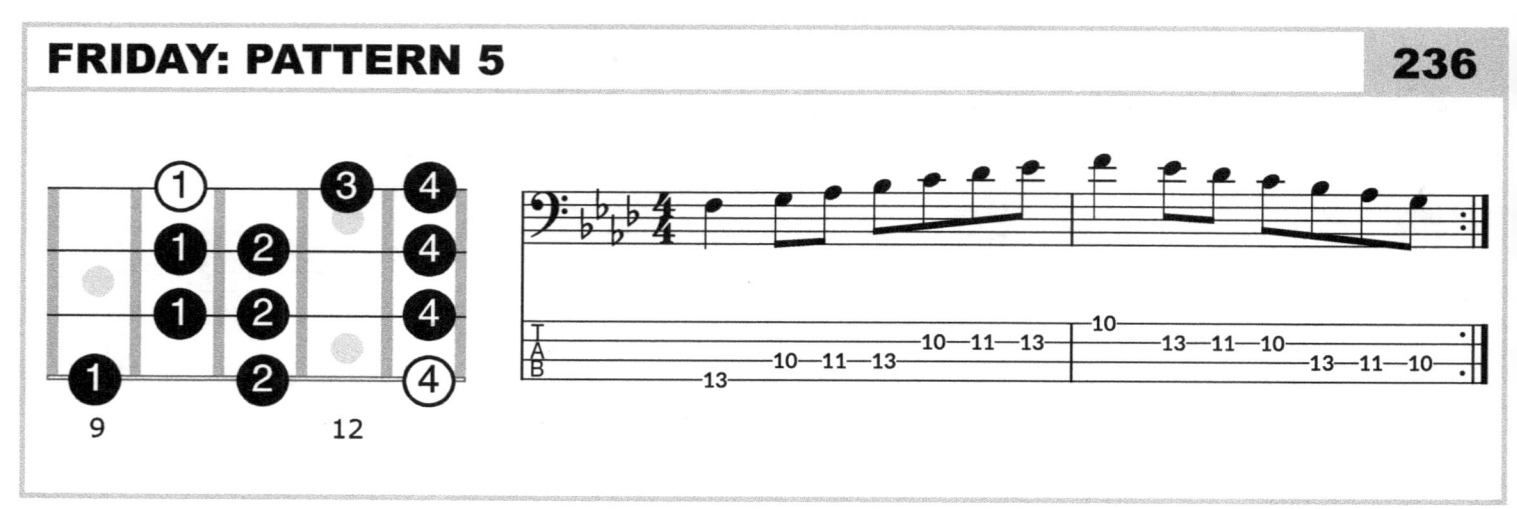

SATURDAY: HORIZONTAL PATTERN 237

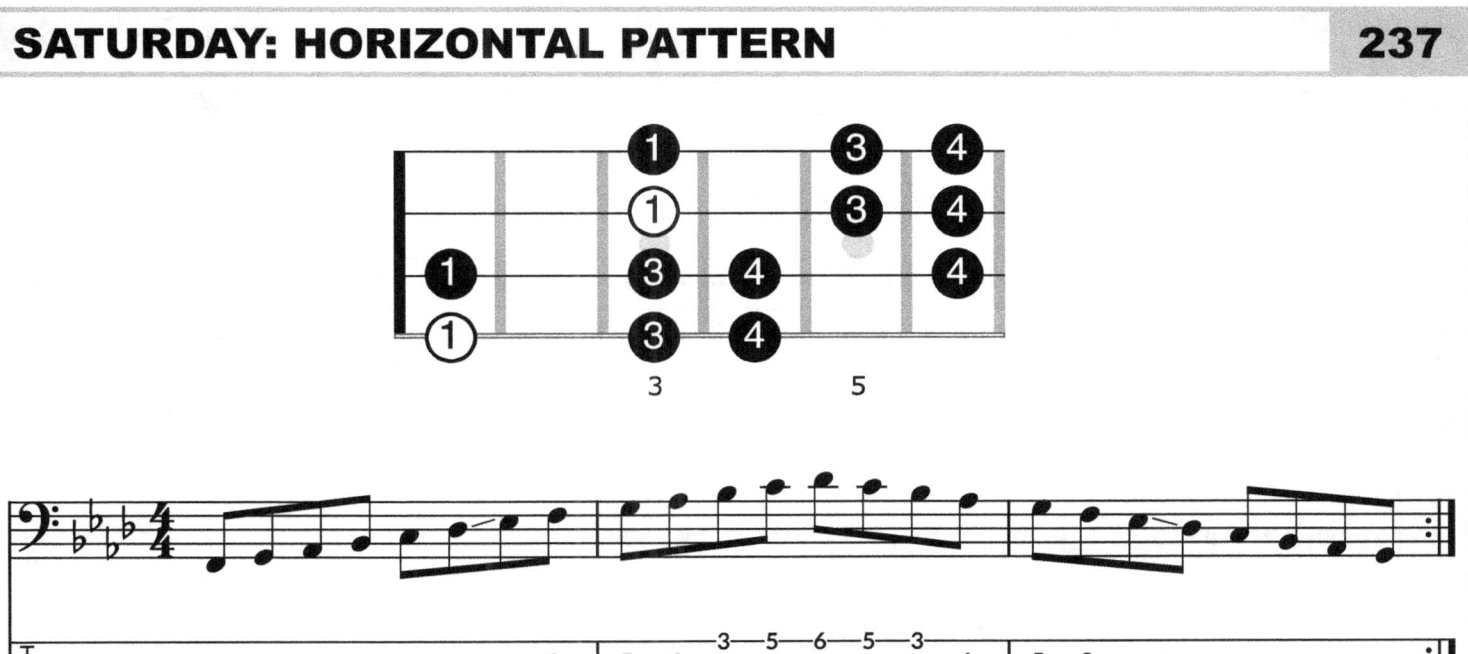

SUNDAY: SCALE APPLICATION 238

In Week 22, we learned how 5ths can be used to spice up a bass line. In addition to going from the root up to the 5th, you can also find the 5th below the root. When you're on strings 1, 2, or 3, you'll find the 5th right below the root, as it's on the same fret, just one string lower. Observe how the first chord uses this idea with the previous 5ths shape to add variety.

WEEK 35: F MAJOR PENTATONIC

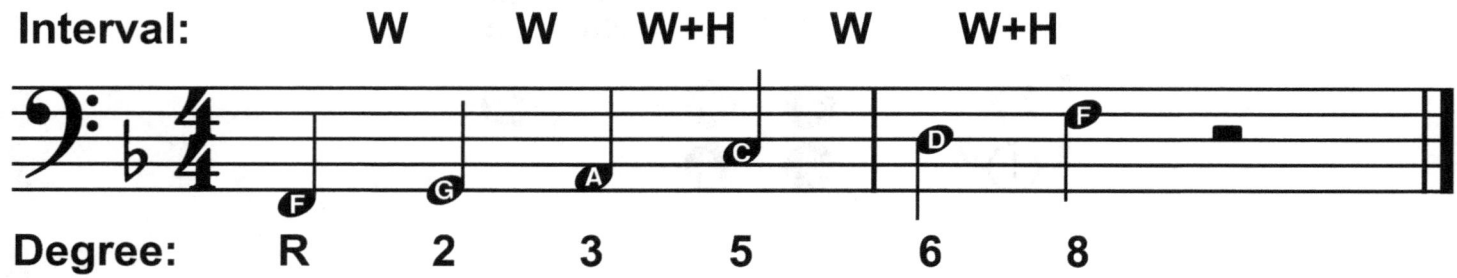

MONDAY: OPEN-STRING PATTERN 2   239

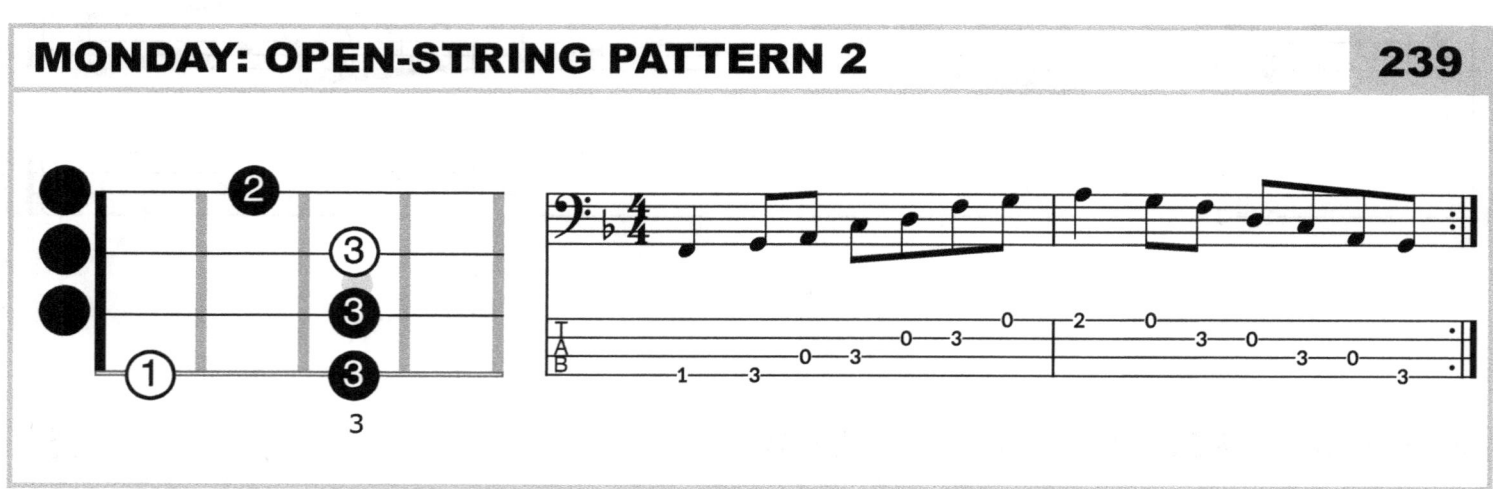

TUESDAY: PATTERN 3   240

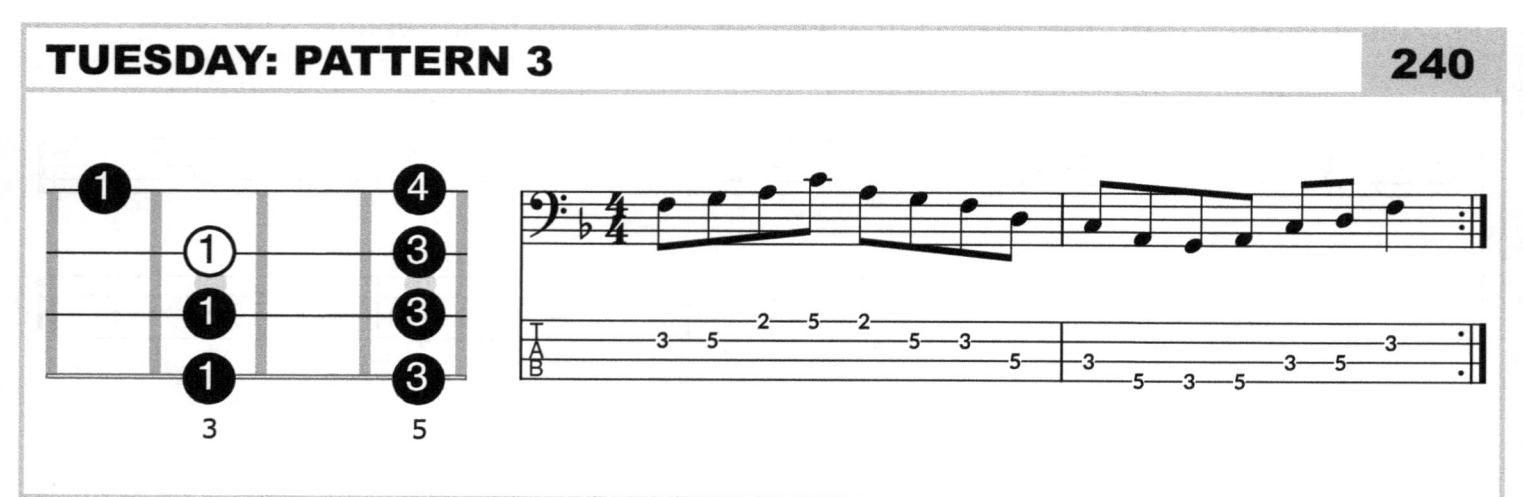

WEDNESDAY: PATTERN 4

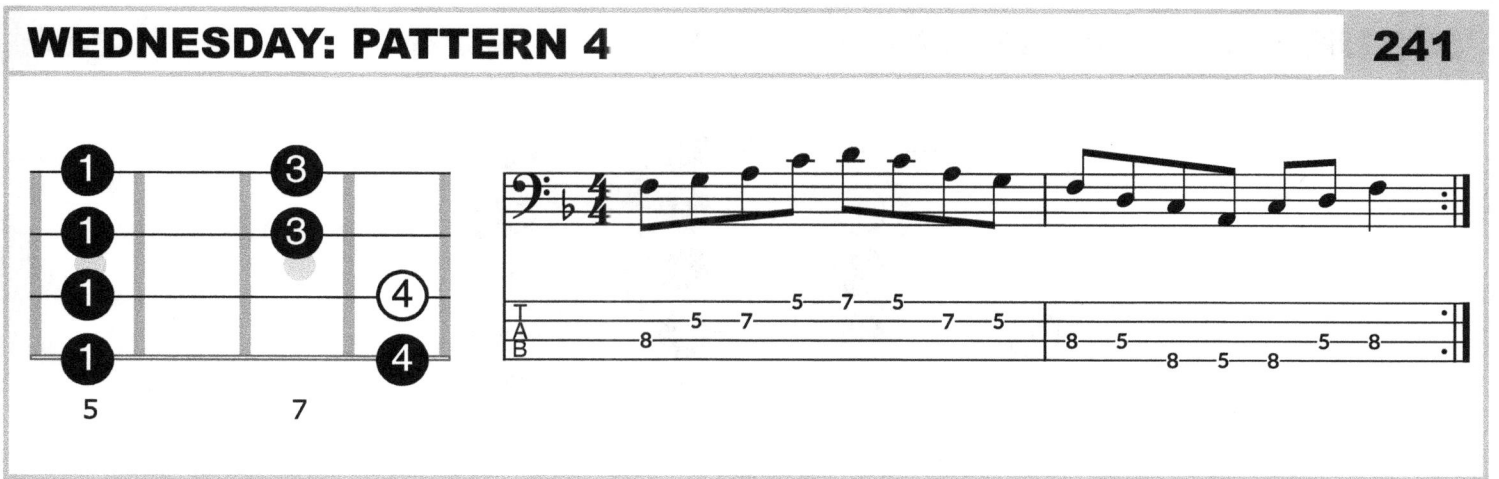

THURSDAY: PATTERN 5

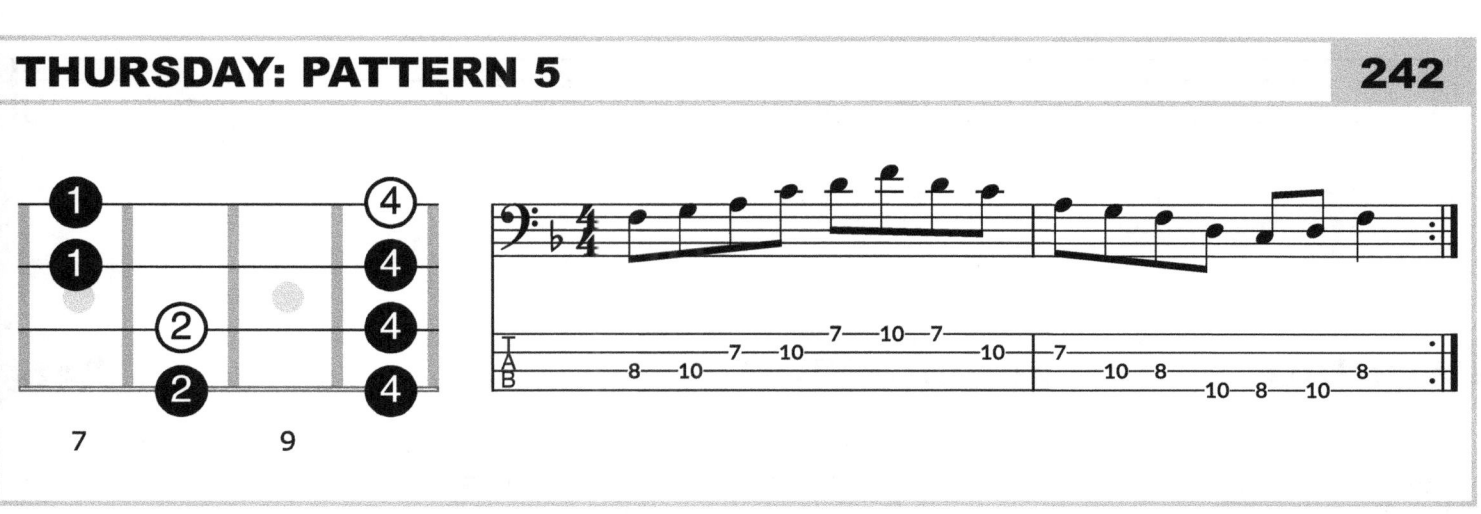

FRIDAY: PATTERN 1

SATURDAY: HORIZONTAL PATTERN 244

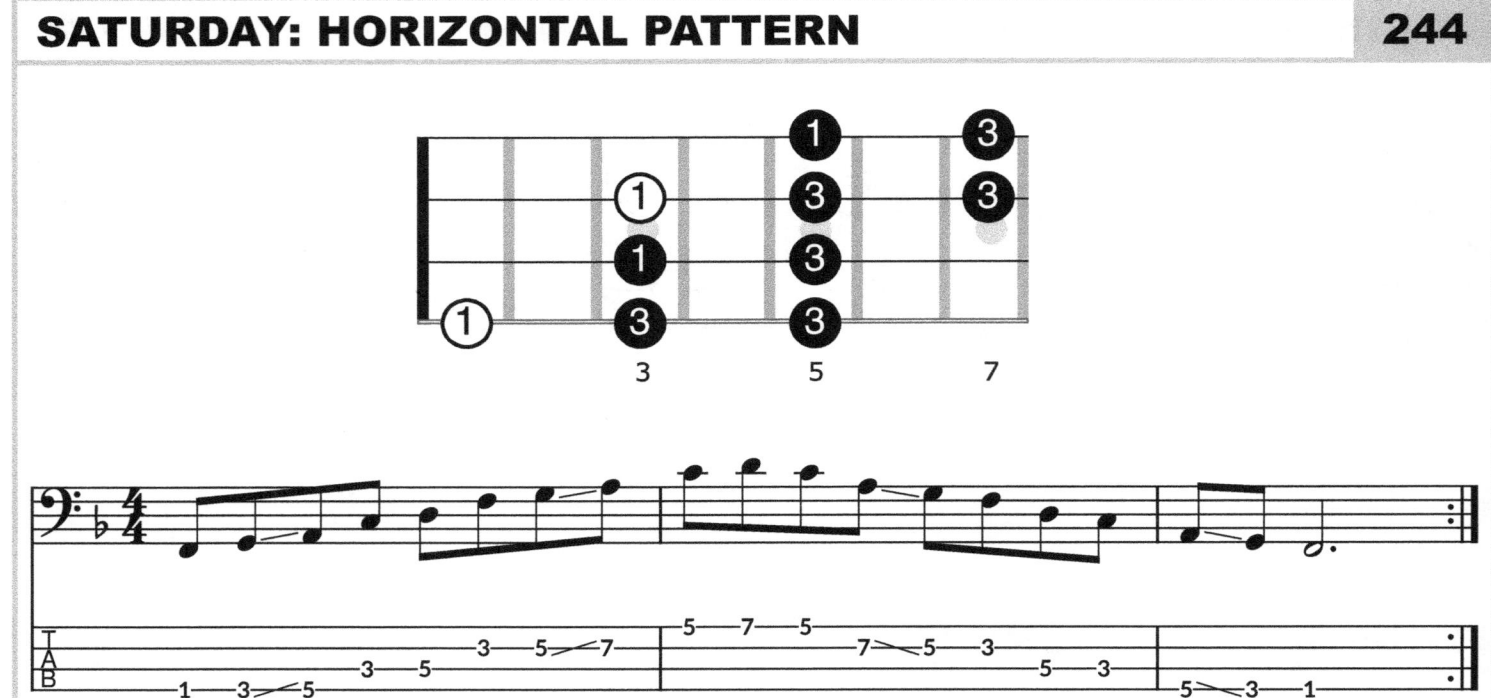

SUNDAY: SCALE APPLICATION 245

A common way bassists descend and ascend in 4s is to move the pattern to a different set of strings. The half note gives the listener a break while creating an ending to the phrase. Be ready for the octave jump in measure 4. For additional study, you can experiment with moving this idea to any of the pentatonic patterns.

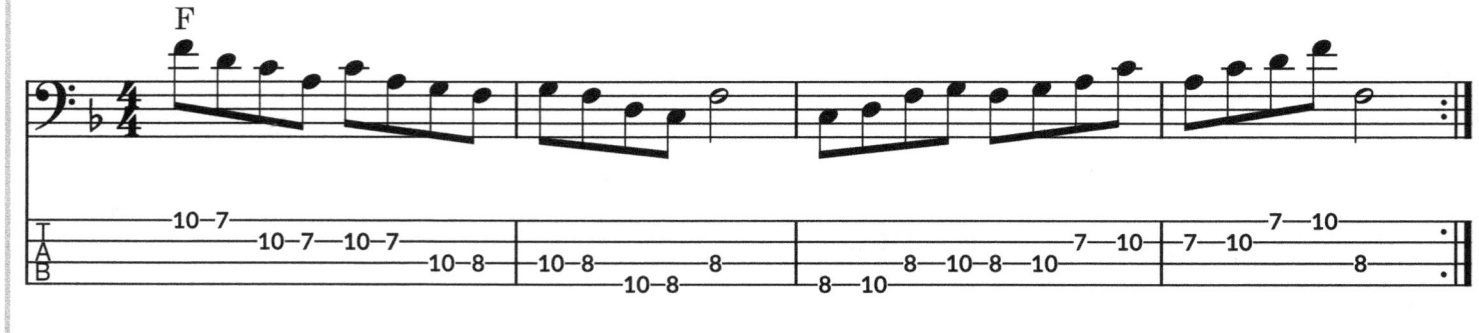

WEEK 36: F MINOR PENTATONIC

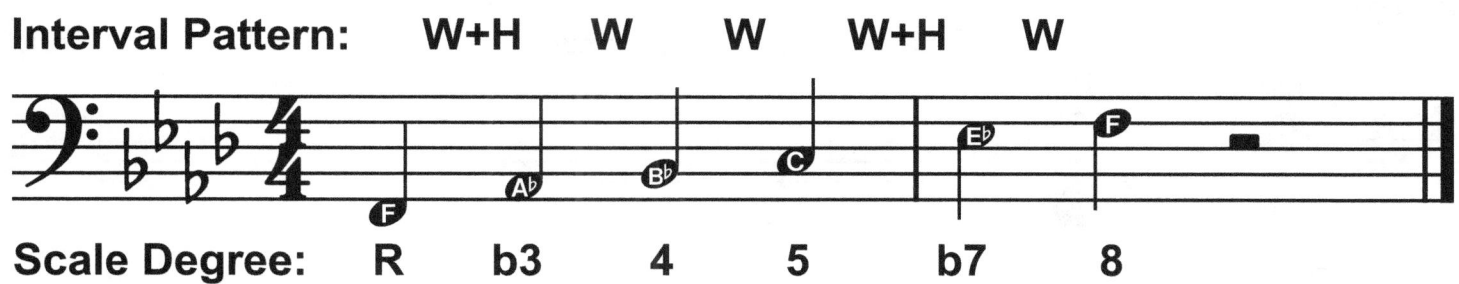

MONDAY: PATTERN 1 — 246

TUESDAY: PATTERN 2 — 247

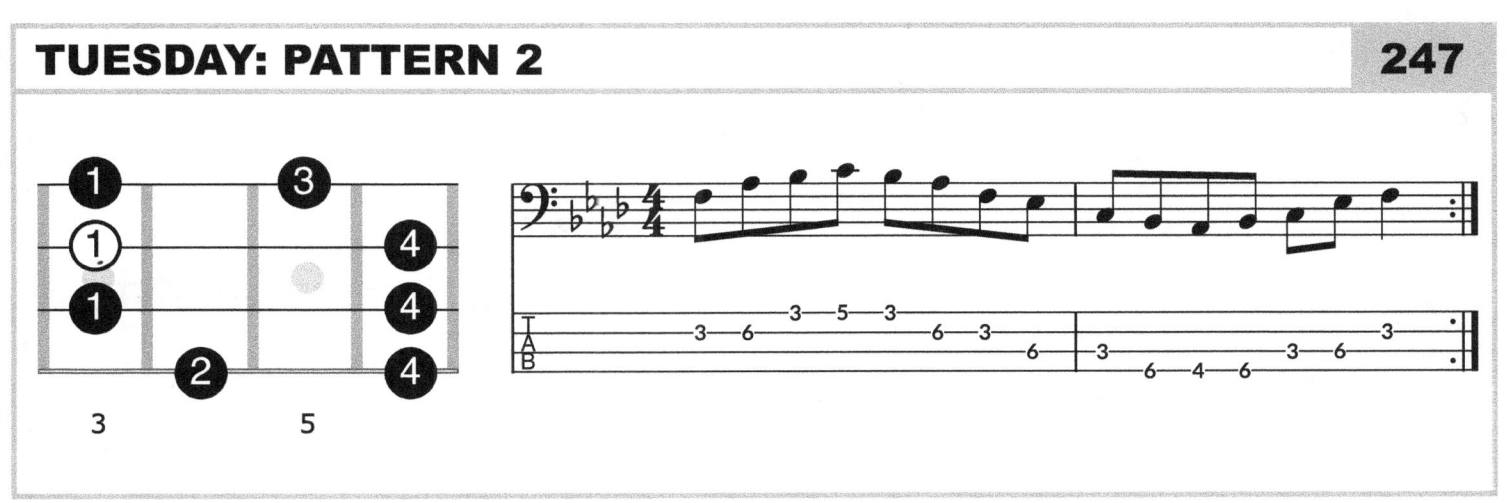

WEDNESDAY: PATTERN 3 — 248

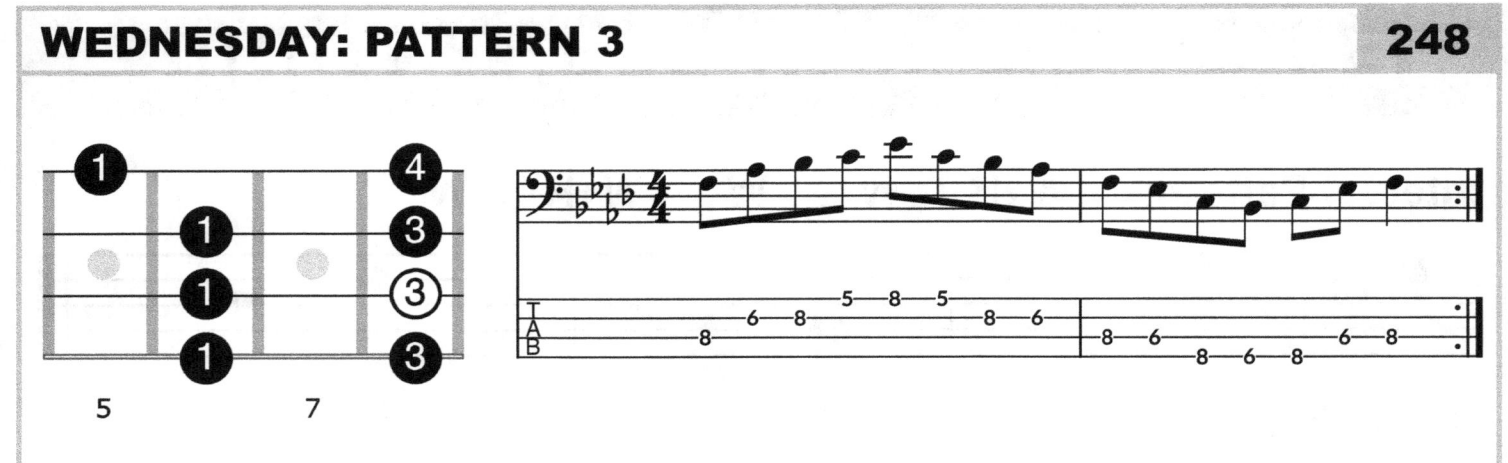

THURSDAY: PATTERN 4 — 249

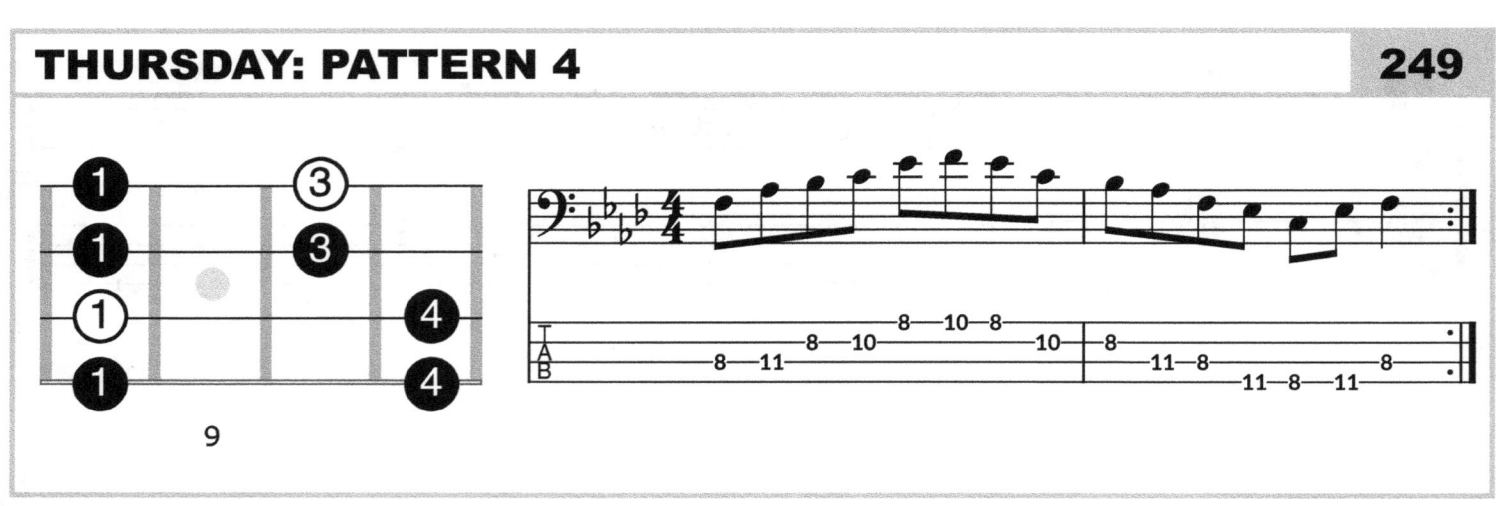

FRIDAY: PATTERN 5 — 250

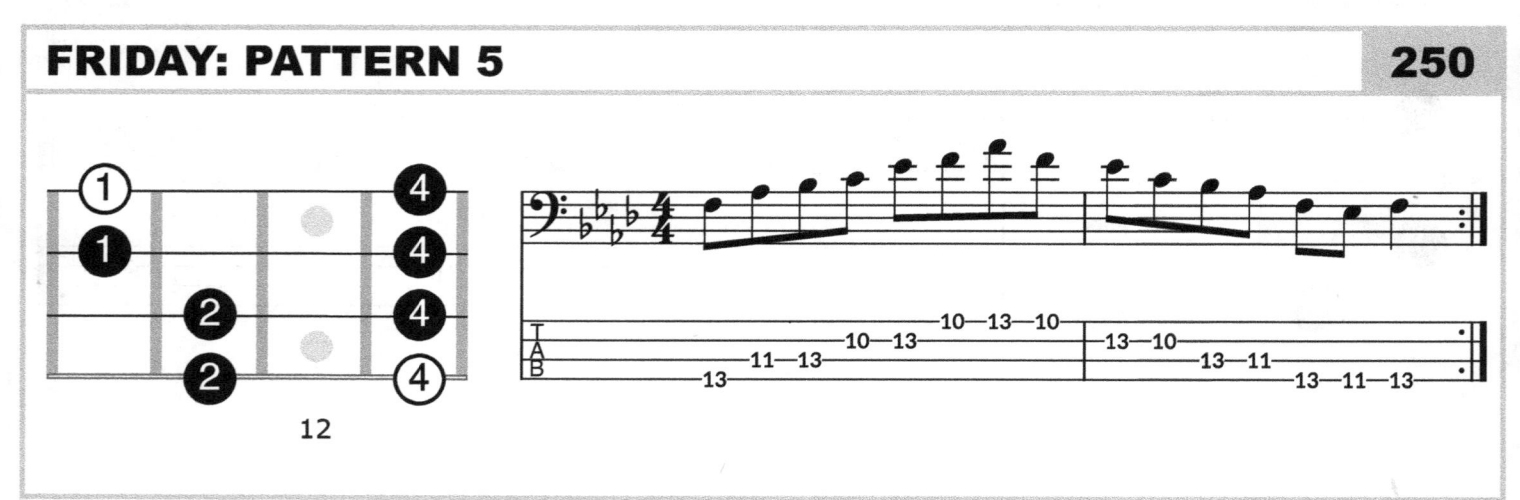

SATURDAY: HORIZONTAL PATTERN   251

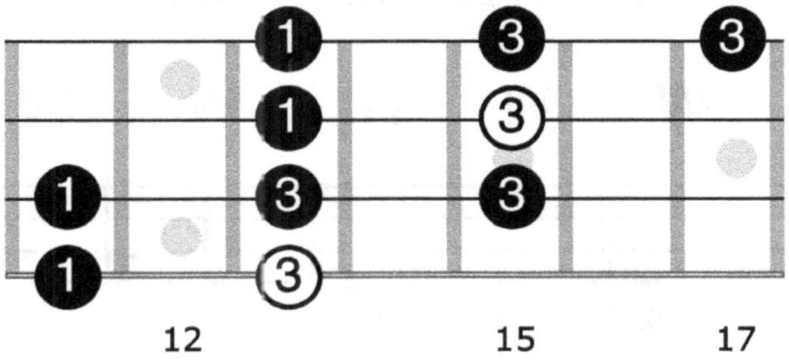

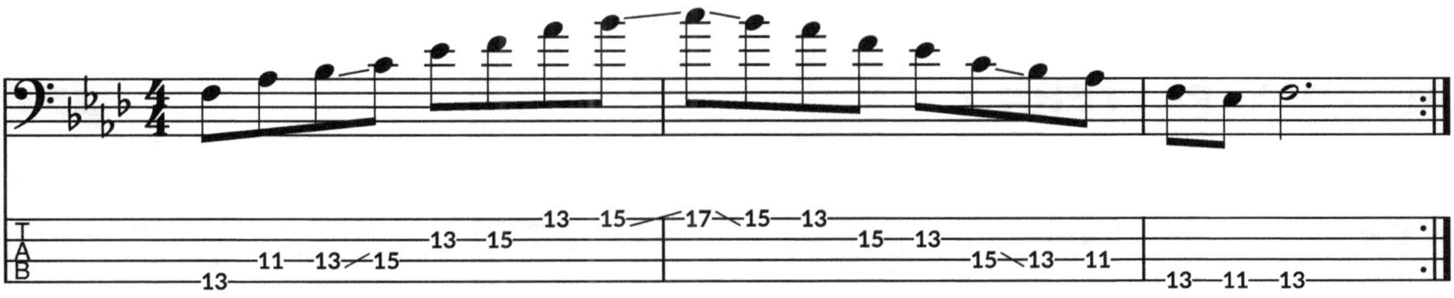

SUNDAY: SCALE APPLICATION   252

In Week 24, we learned about the Downtown Blues box pattern. Today, we'll reverse the idea and learn an Uptown Blues. As its name implies, Uptown Blues is always ascending and can be referenced by its scale degrees: 1, 5, ♭7, 8. Like a standard blues progression, we will move to the 4-chord in measure 2 (the notes still fit within Pattern 1).

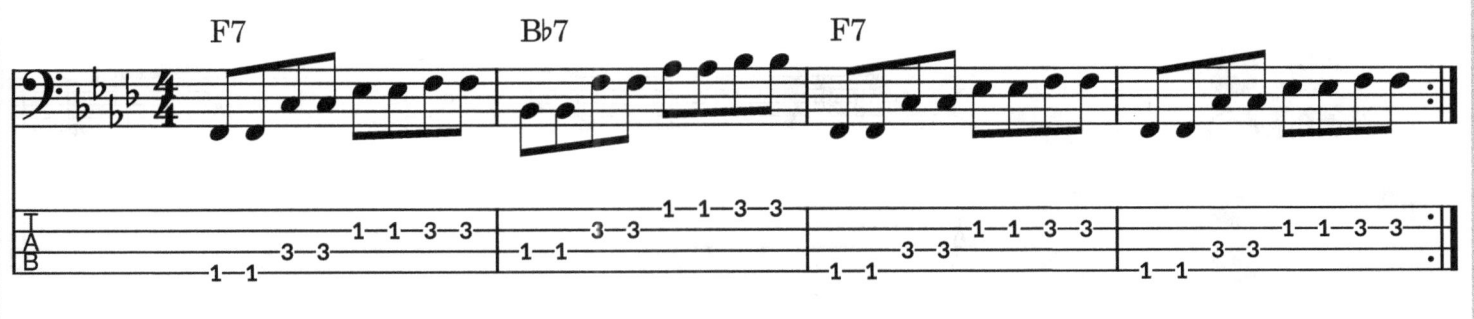

WEEK 37: F♯ MAJOR

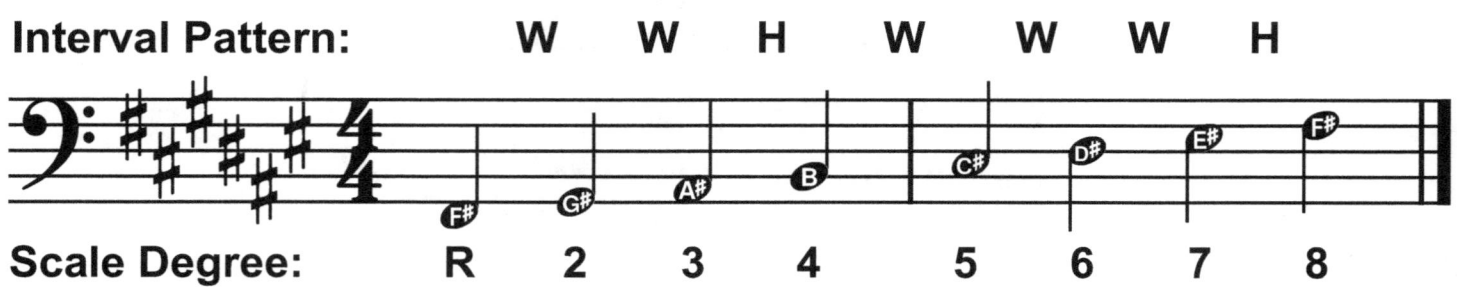

MONDAY: PATTERN 2 — 253

TUESDAY: PATTERN 3 — 254

WEDNESDAY: PATTERN 4

THURSDAY: PATTERN 5

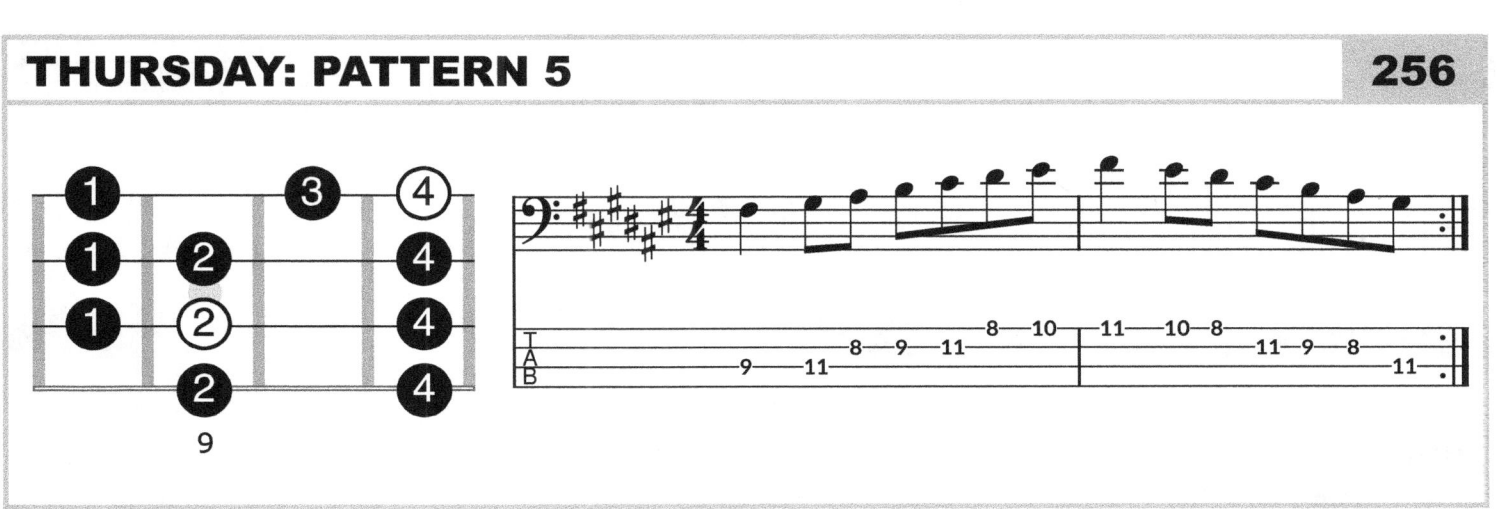

FRIDAY: PATTERN 1

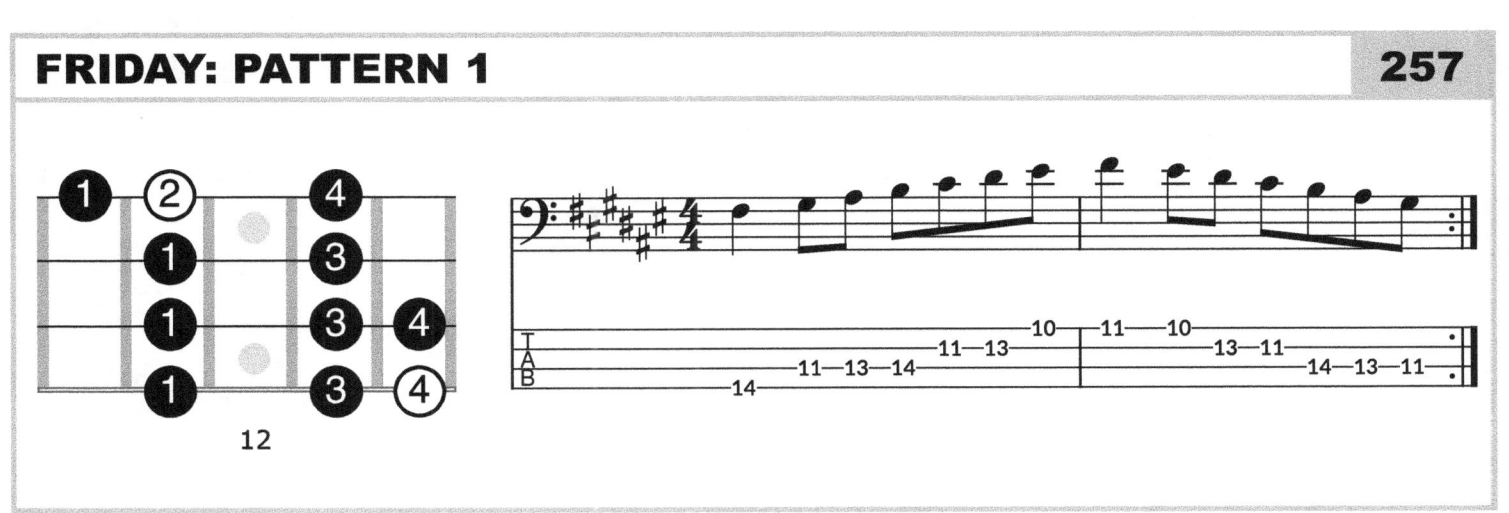

SATURDAY: HORIZONTAL PATTERN   258

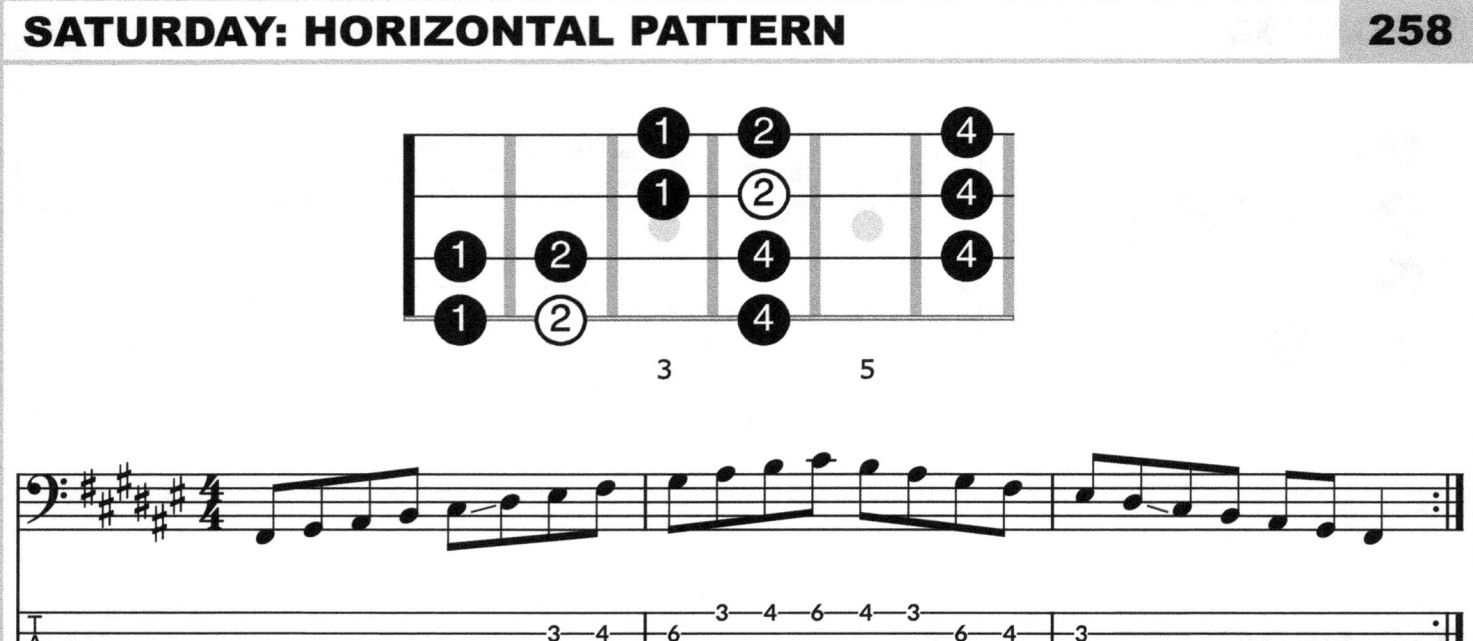

SUNDAY: SCALE APPLICATION   259

Stepwise scale motion is also a great way to connect one chord to the next. The following example walks up and down the scale to reach the root of the next chord while using the 5th above and below the root.

WEEK 38: F# MINOR

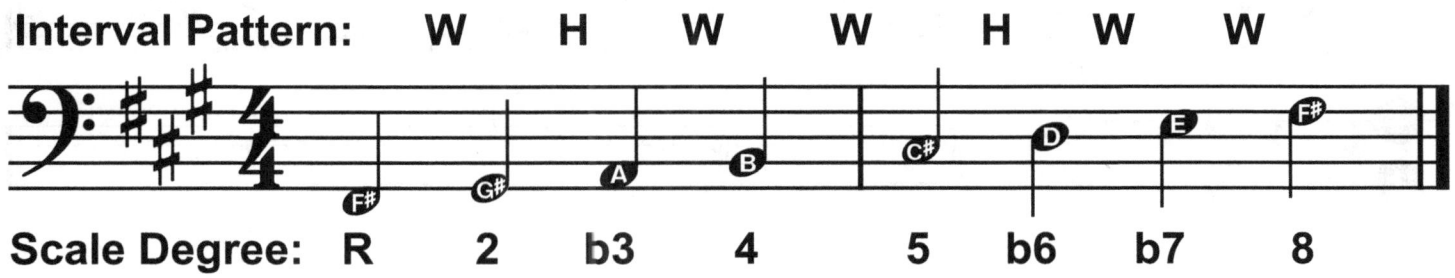

MONDAY: PATTERN 1 — 260

TUESDAY: PATTERN 2 — 261

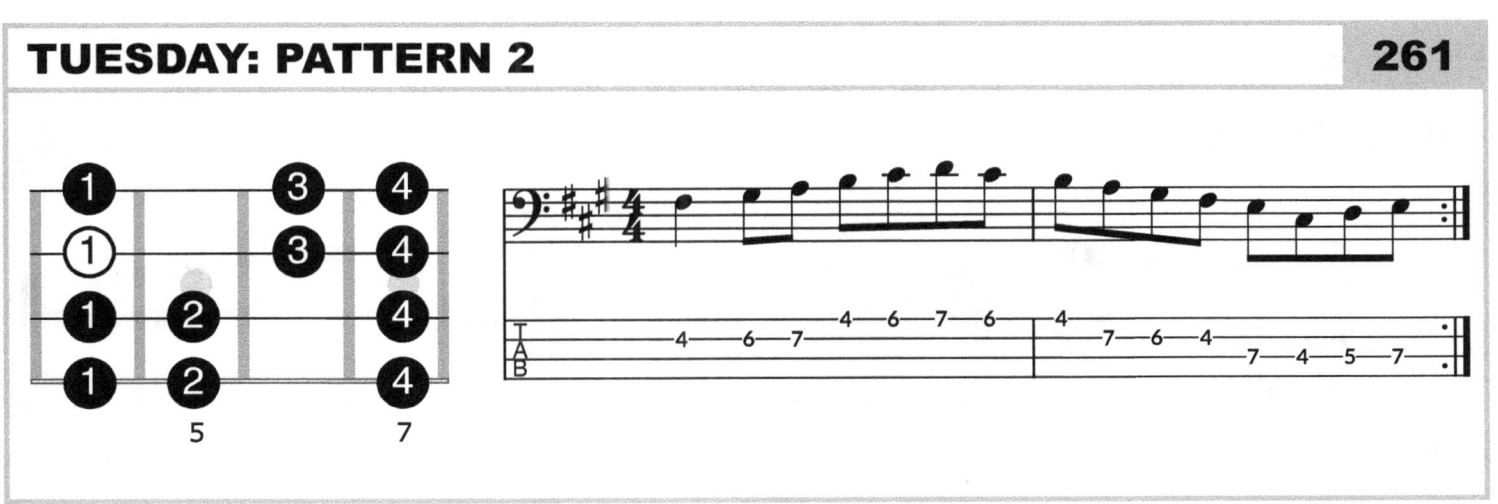

WEDNESDAY: PATTERN 3

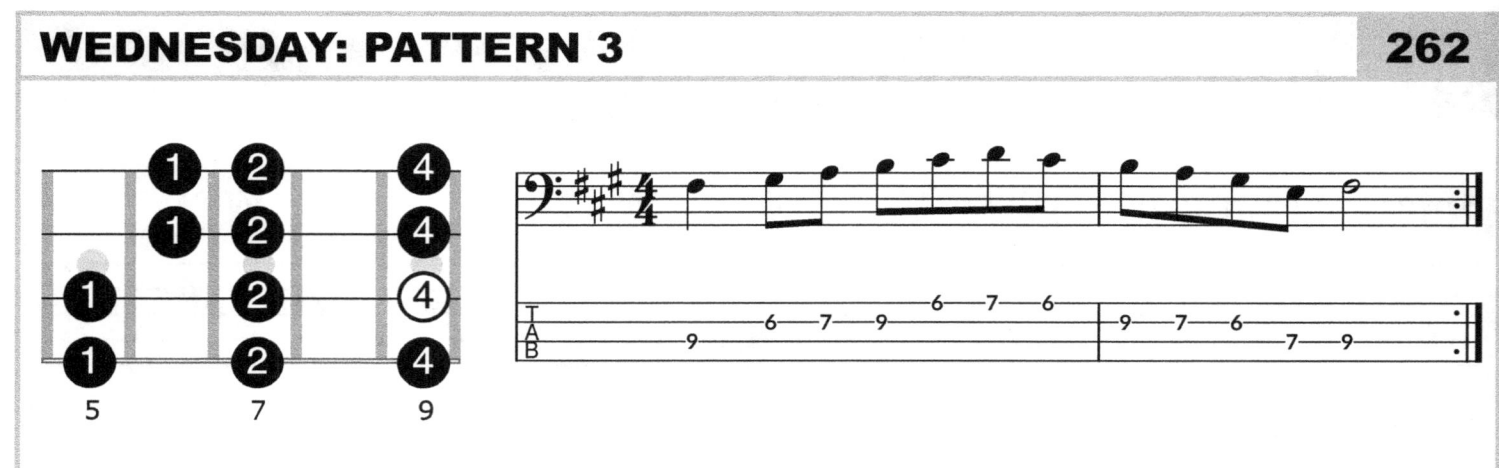

THURSDAY: PATTERN 4

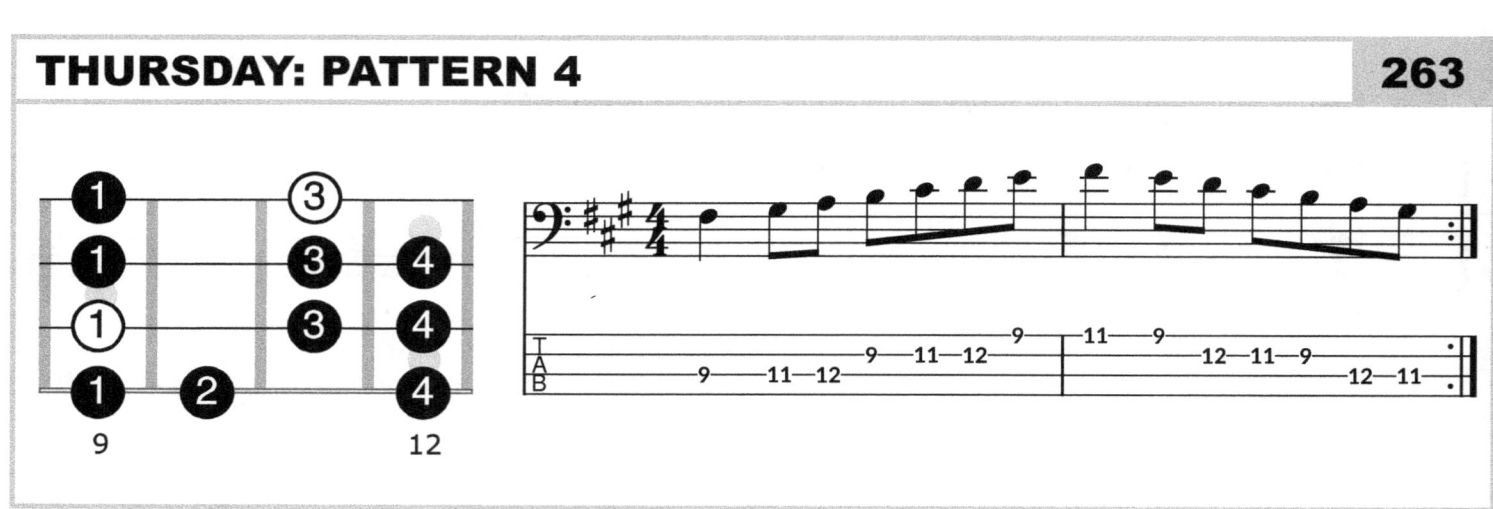

FRIDAY: PATTERN 5

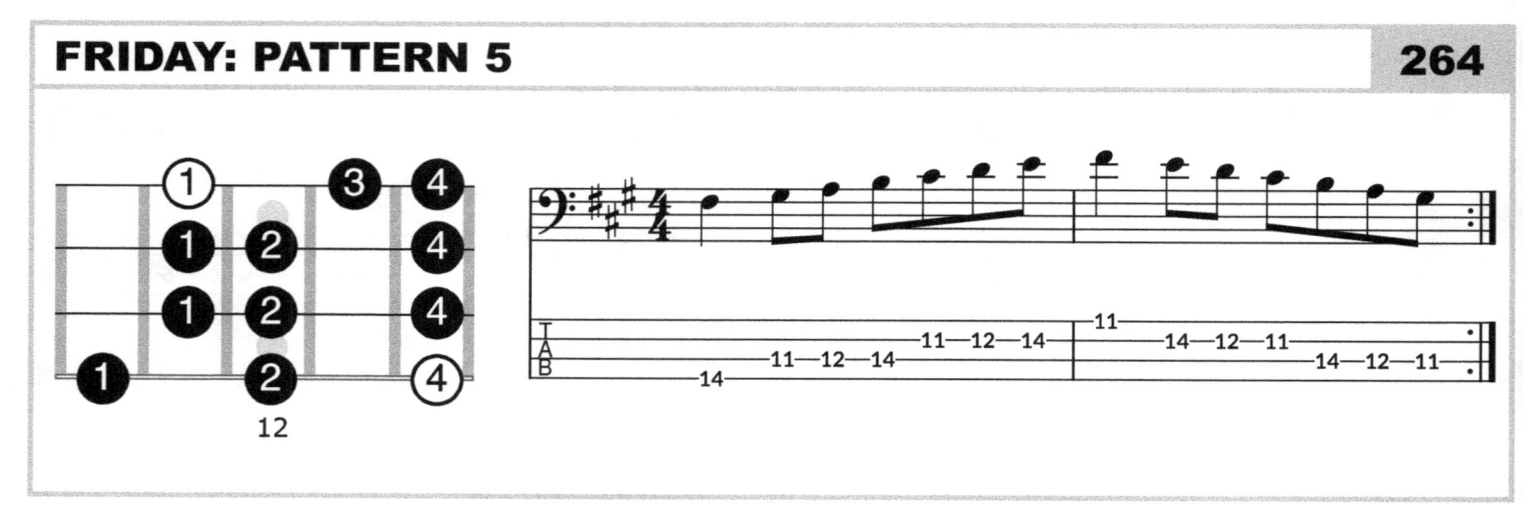

SATURDAY: HORIZONTAL PATTERN 265

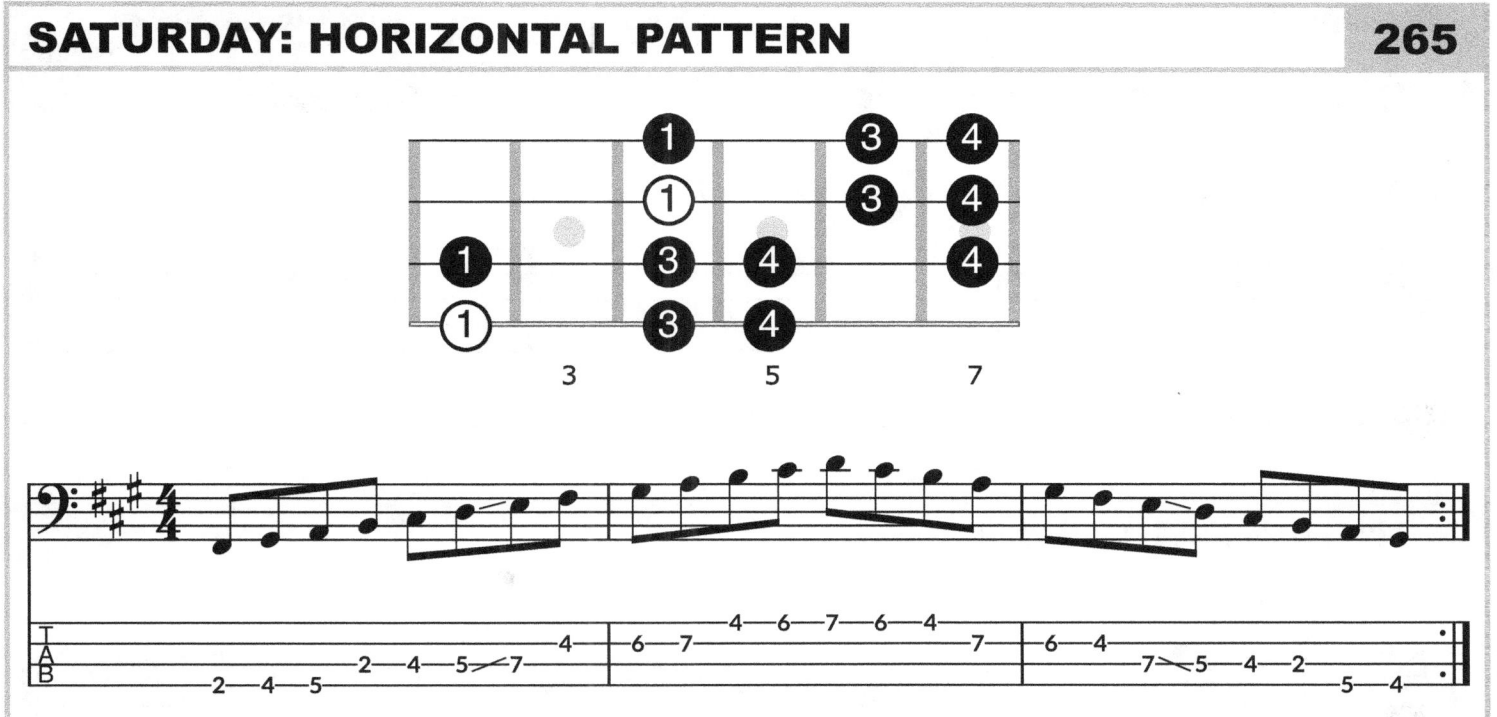

SUNDAY: SCALE APPLICATION 266

In addition to stepwise motion, chords can also be connected by using chromatic notes. The following example does both while staying within Pattern 3.

WEEK 39: F# MAJOR PENTATONIC

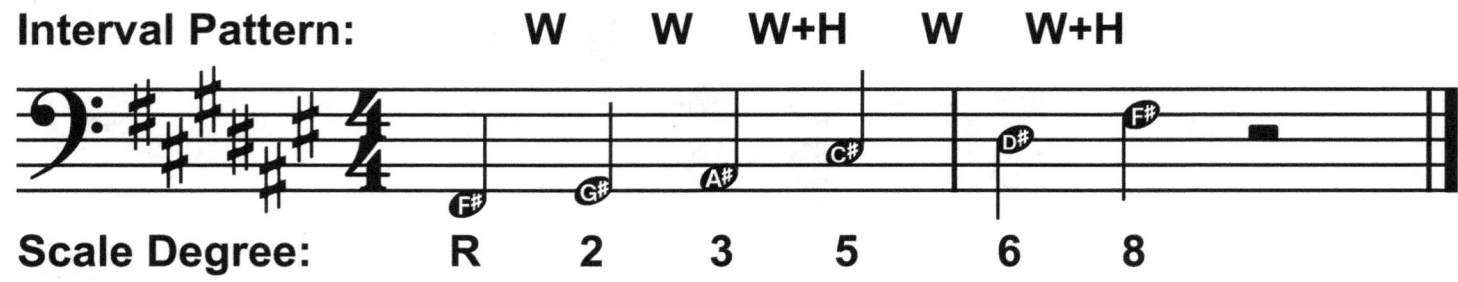

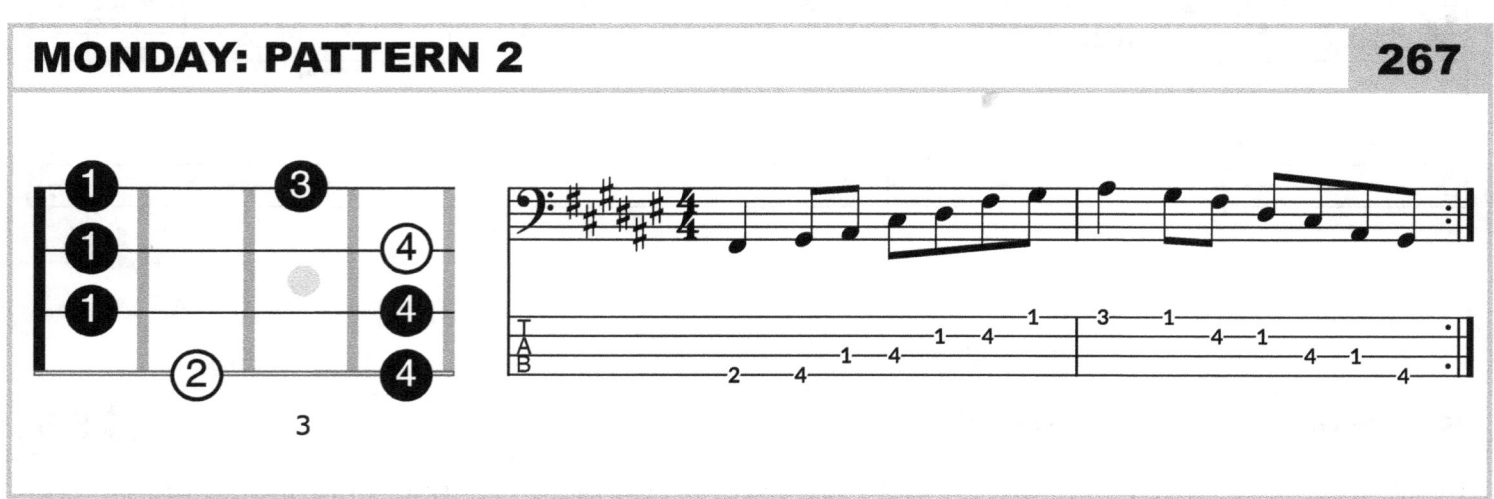

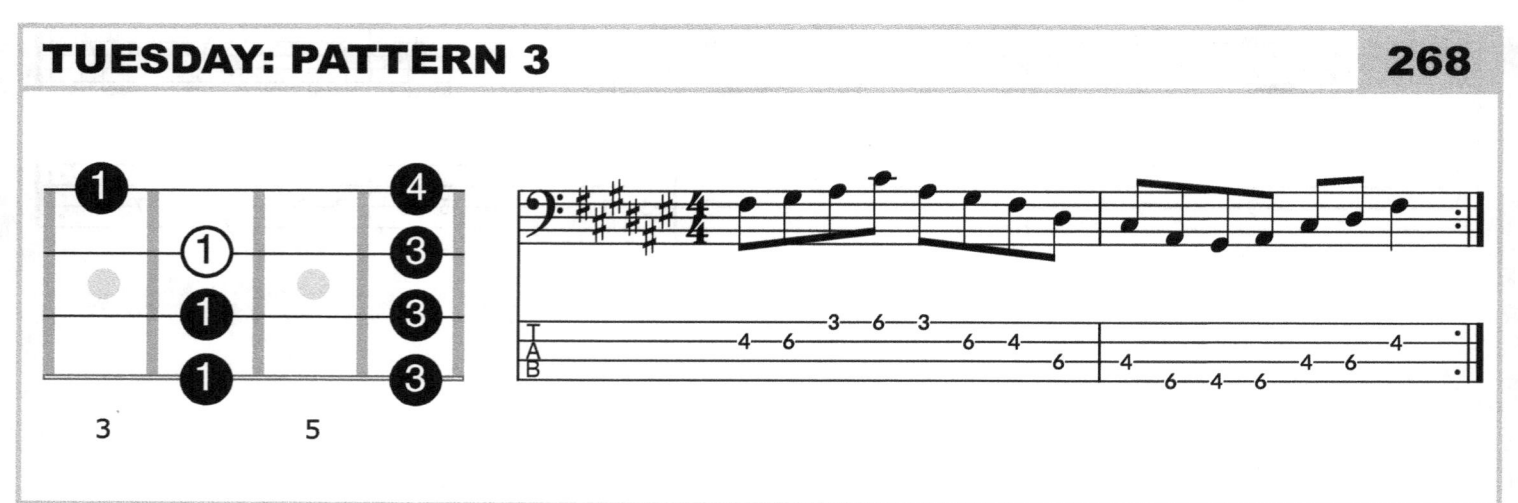

WEDNESDAY: PATTERN 4 — 269

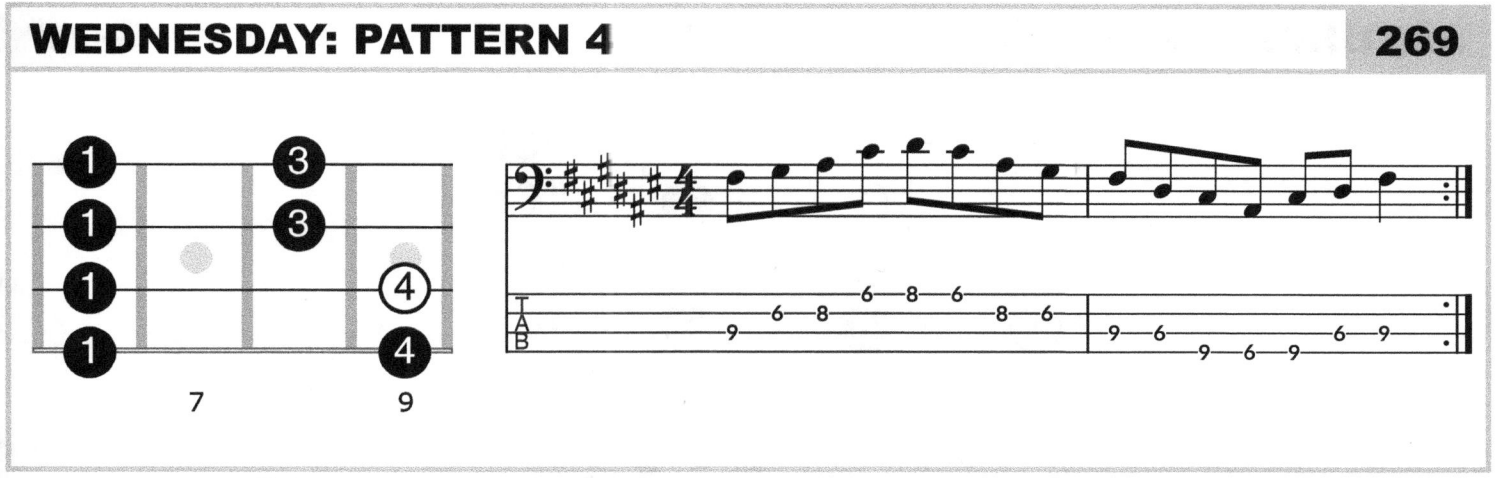

THURSDAY: PATTERN 5 — 270

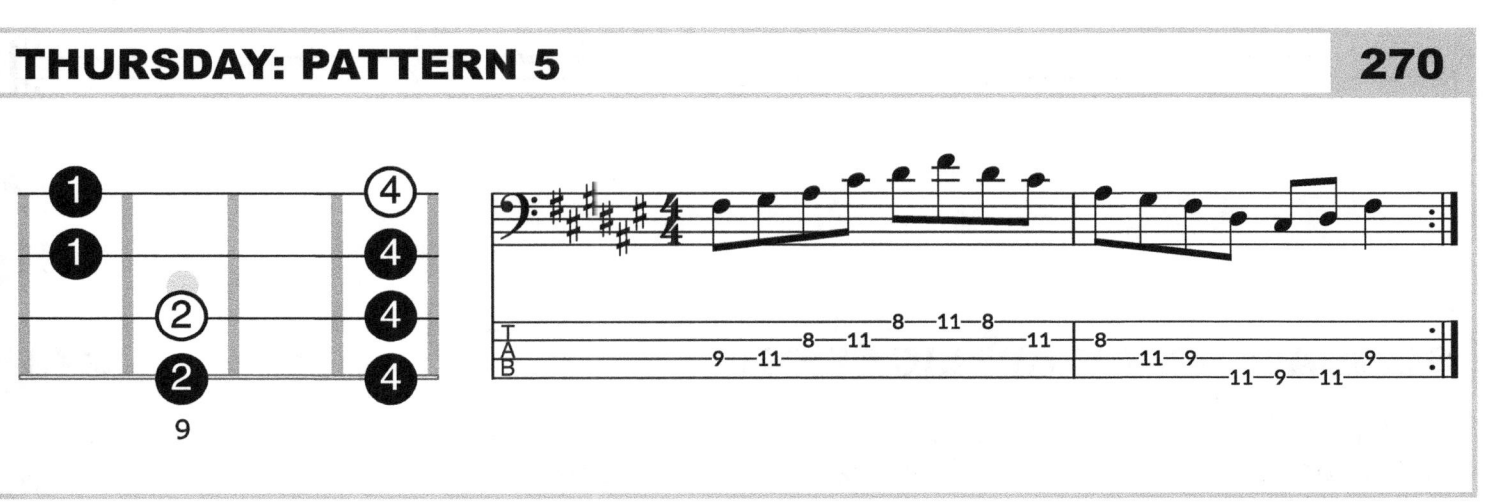

FRIDAY: PATTERN 1 — 271

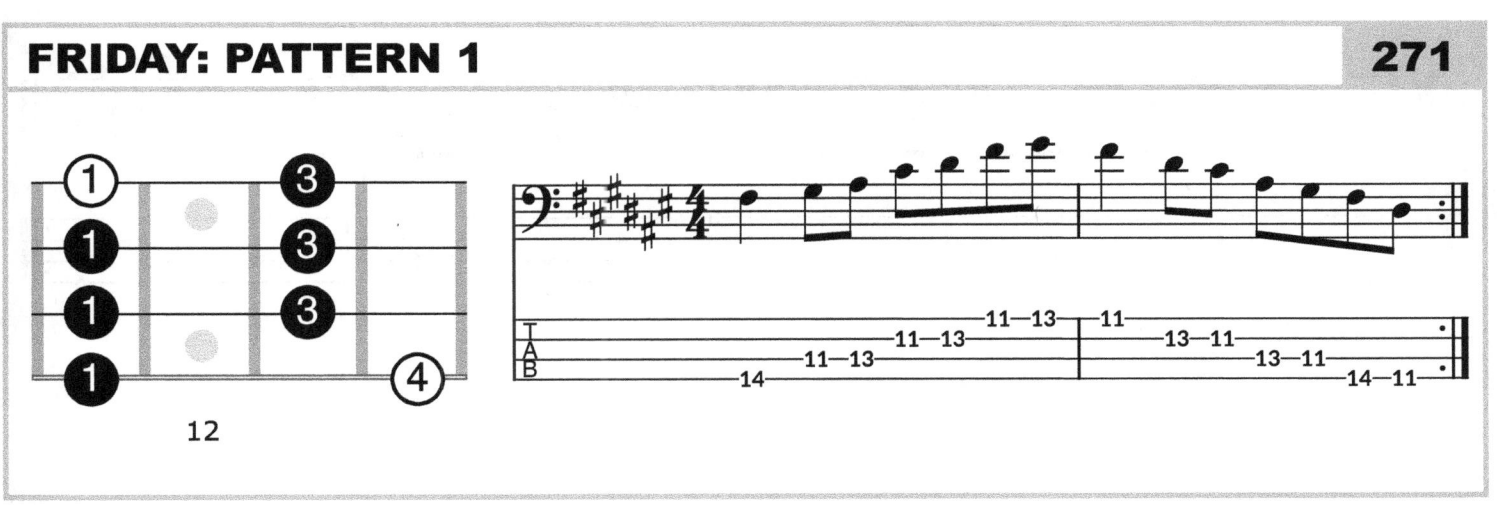

SATURDAY: HORIZONTAL PATTERN 272

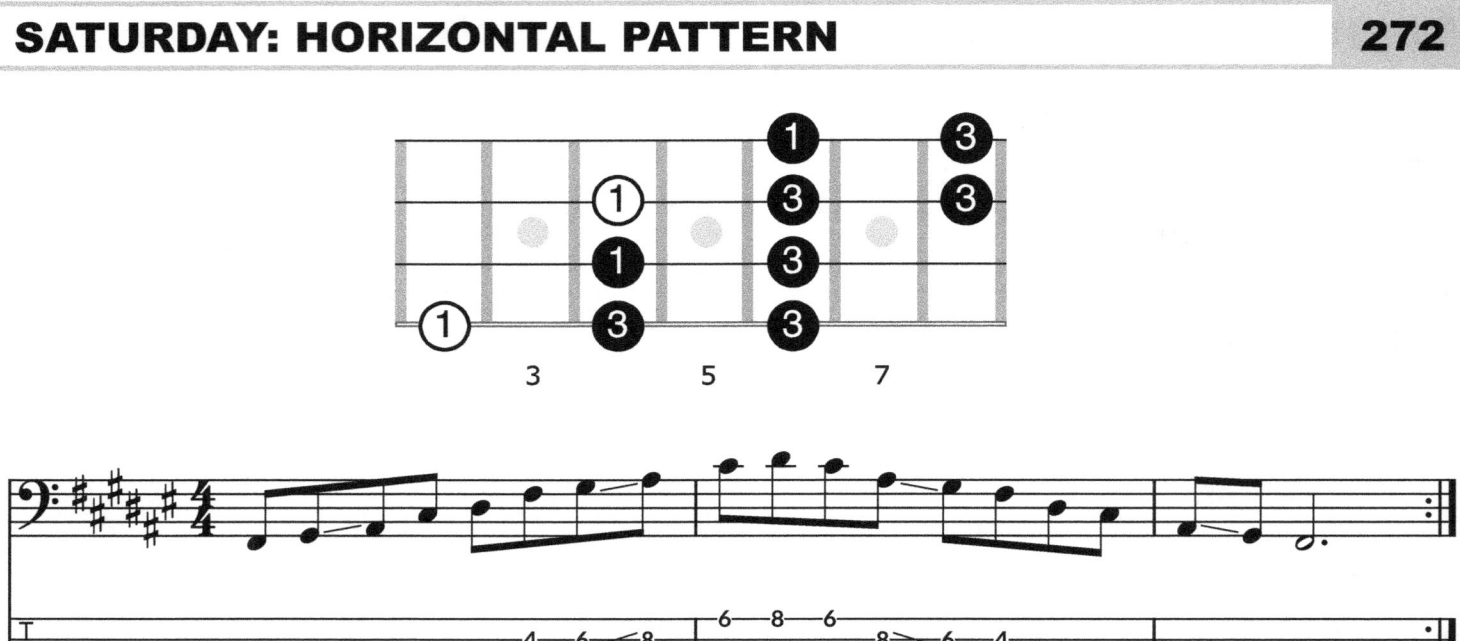

SUNDAY: SCALE APPLICATION 273

Rhythmic displacement is a musical technique whereby a musical element, such as the three-note figure starting on the "and" of beat 1 in our next example, is moved slightly earlier or later in the music. This creates an interesting tension-and-release pattern that resolves every two measures. This riff changes the last three notes of our two-measure phrase to create a question-and-answer effect.

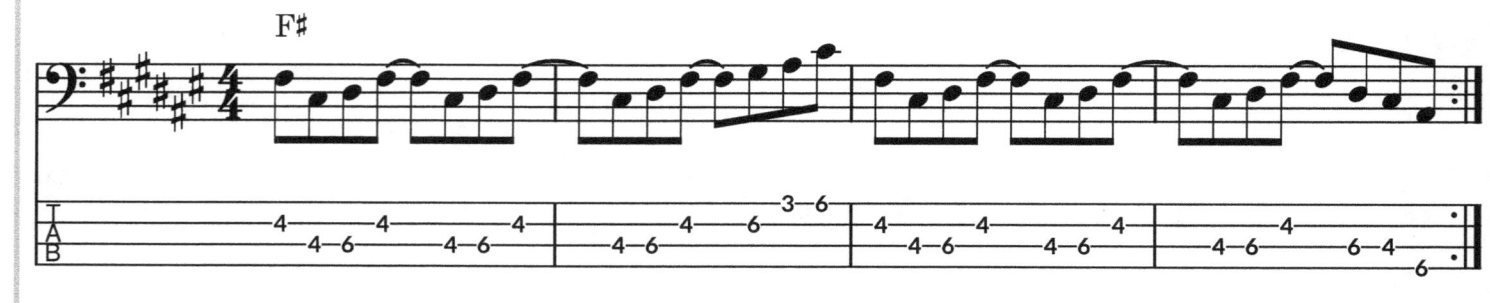

WEEK 40: F# MINOR PENTATONIC

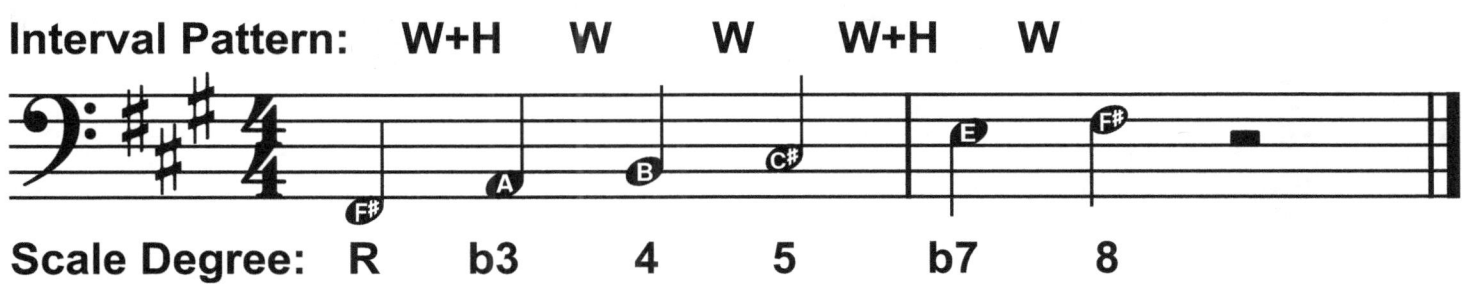

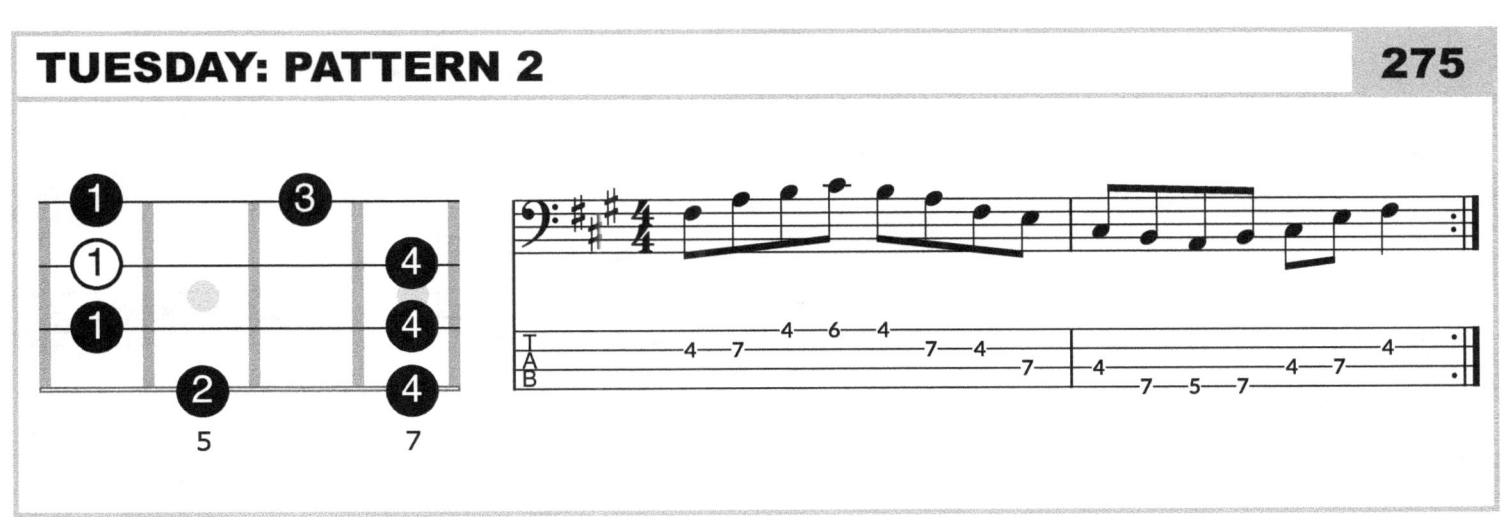

WEDNESDAY: PATTERN 3

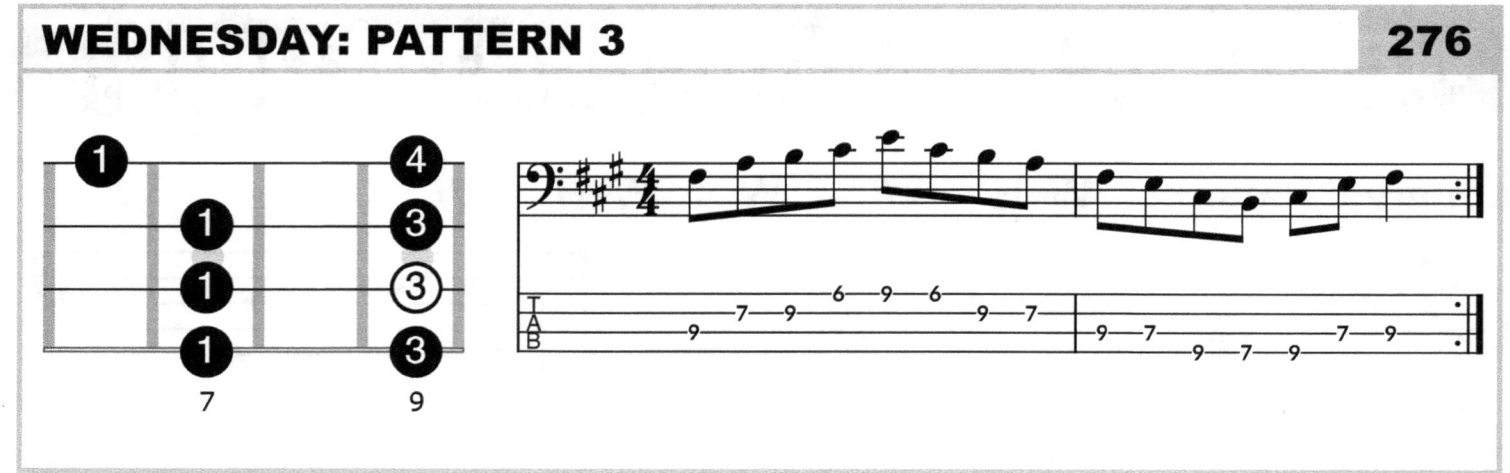

THURSDAY: PATTERN 4

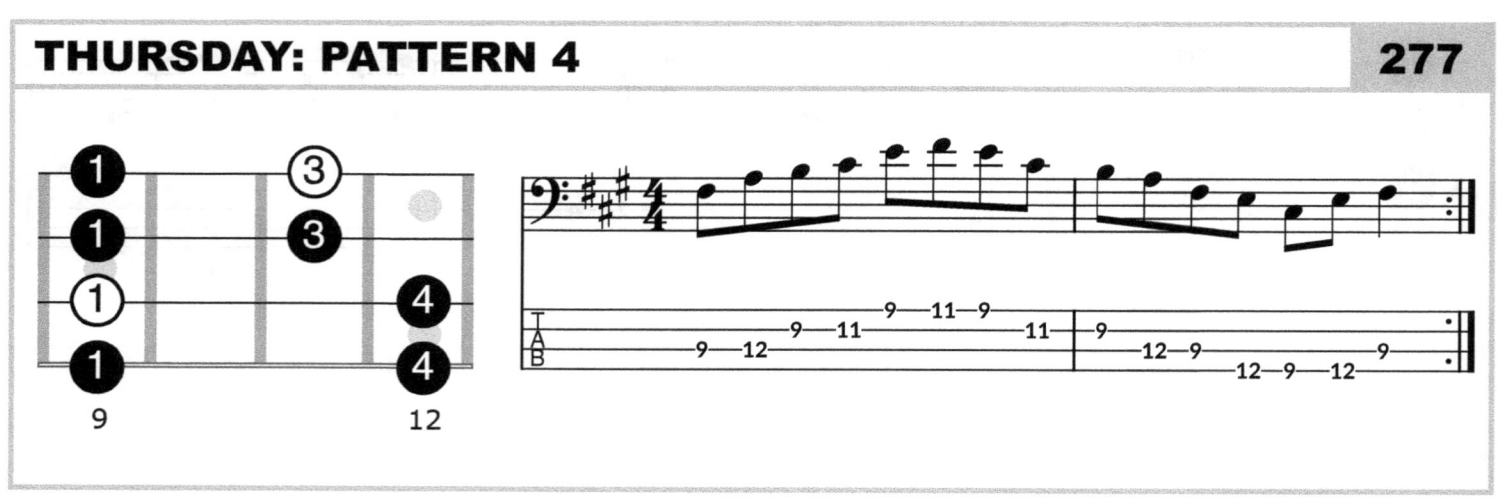

FRIDAY: PATTERN 5

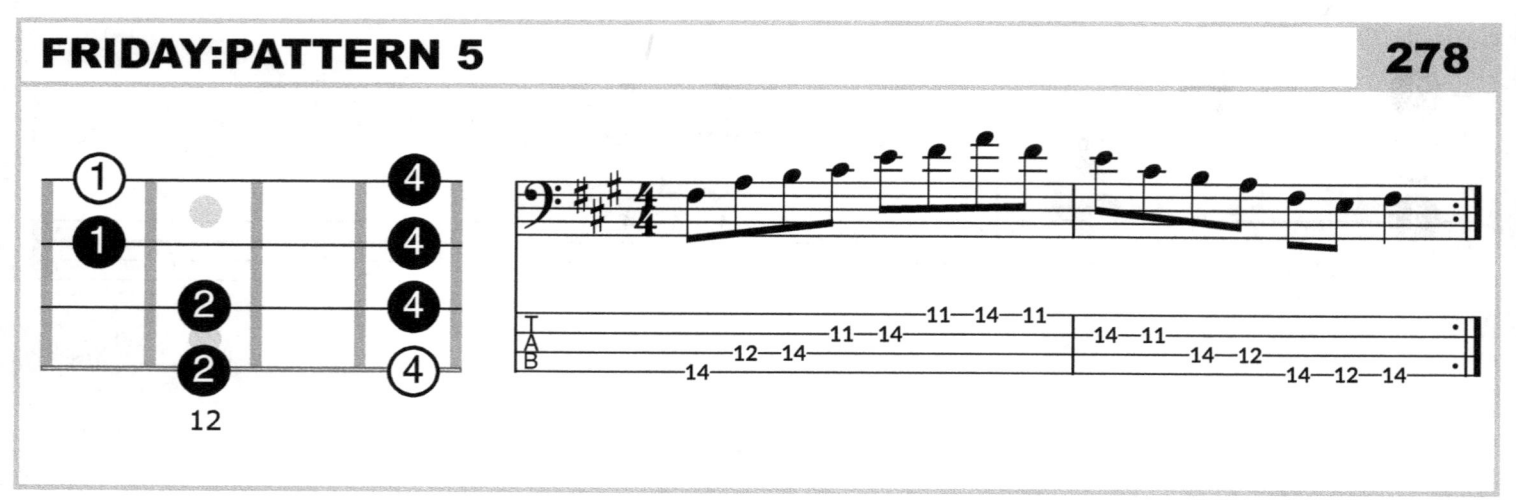

SATURDAY: OPEN-STRING HORIZONTAL PATTERN 279

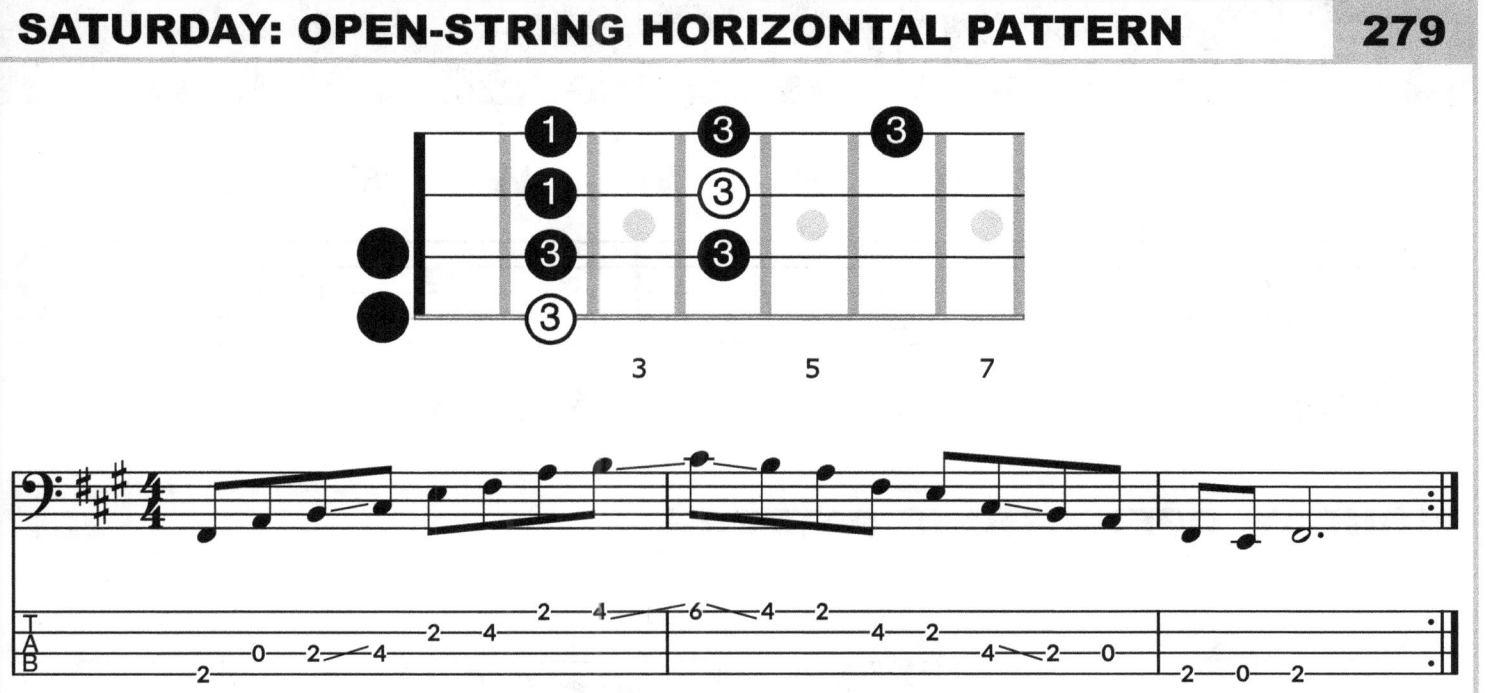

SUNDAY: SCALE APPLICATION 280

Our next riff introduces a very useful bass technique that combines the octave, 5th, and root in descending fashion. Fret the 1st-string note with the pad of your 3rd finger with your first knuckle collapsed. Roll up to the tip as you move to the 2nd string on the same fret. Try "dragging" a finger of your picking hand across strings 1, 2, and 3 as you descend octave–5th–root.

WEEK 41: G MAJOR

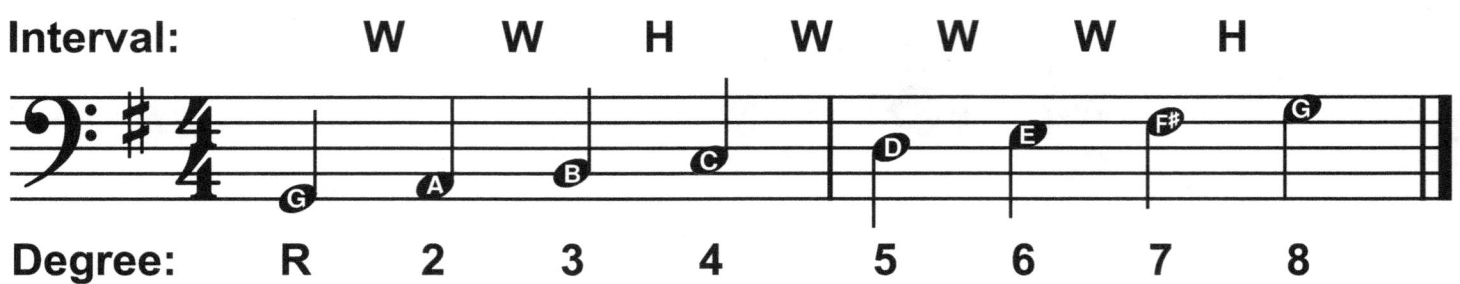

MONDAY: OPEN-STRING PATTERN   281

TUESDAY: PATTERN 2   282

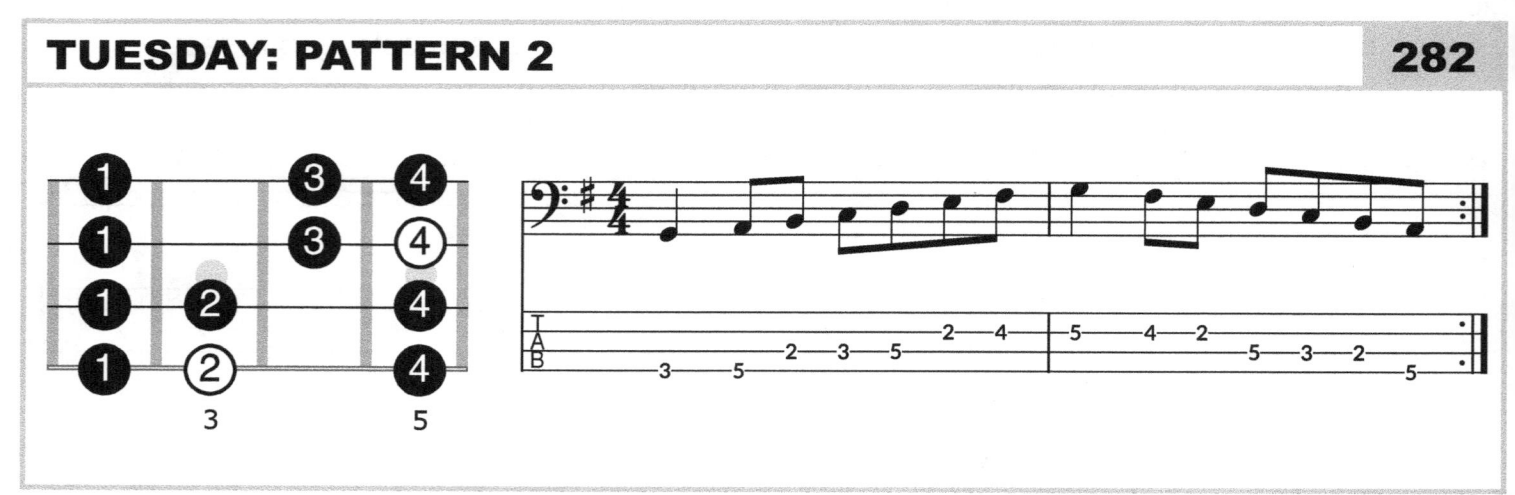

WEDNESDAY: PATTERN 3

283

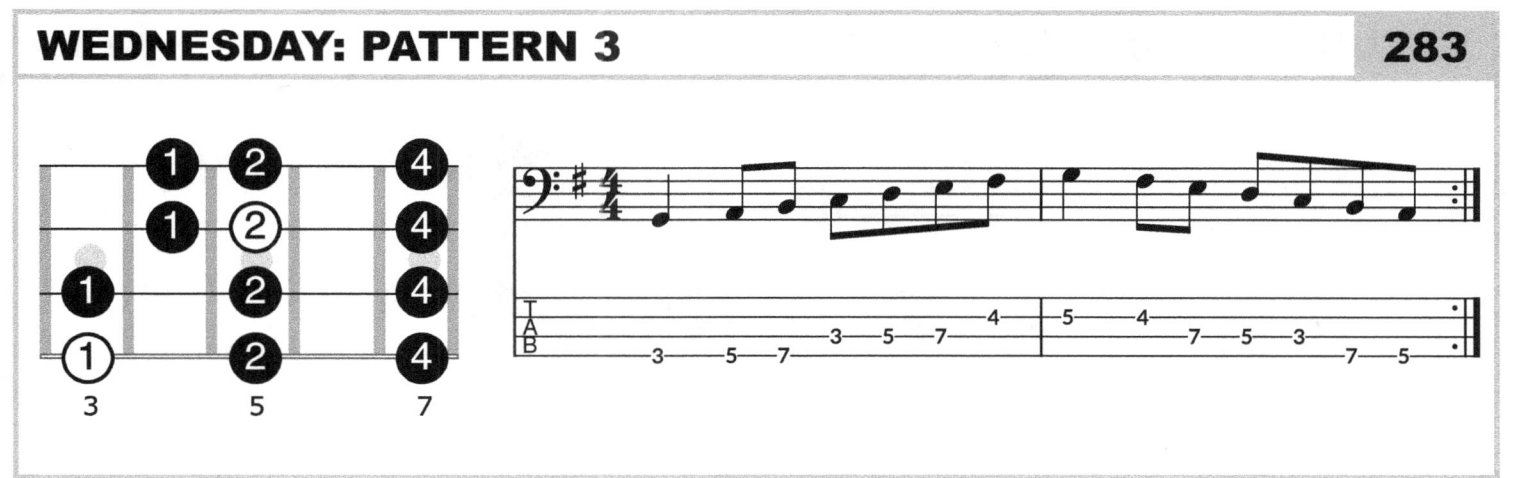

THURSDAY: PATTERN 4

284

FRIDAY: PATTERN 5

285

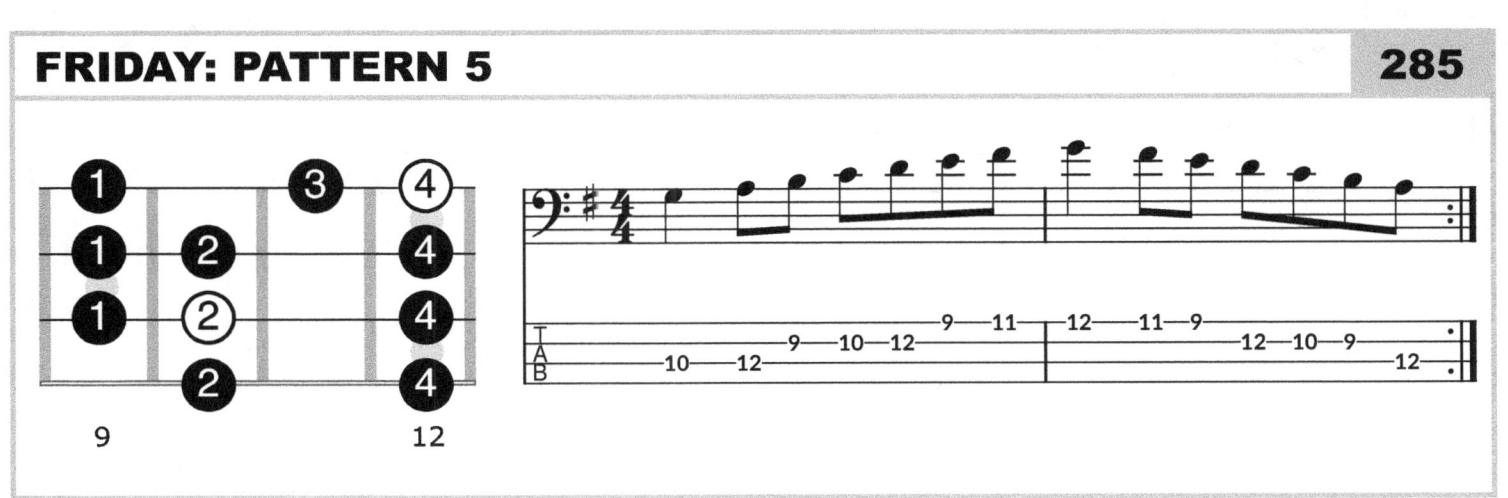

SATURDAY: HORIZONTAL PATTERN 286

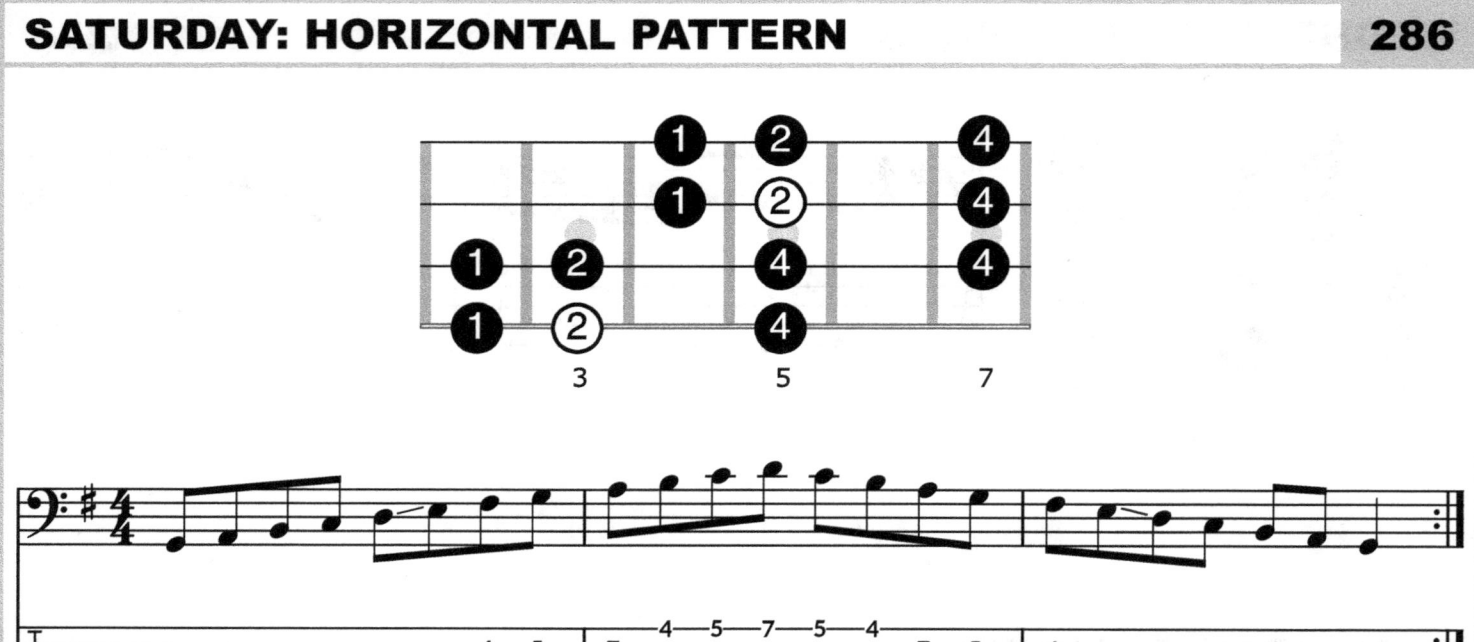

SUNDAY: SCALE APPLICATION 287

Horizontal patterns offer an opportunity to move a bass line through different octaves while maintaining the same fingering. In the first two measures, use your middle finger for the last note of each measure—a logical choice that makes fingering the next part easier.

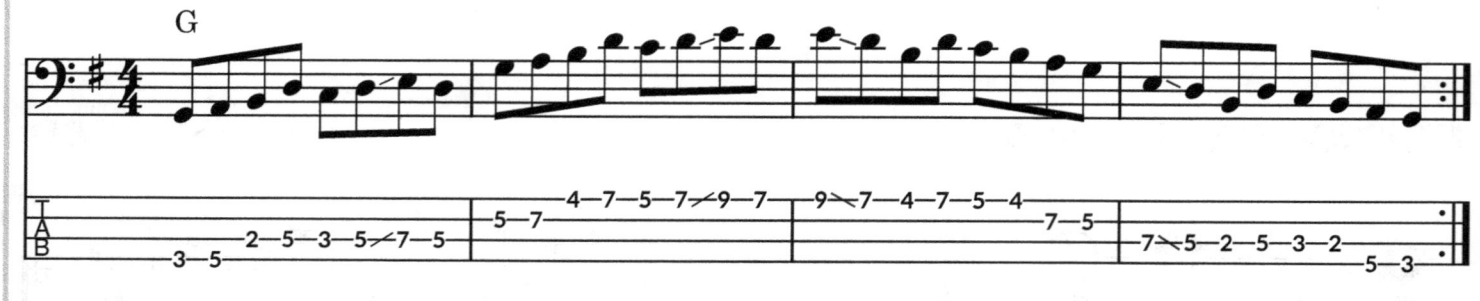

WEEK 42: G MINOR

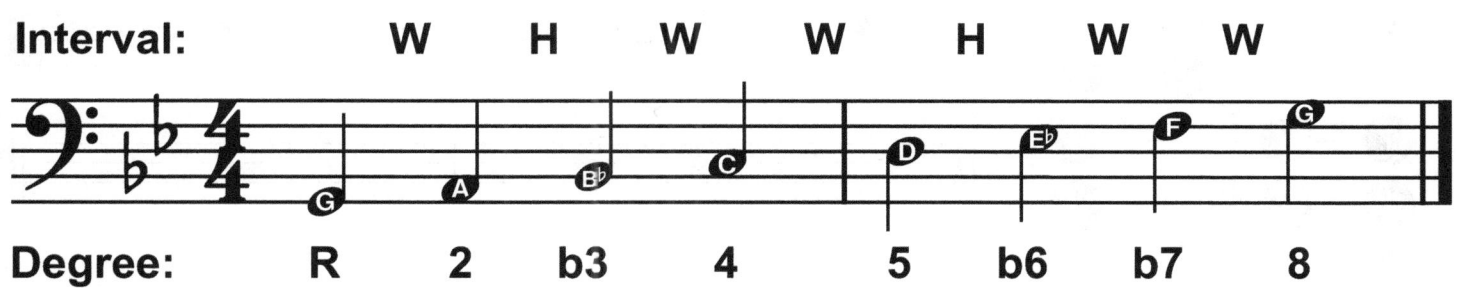

MONDAY: OPEN-STRING PATTERN 5 — 288

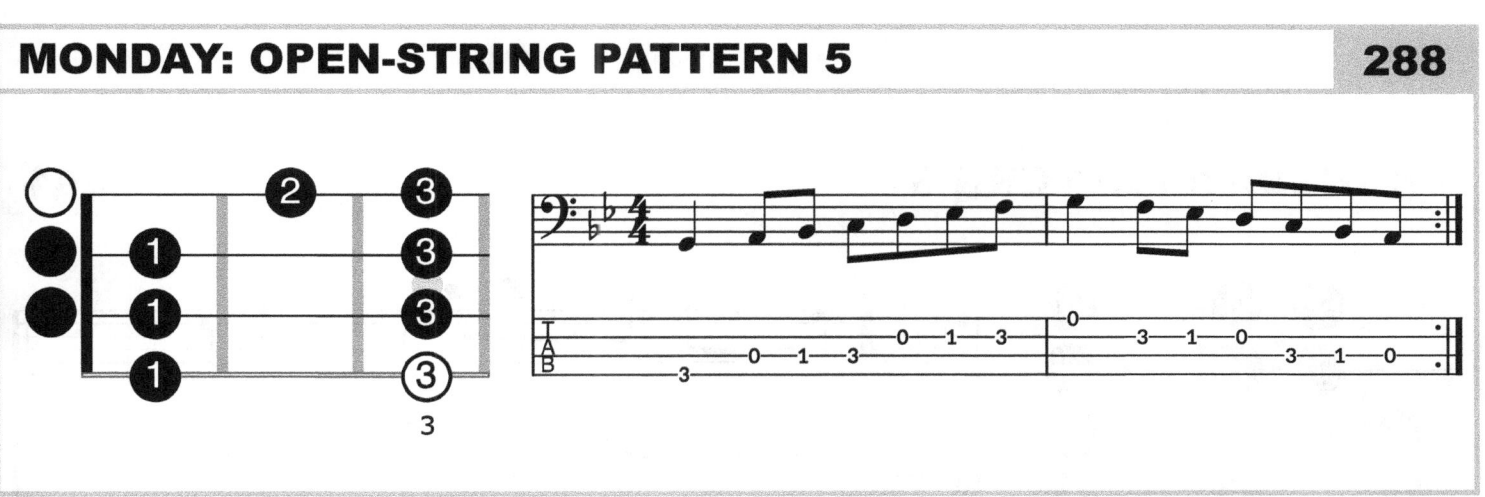

TUESDAY: PATTERN 1 — 289

WEDNESDAY: PATTERN 2
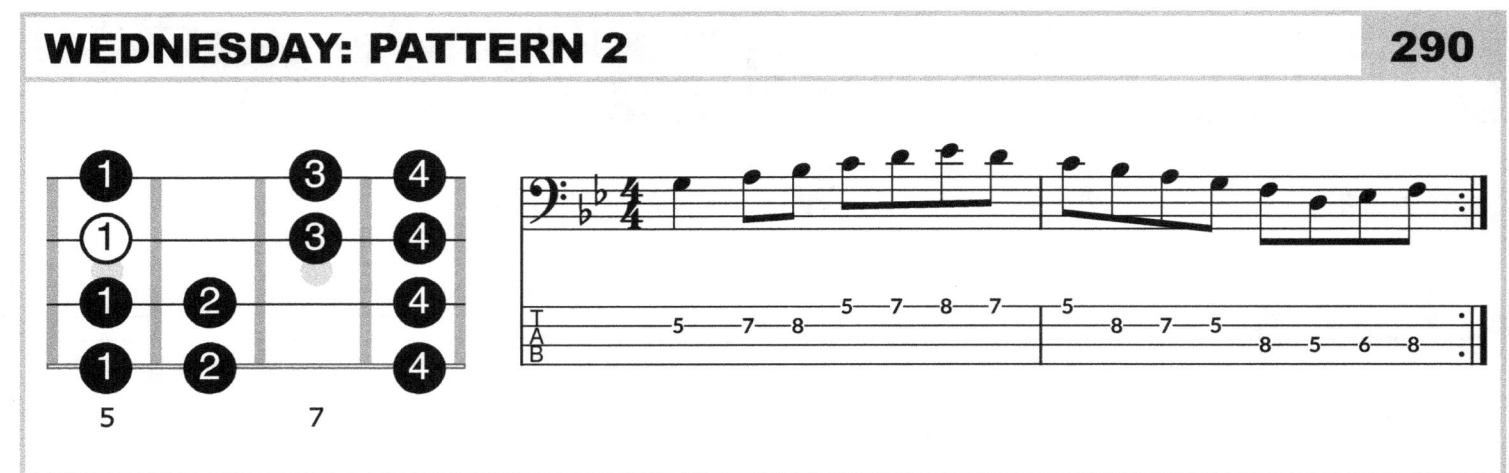

THURSDAY: PATTERN 3
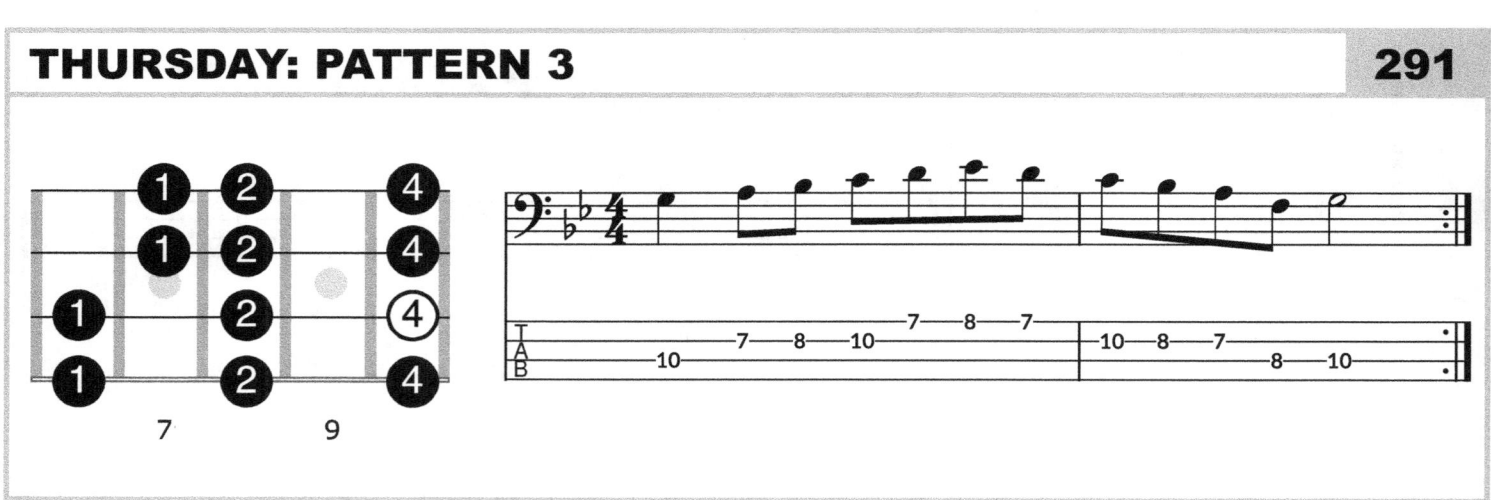

FRIDAY: PATTERN 4
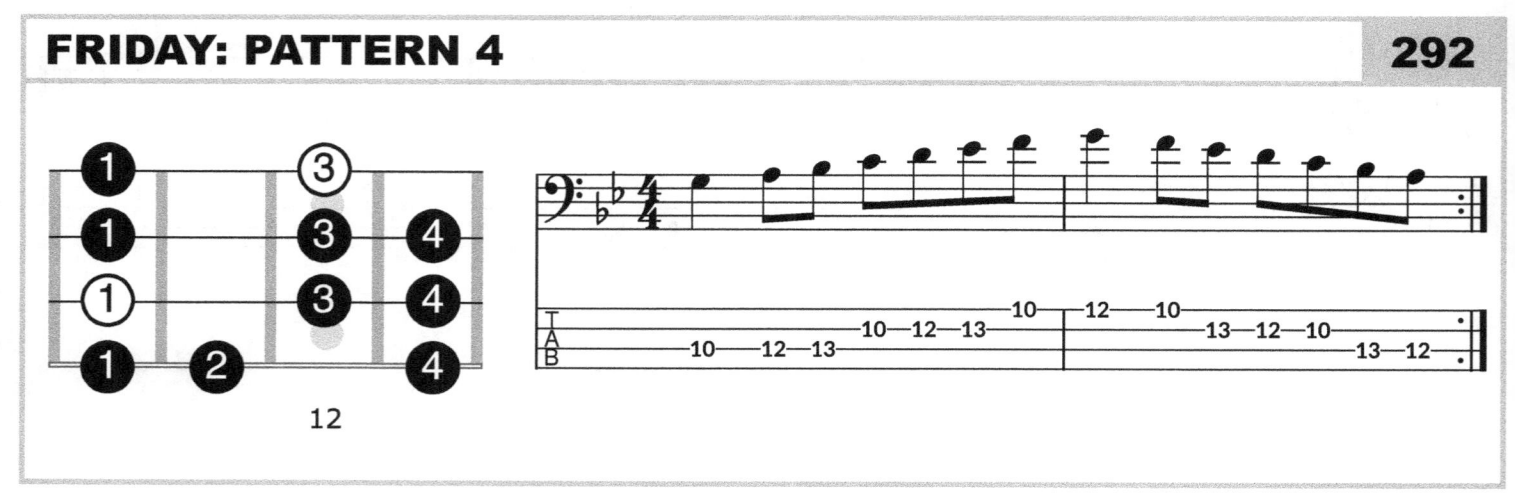

SATURDAY: HORIZONTAL PATTERN 293

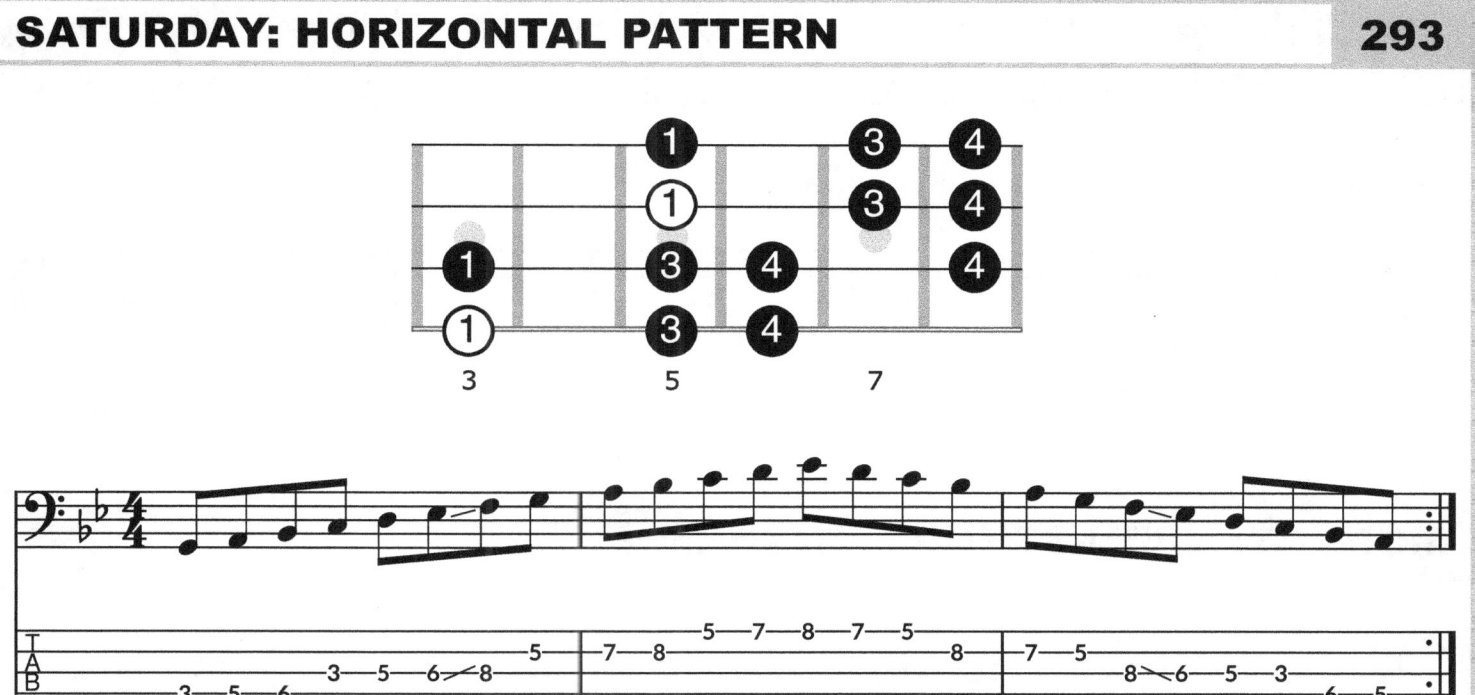

SUNDAY: SCALE APPLICATION 294

Let's continue exploring ways to connect the chord changes while using ideas we've learned along the way. While using Pattern 5, we'll incorporate stepwise motion, 5ths below the root, the 8–5–root descending phrase, and the stepwise up 3, down a 3rd pattern to bring us back to the beginning.

WEEK 43: G MAJOR PENTATONIC

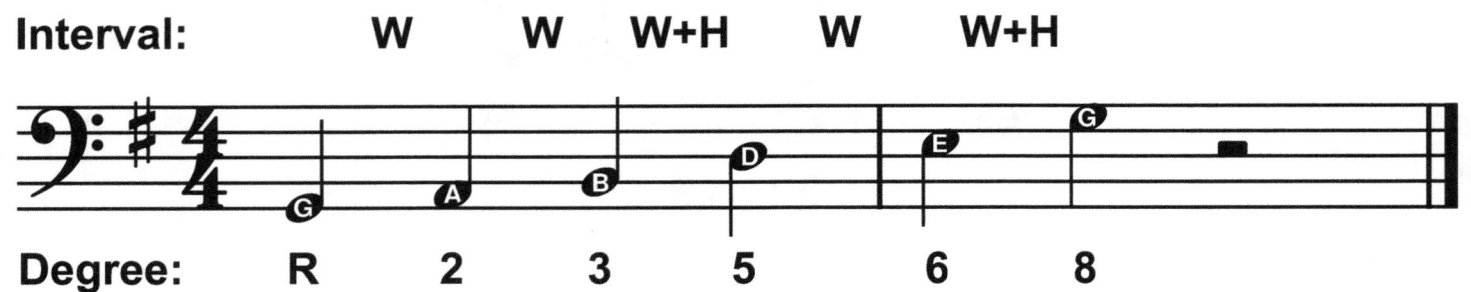

MONDAY: OPEN-STRING PATTERN 1 — 295

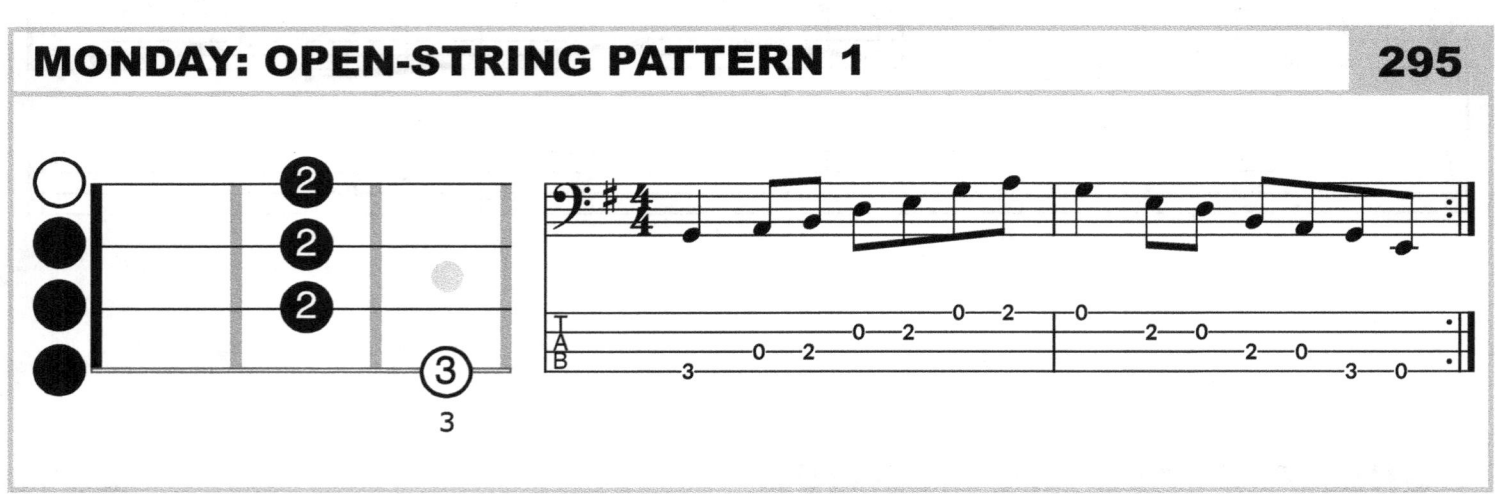

TUESDAY: PATTERN 2 — 296

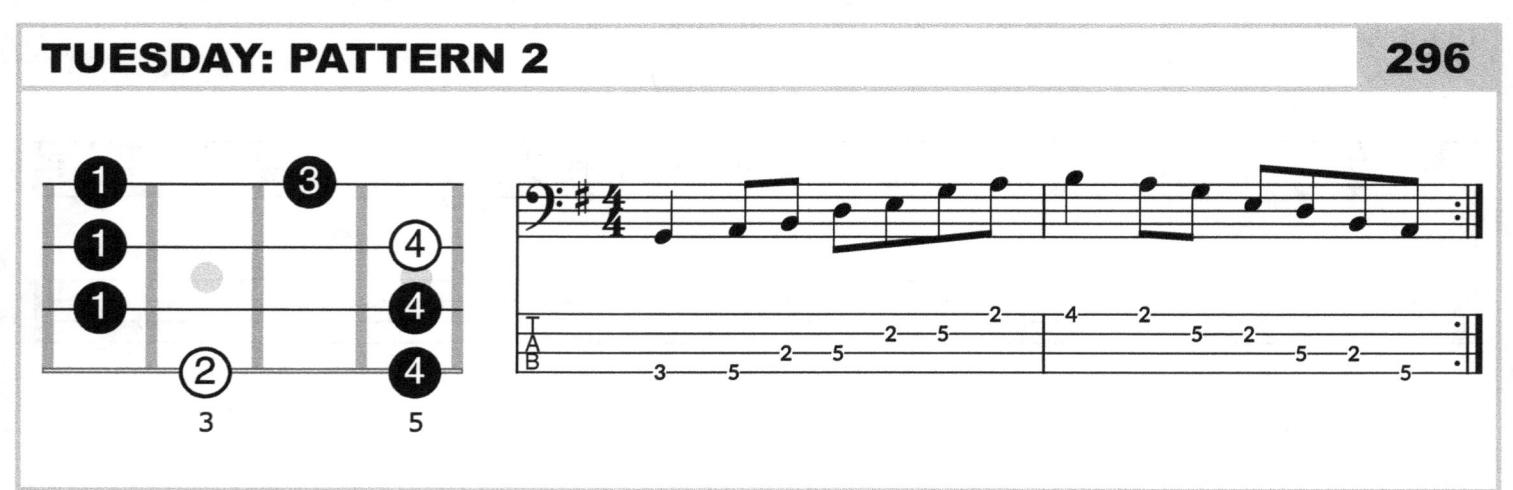

WEDNESDAY: PATTERN 3   297

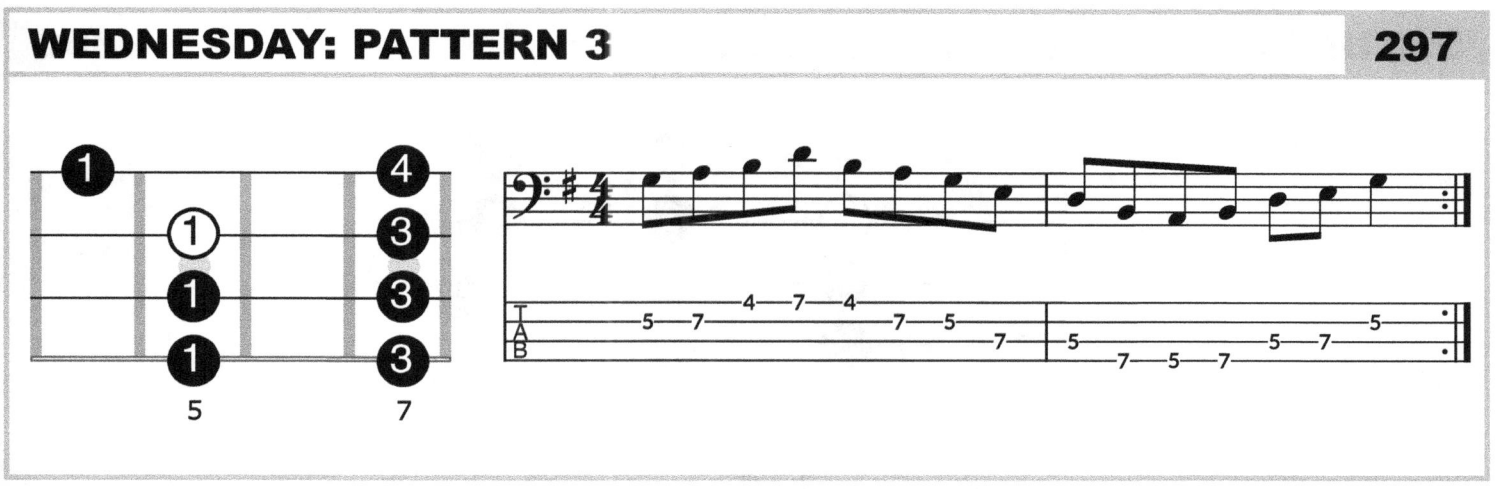

THURSDAY: PATTERN 4   298

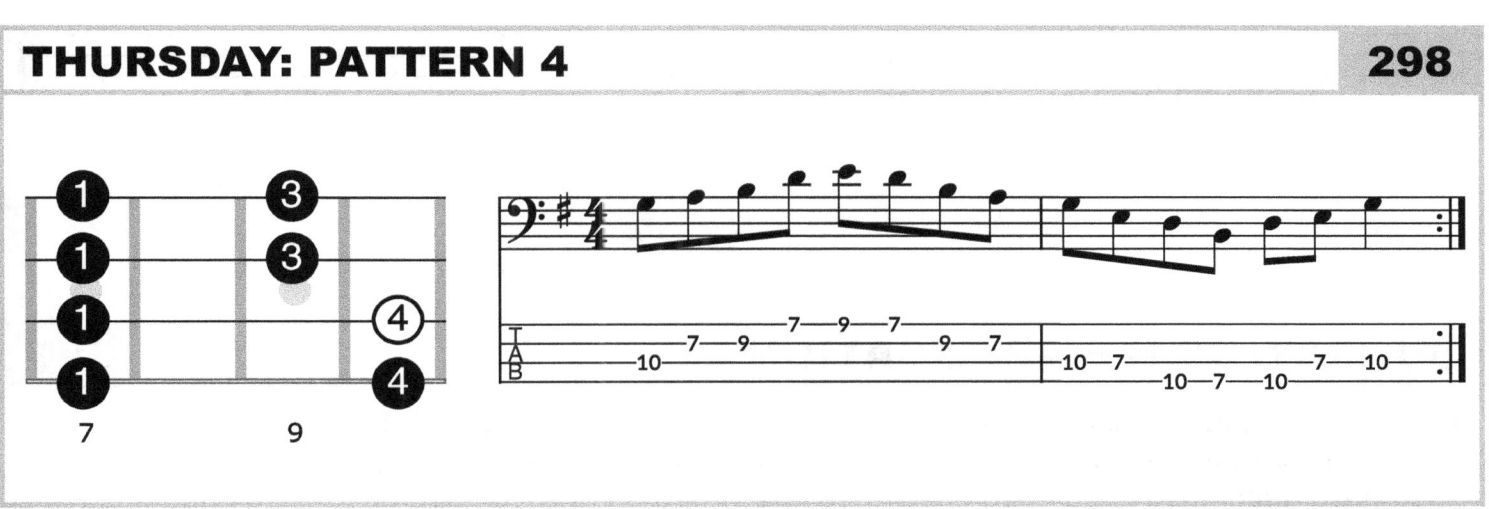

FRIDAY: PATTERN 5   299

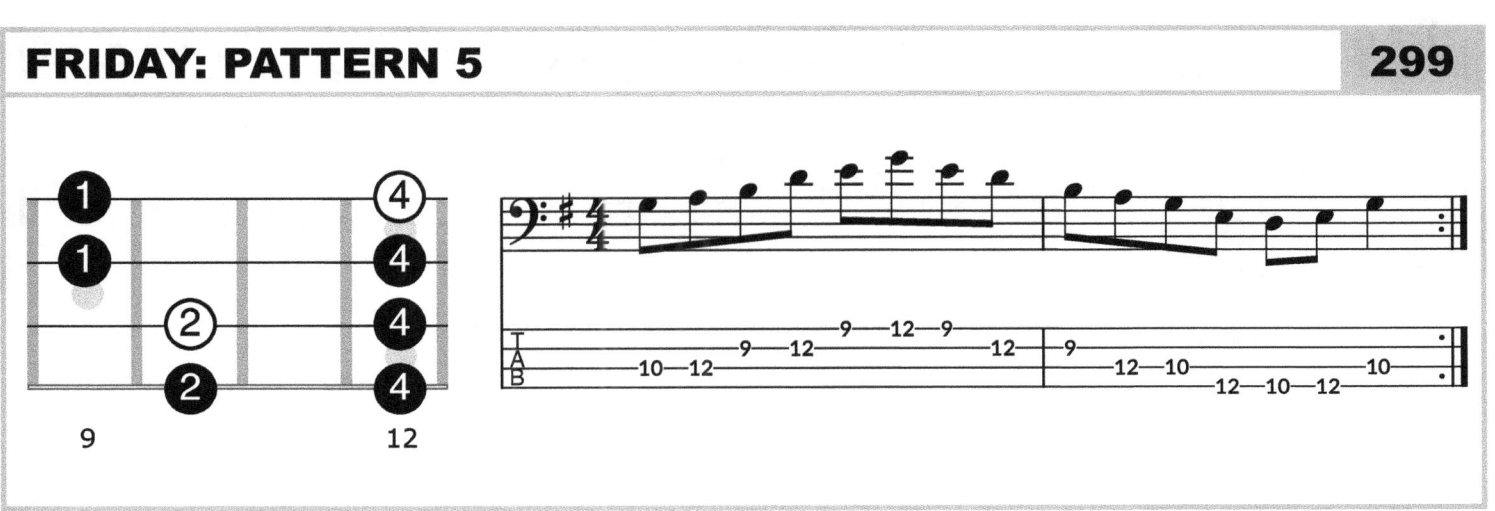

SATURDAY: HORIZONTAL PATTERN 300

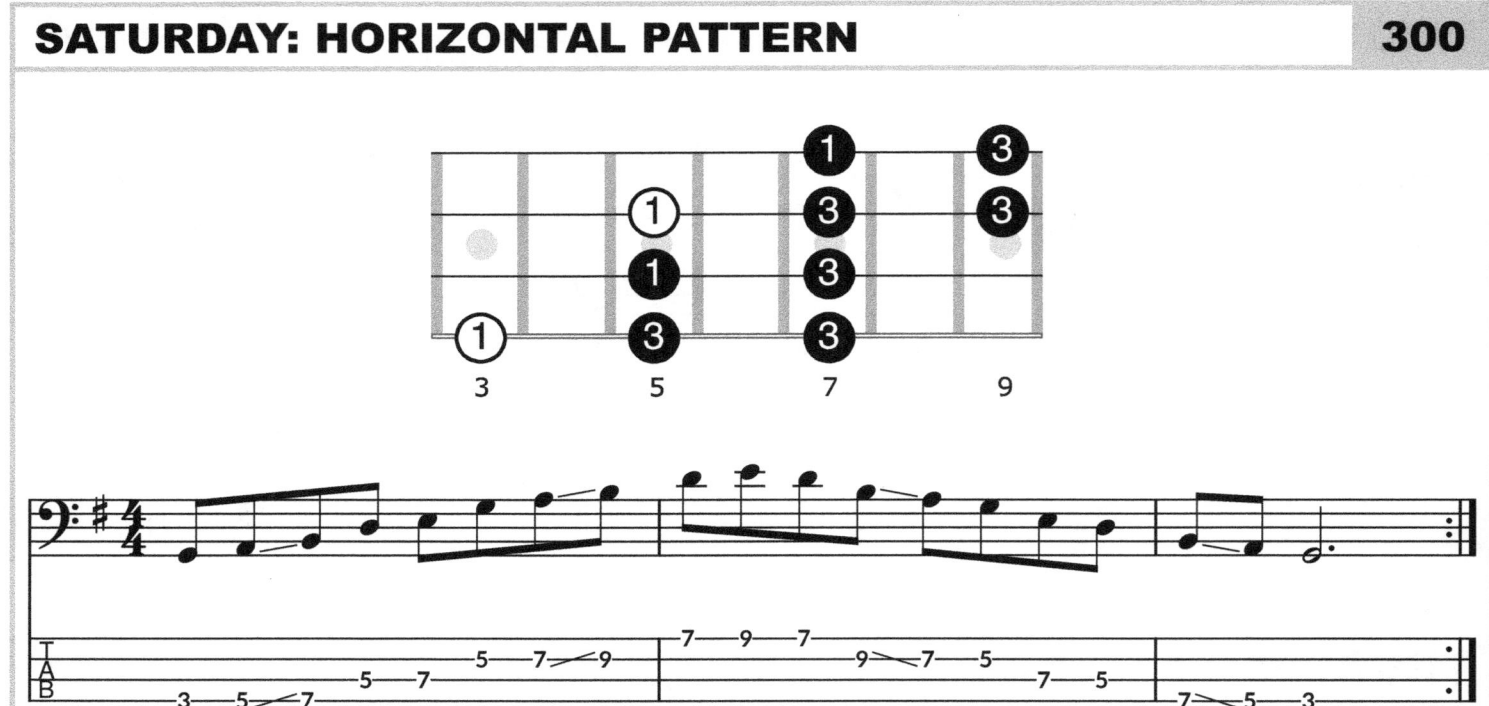

SUNDAY: SCALE APPLICATION 301

Here is a popular riff using notes from the major pentatonic scale. Our example will shift from the 1 (G) chord to the 4 (C) chord in the second measure. We will shift from Pattern 2 (G major) to Pattern 5 (C major) to accommodate. Notice how we keep the two-measure riff going across the chord change.

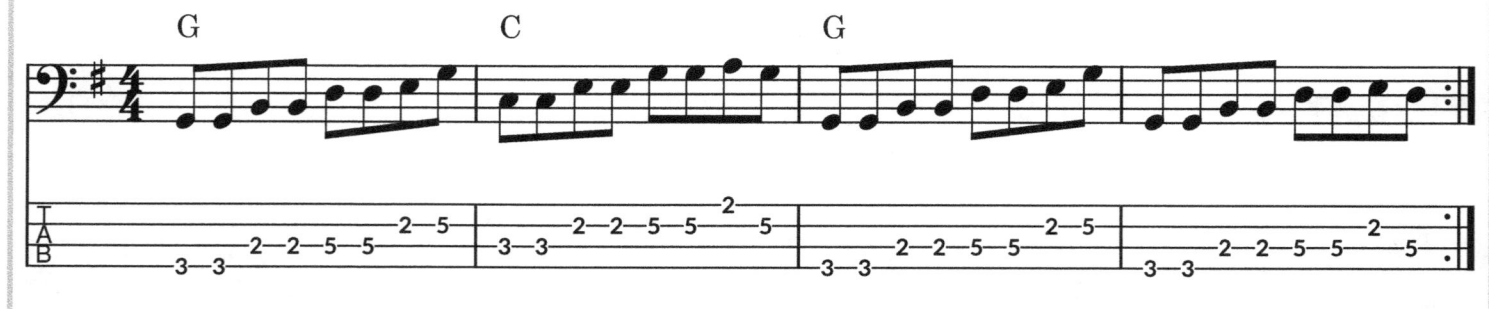

WEEK 44: G MINOR PENTATONIC

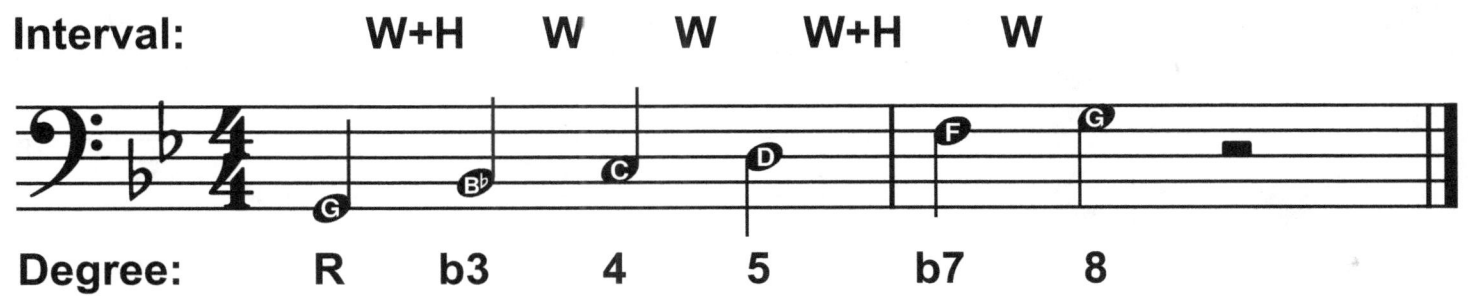

MONDAY: OPEN-STRING PATTERN 5 — 302

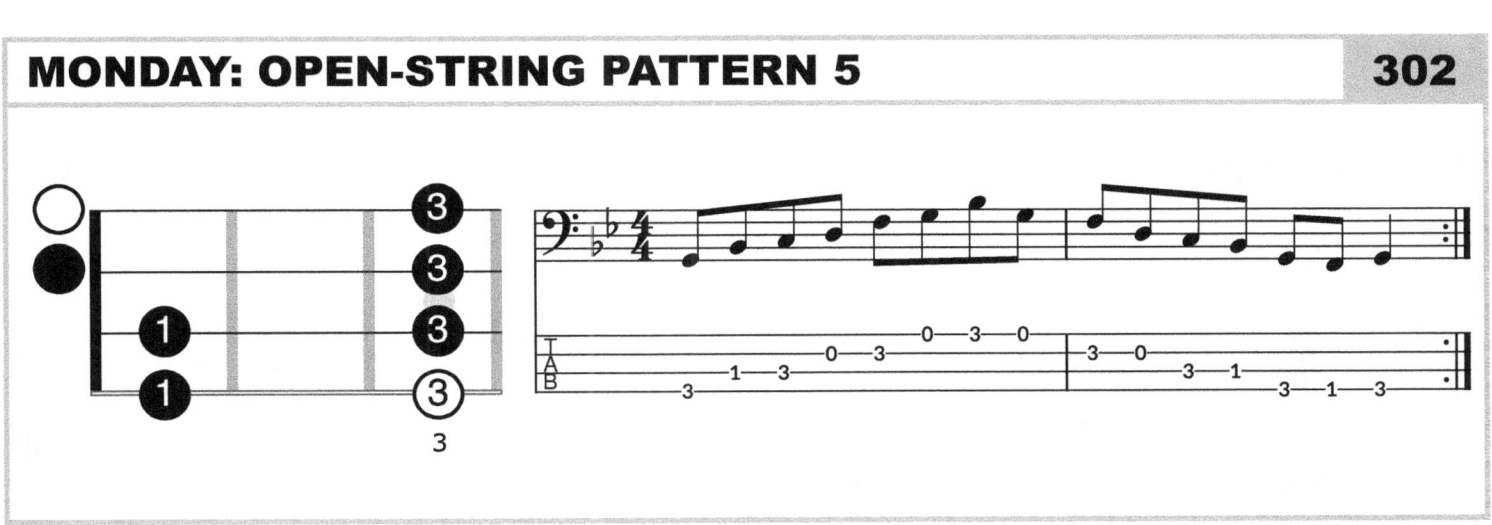

TUESDAY: PATTERN 1 — 303

WEDNESDAY: PATTERN 2

304

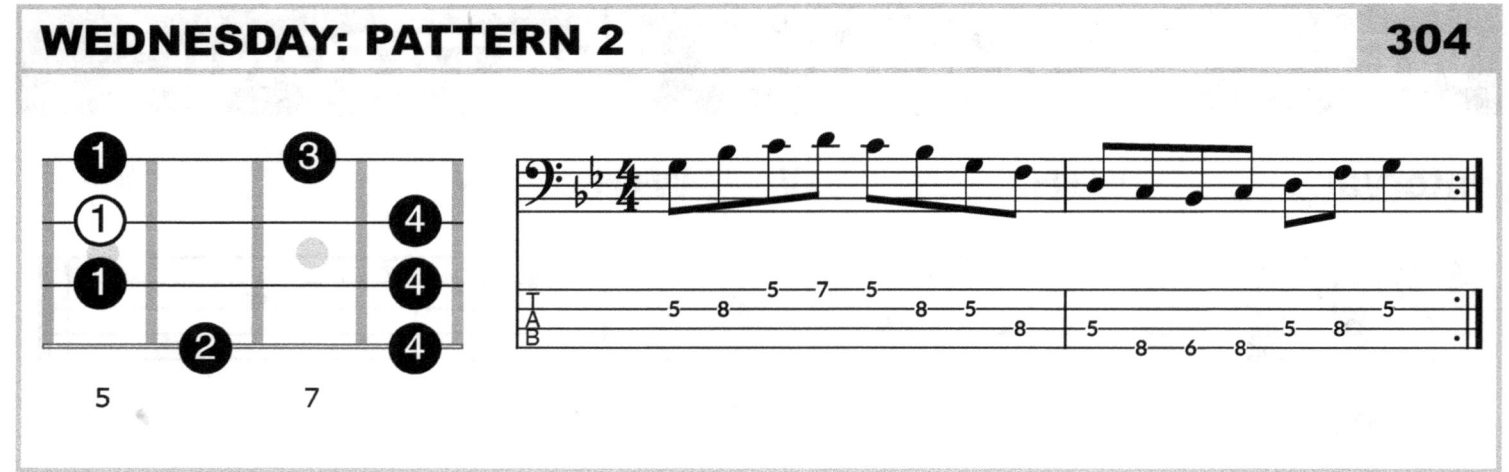

THURSDAY: PATTERN 3

305

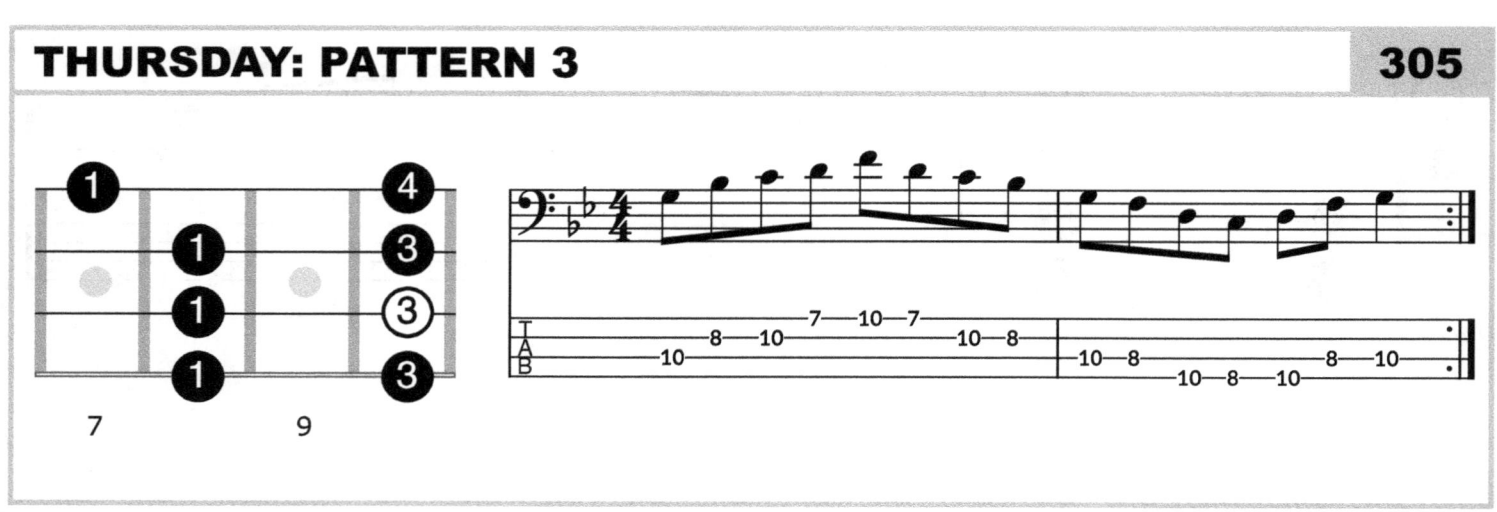

FRIDAY: PATTERN 4

306

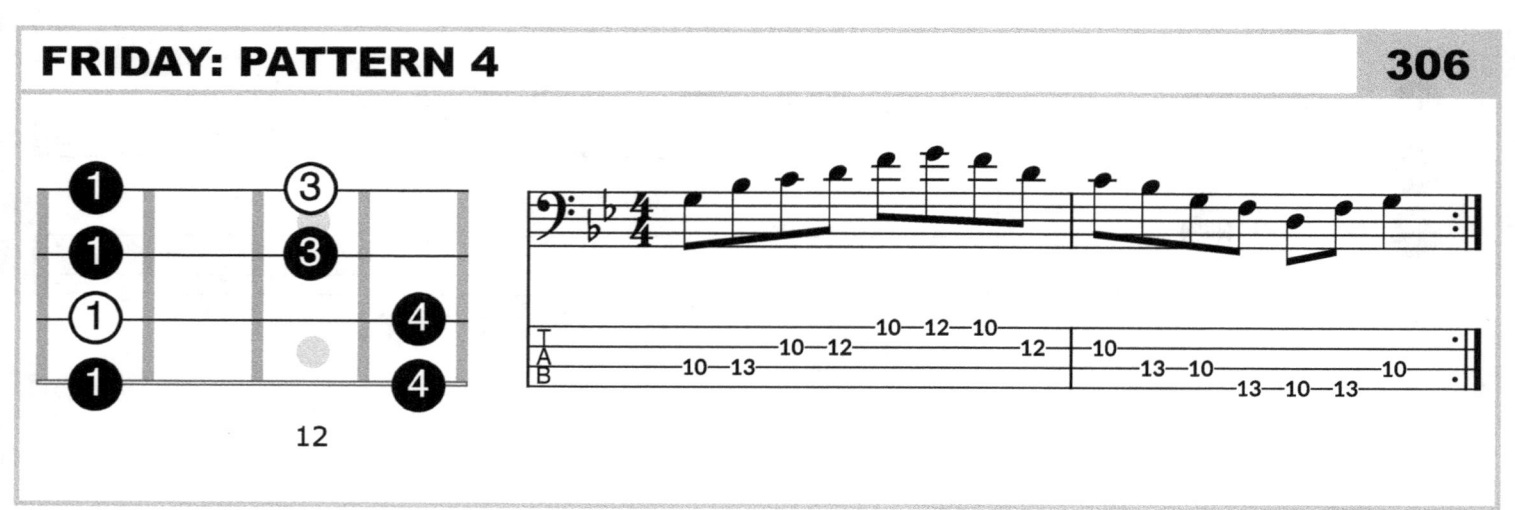

SATURDAY: HORIZONTAL PATTERN 307

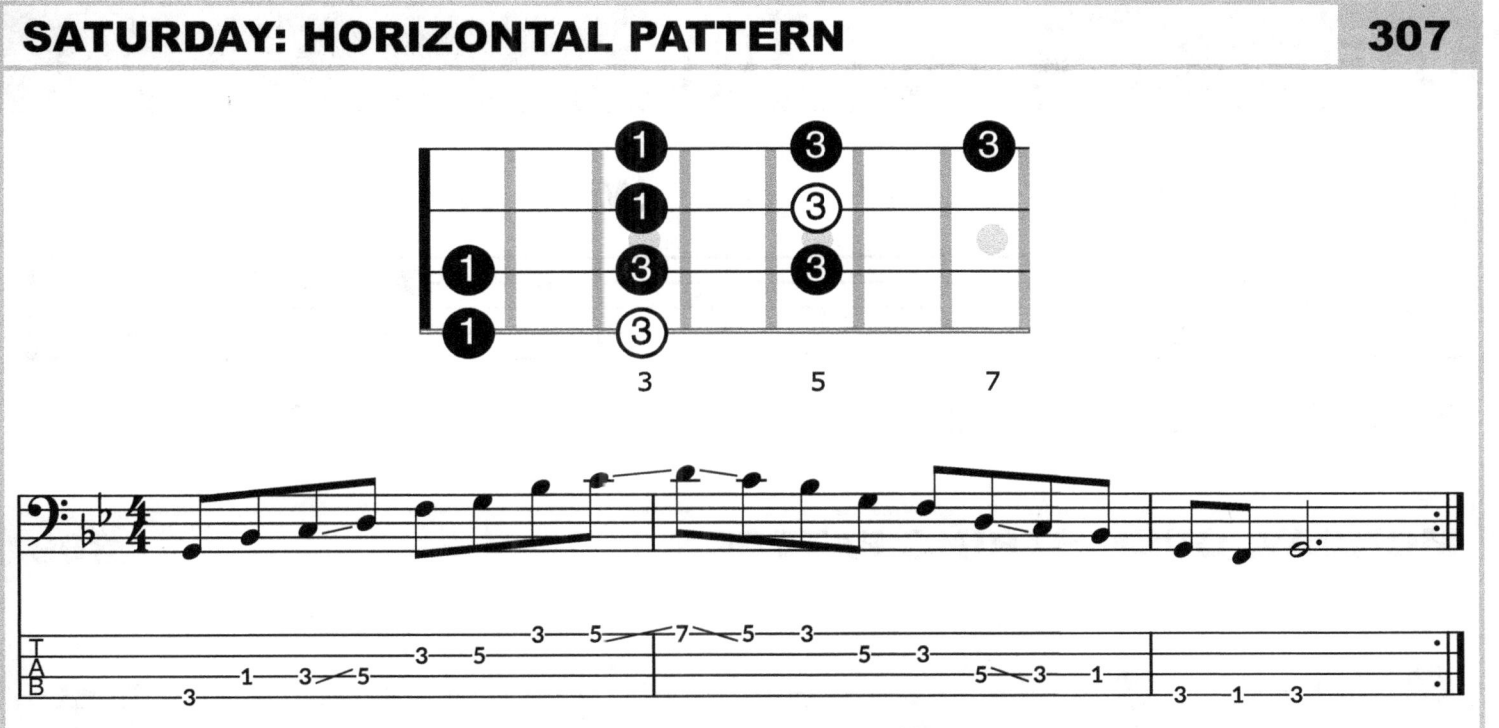

SUNDAY: SCALE APPLICATION 308

Changing direction in groups of 3 fits like a glove when using triplets, and triplets fit like a glove when playing blues. This phrase ascends through the full range of the Horizontal Pattern. Shift positions on your 3rd finger throughout.

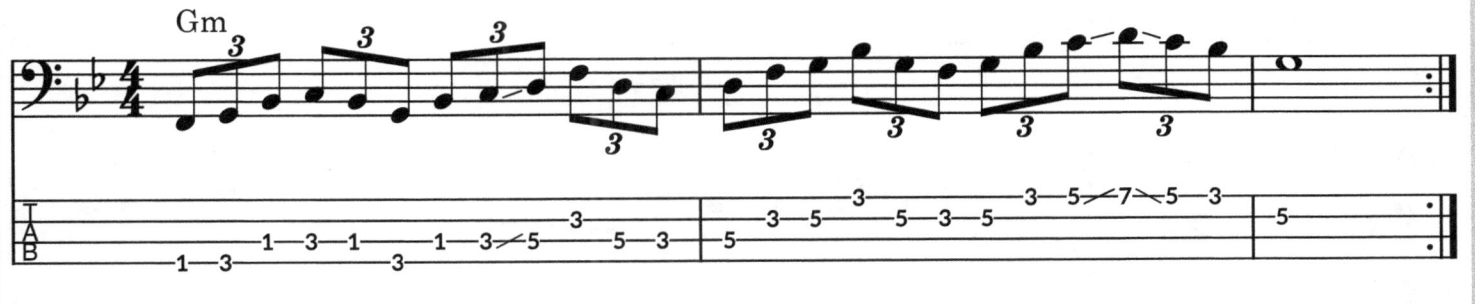

WEEK 45: A♭ MAJOR

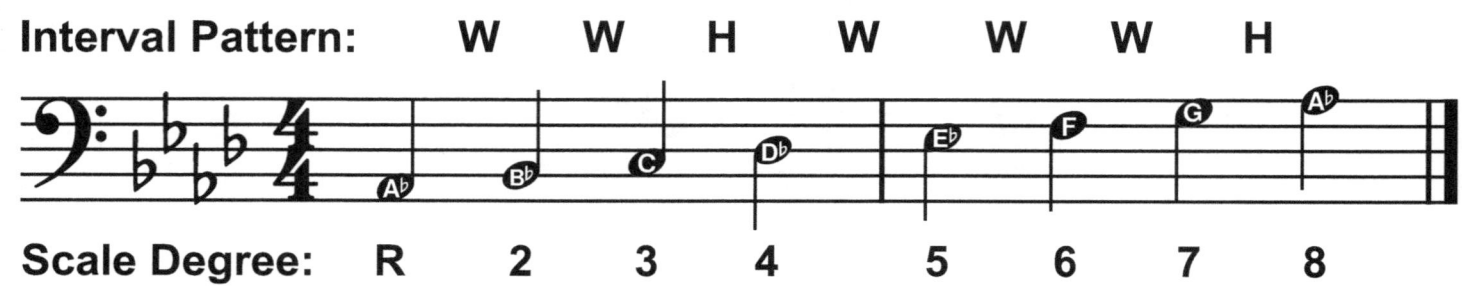

MONDAY: OPEN-STRING PATTERN 1 — 309

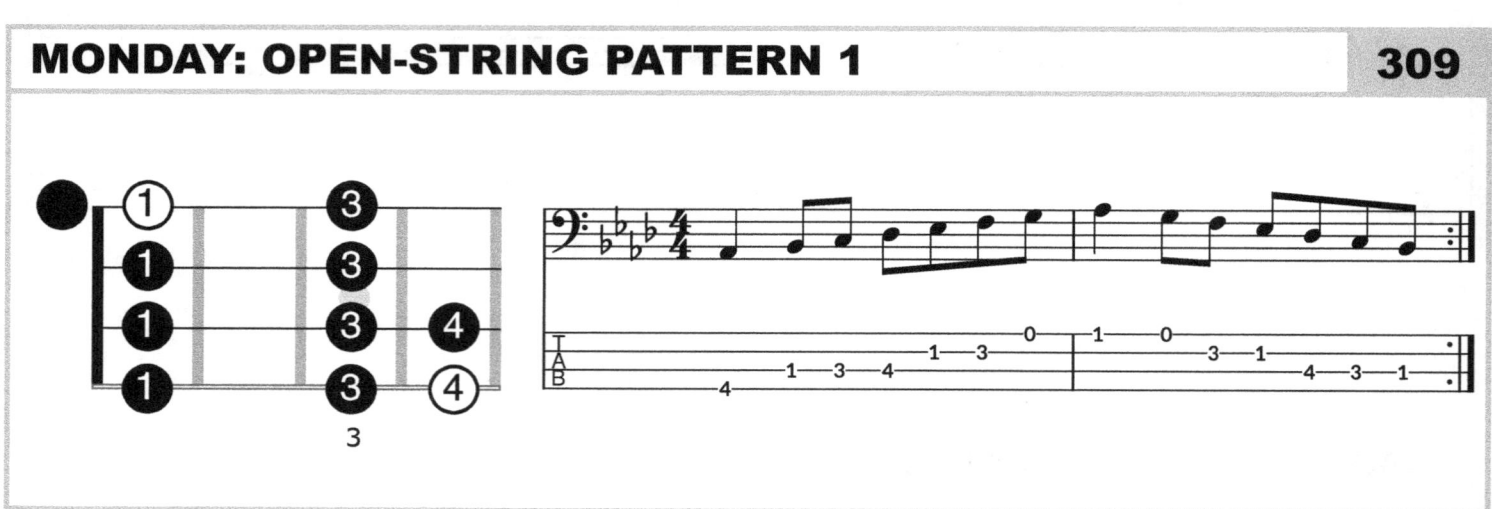

TUESDAY: PATTERN 2 — 310

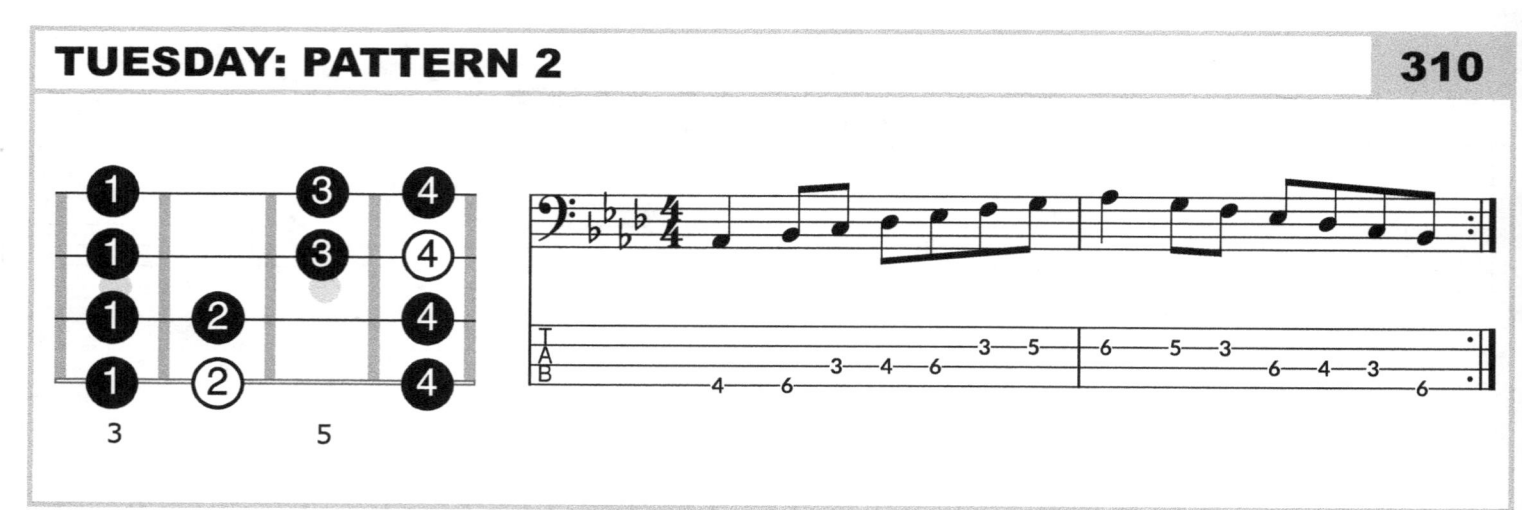

WEDNESDAY: PATTERN 3

311

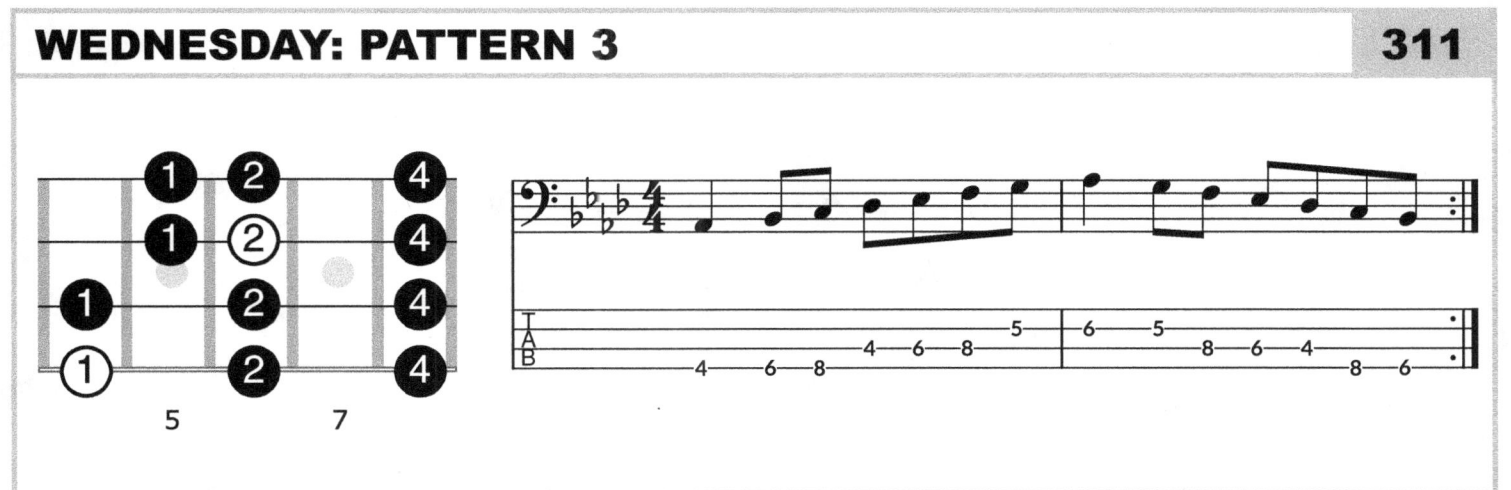

THURSDAY: PATTERN 4

312

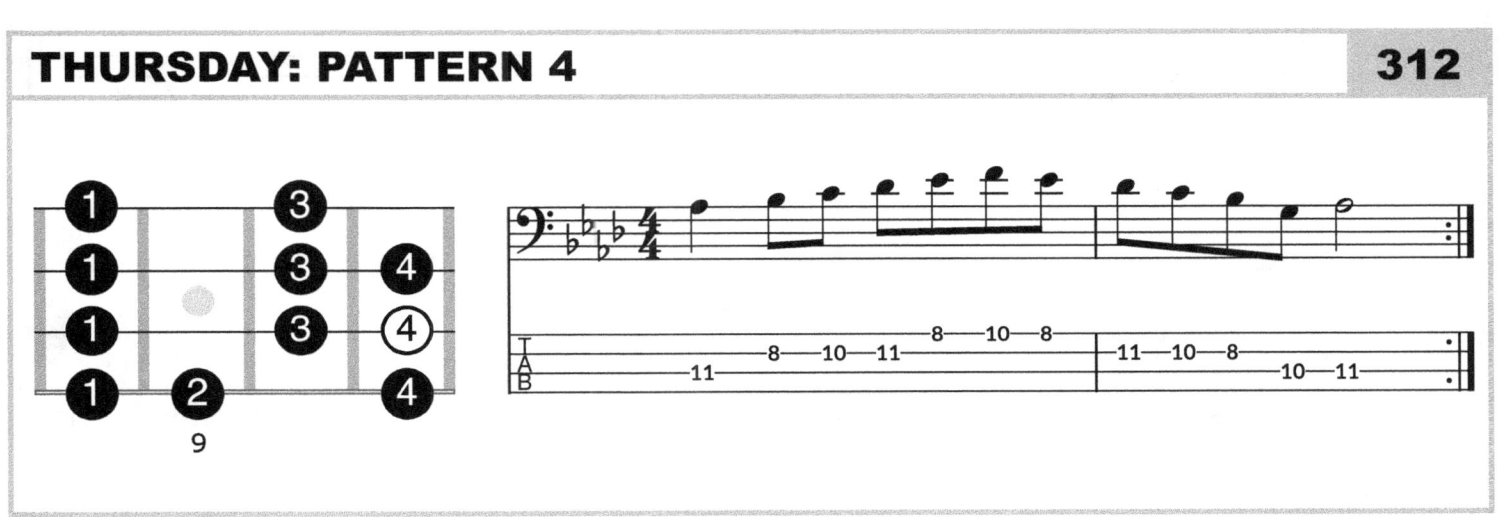

FRIDAY: PATTERN 5

313

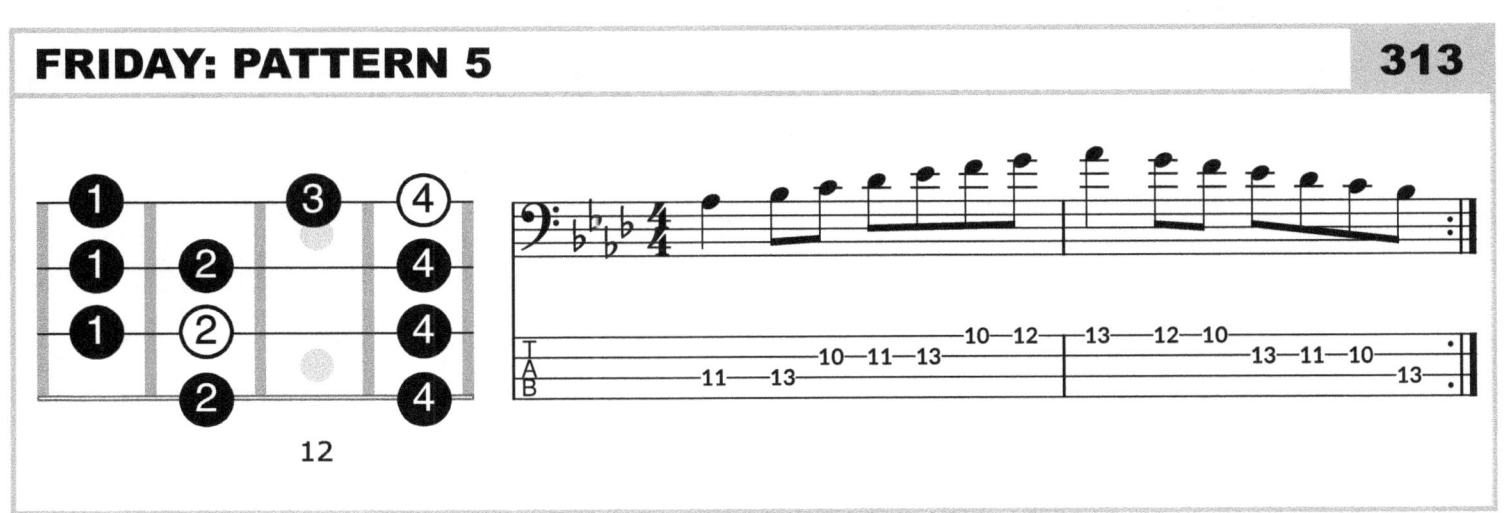

SATURDAY: HORIZONTAL PATTERN 314

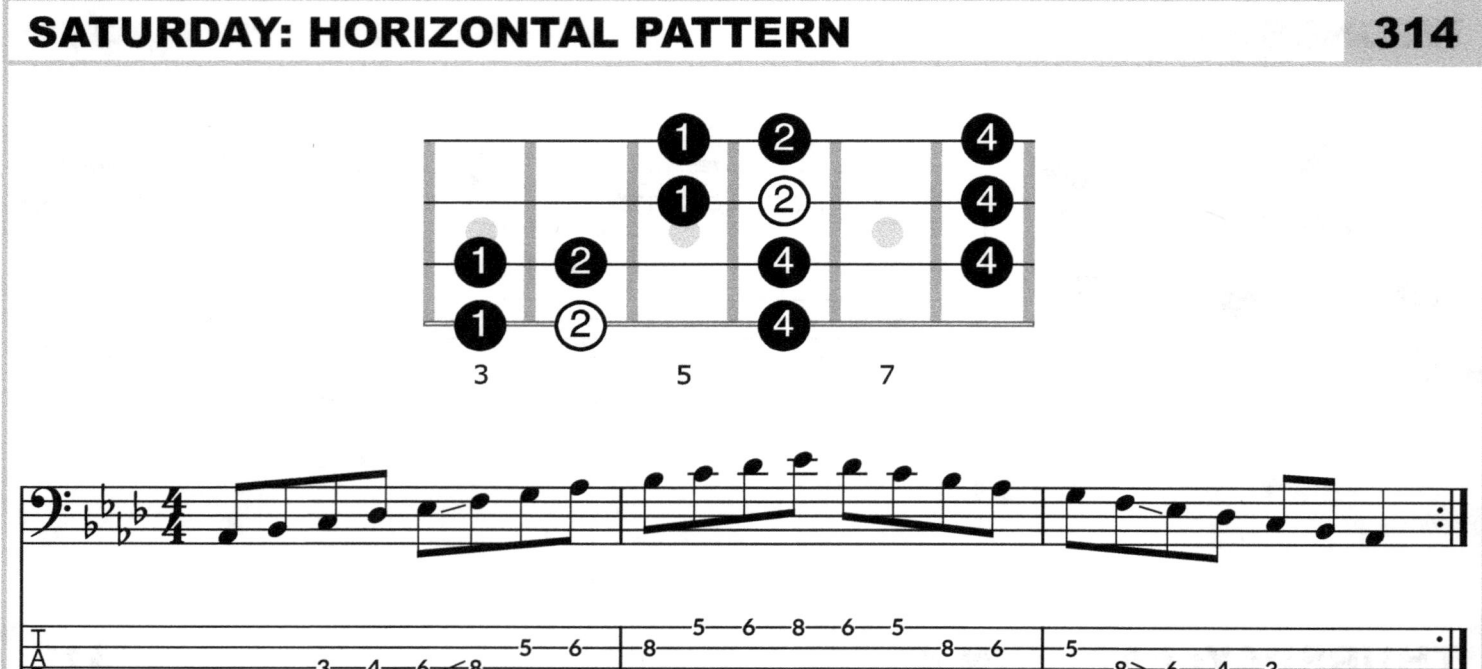

SUNDAY: SCALE APPLICATION 315

This bass line makes use of stepwise connecting phrases and root–5th–octave patterns. Staying within Pattern 2 dictates where we ascend root–5th–octave or descend root to 5th.

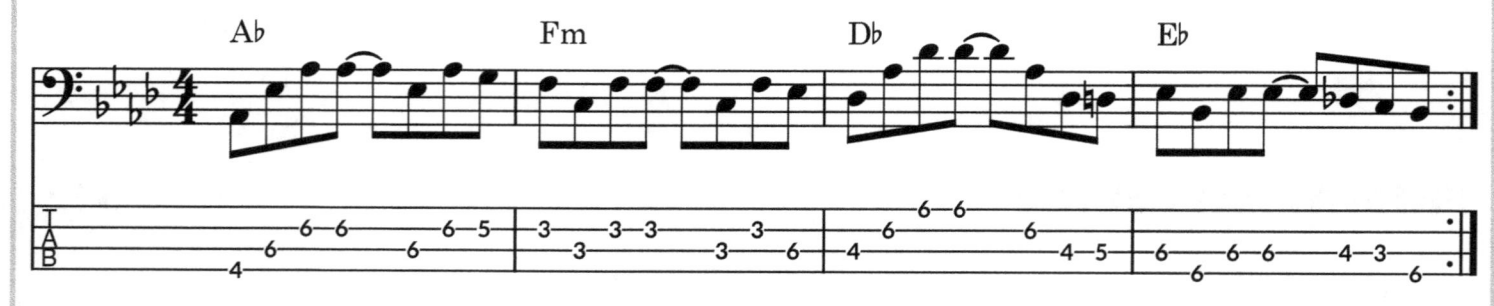

WEEK 46: A♭ MINOR

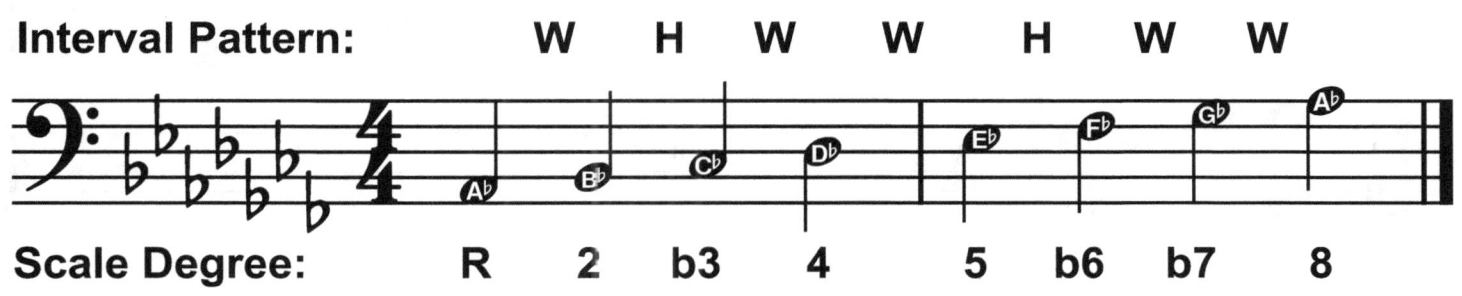

MONDAY: PATTERN 5   316

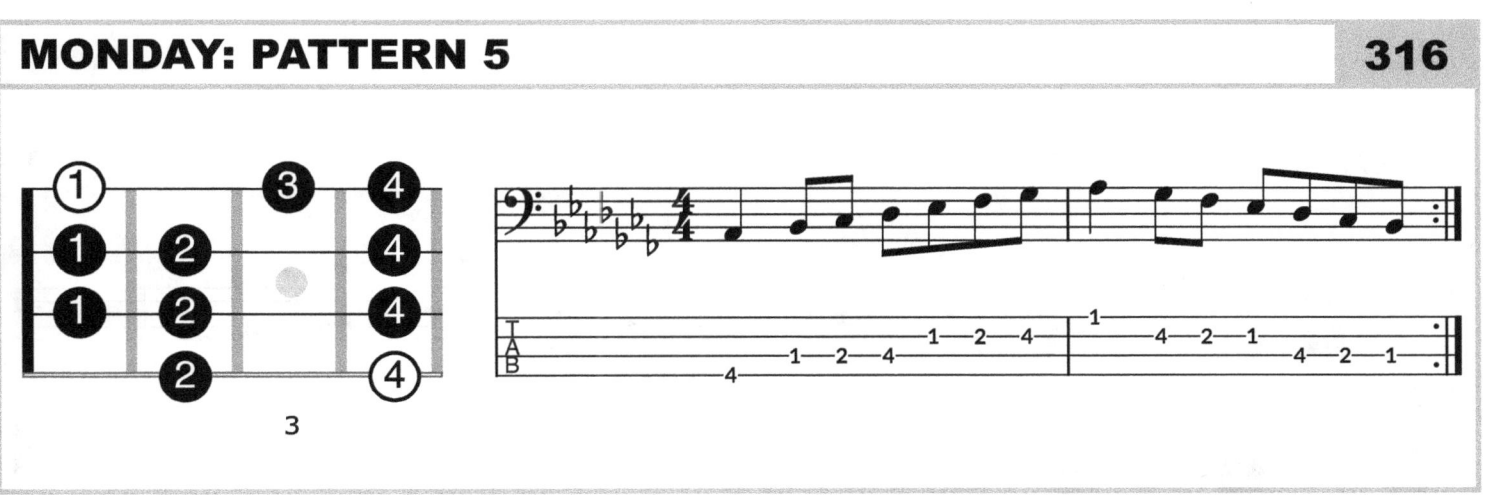

TUESDAY: PATTERN 1   317

WEDNESDAY: PATTERN 2   318

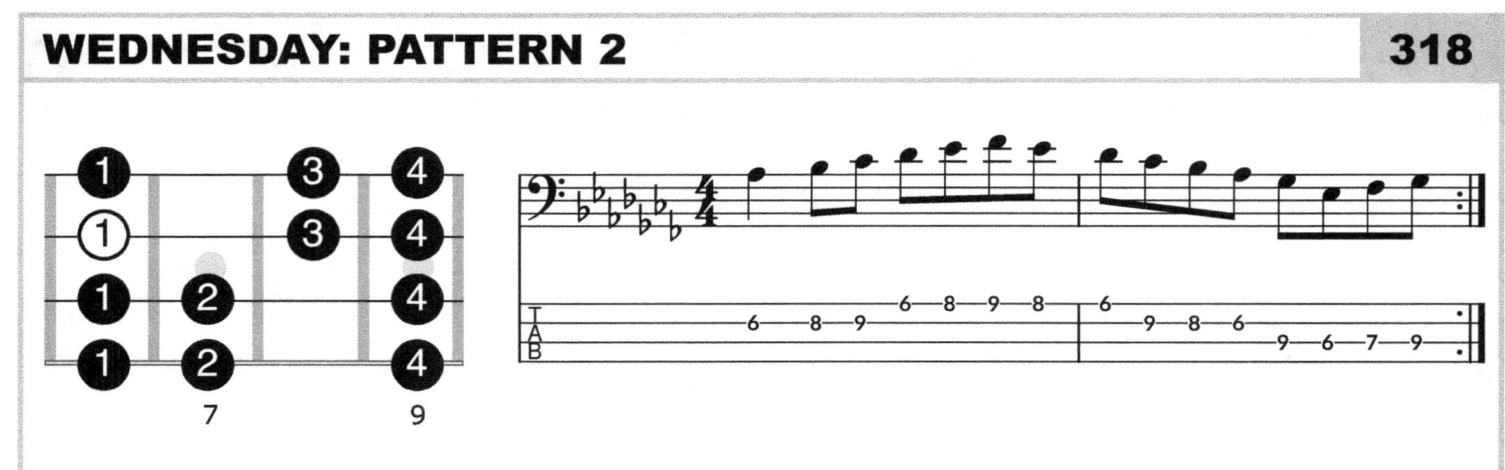

THURSDAY: PATTERN 3   319

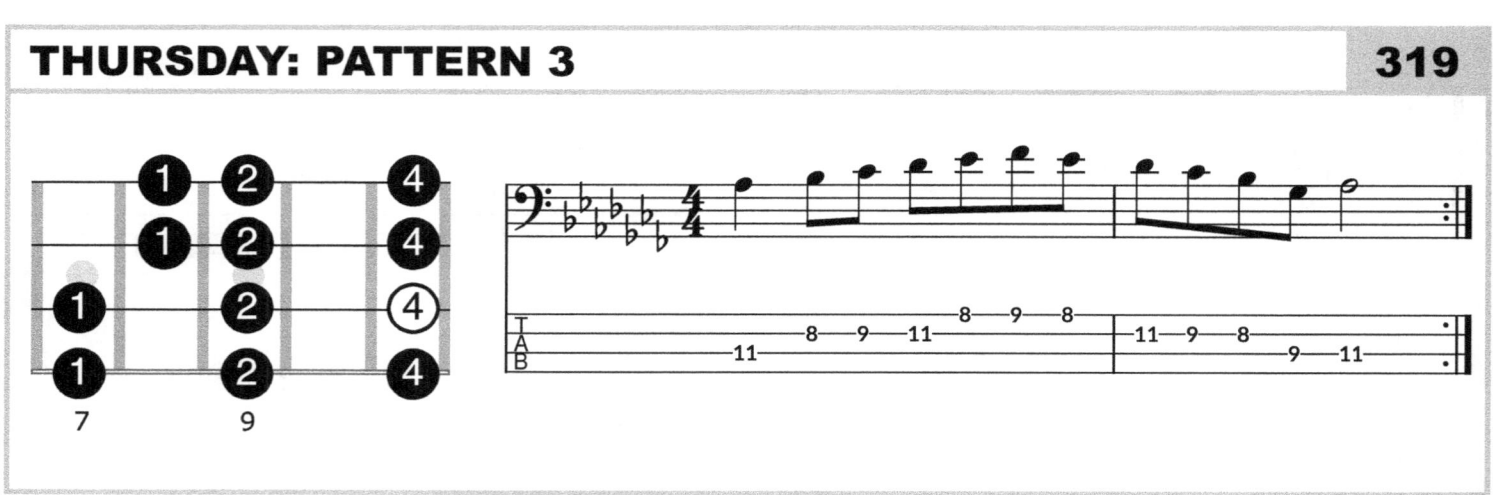

FRIDAY: PATTERN 4   320

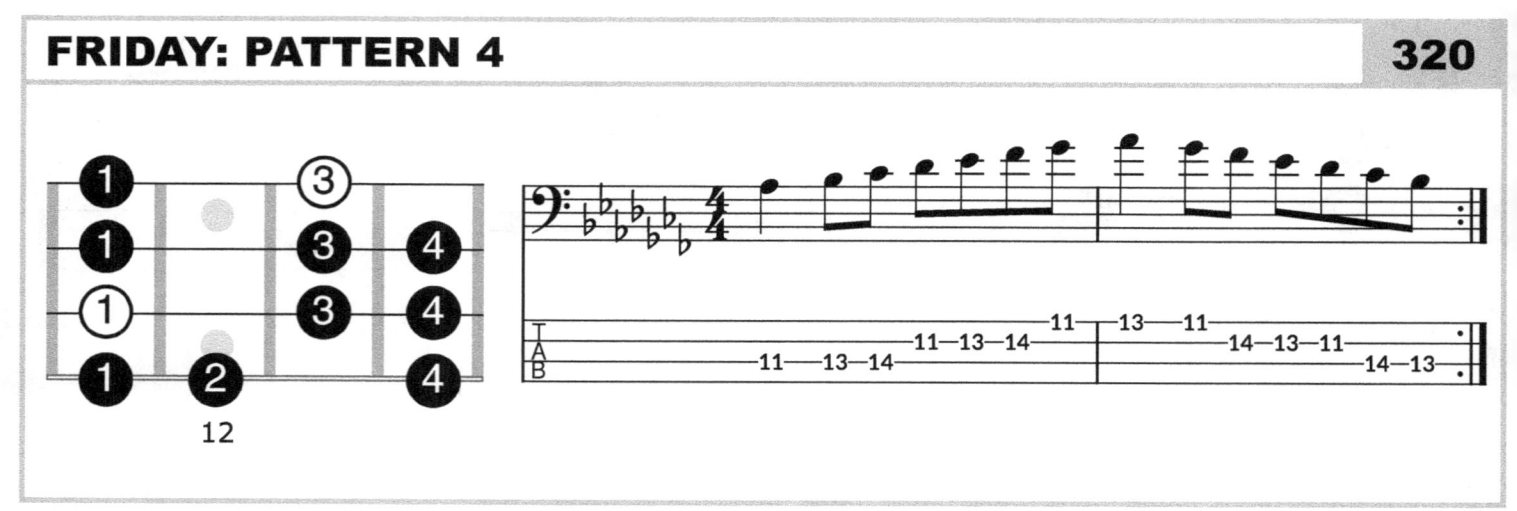

SATURDAY: HORIZONTAL PATTERN   321

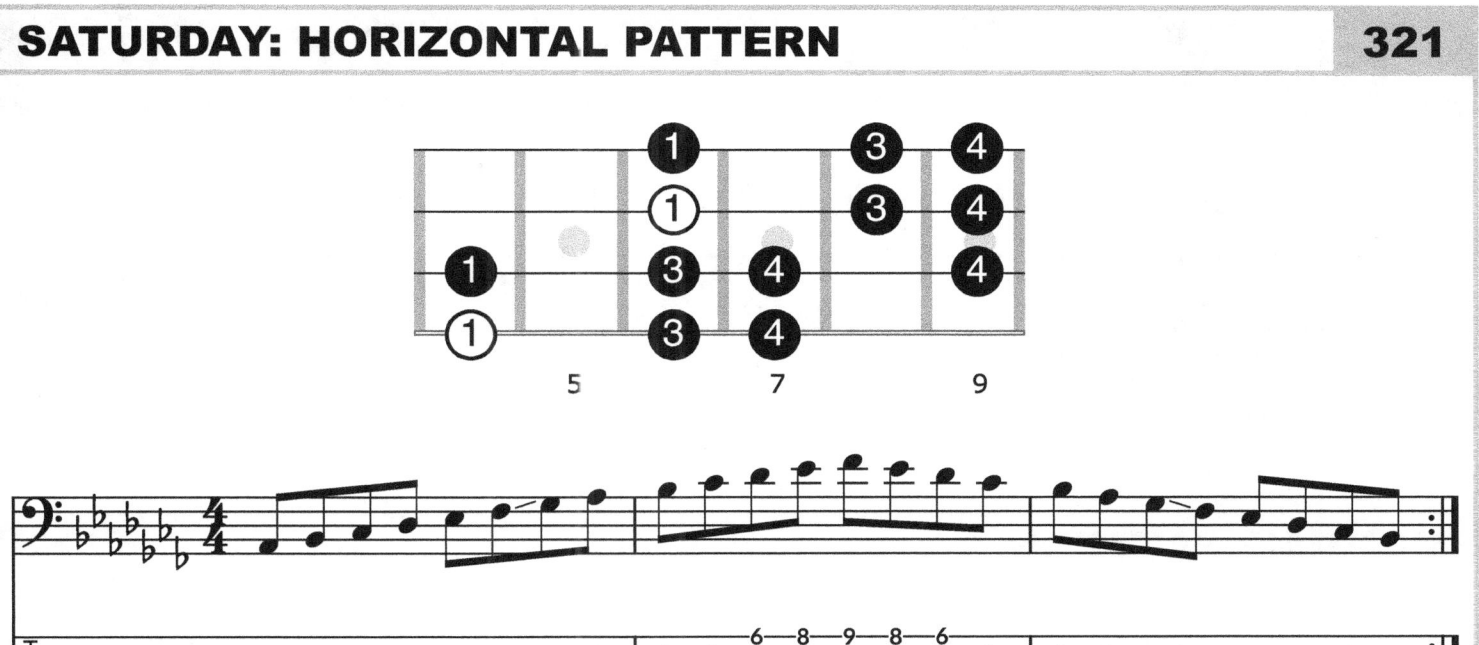

SUNDAY: SCALE APPLICATION   322

In our last minor scale example, we'll explore developing a theme while using the Horizontal Pattern. The similarity in fingering makes it easy to move an idea across octaves. Again, the change of rhythm in bar 4 creates a question-and-answer response within the four-measure bass line.

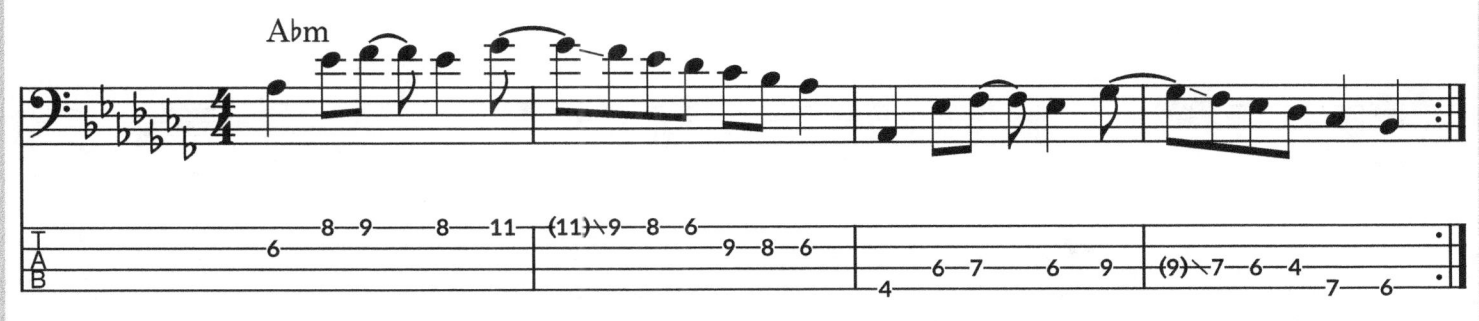

WEEK 47: A♭ MAJOR PENTATONIC

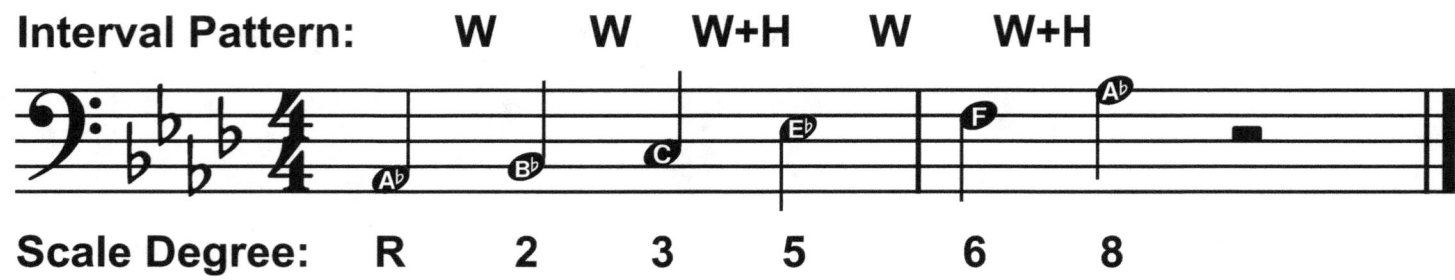

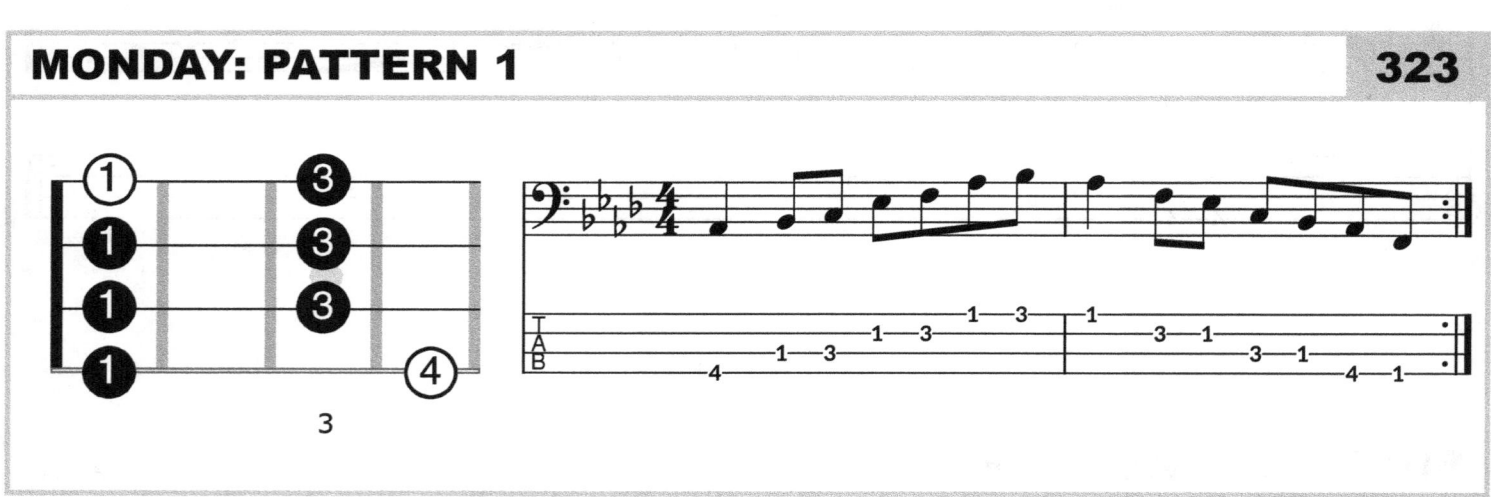

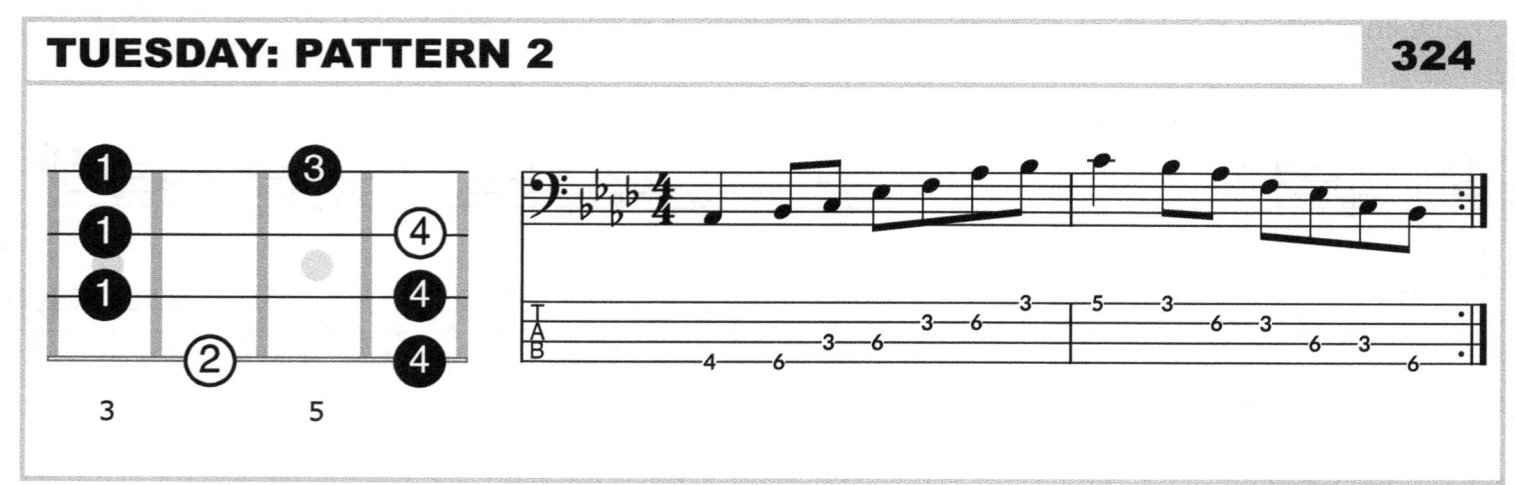

WEDNESDAY: PATTERN 3 — 325

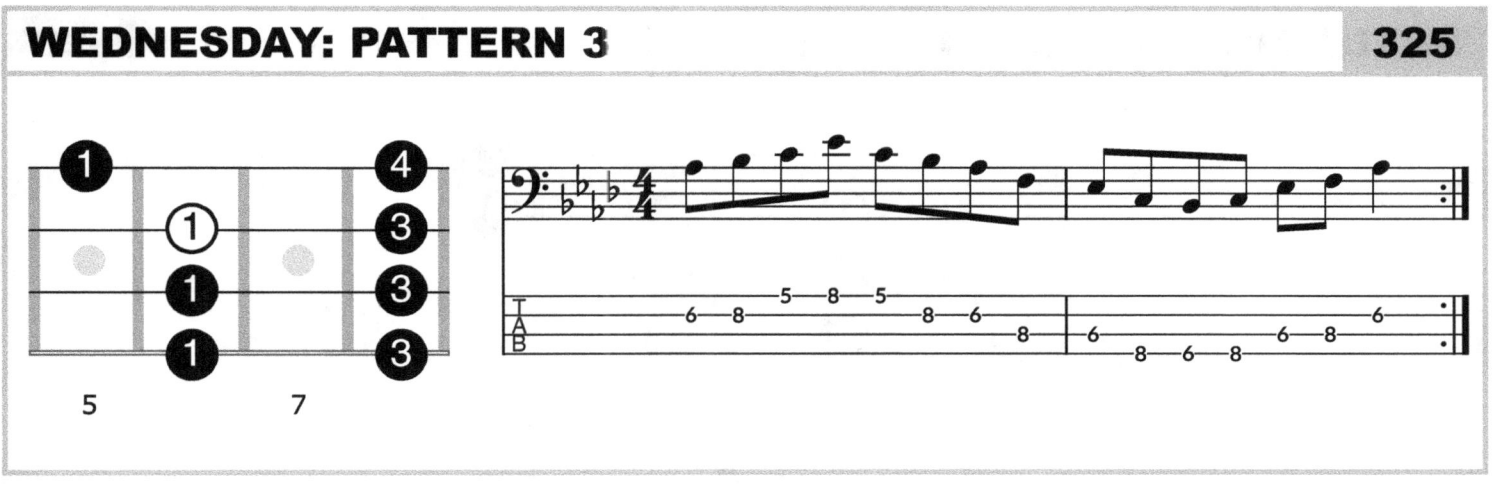

THURSDAY: PATTERN 4 — 326

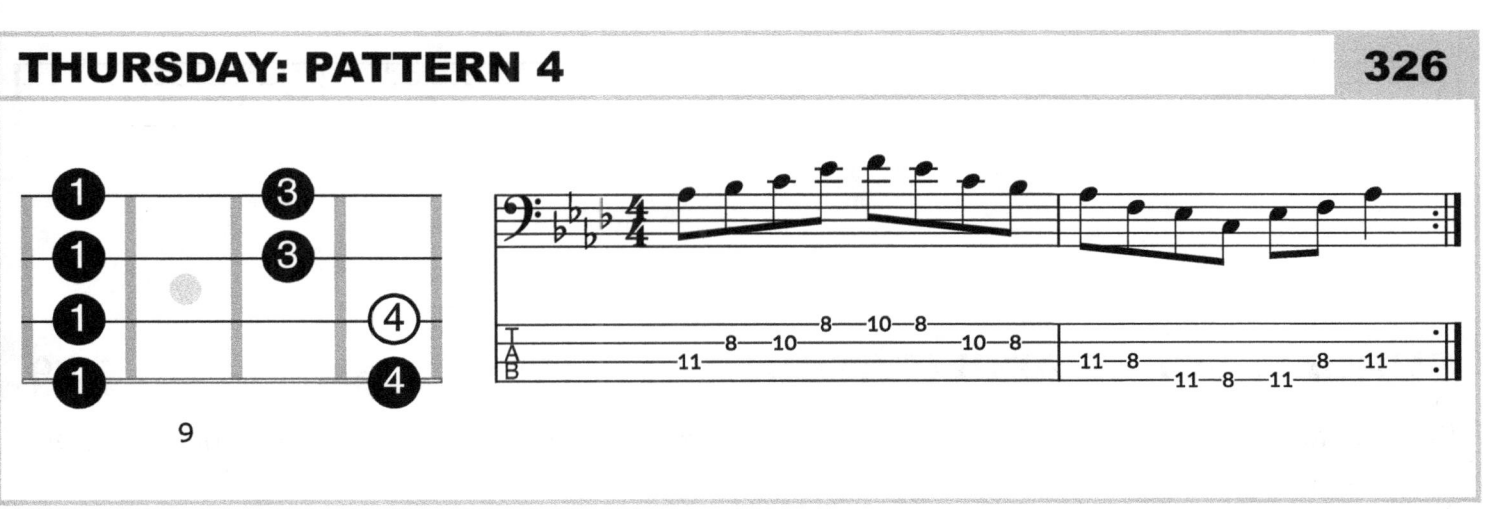

FRIDAY: PATTERN 5 — 327

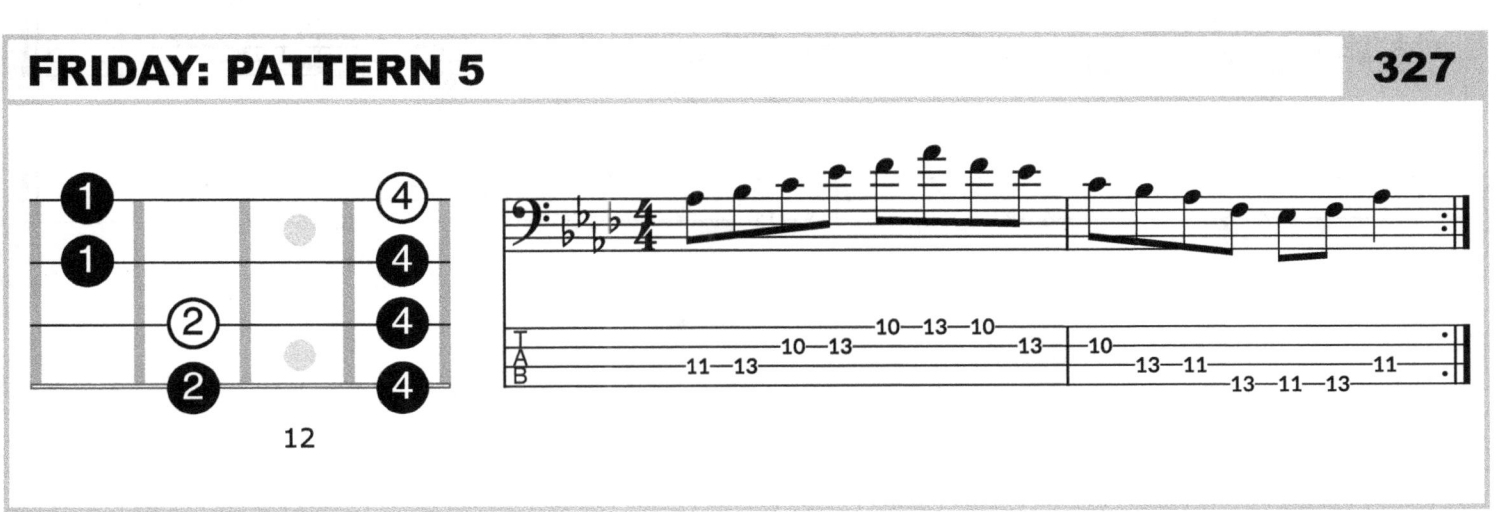

SATURDAY: HORIZONTAL PATTERN   328

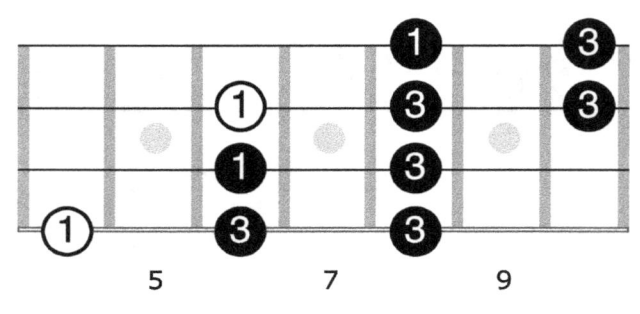
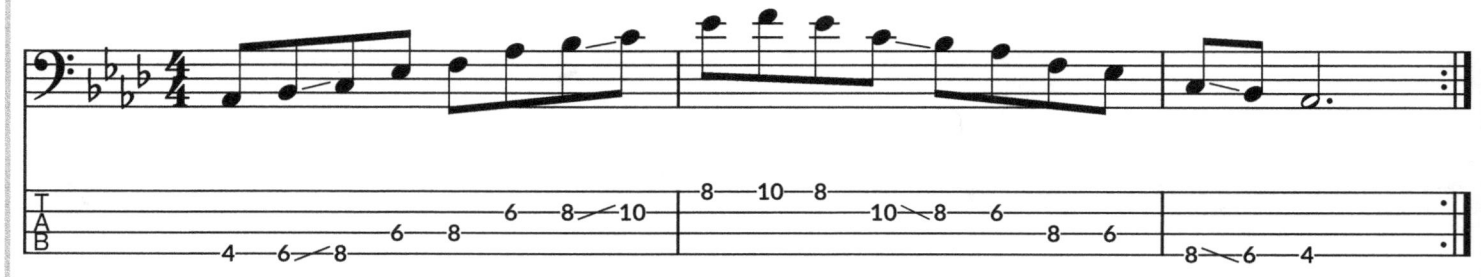

SUNDAY: SCALE APPLICATION   329

For our final pentatonic scale sequences, we'll explore groups of 6. We'll ascend six notes from the lowest note in each pattern, then immediately move to the next without pause. This reinforces each pattern and your ability to shift between them!

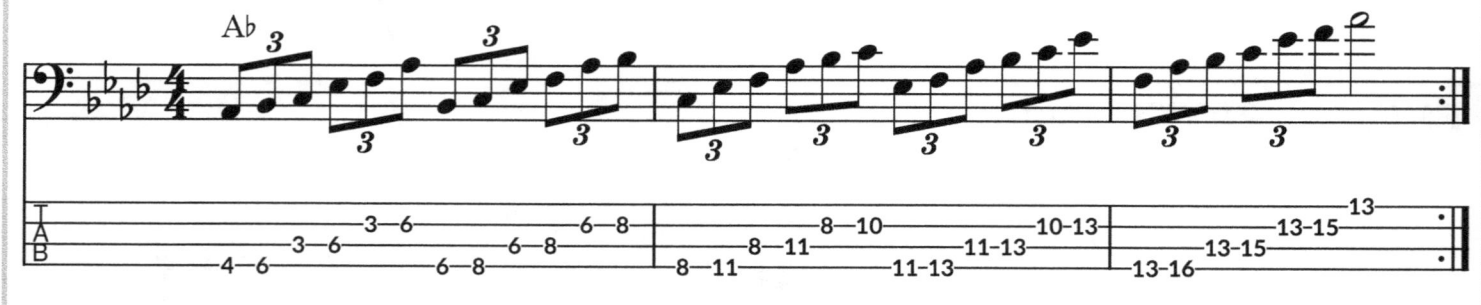

WEEK 48: A♭ MINOR PENTATONIC

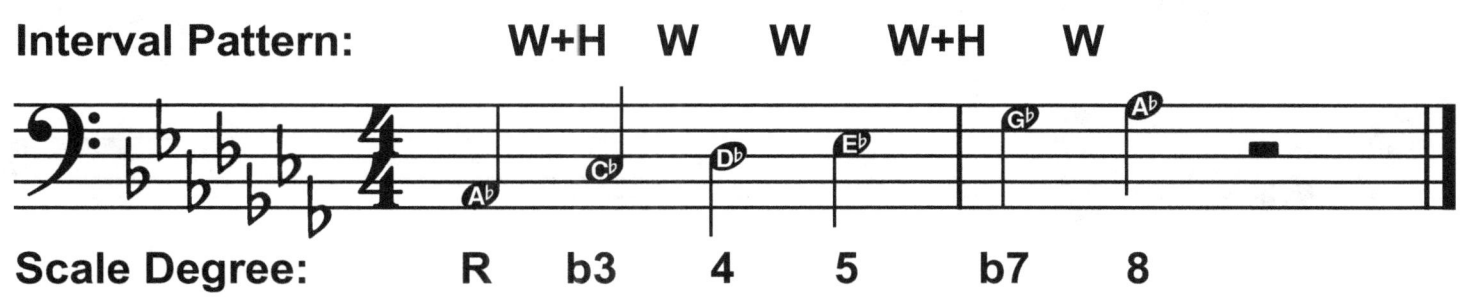

MONDAY: PATTERN 5 330

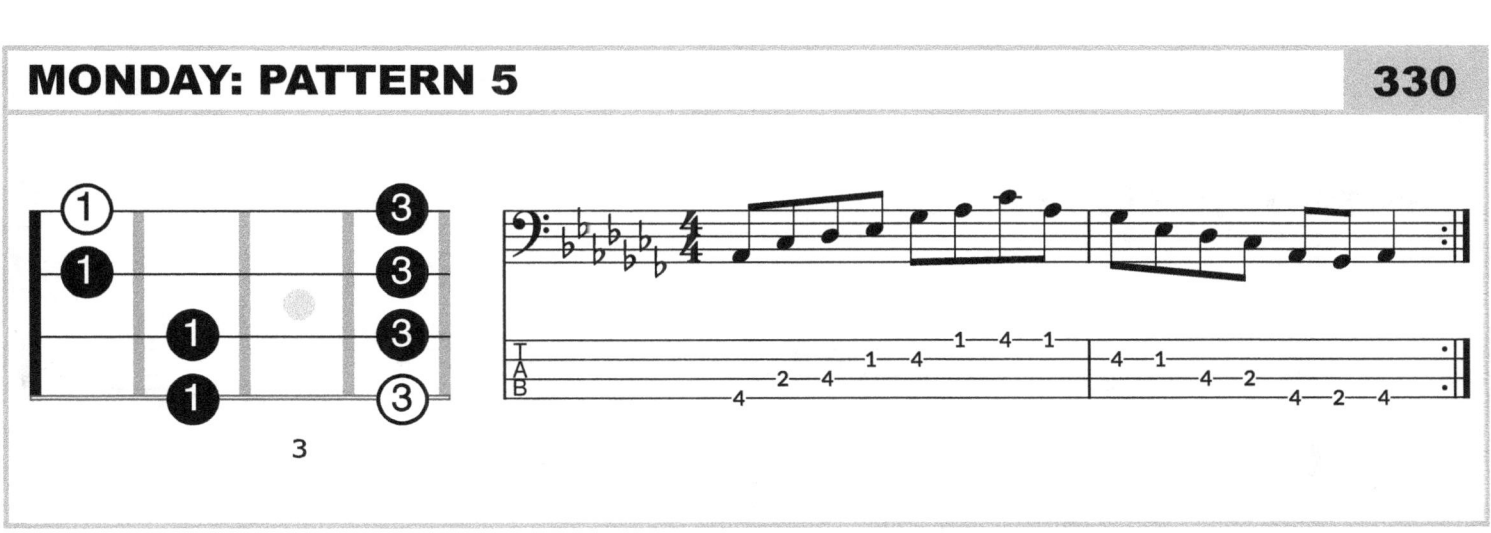

TUESDAY: PATTERN 1 331

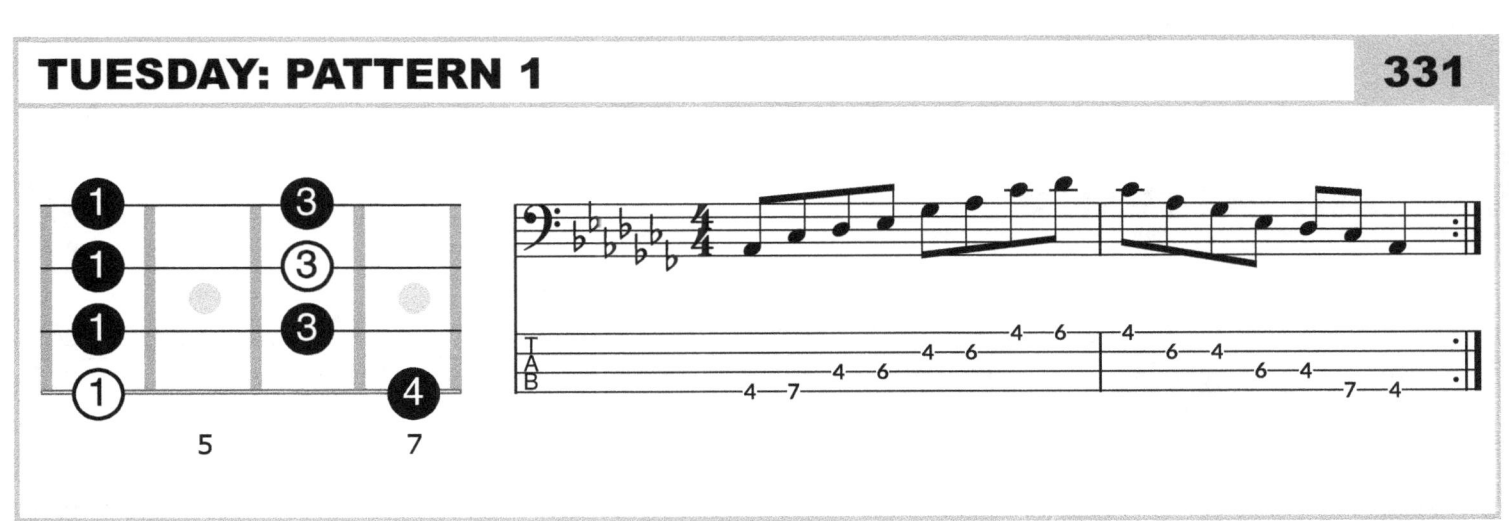

WEDNESDAY: PATTERN 2 — 332

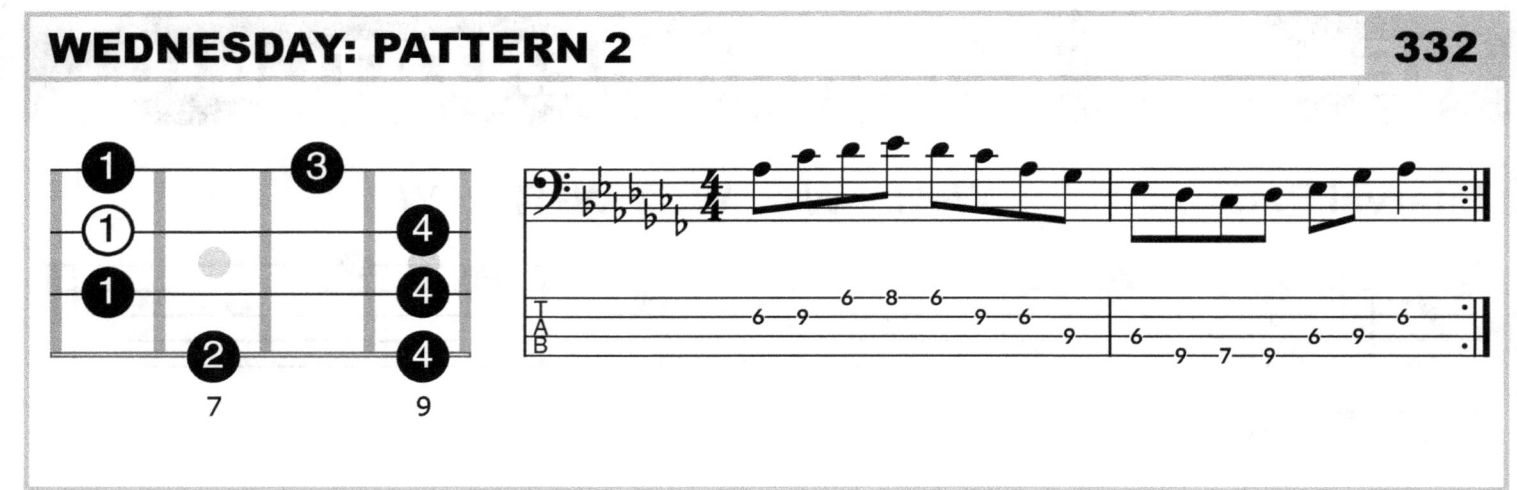

THURSDAY: PATTERN 3 — 333

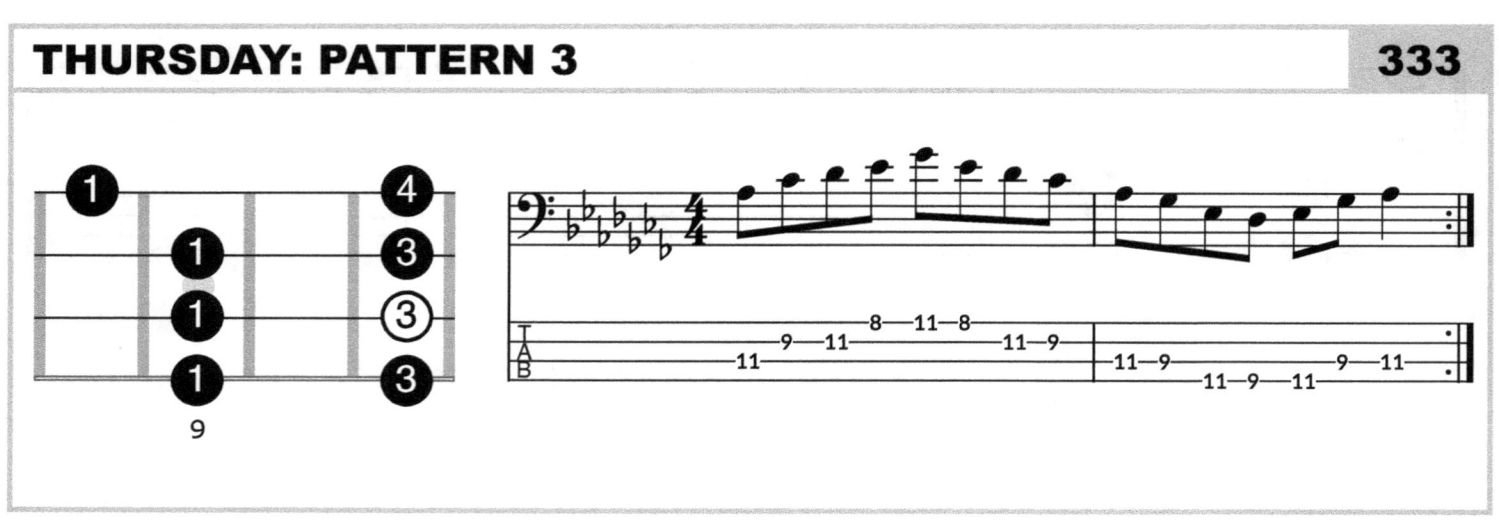

FRIDAY: PATTERN 4 — 334

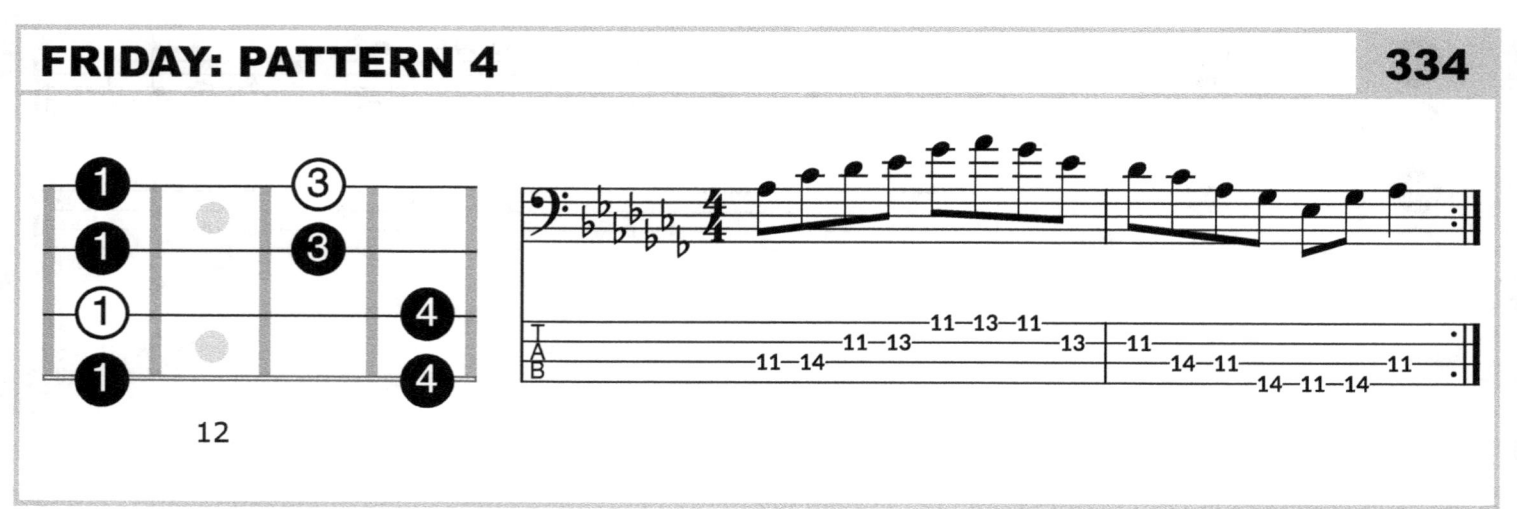

SATURDAY: HORIZONTAL PATTERN   335

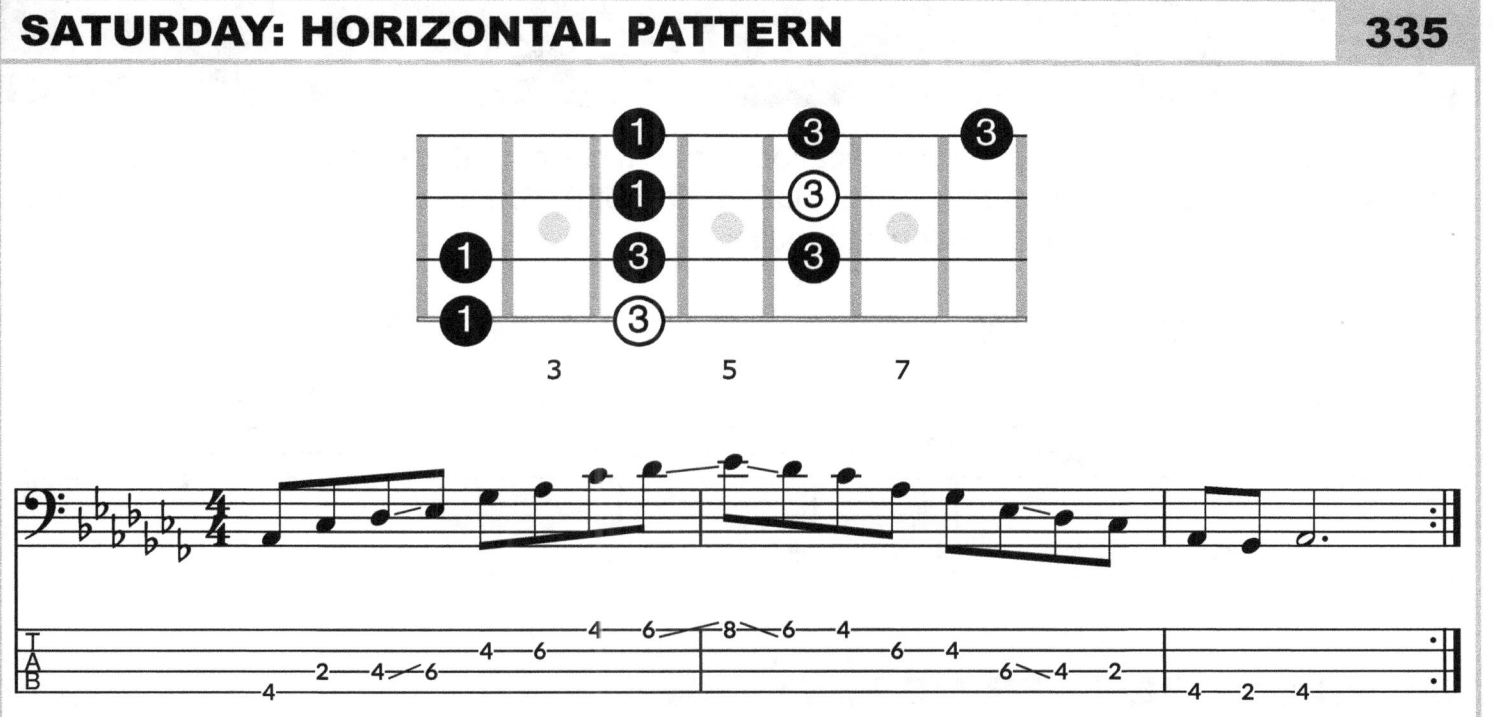

SUNDAY: SCALE APPLICATION   336

Today's pentatonic sequence descends each pattern in 6-note groups, changing direction from last week. We'll work down the fretboard in descending fashion through each pattern, focusing on the highest three strings. Take your time transitioning between patterns.

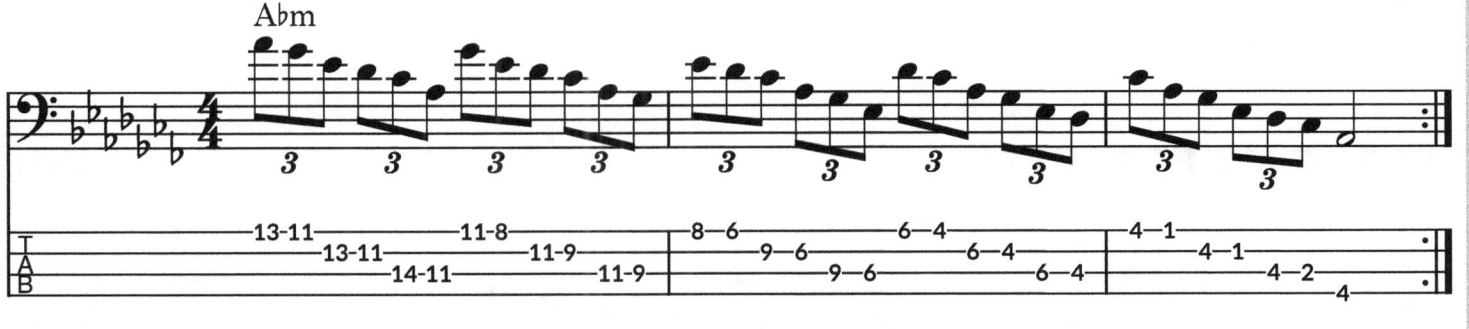

WEEK 49: THE BLUES SCALE

The *blues scale* is a very popular modification of the minor pentatonic scale you already know and is used in many styles of music. The flatted 5th (♭5th), commonly referred to as the "blue note," is added to the minor pentatonic formula.

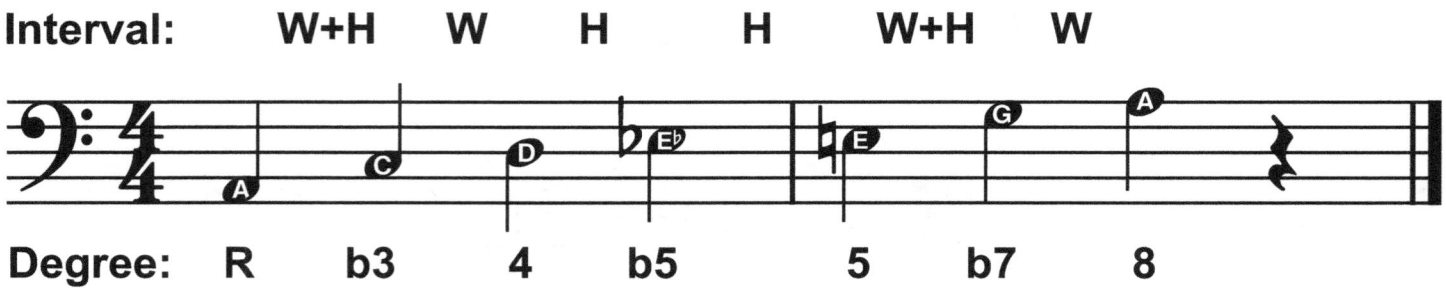

MONDAY: OPEN-STRING PATTERN 4 — 337

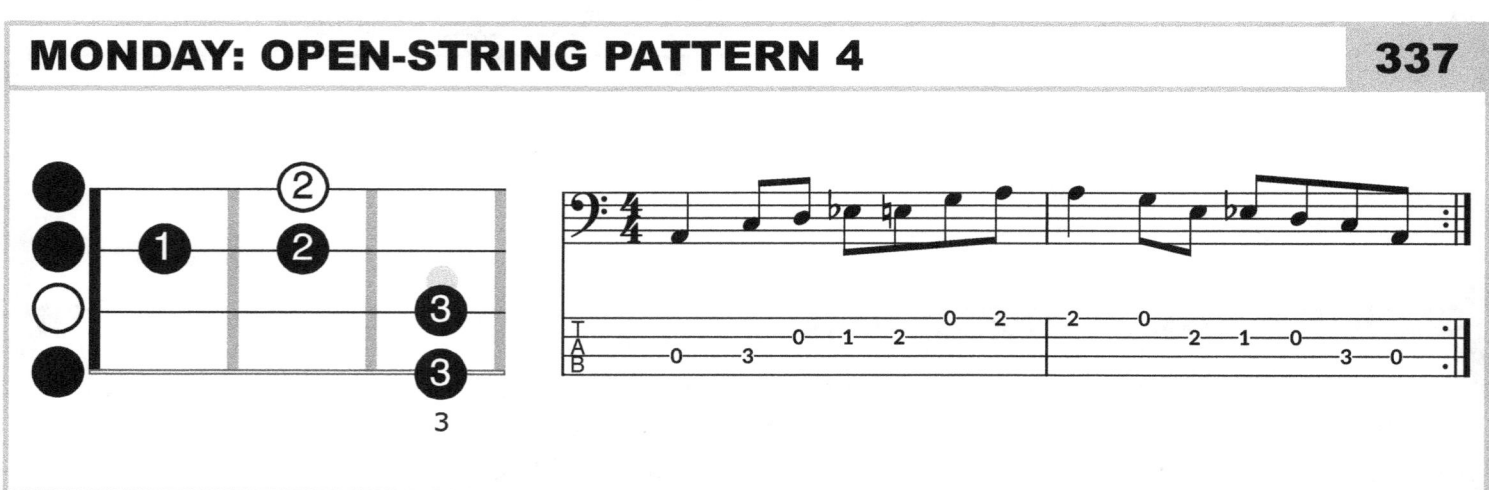

TUESDAY: PATTERN 5 — 338

WEDNESDAY: PATTERN 1   339

THURSDAY: PATTERN 2   340

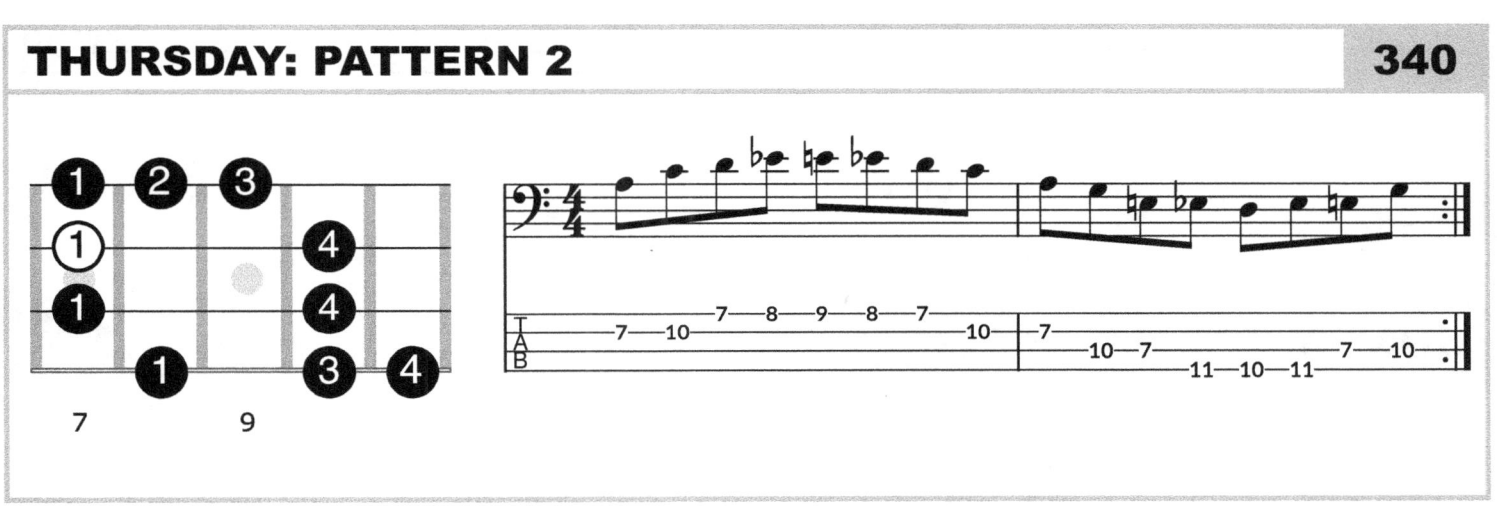

FRIDAY: PATTERN 3   341

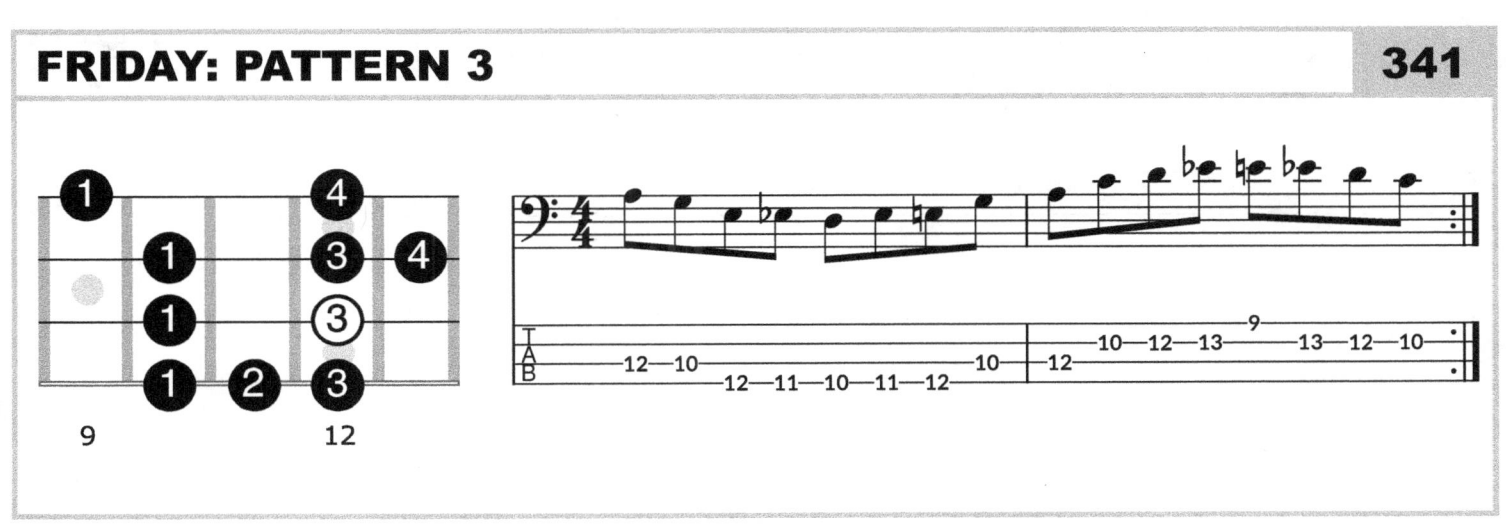

SATURDAY: HORIZONTAL PATTERN 342

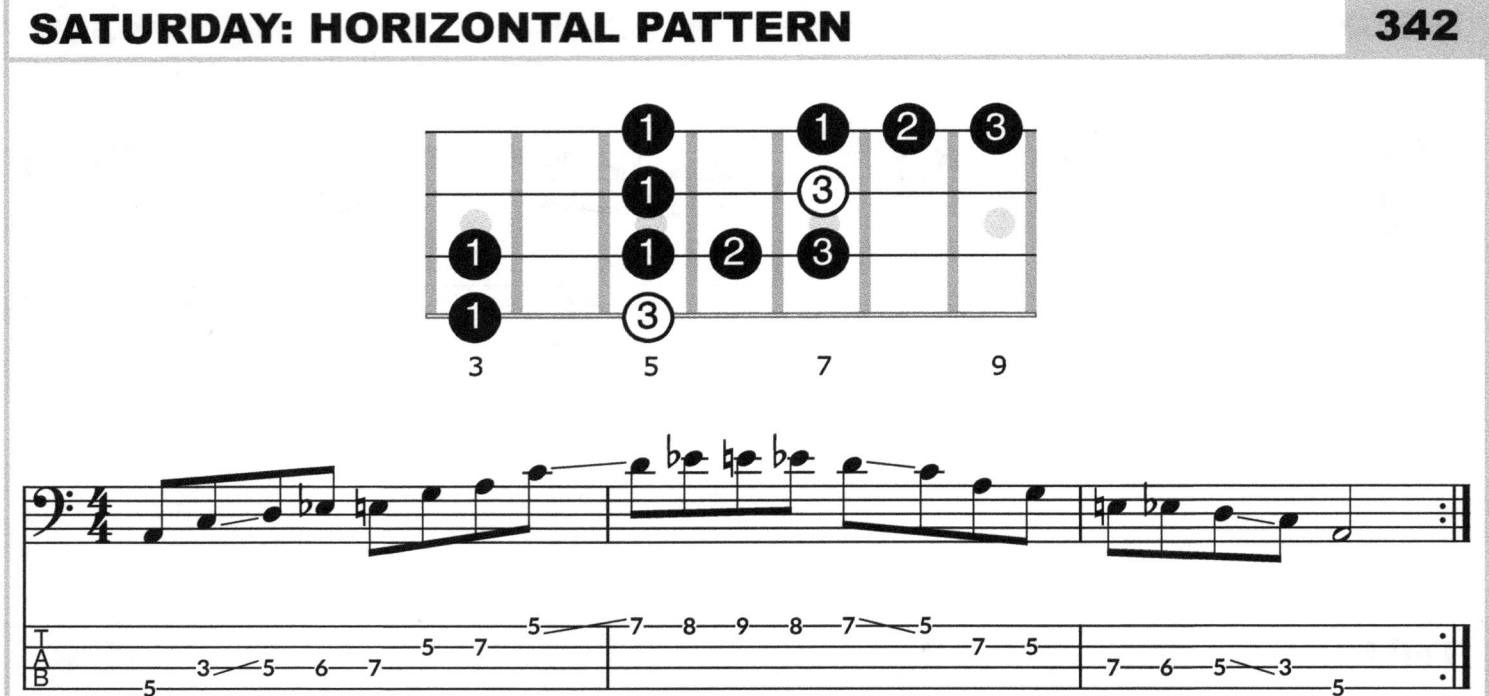

SUNDAY: SCALE APPLICATION 343

Since we're already familiar with the Downtown Blues pattern, we'll enhance its flavor by incorporating the ♭5th. A triplet on beat 4 also adds forward momentum. Although this riff is repeated four times in a row, you can insert it occasionally as a fill to create surprise in your bass line.

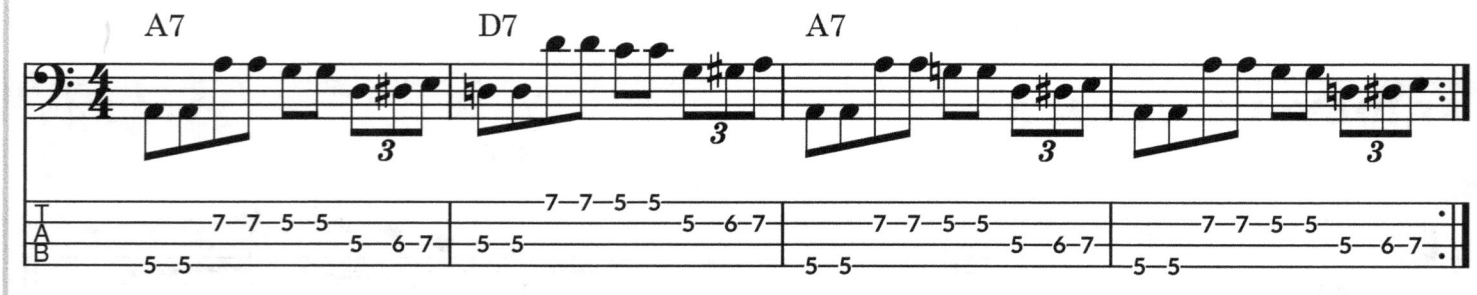

WEEK 50: HARMONIC MINOR

The *harmonic minor scale* is a popular modification of the natural minor scale. The (minor) 7th degree of the scale is raised to a major 7th, creating increased pull back to the root note.

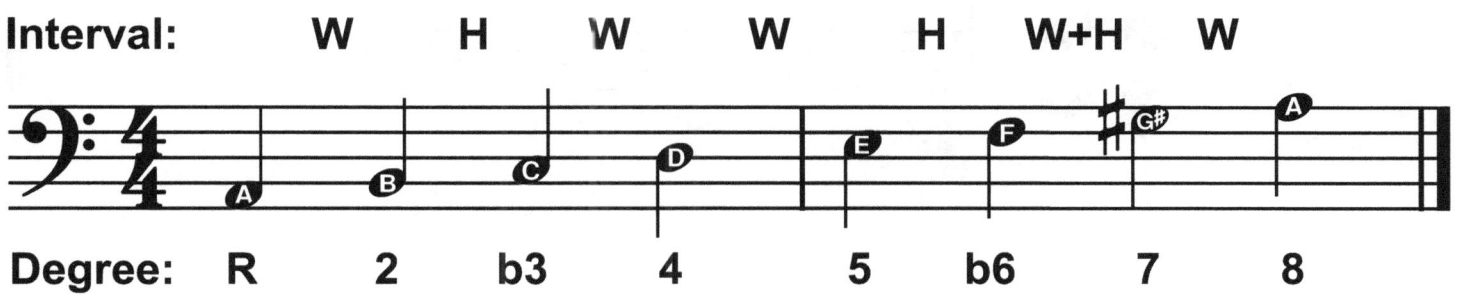

MONDAY: OPEN-STRING PATTERN 4 — 344

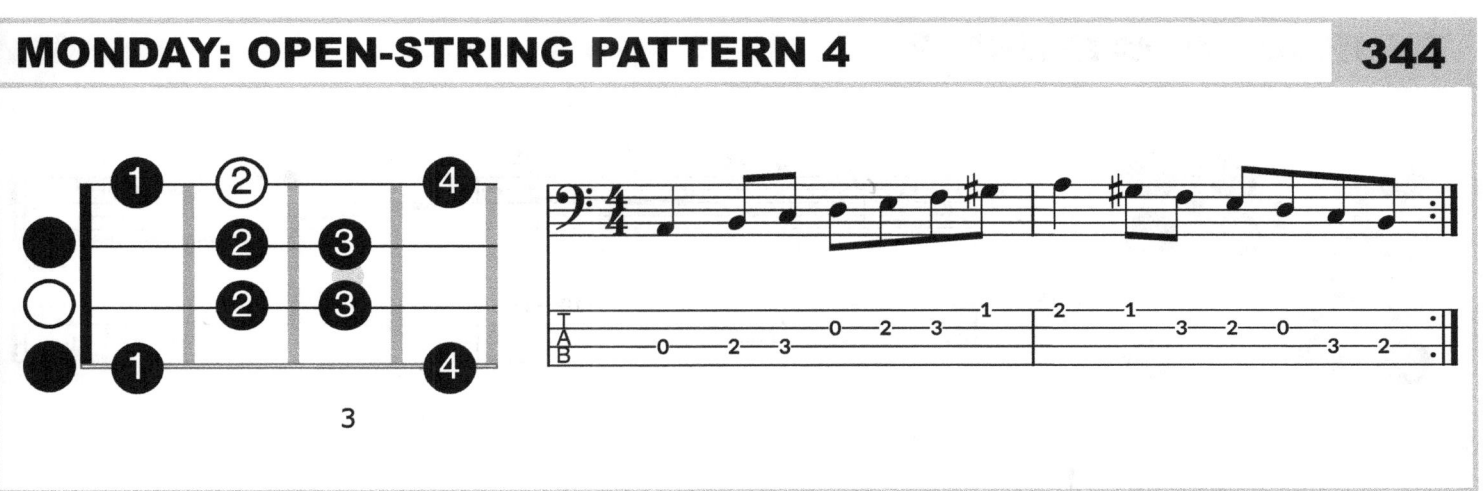

TUESDAY: PATTERN 5 — 345

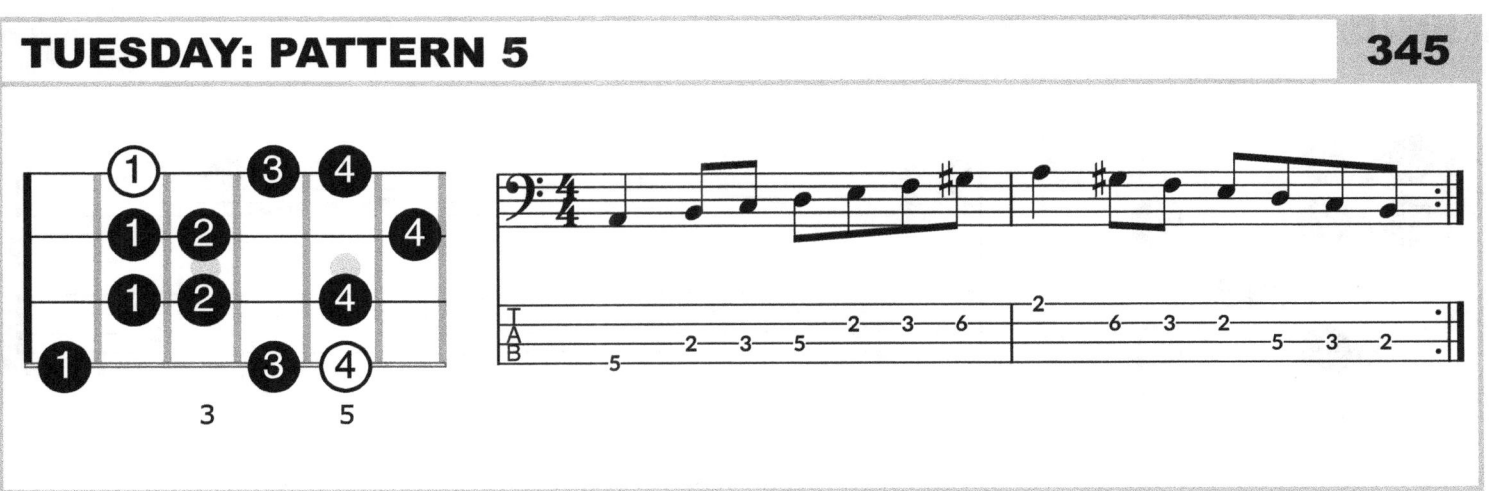

WEDNESDAY: PATTERN 1   346

THURSDAY: PATTERN 2   347

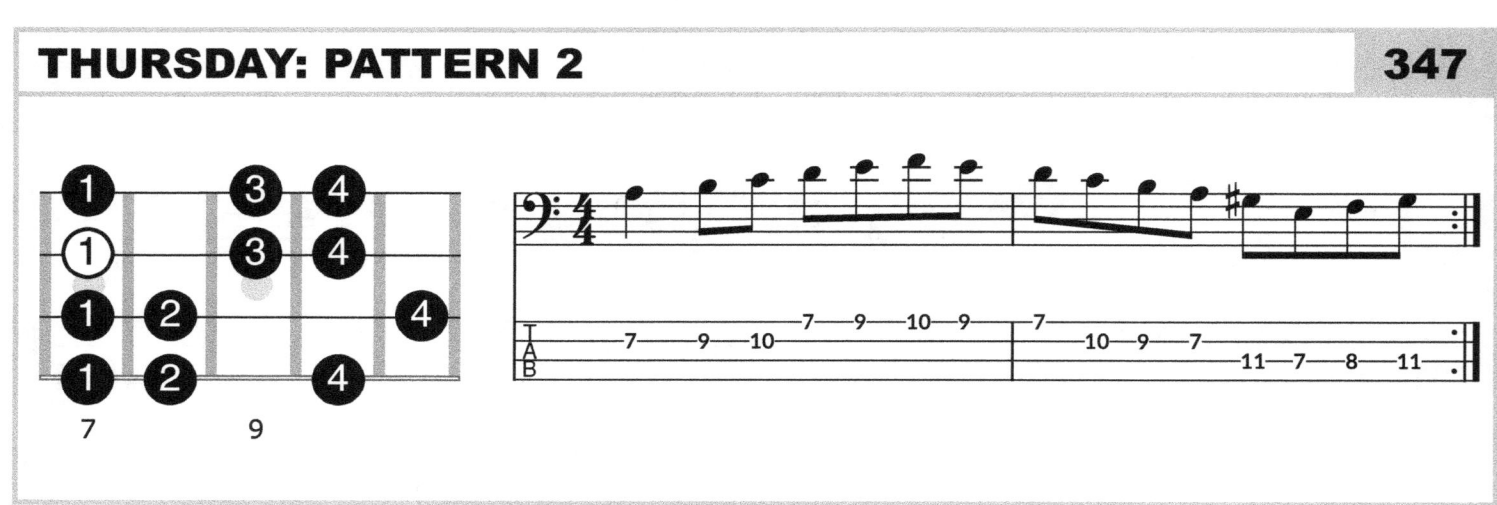

FRIDAY: PATTERN 3   348

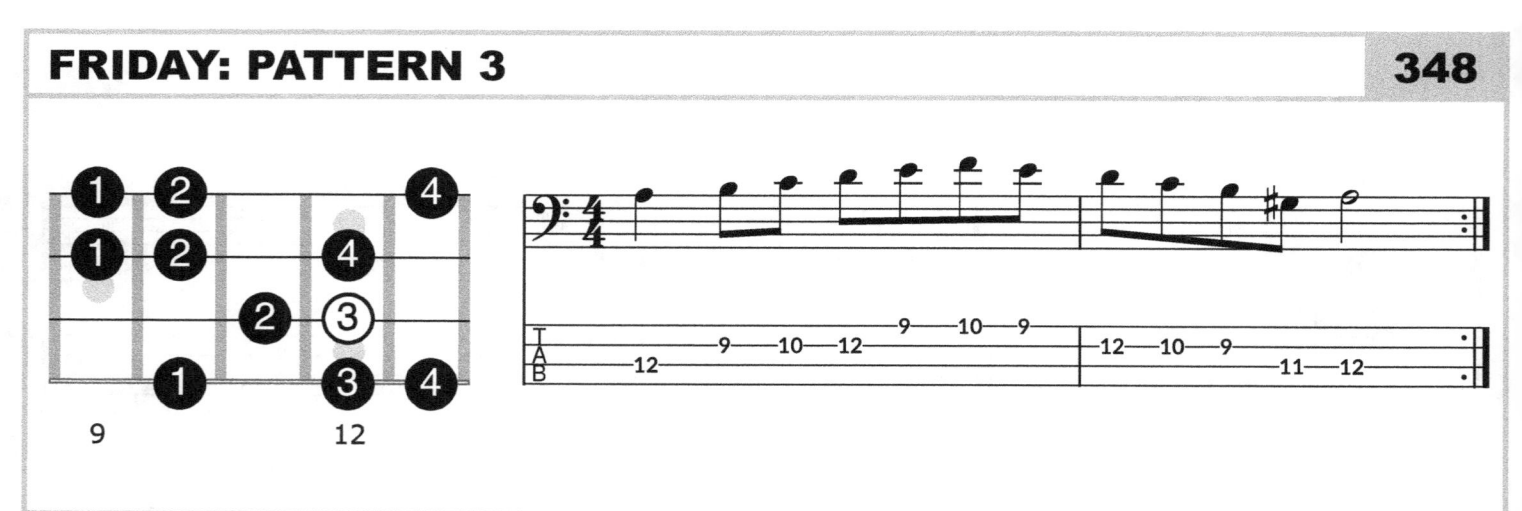

SATURDAY: HORIZONTAL PATTERN   349

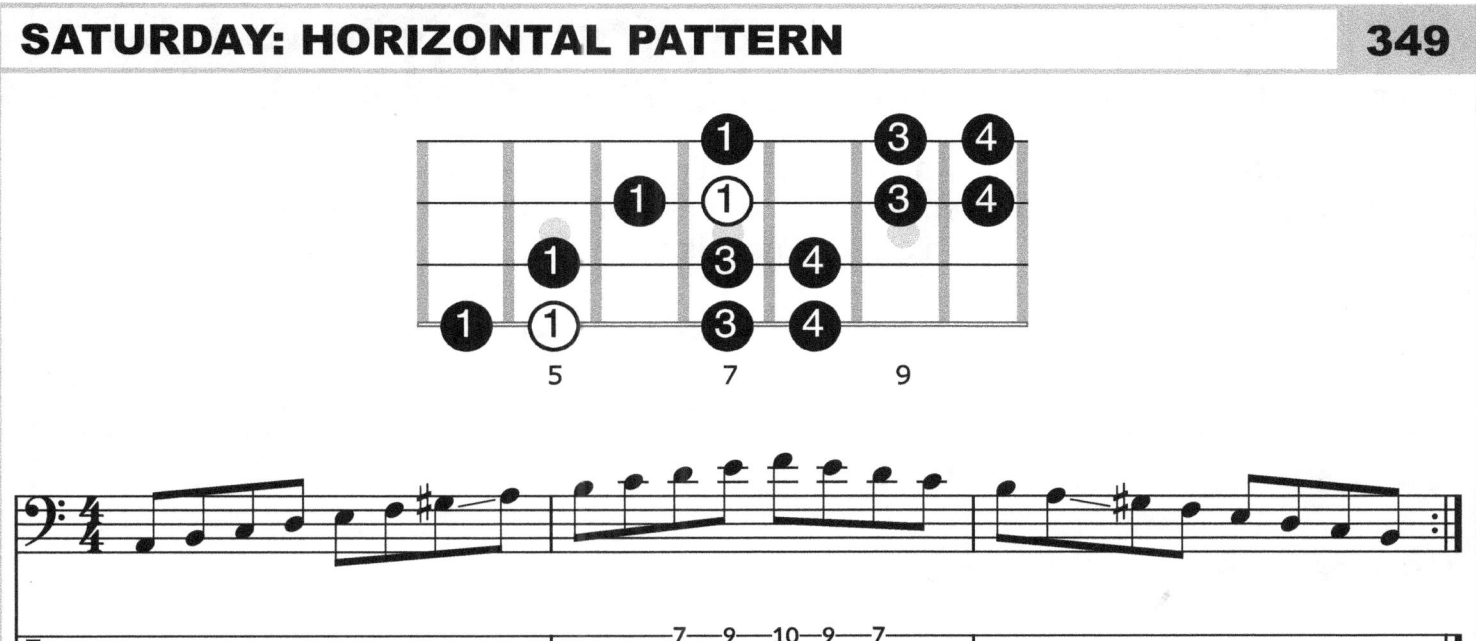

SUNDAY: SCALE APPLICATION   350

The harmonic minor scale is an excellent choice for a minor 2–5–1 chord progression, as demonstrated in this walking bass style. Notably, the 7th degree of the scale (G♯) also serves as the 3rd degree of the 5-chord (E7♭9). Most walking bass lines start with the root of each new chord on beat 1. This line employs notes that approach these root notes by way of stepwise motion. For instance, E7♭9 and Bm7♭5 are approached by scale notes positioned below their roots, while Am is approached from above. These are concepts that you can apply when crafting your own walking bass lines.

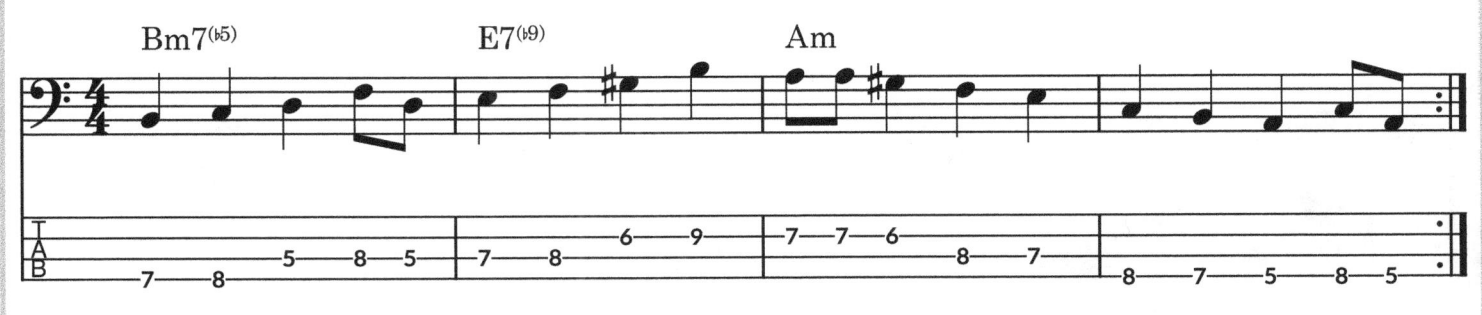

WEEK 51: MELODIC MINOR

The *melodic minor scale* utilizes a major 6th and 7th scale degree. You might think of it as raising the 6th and 7th of the natural minor scale or lowering the 3rd of a major scale. "Yesterday" by The Beatles is a great example of its sound and usage.

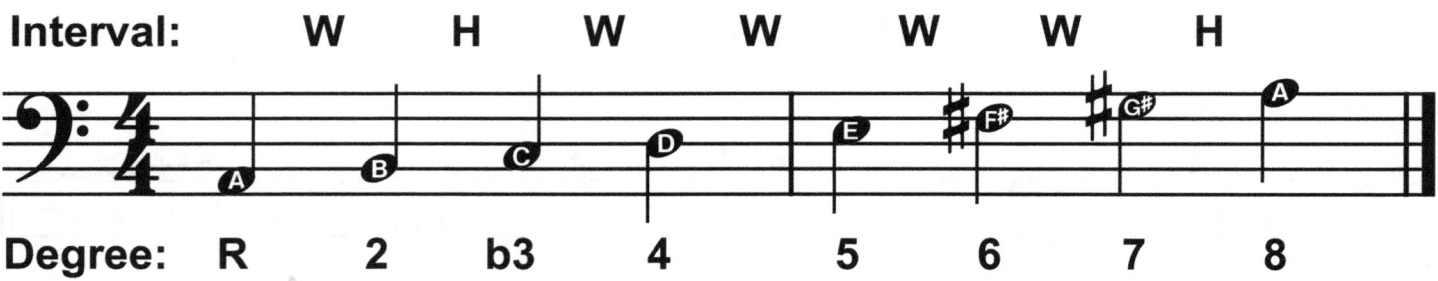

MONDAY: OPEN-STRING PATTERN 4 — 351

TUESDAY: PATTERN 5 — 352

WEDNESDAY: PATTERN 1 — 353

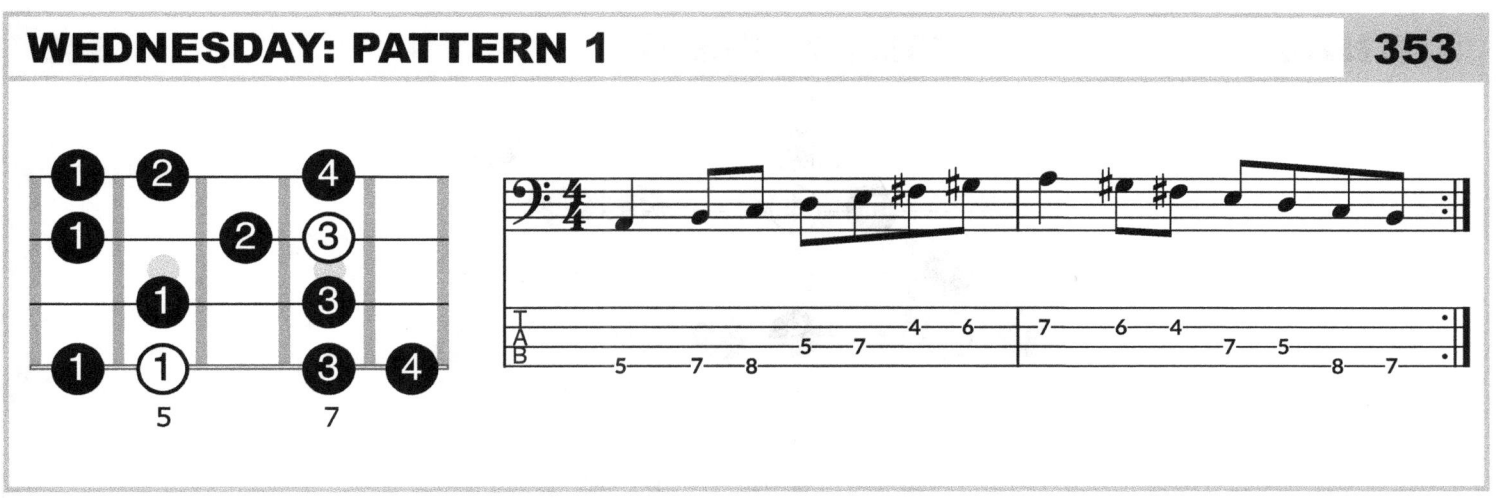

THURSDAY: PATTERN 2 — 354

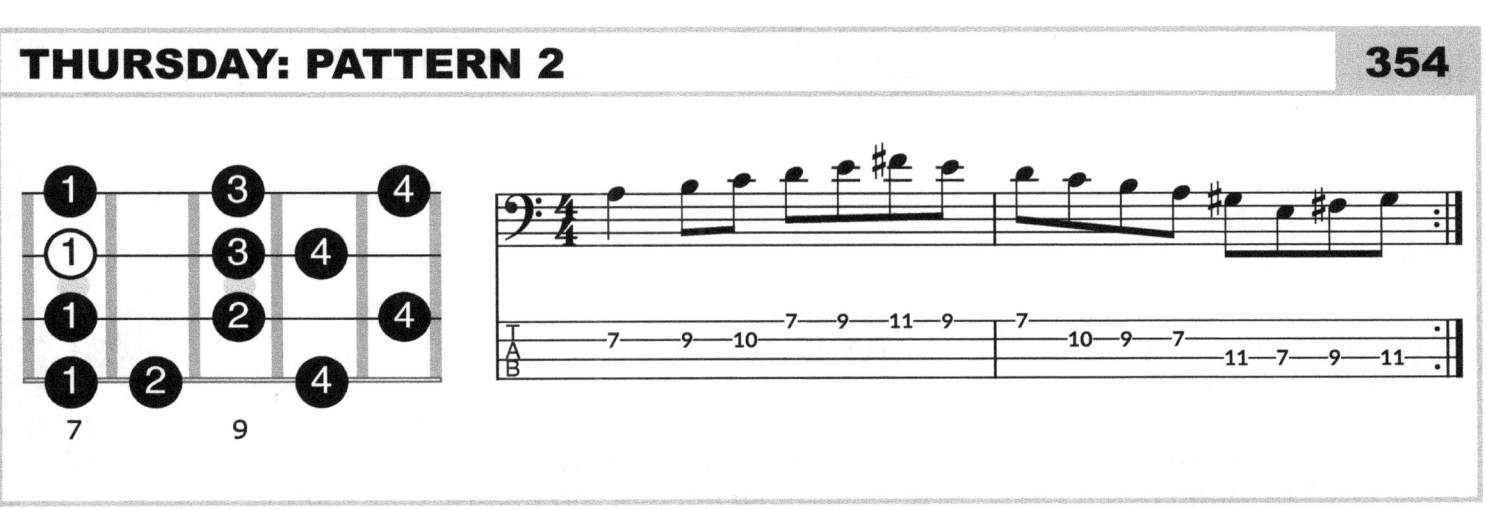

FRIDAY: PATTERN 3 — 355

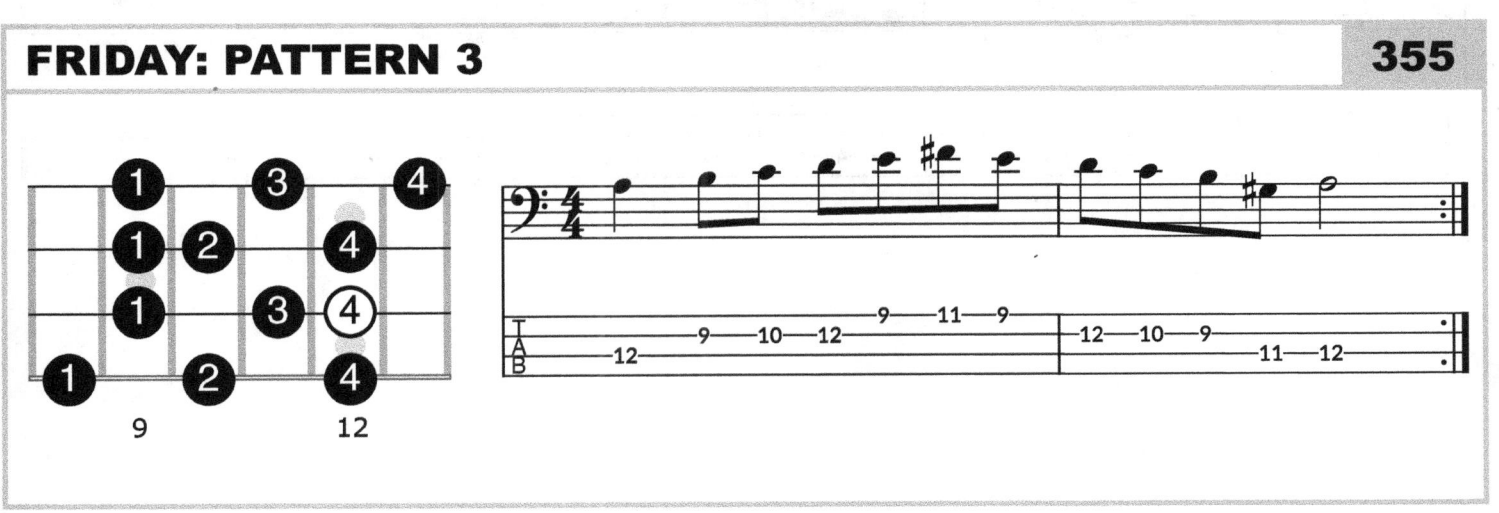

SATURDAY: HORIZONTAL PATTERN   356

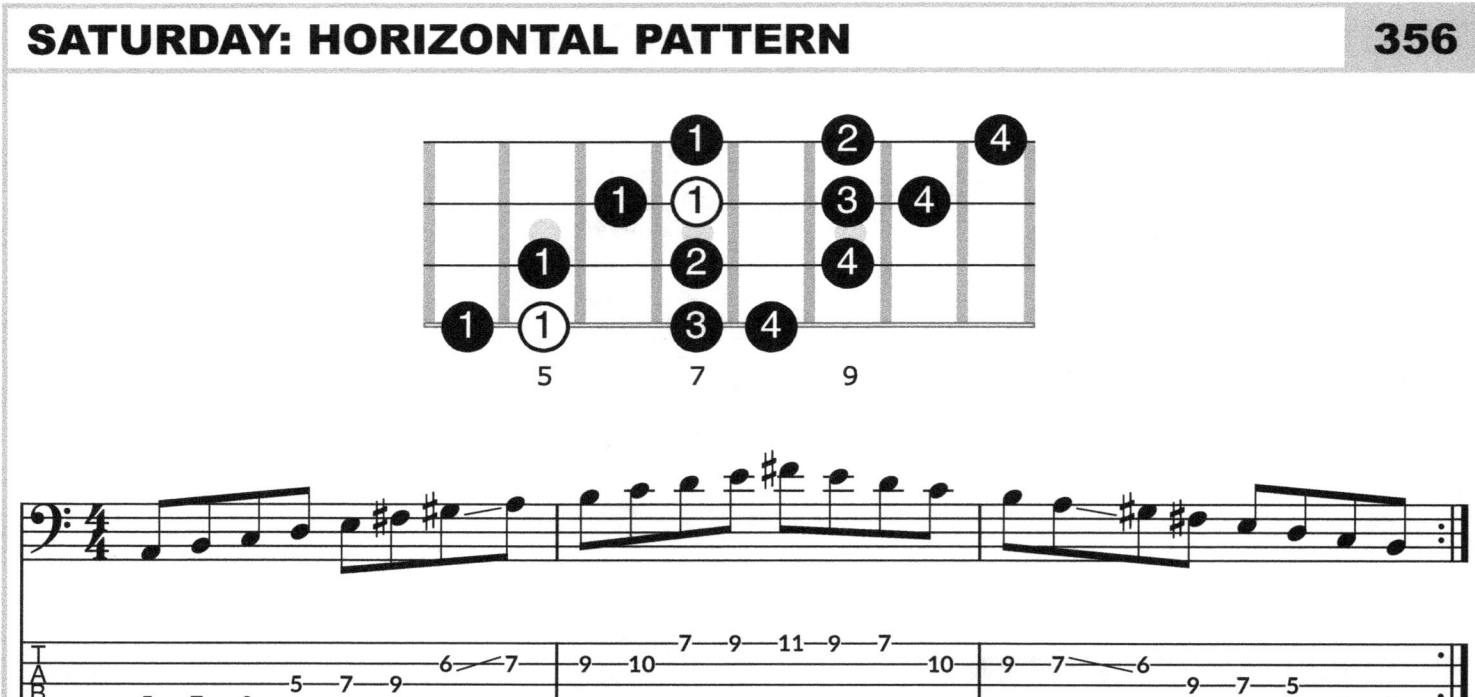

SUNDAY: SCALE APPLICATION   357

The melodic minor scale can often be found in classical and jazz music. Today's example is an excerpt from Bach's *Bourrée in Em*. As demonstrated in measure 2 of this melody, classical compositions often use melodic minor when ascending and natural minor when descending.

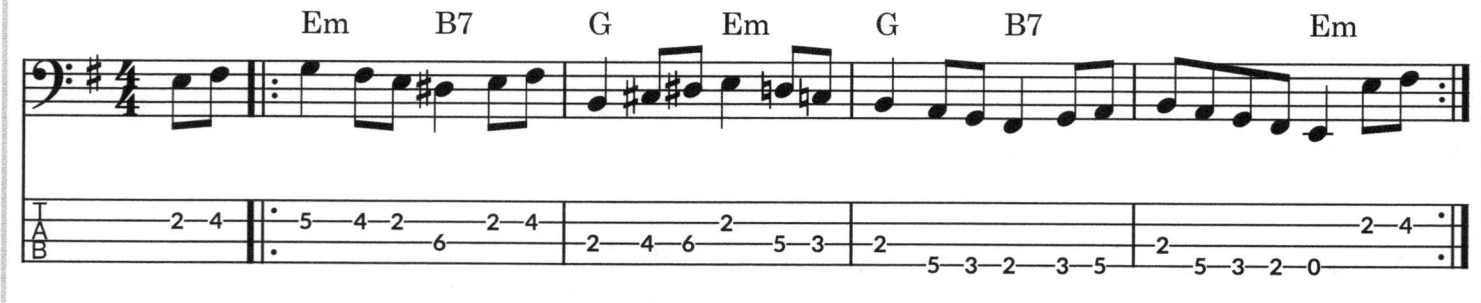

WEEK 52: THE MODES

Throughout this book, we've examined how the starting note of a scale directly influences its sound. Changing the starting pitch of the major scale creates a new interval pattern when it returns to that pitch eight notes (one octave) higher. Since there are seven notes in the major scale, there are seven different scale degrees from which to start, and these are commonly referred to as "The Modes." These modes, based on Greek music theory, have been used since the Middle Ages and are named after different regions of Greece.

Each mode has its own sound or musical flavor. Let's explore how this works by using Pattern 2 in the key of G Major. We'll begin by reviewing the construction of the G major scale.

IONIAN: THE MAJOR SCALE

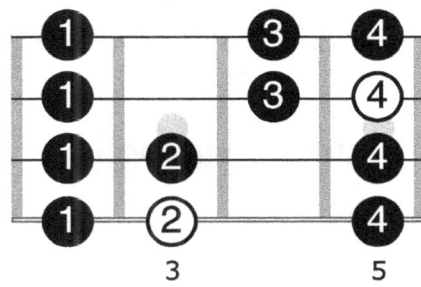

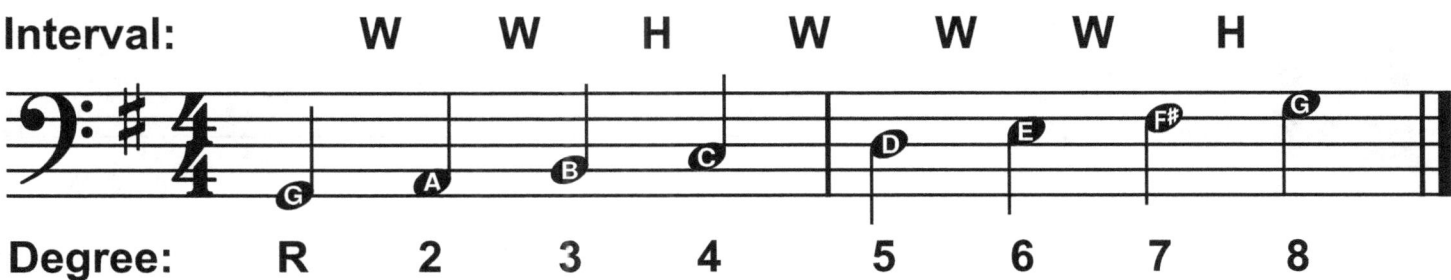

MONDAY: DORIAN   358

To build the Dorian mode, we'll simply start the G major scale from its 2nd note, playing the scale from A to A an octave higher. By doing so, we have made the A note the 1st scale degree, or root, and now call the scale A Dorian.

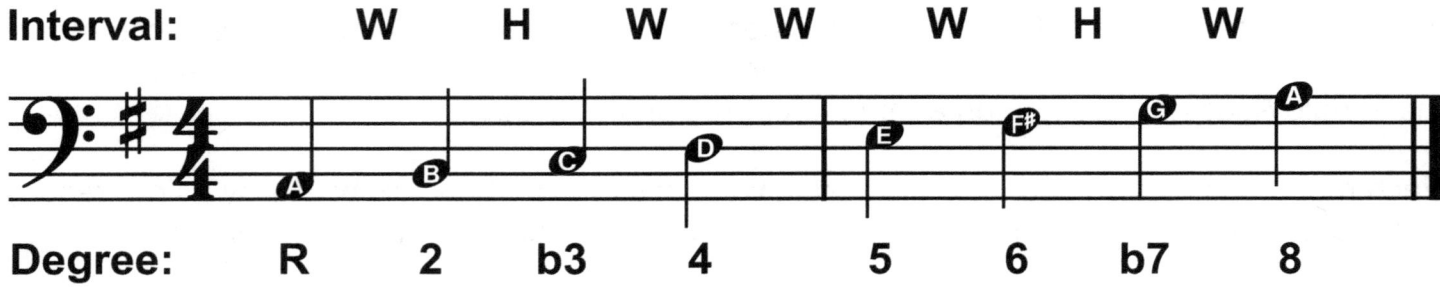

Notice how the interval pattern has shifted. In analyzing what is different from a standard A major scale, you'll find the 3rd and 7th degrees have been lowered. When you have a lowered 3rd, the scale is considered minor.

On the fretboard, we will shift the Pattern 2 starting note one note, as well. Observe the positioning of the white dots.

TUESDAY: PHRYGIAN   359

To build the B Phrygian mode, start the G major scale from its 3rd note, playing the scale from B to B. When compared to B Major, you'll find a lowered 2nd, 3rd, 6th, and 7th. The presence of a lowered 3rd makes it a minor scale.

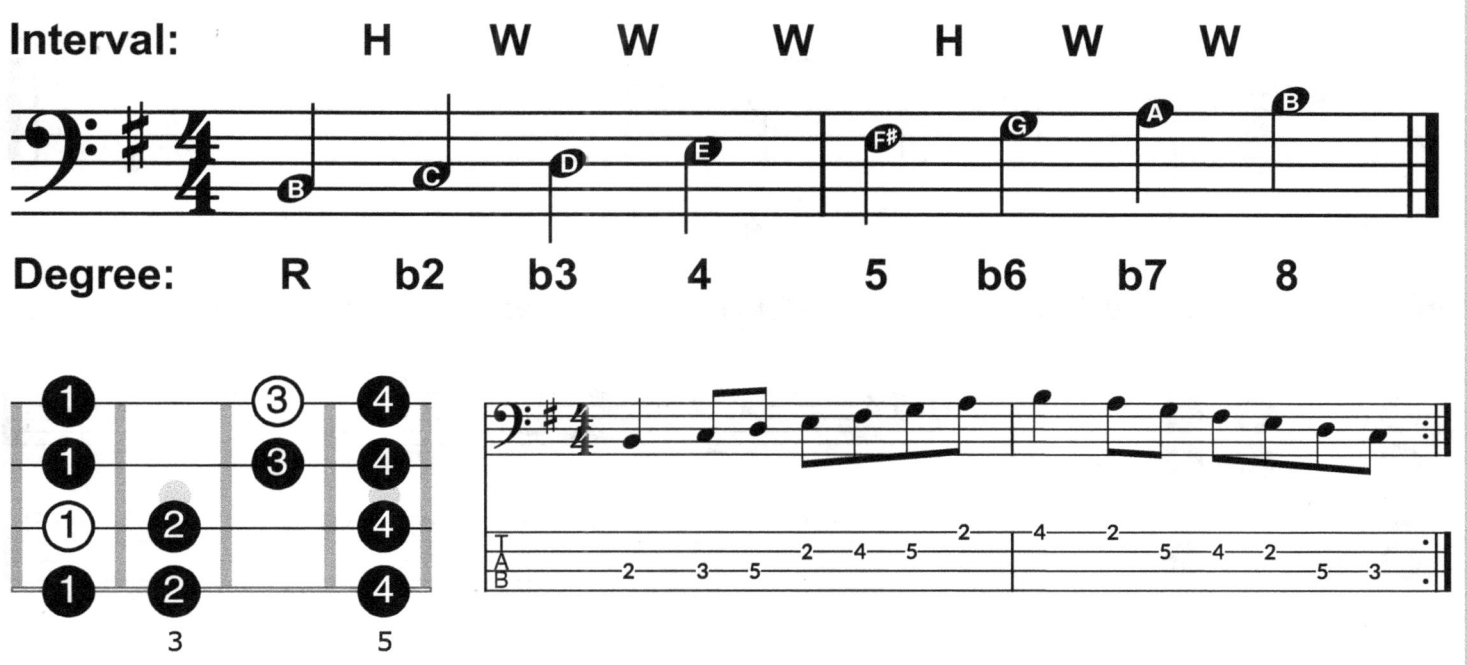

WEDNESDAY: LYDIAN   360

Following the idea, to build C Lydian, we'll start the G major scale from its 4th note. Doing so raises the 4th scale degree from a standard C major scale and provides us with a new major sound.

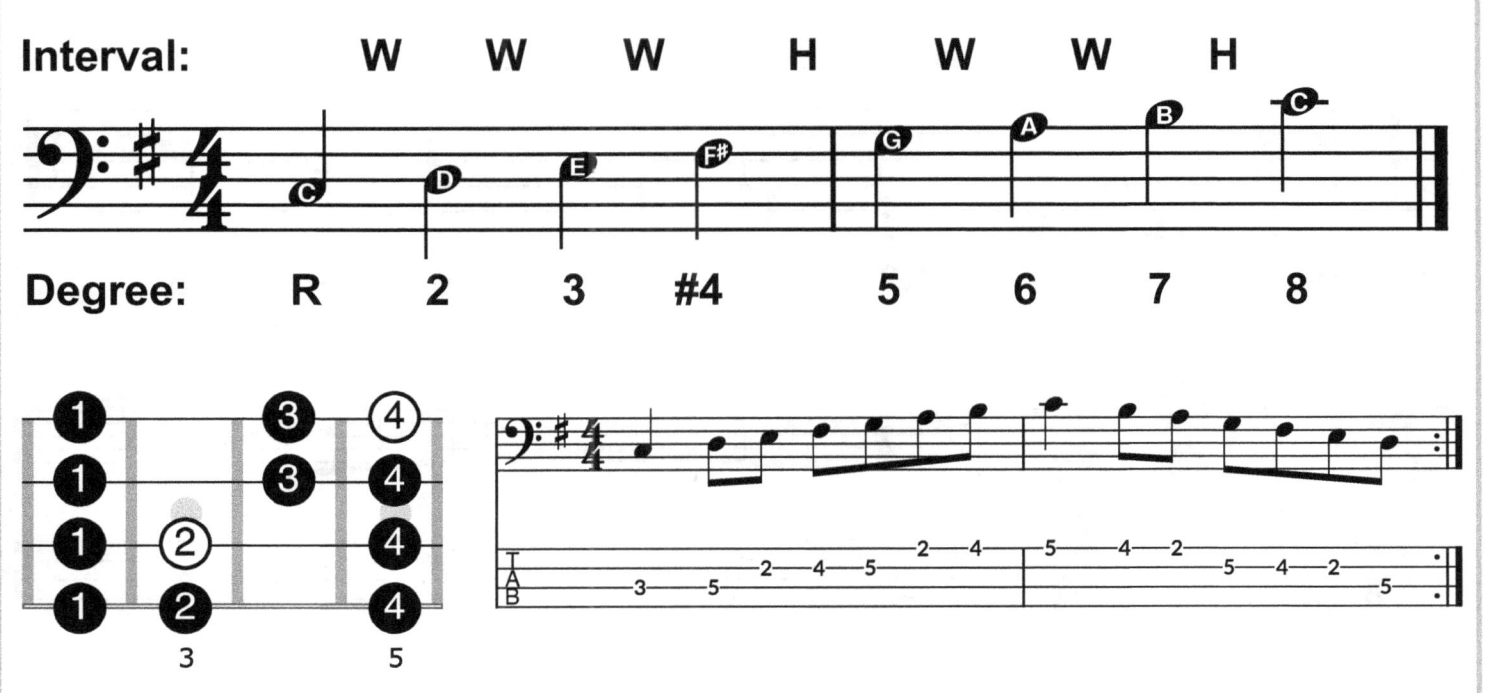

THURSDAY: MIXOLYDIAN   361

D Mixolydian is created by playing G Major from its 5th step. You could think of it as a major scale with a lowered 7th.

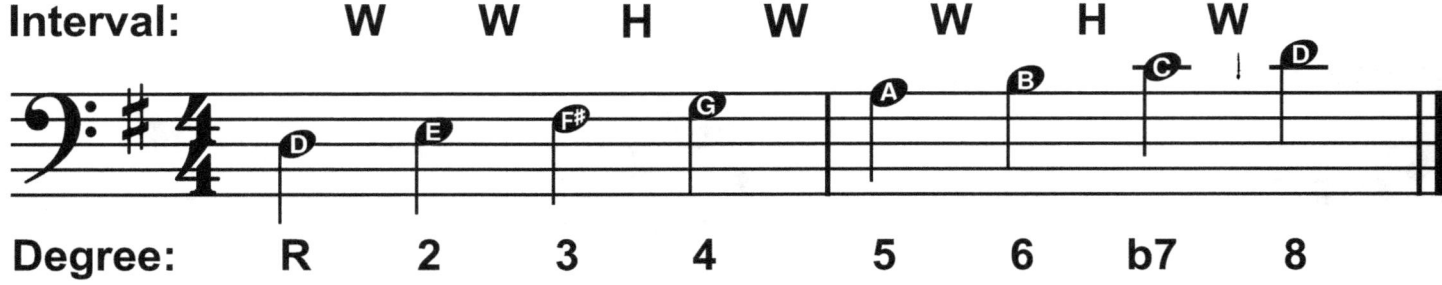

In our next example, we'll add a position shift to Pattern 3 to resolve the scale on its root note, D.

FRIDAY: AEOLIAN   362

Playing G major from its 6th creates E Aeolian. Aeolian is the most commonly used mode. In fact, we've been playing it throughout the book, as it's also referred to as *natural minor* or *relative minor*.

SATURDAY: LOCRIAN 363

Our last mode, F# Locrian, is built by playing G major from its 7th degree and contains the most alterations from its major counterpart, F# major: b2nd, b3rd, b5th, b6th, and b7th.

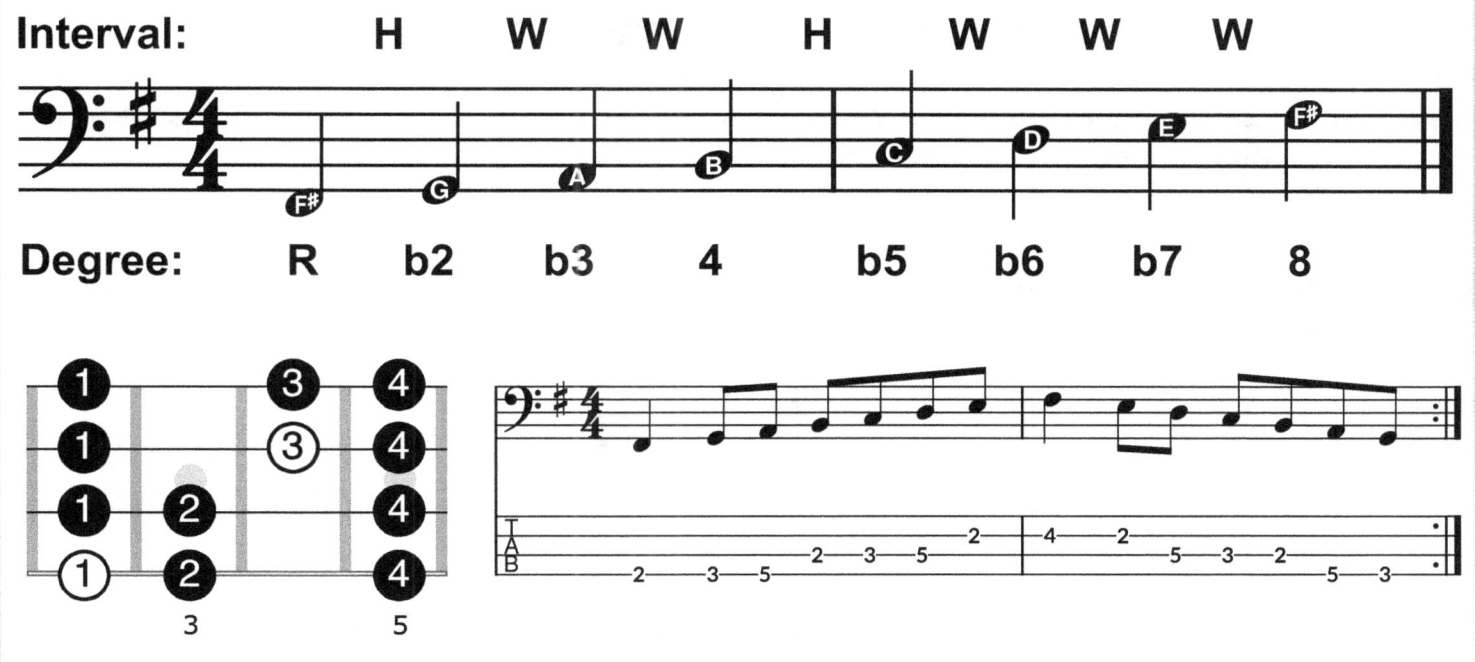

SUNDAY: SCALE APPLICATION 364

Our next example illustrates the sound of each mode by playing the triad built from each scale degree, literally outlining each mode's strongest notes. For further study, you can turn each of the patterns into each of the modes (the fingerings will remain the same). To play the last G triad in measure 4, shift into the Horizontal Pattern and use fingers 2, 1, and 4. This keeps the fingering identical to the lower-octave version that begins the example.

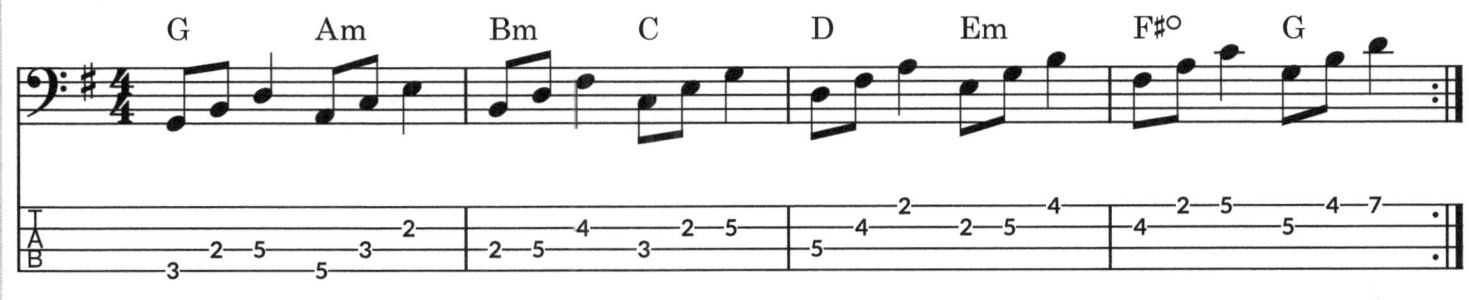

WEEK 53: DAY 365

MONDAY   365

Firstly, a huge congratulations on making it to the end of the book! At this point, you've earned a command of scale patterns while building a vocabulary of musical phrases. Our final example is a 12-bar blues in A that employs a variety of scales and musical devices we've learned. See how many you can identify while learning it.

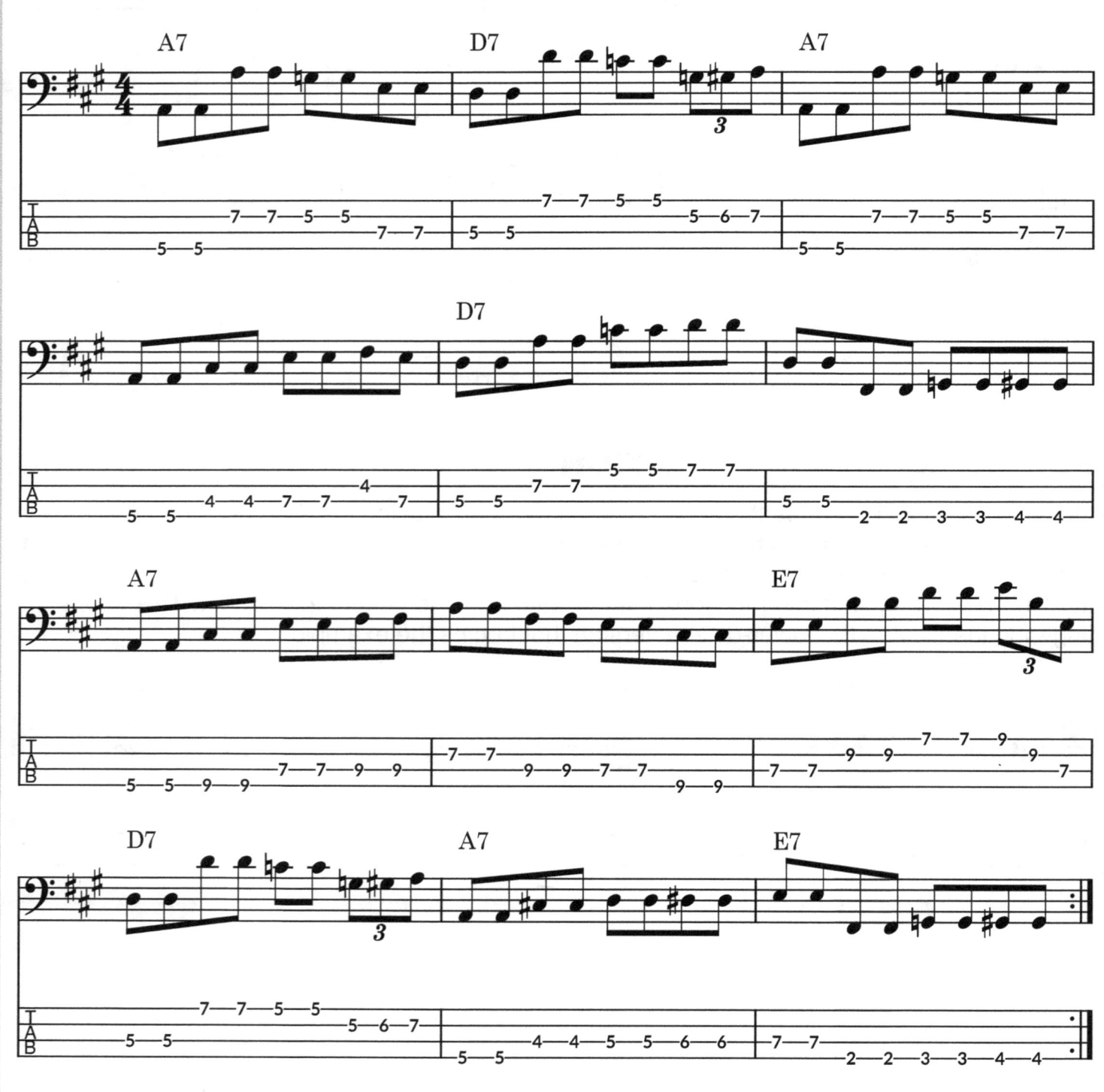

ABOUT THE AUTHOR

Since he was just three years old, Milwaukee-area guitarist **Kirk Tatnall** has been chasing music via his favorite vehicle: the guitar. In addition to authoring instructional books, Kirk continues to perform, compose, record, and release original music, teach guitar, and lend his playing to other artists and various commercial music sessions. For more details, please visit his website: *kirktatnall.com*.

www.ingramcontent.com/pod-product-compliance
Lightning Source LLC
Chambersburg PA
CBHW080441110426
42743CB00016B/3231